PROPERTY OF OAKLAND SCHOOLS
William J. Emerson, Supt.
PONTIAC, MICHIGAN

RESEARCH IN COUNSELING

CONTRIBUTORS

Robert P. Anderson
Gordon V. Anderson
David J. Hebert
Albert Rosen
Frances F. Fuller
Maurice Lorr
David H. Mills
Norman Abeles
Robert L. Milliken
John J. Paterson
John M. Branan
Kenneth U. Gutsch
William D. Bellamy
David G. Zimpfer
Ernest Spaights
John W. McDavid
Martin Katahn
Stuart Strenger
Nancy Cherry
Stuart H. Gilbreath
Betty J. Bosdell
John Teigland
Jack D. Orsburn
Harry J. Waters
Weldon F. Zenger
Donald A. Pool
Dale G. Andersen
Robert A. Heimann
Harvey W. Wall
Samuel H. Osipow
Jefferson D. Ashby
Donivan J. Watley
Harry E. Leubling
Charles F. Combs
Charles B. Truax
Albert H. Krueger
Kenneth Heller
John D. Davis
Roger A. Myers
Robert R. Carkhuff
Todd Holder
Bernard G. Berenson
Mae Alexik
Neal Richard Gamsky
Gail F. Farwell
June E. Holmes
Richard T. Knowles
Bruce Shertzer
Car M. Foster
Thomas J. Sweeney
Philip A. Perrone
Mary L. Weiking
Elwyn H. Nagel
Marilyn Heilfron
George M. Gazda
Hubert M. Clements
Jack A. Duncan
Carol L. Martin
Jane S. O'Hern
Dugald S. Arbuckle
Joseph A. Johnston
Norman C. Gysbers
James D. Linden
Shelley C. Stone
M. Ronald Minge
Laura North Rice
Orville A. Schmieding
Bernard C. Kinnick
Jack T. Shannon
David P. Campbell

RESEARCH IN COUNSELING

EDITED BY

LAWRENCE LITWACK
RUSSELL GETSON
GLENN SALTZMAN
Kent State University

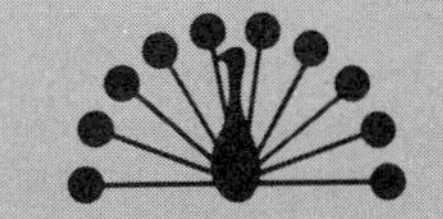

F. E. PEACOCK PUBLISHERS, INC.
Itasca, Illinois

Library of Congress
Catalog Card Number 68-21873

*

PREFACE

This book is designed to fill an existing void in the literature available to counselors and counselor educators. It is dedicated to those individuals who truly can be called professionals in the social sciences—those who are interested in learning more about what we do and how we do it, and who are dissatisfied with operating on the basis of untested hypotheses and value judgments. It is designed to serve a twofold purpose. First, it is intended to be a source of information for practicing counselors, students preparing to become counselors, and counselor educators. Second, it is hoped that this book will serve to emphasize the importance of continuing research.

The editors would like to express their deep appreciation to those who have made this book possible—the authors who conducted the research on which these articles and papers are based, and who consented to share their research by allowing their studies to be part of this book. Appreciation is also due to the organizations publishing journals, which proved so cooperative in allowing us to reprint material.

The editors realize that there are many other topics and many other good studies which might have been included in this book. The choices made were primarily based on relevancy to the topics selected and recency of publication. Much significant research accomplished prior to 1964 is already either printed fully in other references or reported elsewhere in sufficient detail to make inclusion here an unnecessary duplication.

It is our hope that the material in this book will prove as useful and informative to others as it has proven to be for us.

The authors would like to express their appreciation to William Bates, Thomas Fagan, Phyllis Krug, and Janet Sivy for their help in the preparation of this book.

Kent, Ohio
1968

LAWRENCE LITWACK
RUSSELL F. GETSON
GLENN A. SALTZMAN

*

INTRODUCTION

Investigating the human relationship called counseling is somewhat analogous to searching for a needle in a haystack or the mythological task of Sisyphus—i.e., attempting the difficult, if not the impossible. Depending on the point of view of the reader, a book containing reports of research in counseling may be seen as vital, superfluous, or virtually impossible, because the research reported attempts to deal with an area that seems relatively unresearchable due to the large number of uncontrolled variables involved.

It is comparatively simple to reach agreement on a working definition of research. For example, a recent dictionary defines research as a "careful, systematic, patient study and investigation in some field of knowledge, undertaken to establish facts or principles."[1] Such a definition represents a broad description of a method designed to advance the frontiers of knowledge. However, this is perhaps the last point upon which there would be general agreement, particularly when the topic under discussion relates to research into counseling theory and practice. From this point on, several divergent points of view begin to emerge. These differences of opinion may be best exemplified by a discussion provoked by the following questions:

(1) Is there a need for research in counseling theory and practice?
(2) Can scientific methods of research be applied to counseling theory and practice?
(3) What research in counseling is being done, and by whom?

Since a discussion of the implications of these questions raises a number of crucial issues in counseling and counselor education, and serves as the underlying justification for a book such as this, they seem worth examining in some detail.

[1]*New World Dictionary of the English Language* (Cleveland: World Publishing Co., 1966), p. 1237.

The Need for Research

Whether one starts with the investigation resulting from the works of Wundt, Galton, or Freud, or with the more recent investigations growing out of activities resulting from federal legislation affecting education and counseling, he would find that society has a great many people engaged in a specialty in which little can be supported by empirical evidence. Such interest clearly identifies an area of great concern and significance.

In recent years education has been the focal point for a number of attacks both from internal and external sources. As the number of persons expressing views on education increases, these criticisms may be expected not only to continue but also to increase in both number and intensity. Education is often viewed as the source of all the ills of modern society. Assaults have been made generally against education, and more specifically against such areas as testing, reading, and curriculum planning. It is reasonable to expect that counseling too might well be exposed to critical examination. The existence of attacks is further evidence of the significance of all of these areas of activity in popular opinion. But the criticism needs to be examined and answered.

The defense of education is difficult because it is primarily and predominantly built upon the shifting quicksand of "expert" opinion. For example, what empirical evidence exists to support such administrative decisions as the age at which a child must start or depart from school? When we begin to question seriously everything we do in the field of education, we may shake American education down to its foundations. Pupil personnel services are no less vulnerable to criticism and debate. For example, what is the nature of the evidence that supports the expenditure of funds on guidance and counseling? The criteria of its value are vague and the findings at least contentious. Yet recommendations suggested by some authorities indicate that schools should provide a counselor for each 250–300 students. But difficulty of investigation is not sufficient grounds for failure to attempt to find answers to questions raised.

Counseling and the education of counselors represents an extremely diffuse and ambiguous field. The close, human relationship that exists in many of the social service fields represents an area of knowledge in which much remains to be learned. Those involved in the counseling process often indicate that they recognize this fact. Efforts are being made to increase understanding of the counseling relationship, but there is much yet to do before counselors can speak with authority about their art and science.

Counseling—Fact or Feeling

Can scientific methods of research be applied to counseling theory and practice? At this point we are confronted with a diversity of opinion that makes response difficult. Arbuckle argues that counseling is much closer to philosophy than science, and therefore we cannot use scientific methods of research. He states, "One might be scientific in his attempts to evaluate what happens as a result of his counseling, what might happen if he does this instead of that, what happens if a certain variable . . . is introduced, and so on, but how scientific can he be in his actual relationship with the client, which after all is what counseling is."[2]

Bixler approaches the question from a different point of view. He states, "Until these workers can offer evidence that their techniques are more effective than placebos, we must look upon their contributions as no more than that. Faith and *ad hominem* arguments about the 'worth and dignity and integrity' of man may be temporarily persuasive but they are very poor substitutes for evidence. Such arguments are illustrative of the attempts throughout history to rebut the findings of science when these have been devastating to cherished but unwarranted positions."[3]

Each of the above positions suggests a framework for research. Arbuckle would look for his answers in investigations of counseling outcomes, techniques, and environments. But he sees an area that is highly significant and yet resistant to investigation, the human relationship. Bixler believes that all aspects of counseling must be open to investigation if there is such a discipline, art, or skill. The difference in position results in differences in investigations. Each makes its contribution to the growth of understanding in the field of counseling. While the editors may lean to the position of Bixler, they would be hard put to refute, with evidence, Arbuckle's contention that the counseling relationship is beyond our powers to express quantitatively and/or qualitatively.

Research in Counseling: A Status Report

Regardless of one's point of view regarding the need for and/or the feasibility of research in counseling, there is no question that research is being done, although the quality of it often leaves much to be

---

[2]"Counseling: Philosophy or Science," *Personnel and Guidance Journal* (September, 1960), p. 13.

[3]"The Changing World of the Counselor II; Training for the Unknown," *Counselor Education and Supervision* (Summer, 1963), p. 170.

desired. There is an abundance of research being published, particularly of the status-type achieved by the survey or questionnaire method. Most role and function studies fall into this category. There is, however, a paucity of research that investigates methodology and success of either counseling or counselor education. The human relationship in counseling is still in the early stages of investigative effort.

Prior to an initial screening of articles for this book, the editors reviewed material representing 135 different authors. It is significant that the vast majority of these authors were located on university campuses. Only 28 came from agencies or organizations not located on college or university campuses. It is also significant that the people who are located where the greatest impact on the population may be made—those counseling in the schools, in job corps centers, in agencies; those working with the educationally or culturally deprived individual—are generally not the people publishing the results of their work. As a consequence we lack information that may lead to new conceptualizations of counseling based upon a rich foundation of experience and creative effort.

It seems to the editors that those involved in counseling need to enter into a research partnership with university faculty in order to strip away some of the veils of ignorance that presently exist. What is needed is a unified effort that includes everyone with a professional commitment to the counseling field.

Summary

With the above as a prologue, it seems appropriate to turn now to the main body of this book—what studies, in the opinion of the editors, represent current significant research in counseling. In addition to the articles selected for this book, the editors have also included, as part of the appendixes, several instruments that show promise of being useful in planning and implementing research. Each chapter has been developed to present the best available contemporary investigations in the area, and the introduction to each chapter is designed to provide a brief overview of the content treated in the articles.

*

CONTENTS

1

The Counseling Relationship

The counseling relationship is a dynamic human interaction. This interaction may be between a counselor and counselee, between a counselor and a group of counselees, or between several counselors and a counselee. The multitude of variables that have an effect on the relationship that is counseling presents a multifaceted problem that both needs research and frustrates researchers. Any examination of counseling methodology, problems, or needs must remain somewhat academic until we know more about what is actually happening in the counseling relationship.

The articles selected for this chapter present a picture of both strength and weakness. As several of the authors suggest, a major problem in examining the dynamics of the counseling relationship revolves around the determination of criteria of success. It is difficult to find any agreement on what constitutes success in counseling. The perceptions of the counselee or counselor, the subsequent actions of the counselee, and the observations of an objective external third party are some of the criteria used in the following studies.

The article by Anderson and Anderson represents an attempt to develop an instrument that can be used to measure rapport in counseling. Their original rating scale, with the weighting and screening by Correll, shows promise of becoming a useful research instrument. The final rating scale is included in Appendix A as one of several promising research tools.

The second article, by Hebert, presents an example of one type of research that can be done, based on the Correll adaptation of the Anderson and Anderson scale. The Hebert study represents an attempt to examine the differential effects of client-counselor personality needs and client-counselor sex similarity. As a guide for further research, it opens the door for analysis of certain aspects of an effective counseling relationship. Within the limitations imposed by the implicit definition of what constitutes success in counseling, it may pave the way toward the assignment of counselees to counselors on criteria related to the probability of the relationship being successful.

The next two articles move into the area of counselee preferences in the counseling relationship. The Rosen article, although not in itself a research article, presents a current review of the literature dealing with client preferences for counselor characteristics and procedures. Two major contributions of this article come from the identification of areas needing study and the comprehensive bibliography. The Fuller article deals with one of the areas indicated by Rosen as needing research. Her study is concerned with client preferences for male or female counselors. Her conclusion that both male and female counselees seem to prefer male counselors has implications for the practice prevalent in many schools of assigning boys to a male counselor and girls to a female counselor.

The Lorr study provides an interesting approach to relating the counselee's perceptions of the counselor's behavior to certain constructs believed to be related to the success of the counseling process. By the use of factor analysis, he has been able to identify five dimensions of such behavior. In addition to providing an empirical basis for the identification of certain related counselor behaviors, he has also provided an instrument for the investigation of constructs proposed by writers in the area of counseling theory.

The final three articles focus attention on the counselor. The Hebert study used the Edwards Personal Preference Schedule (EPPS) to determine counselor-counselee personality similarity and investigate the relationship with counseling session ratings by both counselors and counselees. The Mills and Abeles study also uses the EPPS as a measure of counselor personality and relates this to a dimension called "liking," determined by a semantic differential technique and approach to dependency and hostility as determined through a content-scoring technique. Their investigation provides a test of some of the formulations expressed by Rogers, Reick, Menninger, and Fromm. While providing no clear substantiation of positions, the results and the authors' interpretations are provocative of further investigation and reformulation.

The Mills–Abeles article is supplemented by Abeles' further investigation of the area of counselor-liking for individual counselees and its effect on the counseling relationship.

The Milliken and Paterson study takes one specific area of counselor personality—the extent of dogmatism and prejudice—and relates it to rated counselor effectiveness. It would have been helpful if the authors had included their 16–item Counselor Effectiveness Scale (CES) for others to use in future research. A counseling relationship was contrived to expose counselors to a situation that might be affected by counselor bias related to race. While only one of the eight relationships investigated reached a level that indicated statistical significance, six of the remaining seven were in a direction that supported the hypotheses. A larger sample and metrics that permit the use of parametric statistics may well provide future investigators with the basis for support of the authors' belief relative to the effect of prejudice on counseling. Again, as the Rosen article indicates, much more research is needed into the effects of race on the counseling relationship.

A review of the literature contained in this chapter reveals several points that support statements made in the introduction. The eight articles represent ten investigators; of these, nine are university faculty members and one is a Veterans Administration staff member; and this despite the fact that the editors searched extensively for research material prepared by individuals operating in settings that represent the major sources of counseling in this country.

Using a predominantly university student population and/or a psychiatric population introduces an element of parochialism into the research presented in this chapter. It seems obvious that much more research is needed in the area of counseling relationship that involves a more representative group of counselors, counseling settings, and counselees.

The research in the chapter draws on a varied array of instruments and procedures. A projective instrument, rating scales, preference questionnaires, and a statement inventory are included among the metrics. The statistical procedures include both parametric and nonparametric techniques. While correlation was most frequently used, illustrations of the use of factor analysis (Lorr) and analysis of variance also are included. One study is included that presents information obtained from a review of the literature.

The editors believe that the studies included in this chapter make a valuable contribution by pointing up the imagination involved in the designs developed to investigate the nebulous nature of the counseling relationship. It is hoped that others will continue the difficult task through further refinement and validation of instruments, replication of studies in different settings with different subjects, and innovative activity in preparing new metrics and procedures for investigation of this significant area.

*

DEVELOPMENT OF AN INSTRUMENT FOR MEASURING RAPPORT

ROBERT P. ANDERSON
GORDON V. ANDERSON

There does not appear to be any striking disagreement in the professional literature concerning the meaning of rapport. The term as generally used, however, is defined in such broad terms as to be of limited usefulness as a concept in training or as a variable in research. Fiedler, in his classic studies [*4*, *5*], investigated the concept of the ideal relationship. He found that therapists with different therapeutic orientations, and non-therapists, tend to have similar concepts of the ideal relation. Fiedler's sample of therapists was small, and the items described as indicative of "good" and "poor" relationships were not scaled for quantitative interview ratings. In an unpublished study, Bown [*1*] utilized *Q*-sort methodology. He also concluded that clients and counselors tend to have similar concepts of the ideal relationship. The present study is an attempt to provide an explicit, operational definition of the counseling relationship characterized by ideal rapport. Directly related to this, we were interested in the extent of agreement among a group of clients and counselors concerning the meaning of rapport. The operational defini-

*This article is reprinted from *Personnel and Guidance Journal,* 1962, *41,* 18–24, by permission of the publisher, the American Personnel and Guidance Association, and the authors.

tion was made in terms of attitudes and behaviors of clients and counselors. Assumptions regarding the study were that rapport is of importance early in counseling; it is relevant to communication; it is observable behavior perceived by both participants in the relationship; and it can be assessed by an observer.

Method

A series of 163 items concerned with counselor and client attitudes and behaviors was collected. Items were derived from transcribed case material, clients, counselors, and the *Q*-Universes of Fiedler and Bown. Preliminary screening in terms of the three categories—good-poor rapport, ambiguous or unrelated to rapport, and those defying classification—was carried out by seven psychologists and one psychiatrist. Judges were allowed to put as many items in a category as they wished. Those items on which there appeared to be agreement concerning their relevance as descriptive of rapport were singled out for further study.

Next, a 99-item form of the Rapport Rating Scale was developed. One hundred counseling psychologists were asked to rate each item on a nine-point scale. The extremes of the scale were "good" rapport and "poor" rapport; the items were rated in terms of the ratees' own conceptions of ideal rapport. The psychologists surveyed were all members of Division 12 and/or 17 of the American Psychological Association. A random sample of judges was not obtained; rather, psychologists known to the authors as being actively engaged in counseling activity were contacted.

In addition to the psychologists, 62 clients from the University of Texas Testing and Guidance Bureau were asked to rate the items. The client population was composed of 15 males and 15 females with more than five interviews in counseling; and 16 males and 16 females with less than five interviews. The majority of persons in the short-term group had finished their counseling experience prior to the request for their participation. Clients in the long-term group had had from 6 to 50 interviews. The majority of these clients were still in counseling at the time they received the scales in the mail.

Results

Sixty-nine psychologists (69 per cent) and 34 clients (55 per cent) returned the 99-item version of the scale; 55 of the psychologists were actively engaged in some form of counseling work; 26 had less than 10 years experience; 26 had from 10 to 15 years of experience;

and 17 had over 15 years of experience. The 34 clients returning scales were about equally divided between males and females and between those with less than five interviews and those with more than five interviews.

Each item checked by at least 10 per cent of the counselors as unclassifiable was eliminated from further analysis; using this criterion, 77 items were retained. Medians and quartile deviations were computed for each item. Twenty-eight items indicative of poor rapport had medians ranging from 0.00 to 1.49; 26 items indicative of good rapport had medians ranging from 6.50 to 7.99. Fifty items with a Q-value of 1.00 or less, representing the extremes of good and poor rapport and showing the least amount of disagreement among judges, were selected for inclusion in the Interview Rating Scale.

Medians for each item rated by the clients were computed. Fifty-four differences in medians between the counselors and clients were less than 0.80 score points. Since we were interested in obtaining those items which both groups agreed represented good and poor rapport, the medians of the 50 items selected from the counselors' ratings were correlated with these same item medians from the clients' ratings. The Pearson r's between the two arrays of medians were 0.98. In short, we had a series of items on which both clients and counselors agreed as representing the extremes of rapport.

The final 50-item IRS is evenly divided between items representing good and poor rapport; 18 items refer to client behaviors and attitudes; the remaining refer to counselor behavior.

Examples of each type are as follows:

Positive client: The client has confidence in the counselor.

Negative client: The client feels more like a case than an individual.

Positive counselor: The counselor's tone of voice conveys the ability to share the client's feelings.

Negative counselor: The counselor pushed the client into saying things that aren't really true.

In order to make the scale adaptable for interview ratings by client and counselors, raters are asked in the directions to indicate the degree to which an item describes a behavior or attitude present in a counseling experience. The range is from "always" through "occasionally" to "never," with five points provided for checking on the continuum. The scale is scored in the following manner: (1) weights from 1 to 5 are assigned to the points in the continuum; (2) items indicating good rapport receive a maximum score of 5 for "always" and a minimum of 1 for "never"; (3) items indicating poor rapport are scored in reverse fashion. Scores may range from a maximum of 250 for ideal rapport to a minimum of 50.

Discussion

The results support the findings of Fiedler and Bown; that is, when described in terms of specific behaviors and attitudes, there is a core of agreement among clients and counselors concerning the nature of ideal rapport or the ideal relationship.

It is hypothesized that each of these characteristics may be rated separately for an interview so as to give a score quantifying the level of rapport. Studies by Correll [*3*] and Brams [*2*] support the hypothesis that the scale can be used to provide a measure of the "relationship" in initial interviews. Correll investigated the factors influencing the quality of the communication process in initial counseling interviews. The Interview Rating Scale was used as a criterion measure. Three judges rated 52 interviews with the scale. Two conclusions were: (1) "Expert judges are able to rate typescripts of initial counseling interviews on the basis of what constitutes good and poor communication situations," and (2) "The Interview Rating Scale is a sensitive instrument for determining the quality of the communication within the initial counseling interview." Correll undertook an item analysis of the scale. He found 8 of the 50 items were of little value in differentiating between "good" and "poor" interviews. As a further step in increasing the sensitivity of the scale, Correll determined weights for each response category for the 50 items.

Brams used the scale as a criterion measure in a study of the personality characteristics of counseling trainees and the effectiveness of their ability to communicate with clients. The weights developed by Correll in his item analysis were used in Brams's modification of the scale, which he labeled the Communication Rating Scale. His results suggest that effective communication as measured by the scale is related positively to a counseling trainee's tolerance for ambiguity, although other relationships measured were inconclusive. The author felt, however, that "the CRS appeared to be an adequate measure of effective communication in the counseling relationship."

Both these studies support the original purpose of the scale, i.e., to rate interviews in terms of the effectiveness of communication or, as we termed it, rapport; moreover, further judicious exploration of the scale as a research instrument and as a tool in counselor training is justified by these results.

Summary

The Interview Rating Scale was developed to provide an operational definition of ideal rapport or, as termed by Correll, effective communication in counseling interviews. Items selected for inclusion in the scale represent a consensus among a select group of counselors and clients concerning the meaning of rapport. Research and subsequent modification by independent investigators have supported the effectiveness of the scale as a measure of "rapport" in counseling.

References

1. Bown, O. H. "An investigation of therapeutic relationships in client-centered psychotherapy." Unpublished doctoral dissertation, University of Chicago, 1953.

2. Brams, J. H. "Counselor characteristics and effective communication in counseling." *Journal of Counseling Psychology*, 1961, *8*, 25–30.

3. Correll, P. "Factors influencing communication in counseling." Unpublished doctoral dissertation, University of Missouri, 1955.

4. Fiedler, F. E. "The concept of the ideal therapeutic relationship." *Journal of Consulting Psychology*, 1950, *14*, 239–45.

5. Fiedler, F. E. "Quantitative studies on the role of therapists' feelings toward their patients." In O. H. Mowrer, (ed.), *Psychotherapy, theory, and research.* New York: Ronald Press, 1953, 296–316.

*

CLIENT-COUNSELOR PERSONALITY NEED AND SEX SIMILARITY

DAVID J. HEBERT

In spite of many references in counseling literature to the importance of the nature of the client-counselor relationship, few studies on the topic have been reported. There have been investigations seeking to determine if client personality variables are related to counseling success. A few studies exist on the relevancy of personality variables to counseling success. There have been still fewer studies done on client-counselor adaptation as it affects outcome. This study is concerned with dyadic counseling relationship and the effect of client-counselor personality-need similarity and the sex of the counselor and client.

The identification of a measurable interaction dimension such as personal needs, which may be related to counseling outcome, may be a step toward specifying in advance which counselors and clients might have a greater chance for "successful" encounter. The influence of the sex of the participants in counseling will also be examined and may provide some data which support or refute same or opposite sex dyads.

It is a difficult task in the area of counseling theory to reach complete agreement. However, we are not likely to get much argument about the idea that the client and counselor influence each other during the counseling interview. Bandura, Lipsher, and Miller (1960) conducted an experimental demonstration of this idea. They concluded that, if the therapist avoided the hostile expressions of the client, this led to more avoidance of hostility by the client, and that the therapist's hostile expressions directed toward the client led to

*This article is an original paper, printed here by permission of the author.

more hostile expression of this kind from the client. In recent years the behaviorists have shown the conditioning influence of counselor talk.

Of all the factors that influence counseling, one of the most important is the interpersonal relationship (Brammer and Shostrom, 1960; Cowen and Combs, 1950; Frank, 1959; Whitaker and Malone, 1953). In analyzing the factors which affected the quality of therapeutic relationships, Parloff (1956), over ten years ago, stated:

> The interpersonal relationship between the therapist and patient is widely accepted as basic to psychotherapy. It is assumed that the "better" this relationship, the greater the possibility that the patient will benefit from treatment. Despite this, little attention has been devoted to the problem of matching therapist and patient in order to enhance the quality of the relationship (p. 5).

Little has been added to prevent Parloff from making the same statement today. McGowan and Schmidt (1962) stated, ". . . Even today our knowledge about the actual effects of the personality traits of the counselor on his client and of the client's on the counselor is relatively limited [p. 276]."

Procedure

This study was conducted with 19 counselor trainees who were in their first practicum. These counselors consisted of 12 males and 7 females. The clients were predominantly college freshmen and sophomores. The degree of similarity in personality needs between clients and counselors was determined with the Edwards Personal Preference Schedule (EPPS). The criterion was the Interview Rating Scale (IRS) utilizing Correll's scale (Anderson and Anderson, 1962). This instrument purports to measure effective communication in the counseling relationship.

The counselors were each scheduled with 2 males and 2 females with educational-vocational (EV) problems. Therefore, it was planned for each counselor to work with 4 clients, with the total number of clients being 76. However, as will be seen later, there are only 73 cases represented in this study. These missing indexes are a result of 3 counselors having worked with only 3 of the required 4 cases. The mean of the 3 obtained indexes was inserted in place of the missing case for each counselor. This produced a loss of three degrees of freedom and therefore required a higher t or F ratio in order to reach significance.

In order to investigate the effect of the sex of client and counselor it was necessary for each counselor to have worked with both males and females. Similarly, in order to control for case-type influencing the ratings, it was necessary for each counselor to have worked with the same type of case. The cases in this study were diagnosed as educational-vocational (EV) by inspection of the intake form. The cases were either substantiated or refuted as being EV by the counselor and an observer. Those finally diagnosed as EV were retained and those which were diagnosed as personal-social were eliminated from the study. This was done with full knowledge of the fact that most EV cases also included personal-social concerns. However, an effort was made to limit the study to those cases evaluated as being concerned primarily with educational-vocational matters.

Before beginning their practicum assignments the counselor trainees were administered the EPPS. The clients were administered the EPPS as part of an intake procedure. The IRS was administered to the client and the counselor at the end of the second interview in order to standardize the length of exposure of client to the counselor, and thus to control for any effect that might be attributable to different case durations. This study produced an average of 2.09 interviews per case. It should be pointed out that similar averages were reported by the following persons: Callis (1965) showed an average of 2.03 in vocational cases and 2.10 in educational cases, and Mendelsohn (1966) showed an average of 2.36 interviews per case.

PREPARING DATA FOR ANALYSIS

Step 1. A Spearman rank order coefficient of correlation was computed between the ranks of the 15 scale scores of the client and counselor on the EPPS. The resultant index, decimal point deleted, served as a measure of the personality need similarity between the client and counselor.

Step 2. The results of the IRS were tabulated. This involved the client ratings of the interview and the counselor self-ratings of the interview. The weights assigned for the five possible responses to each item by Correll in Anderson and Anderson (1962) were utilized.

Step 3. A Spearman rank order coefficient of correlation was computed to determine if there was a significant relationship between the personality need similarity indexes of client and counselor and the client ratings of the counselor. A similar computation was carried out for the counselor self-ratings of the interview.

Step 4. The difference in client ratings in various client-counselor sex dyads was investigated. This was accomplished by using

Guilford's (1956) *t*-formula for testing differences between correlated pairs of means.

Step 5. An analysis of variance was applied to a $2 \times 2 \times 2$ factorial design. The three factors were counselor, degree of similarity, and clients. The levels were male-female counselor, high-low similarity and male-female clients. The dependent variable was client ratings of the interview. A similar analysis was applied using counselor self-ratings as the dependent variable.

Findings

H_{01}—It was hypothesized that no relationship would be found to exist between the similarity of the client and the counselor on the EPPS and the client ratings on the IRS. The obtained rho was .148 and was not significant at the .05 level; therefore, the hypothesis of no relationship could not be rejected.

H_{02}—It was hypothesized that no relationship would be found to exist between the similarity of the client and the counselor on the EPPS and the counselor self-rating of the relationship on the IRS. The obtained rho was .177 and was not significant at the .05 level; therefore, the hypothesis of no relationship could not be rejected.

H_{03}—It was hypothesized that no differences would be found in the client rating given male counselors by male or female clients. The obtained *t*-ratio was 2.428 and was significant at the .05 level; therefore, the hypothesis of no difference was rejected. Inspection of the data (Table 1) showed that male clients gave a higher rating to male counselors than did the female clients.

H_{04}—It was hypothesized that no differences would be found in the client ratings given female counselors by male or female clients. The obtained *t*-ratio was 1.865 and was not significant at the .05 level; therefore, the hypothesis of no difference was not rejected.

H_{05}—It was hypothesized that no difference would be found in the counselor self-ratings of male counselors whether their clients are male or female. The obtained *t*-ratio was 1.666 and was not significant at the .05 level; therefore, the hypothesis of no difference was not rejected.

H_{06}—It was hypothesized that no difference would be found in the counselor self-ratings of female counselors whether their clients are male or female. The obtained *t*-ratio was 1.445 and was not significant at the .05 level; therefore, the hypothesis of no difference was not rejected.

H_{07}—It was hypothesized that no difference would be found between the relationship of client rating and similarity index when

TABLE 1

RATINGS GIVEN TO MALE COUNSELORS BY CLIENTS OF SAME AND OPPOSITE SEX

	Clients Same Sex			*Clients Opposite Sex*				*Difference of Sums*
Male Counselors	*A*	*B*	*Sum (X)*	*C*	*D*	*Sum (Y)*	*Total*	*(X—Y)*
1	45	73	118	—31	62	31	149	+87
2	96	89	185	72	100	172	357	+13
3	95	—1	94	90	54	144	238	—50
4	68	61	129	1	48	49	178	+80
5	19	87	106	90	70	160	266	—54
6	20	97	117	44	24	68	185	+49
7	71	30*	102	1	17	18	120	+84
8	60	63	123	50	75	125	248	+ 2
9	91	84	175	102	37	139	314	+36
10	93	74	164	66	88	154	318	+10
11	91	58	149	55	37	92	241	+57
12	94	98	192	73	88*	161	353	+31

*Inserted score.

the client and the counselor are of the same sex and the relationship obtained when client and counselor are not of the same sex. The obtained *F*-ratio was 2.320 and was not significant at the .05 level; therefore, the hypothesis of no difference was not rejected.

H_{08}—It was hypothesized that no difference would be found between the relationship of counselor self-rating and similarity index when the client and the counselor are not of the same sex. The obtained *F*-ratio was 2.509 and was not significant at the .05 level; therefore, the hypothesis of no difference was not rejected.

With respect to the interaction analysis, it should be noted that a significant interaction did occur between the sex of the counselor, degree of similarity, and the sex of the client ($F = 4.596$, p less than .05) when counselor self-rating was used as the dependent variable. This would seem to indicate that there are such influences present. Further research is needed to extract and identify them.

DISCUSSION

Counselor-Client Sex.—The findings indicate that male counselors received a significantly higher rating from male clients than they did from female clients. It might be interesting to speculate why this result was obtained. Is it possible that, since these cases were of an educational-vocational nature, male clients believe that men know more about the world of work than women and therefore rated male counselors higher than female counselors? Perhaps the female clients are not as sure about the male counselor's knowledge of the world of work that has relevance for them. There is a second possible explanation of the difference in ratings. It has been noted in the past that the female clients who present themselves to the counseling center for educational-vocational problems are also experiencing some personal-social problems. This was reported in a study by Heisey (1964). It is possible, then, that the male clients feel that their problem has been resolved by educational-vocational counseling and give high ratings to the counseling relationship. On the other hand, the female clients, after being exposed to educational-vocational counseling, are still experiencing some anxiety about some other problems and therefore tend to rate the counseling relationship low. The writer is not saying that every female client has an educational-vocational problem that includes an intense personal-social problem. He is rather suggesting that the tendency may result in more personal-social involvement in the cases selected that included female counselees. This therefore presents some problems in controlling for case type.

In general it would appear that same sex dyads result in better counseling effectiveness as rated by the clients. Garfield, Blek, and Melker (1952) suggested that the sex of the counselor is important only where cultural mores prohibit expression of aroused needs. In contrast to this study, it would appear that the sex of the counselor is important even in the supposed nonthreatening atmosphere of educational-vocational counseling.

It may be desirable to assign male clients to male counselors and female clients to female counselors. However, this study should be replicated at other institutions in order to determine if the situation may be peculiar to the locale in which the study was conducted.

Personality-Need Similarity.—The conclusions indicate that positive correlations exist between the degree of personality-need similarity and the rated counseling relationship. These correlations, however, were not significant at the generally acceptable levels.

These nonsignificant findings may result from the brief counselor-client contact prior to the rating. Therefore, the effect of the need variable was not given ample time to have any marked influence. It is also possible that the EPPS was not sensitive enough to adequately express difference in the personal needs of the counselor and client.

It is interesting to note that some other studies using personality inventories, such as were used in this study, found curvilinear relationships between similarity and degree of rated success. Carson and Heine (1962) with the MMPI, Schopler (1958) with Leary's Interpersonal Check List, and Mendelsohn and Geller (1963) using the Myers-Briggs Type Indicator found curvilinear relationships. The study being presented here was checked for curvilinear trends and none was found to exist.

Interaction of Personality-Needs and Sex.—The finding was that there is no difference between the relationship of client rating and similarity index when the client and the counselor are of the same sex and the relationship obtained when the client and the counselor are not of the same sex. The same finding resulted when the counselor self-rating was inserted as the criterion. It is noted, however, that a significant interaction did occur in the grouping of counselor sex, degree of similarity, and client sex when the counselor self-rating was used as the criterion.

In the final analysis, the significance of the counselor sex, degree of similarity, and client sex would seem to imply that these are influences operating on the counseling relationship. Further research is necessary to extract and identify them.

References

Anderson, R. P., & Anderson, G. V. "Development of an Instrument for Measuring Rapport." *Personnel and Guidance Journal,* 1962, *41,* 18–24.

Bandura, A., Lipsher, D. H., & Miller, P. "Psychotherapists' Approach-Avoidance Reactions to Patients' Expressions of Hostility." *Journal of Consulting Psychology,* 1960, *24,* 1–8.

Brammer, L. M., & Shostrom, E. L. *Therapeutic Psychology.* Englewood Cliffs, N.J.: Prentice-Hall, 1960.

Callis, R. "Diagnostic Classification as a Research Tool." *Journal of Counseling Psychology,* 1965, *12,* 238–43.

Carson, R. C., & Heine, R. W. "Similarity and Success in Therapeutic Dyads." *Journal of Consulting Psychology,* 1962, *26,* 38–43.

Correll, P. T. "Factors Influencing Communication in Counseling." Unpublished doctoral dissertation, University of Missouri, 1958.

Cowen, E. L., & Combs, A. W. "Follow-up Study of 32 Cases Treated by Non-Directive Psychotherapy." *Journal of Abnormal and Social Psychology,* 1950, *45,* 232–58.

Frank, J. D. "The Dynamics of the Psychotherapeutic Relationship; Determinants and Effects of the Therapist's Influence." *Psychiatry,* 1959, *22,* 17–39.

Garfield, S. L., Blek, L., & Melker, F. "The Influence of Method of Administration and Sex Differences on Selected Aspects of TAT Stories." *Journal of Consulting Psychology,* 1952, *16,* 140–44.

Guilford, J. P. *Fundamental Statistics in Psychology and Education.* New York: McGraw-Hill, 1956.

Heisey, M. J. "A Critical Study of the Counseling Records in the Kent State University Guidance Laboratory from 1957 through 1963." Unpublished master's thesis, Kent State University, 1964.

McGowan, J. F., & Schmidt, L. D. *Counseling: Readings in Theory and Practice*. New York: Holt, Rinehart & Winston, 1962.

Mendelsohn, G. A. "Effects of Client Personality and Client-Counselor Similarity on the Duration of Counseling: A Replication and Extension." *Journal of Counseling Psychology,* 1966, *13,* 228–34.

Mendelsohn, G. A., & Geller, M. H. "Effects of Counselor-Client Similarity on the Outcome of Counseling." *Journal of Counseling Psychology,* 1963, *10,* 71–77.

Parloff, M. B. "Some Factors Affecting the Quality of Therapeutic Relationships." *Journal of Abnormal and Social Psychology,* 1956, *52,* 5–10.

Schopler, J. H. "The Relation of Patient-Therapist Personality Similarity to the Outcome of Psychotherapy." Unpublished doctoral dissertation, University of Colorado, 1958.

Whitaker, C. A., & Malone, T. P. *The Roots of Psychotherapy.* New York: Blakiston, 1953.

*

CLIENT PREFERENCES: AN OVERVIEW OF THE LITERATURE

ALBERT ROSEN

The perceptions, biases, expectations, values, and "hypotheses" of clinicians and clients are coming more sharply into focus as a result of investigations of clinical interactions (Kintz, Delprato, Mettee, Persons, and Schappe, 1965; Masling, 1966; Orne, 1962; Rosenthal, 1963). Expectations of counselors and clients regarding the counseling process have received considerable study (Cundick, 1963; Goldstein, 1962; Klein, 1958). The characteristics of desirable clients from the standpoint of the therapist have been described in annual reviews of psychotherapy and counseling research (see Dittmann, 1966, and Patterson, 1966, as well as prior volumes).

One area of research has received relatively little attention, how-

---

*This article is reprinted from *Personnel and Guidance Journal,* 1967, *45,* 785–89, by permission of the publisher, the American Personnel and Guidance Association, and the author.

ever, especially in light of its potential importance. This has to do with the *preferences of clients* regarding characteristics and behavior of counselors. In fact, the study of certain kinds of preferences of either clients or counselors, such as religion, race, marital status, or physical attractiveness, seems to be a "taboo topic" (cf. Farberow, 1963).

Inasmuch as the literature on client preferences for characteristics of counselors or psychotherapists has apparently never been brought together, a brief but comprehensive review would seem to be in order. In any selection from the literature there will be some disagreement about what should be included. Some reports were excluded because they dealt with clients' expectations or their perceptions of, or reactions to, therapists. Several investigations or comments are in a gray area because they involved preferences primarily inferred from measures of client satisfaction with counseling. For completeness they are cited: Barahal, Brammer, and Shostrom, 1950; Forgy and Black, 1954; Goodstein and Grigg, 1959; Grigg and Goodstein, 1957; Patterson, 1958; Patterson, 1959.

Although in some studies clients (and researchers) may have interpreted "expectations" to include "preferences," these are not included because the intent or set is too uncertain. An example of this overlap in meaning occurred in one investigation in which instructions to two comparable groups of students changed from a request for the behavior the counselor "would" manifest to what he "should" do (Worby, 1955). An attempt at clearly differentiating expectations and preferences is exemplified by the research of Mendelsohn (1963). Only reports involving the collection of original data will be presented. Other relevant papers containing heuristic theory or observations would have been cited but none was located. The literature will be summarized under six headings, according to type of subject and setting.

Clients of University Counseling Centers.—Seven studies, primarily of clients at university counseling centers, reported the following major results: (1) Males showed a stronger preference for male counselors than did female students for female counselors, and clients who initially perferred a female counselor were more likely to change this preference after counseling than were those originally desiring a male counselor (Fuller, 1964). (2) Clients with no preference regarding sex of counselor expressed more feeling in counseling sessions than those who preferred male counselors (Fuller, 1963). (3) Clients who deemed counselor affective characteristics (warm, friendly, kind, accepting) more important than cognitive ones(logical, knowledgeable, efficient, poised) focused more on personal-social than educational-vocational problems in the first interview than did those clients favoring cognitive characteristics (Grater, 1964). (4) Students considered questions relating to vocational choice most "appropriate" for discussion at the university counseling center; difficulties in adaptation to the academic routine, next most preferred for discussion; and problems of personal-social adjustment, least appropriate for such interaction (Warman, 1960). (5) Although clients' preferences changed during counseling, there was still much divergence at the end of counseling between preferred and actual counselor behaviors (Pohlman, 1961). (6) There was no relationship between success of counseling as rated by clients and counselors and the degree to which clients perceived counselors had followed preferred procedures (Pohlman, 1964). (7) Students reacted with a significant degree of annoyance to questionnaire statements indicating lack of interest or respect for clients, with mild dislike to counselors with visual or hearing handicaps, with neutrality to Jewish or Negro counselors; women students more often than men disliked a male counselor of similar age (Pohlman and Robinson, 1960). This is the only study that could be located that reported any empirical data on preferences regarding religion and race, and one of two dealing with age of the counselor.

Patients in Psychiatric Settings.—Four studies dealt with psychiatric patients. In a Veterans Administration hospital, patients, primarily of lower socio-economic status, preferentially rated psychotherapy near the bottom of a list of 12 rehabilitation and treatment activities (Stotsky, 1956). Out-patients ranked the five most helpful topics to be discussed in group therapy as sex, symptoms and anxieties, shame and guilt, childhood memories, and quarrels. There was a close correspondence between topics judged to be both helpful and disturbing, with $r = .79$, $N = 43$ (Talland and Clark, 1954). Two schizophrenic patients and their therapist showed interesting phasic changes of agreement in ranking the importance of topics discussed during each therapy hour (Parloff, Iflund, and Goldstein, 1958). A patient who talked to a supposed (but non-existent) therapist on the other side of a one-way mirror endowed him with various characteristics, perhaps preferred ones (Dimascio and Brooks, 1961).

Non-Client College Students.—Non-client college students did not wish to discuss with anyone 40 per cent of the problems they identified, but when they desired help they slightly preferred a professionally trained counselor or psychologist over other sources of assistance. Each sex tended to prefer a same-sex counselor, with men much more partial to their own sex (Koile and Bird, 1956). Preference for a "directive" counselor response was greater for college sophomores than seniors, men than women, and private school than public school students. Women with greater preference for initial counselor directiveness were reported to be more extroverted than the other women students (M. Rogers, 1957). A sample of students, primarily non-clients, indicated they would be more amenable to using the counseling center for educational and vocational problems than for personal and social ones (King and Matteson, 1959). Only 20 per cent of deaf college students stated a definite preference for deaf counselors. Students with least severe deafness and poorer ability to communicate by the language of signs showed greatest preference for hearing counselors (Rosen, 1966).

High School Students.—High school students, clients and non-clients, saw their school counselors as primarily helpful with educational-vocational problems, usually preferring others for discussion of personal-emotional difficulties (Grant, 1954; Jenson, 1955). Specifically, they were most resistant to seeking help for problems concerning members of the same sex, parents, and personal appearance (Holman, 1955). Almost unanimously they preferred a helping person of the same sex, at least nine years older, generally between 25 and 40 years of age (Worby, 1955). The great majority of high school seniors preferred directive to client-centered counseling, but a significantly higher proportion of equalitarian, as compared to authoritarian, personalities preferred the client-centered approach (Sonne and Goldmann, 1957).[1] Preference for a directive counselor reaction to a statement of the student's problem was expressed to a greater degree by high school juniors than seniors, girls than boys, private than public school students (Maher, 1952), and by high school than college students (M. Rogers, 1957). With decisions relating to college attendance, high school students preferred obtaining help primarily from parents and school counselors, in that order (Kerr, 1962).

College Experimental Subjects.—Two experiments involved interviews with non-client college students. Kanfer and Marston (1964) found that (a) subjects preferring interpretive rather than reflective interviewers scored higher on the Minnesota Multiphasic Personality Inventory (MMPI) Schizophrenia Scale and lower on measures of defensiveness and social conformity, (b) those subjects aware that the interviewer's role was to change them requested interviewer re-

---

[1]Data from Section C of Table 2 in Sonne and Goldman (1957) have been recomputed in order to more appropriately test their major hypothesis. The most appropriate test with the available discrete data gives an overall $\chi^2 = 8.50$, $df = 1$, $p = .02$, supporting the difference in preference of authoritarians and equalitarians.

actions less frequently when he consistently disagreed with their comments, and (c) less-conforming subjects increased over time their avoidance of interviewer reactions. Those students whose counselor followed their preference for a "personal" or "objective" vocational counseling interview rated the interview more positively than did those who had the non-preferred interview (Mendelsohn, 1963).

Counselors and Graduate Students in Advanced Counselor Training.—Two groups of graduate student counselor trainees were asked to state preferences for counselors within their own ranks. Those selected most often showed better adjustment on the MMPI and higher interest scores (Kuder Preference Record) in the social service, persuasive, literary, and scientific areas than those choosing them (Arbuckle, 1956). There was no relationship between chosen (or rejected) counselors and those choosing (or rejecting) them in personality, age, and intelligence (Stefflre and Leafgren, 1964). Those most frequently chosen, as compared to a least-often chosen group, were higher in academic performance, had higher Strong Vocational Interest Blank scores in several social service occupations, and were lower on a test of dogmatism (Stefflre, King and Leafgren, 1962).

Discussion

Although the literature on client preferences for certain characteristics and procedures of psychotherapists is not yet sufficiently developed to warrant major interpretation, some suggestions regarding future research are relevant. Certainly the research to date, as well as clinical impressions, suggests that potential and actual clients have implicit and explicit ideas concerning the characteristics they would like manifested in their counselors. These preferences might determine to a significant degree whether or not they seek counseling, length of counseling, various aspects of client-counselor interaction, their subsequent evaluation of the experience, and other measures of the effectiveness of counseling.

There is a remarkable paucity of knowledge of the relationship of client preferences regarding counselors to counseling processes and outcomes. Needed are the following kinds of studies: (a) clients' preferences concerning counselors' age, marital status, race, religion, sex, personality characteristics, physical appearance and attractiveness, professional discipline, and counseling procedures; (b) clients' personality and cultural background as related to these preferences; (c) patients' preferences with respect to *any* relevant behavior, procedures, or characteristics of psychotherapists in psychiatric settings; and (d) clients' ability to discriminate between preferences and expectations. One finding has received considerable confirmation, namely, that students are generally averse to discussing personal-social, as compared with educational-vocational, problems with high school and university counselors. More research should be focused on the bases and impact of such attitudes.

Almost all of the studies on client preferences have relied on the correlational or sample survey design and the questionnaire method of data collection for measurement of preferences and their correlates. Although these are useful exploratory studies, other approaches are also recommended: (a) application of the experimental design for control and measurement of selected variables in the study of preference as an independent or dependent variable (e.g., see Mendelsohn, 1963; Kanfer and Marston, 1964); and (b) the use of skillful interviewing (Spielberger and DeNike, 1962) as well as more oblique and subtle methods for gaining information about preferences, especially the sensitive ones pertaining to race and religion. These are, of course, easier to recommend than to carry out. The Dimascio and Brooks (1961) method, although not originally tried with this purpose in mind, is suggestive. Eliciting patients' reactions to pictures of patient-therapist interactions after a therapy session seems to be too transparent a method, perhaps measuring docility more than preference (Libo, 1957). This method may be amenable to subtle instrumentation, however. Likewise, the sentence completion approach, which in one study apparently elicited what the subjects believed they were expected to produce (Worby, 1955), may prove useful if the research method anticipates this problem of subjects' "hypotheses" (Orne, 1962).

Research on client preferences may prove useful in the study of personality and of cultural influences on behavior. As in the case of preferences elicited in personality and interest tests, preferences regarding counselors may be related to significant attitudes and behavior, especially those toward parents and authority figures (Kapit, 1956; Sechrest, 1962).[2]

References

Arbuckle, D. S. "Client Perception of Counselor Personality." *Journal of Counseling Psychology,* 1956, *3,* 93–96.

Barahal, G. D., Brammer, L. M., & Shostrom, E. L. "A Client-Centered Ap-

[2]The writer has developed a questionnaire for exploratory research on client preferences in school, university, clinic, and social agency settings. See Appendix B.

proach to Vocational Counseling." *Journal of Consulting Psychology,* 1950, *14,* 256–60.

Cundick, B. P. "The Relation of Student and Counselor Expectations to Rated Counseling Satisfaction." Unpublished doctoral dissertation, Ohio State Univ. 1962. *Dissertation Abstracts,* 1963, *23*(8), 2983–84.

Dimascio, A., & Brooks, G. "Free Association to a Fantasied Psychotherapist." *Archives of General Psychiatry,* 1961, *4,* 513–16.

Dittmann, A. T. "Psychotherapeutic Processes." *Annual Review of Psychology,* 1966, *17,* 51–78.

Farberow, N. L. (Ed.) *Taboo Topics.* New York: Atherton Press, 1963.

Forgy, E. W., & Black, J. D. "A Follow-up after Three Years of Clients Counseled by Two Methods." *Journal of Counseling Psychology,* 1954, *1,* 1–8.

Fuller, Frances F. "Influences of Sex of Counselor and of Client on Client Expressions of Feeling." *Journal of Counseling Psychology,* 1963, *10,* 34–40.

Fuller, Frances F. "Preferences for Male and Female Counselors." *Personnel and Guidance Journal,* 1964, *42,* 463–67.

Goldstein, A. P. *Therapist-Patient Expectancies in Psychotherapy.* New York: Macmillan, 1962.

Goodstein, L. D., & Grigg, A. E. "Client Satisfaction, Counselors, and the Counseling Process." *Personnel and Guidance Journal,* 1959, *38,* 19–24.

Grant, C. W. "How Students Perceive the Counselor's Role." *Personnel and Guidance Journal,* 1954, *32,* 386–88.

Grater, H. A. "Client Preferences for Affective or Cognitive Counselor Characteristics and First Interview Behavior." *Journal of Counseling Psychology,* 1964, *11,* 248–50.

Grigg, A. E., & Goodstein, L. D. "The Use of Clients as Judges of the Counselor's Performance." *Journal of Counseling Psychology,* 1957, *4,* 31–36.

Holman, Miriam. "Adolescent Attitudes Toward Seeking Help with Personal Problems." *Smith College Studies in Social Work,* 1955, *25*(3), 1–31.

Jenson, R. E. "Student Feeling About Counseling Help." *Personnel and Guidance Journal,* 1955, *33,* 498–503.

Kanfer, F. H., & Marston, A. R. "Characteristics of Interactional Behavior in a Psychotherapy Analogue." *Journal of Consulting Psychology,* 1964, *28,* 456–67.

Kapit, Hanna E. "Relationships Between Attitudes Toward the Therapist and Attitudes Toward Parents." Unpublished doctoral dissertation, Columbia University, 1956.

Kerr, W. D. "Student Perceptions of Counselor Role in the College Decision." *Personnel and Guidance Journal,* 1962, *41,* 337–42.

King, P. T., & Matteson, R. W. "Student Perception of Counseling Center Services." *Personnel and Guidance Journal,* 1959, *37,* 358–64.

Kintz, B. L., Delprato, D. J., Mettee, D. R., Persons, C. E., & Schappe, R. H. "The Experimenter Effect." *Psychological Bulletin,* 1965, *63,* 223–32.

Klein, F. L. "An Experimental Approach to Modifying Clients' Perceptions of Counseling." Unpublished master's thesis, University of Maryland, 1958.

Koile, E. A., & Bird, Dorothy J. "Preferences for Counselor Help on Freshman Problems." *Journal of Counseling Psychology,* 1956, *3,* 97–106.

Libo, L. M. "The Projective Expression of Patient-Therapist Attraction." *Journal of Clinical Psychology,* 1957, *13,* 33–36.

Maher, T. P. *The Attitude of High School Juniors and Seniors Toward Counseling Procedure with Reference to Certain Personality Factors and*

Personal Problem Frequency. Washington, D. C.: Catholic University of America Press, 1952.

Masling, J. "Role Related Behavior of the Subject and Psychologist and Its Effects upon Psychological Data." In *Nebraska Symposium on Motivation.* Lincoln: University of Nebraska Press, 1966.

Mendelsohn, R. A. "The Effects of Cognitive Dissonance and Interview Preference upon Counseling-type Interviews." Unpublished doctoral dissertation, University of Michigan, 1963.

Orne, M. T. "On the Social Psychology of the Psychological Experiment: With Particular Reference to Demand Characteristics and Their Implications." *American Psychologist,* 1962, *17,* 776–83.

Parloff, M. B., Iflund, B., & Goldstein, N. "Communication of 'Therapy Values,' Between Therapist and Schizophrenic Patients." *Journal of Nervous and Mental Disease,* 1958, *130,* 193–99.

Patterson, C. H. "Client Expectations and Social Conditioning." *Personnel and Guidance Journal,* 1958, *37,* 136–38.

Patterson, C. H. "Comments." *Personnel and Guidance Journal,* 1959, *38,* 25–26.

Patterson, C. H. "Counseling." *Annual Review of Psychology,* 1966, *17,* 79–110.

Pohlman, E. "Changes in Client Preferences During Counseling." *Personnel and Guidance Journal,* 1961, *40,* 340–43.

Pohlman, E. "Should Clients Tell Counselors What To Do?" *Personnel and Guidance Journal,* 1964, *42,* 456–58.

Pohlman, E., & Robinson, F. P. "Client Reaction to Some Aspects of the Counseling Situation." *Personnel and Guidance Journal,* 1960, *38,* 546–51.

Rogers, Mary E. "The Attitude of College Sophomores and Seniors Toward Counseling Procedure with Reference to Certain Personality Factors and Personal Problem Frequency." Unpublished doctoral dissertation, St. Louis University, 1957.

Rosen, A. "Deaf College Students' Preferences Regarding the Hearing Status of Counselors." Unpublished manuscript, Gallaudet College, Washington, D. C., 1966.

Rosenthal, R. "Experimenter Attributes as Determinants of Subjects' Responses." *Journal of Projective Techniques,* 1963, *27,* 324–31.

Sechrest, L. B. "Stimulus Equivalents of the Psychotherapist." *Journal of Individual Psychology,* 1962, *18*(2), 172–76.

Sonne, T. R., & Goldman, L. "Preferences of Authoritarian and Equalitarian Personalities for Client-Centered and Eclectic Counseling." *Journal of Counseling Psychology,* 1957, *4,* 129–35.

Spielberger, C. C., & DeNike, L. D. "Operant Conditioning of Plural Nouns: A Failure To Replicate the Greenspoon Effect." *Psychological Reports,* 1962, *11,* 355–66.

Stefflre, B., King, P., & Leafgren, F. "Characteristics of Counselors Judged Effective by Their Peers." *Journal of Counseling Psychology,* 1962, *9,* 335–40.

Stefflre, B., & Leafgren, F. A. "Mirror, Mirror on the Wall . . . A Study of Preferences for Counselors." *Personnel and Guidance Journal,* 1964, *42,* 459–62.

Stotsky, B. A. "How Important Is Psychotherapy to the Hospitalized Psychiatric Patient." *Journal of Clinical Psychology,* 1956, *12,* 32–36.

Talland, G. A., & Clark, D. H. "Evaluation of Topics in Therapy Group Discussion." *Journal of Clinical Psychology.* 1954, *10,* 131–37.

Warman, R. E. "Differential Perceptions of Counseling Role." *Journal of Counseling Psychology,* 1960, *7,* 269–74.
Worby, Marsha. "The Adolescents' Expectations of How the Potentially Helpful Person Will Act." *Smith College Studies in Social Work,* 1955, *26*(1), 19–59.

*

PREFERENCES FOR MALE AND FEMALE COUNSELORS

FRANCES F. FULLER

To note that the counseling relationship is a dyadic one, that it is dependent upon interaction, has become commonplace. The sophisticated question now is not whether the interaction is influential, but how. In Sanford's words, "The question is, which people, in what circumstances, responding to what therapeutic stimuli" [*16, p. 355*].

Client perceptions and expectations have been hypothesized to be influential in this interaction [*8*]. Hollingshead and Redlich [*12*] and Meyers and Schafer [*15*] have in fact suggested that selective factors may work to limit choice to those patients who are like the therapist in outlook, values, and social background. Fiedler [*5*], in commenting upon the success and failure of therapists in establishing relationships, notes that the "good" therapists in his study were renowned (and presumably favorably perceived by patients) and other therapists were not renowned. He also notes that patients who did not improve were apt to be drawn from a "mental hygiene clinic" population, where, we might suppose, self-selection of patient and therapist was more limited than in private practice.

Mental hygiene clinics are not the only places in which self-selection is limited. In contrast to persons choosing private practitioners,

*This article is reprinted from *Personnel and Guidance Journal,* 1964, *42,* 463–67, by permission of the publisher, the American Personnel and Guidance Association, and the author.

university counseling center clients have little if any information about the counselors to whom they may be assigned and, except in unusual circumstances, such counselors take all comers. Whether the difference in opportunity for selection in the two settings influences the kind of relationships which are established in counseling is not known, but seems worthy of investigation.

A considerable literature on the sex preferences of persons in different age groups, situations, and cultures supports the notion that males and females have distinct preference patterns which are fairly consistent [*1–3*, *10*, *11*, *17–19*, *21*]. The only investigation of preferences for counselors is that of Koile and Bird [*13*] who studied preferences of freshmen for persons from whom they would seek help. Their findings were consistent with those of other studies: although male freshmen preferred a male counselor on far more problems than they preferred a woman counselor and women freshmen preferred a woman counselor on more problems than they preferred a man, the proportionate number of problems on which women were willing to consult a man was greater than the proportionate number on which men were willing to consult a woman. In addition, the men expressed a preference significantly more often than did the women.

Koile and Bird's study apparently has not been utilized, since no investigation of counseling outcome or process seems to have been reported which has taken client preferences into account, and most fail to report the sex composition of the counseling pairs under scrutiny.

At the same time, the literature on influence of examiner upon responses to projective instruments supports the notion that counselor variables such as sex and clients' perceptions of them do influence response [*4*, *6*, *7*].

The purpose of this study was to discover whether clients referring themselves for counseling in a university counseling center do have preferences regarding the sex of the counselor to whom they may be assigned, whether such preferences vary with client sex and presenting problem, and whether preferences change after counseling. An attempt was also made to compare preferences of clients with preferences of non-clients in the same student population, and preferences for friends or personal confidantes with preferences for professional counselors.

Procedure

Students.—Statements regarding sex of person preferred for help with a vocational and a personal problem were secured from 588 university reading program students between 18 and 29 years of age who had never had counseling. Of these 588 students, 303 (195 males and 108 females) were asked to state their preferences if a nonprofessional person (personal confidante) were chosen. The other 285 students (219 males and 66 females) were asked to state their preferences if a professional counselor were chosen. This questionnaire was administered by male instructors.

Clients.—In addition, 534 self-referred clients in the same age group (388 males and 146 females) of a university counseling center were asked on a basic information form filled out before counseling to indicate the nature of their presenting problem and whether they preferred to see a male or female counselor or had no preference. These forms were handed out by a female receptionist as part of regular intake procedure.

Of the 534 clients, 40 clients (20 males and 20 females) were asked to state their counselor preference after counseling as well as before counseling. In each sex group of 20, 8 had initially preferred a male counselor, 8 had had no preference, and 4 had preferred a female counselor. Half of each preference group was counseled by male counselors (2 experienced and 2 inexperienced) and half by female counselors similarly divided. Half of each client preference group and half of each client sex group were assigned in accordance with expressed preference and half of each group assigned in opposition to expressed preference.

Of these 40 clients, 39 presented vocational-educational problems only. One, a male who preferred a female counselor, presented both a vocational and a personal problem, but was included because of the dearth of males who preferred female counselors.

Results

Student Preferences for Personal Confidantes.—As can be seen from Table 1, male students more frequently expressed a preference for a male confidante and less frequently expressed a preference for a female confidante than did female students on both the vocational problem (chi-square = 53.04, $P < 0.01$) and the personal problem (chi-square = 34.61, $P < 0.01$).

Student Preferences for Professional Counselors.—When students were asked to express a preference for a professional counselor (Table 2), males again expressed preferences for male counselors significantly more often and for female counselors less often than did female students on both the vocational problem (chi-square = 18.89, $P < 0.01$) and the personal problem (chi-square = 19.55, $P < 0.01$).

TABLE 1

PERCENTAGES OF NONCLIENT STUDENTS
EXPRESSING PREFERENCES FOR CONFIDANTES

Presented Problem	*Groups*	*—Preferences for Confidantes—* *Prefer Male*	*Prefer Female*	*No Preference*	*N*
Vocational*	Male	49.23	1.03	49.74	195
	Female	12.96	12.04	75.00	108
Personal†	Male	51.28	12.82	35.90	195
	Female	20.37	35.19	44.44	108

†Chi-square = 53.04, $P < 0.01$.
*Chi-square = 34.61, $P < 0.01$.

TABLE 2

PERCENTAGES OF NONCLIENT STUDENTS
EXPRESSING PREFERENCES FOR COUNSELORS

Presented Problem	*Groups*	*—Preferences for Counselors—* *Prefer Male*	*Prefer Female*	*No.Preference*	*N*
Vocational*	Male	63.02	0.90	36.08	219
	Female	40.90	9.10	50.00	66
Personal†	Male	70.32	5.02	24.66	219
	Female	21.22	42.42	36.36	66

*Chi-square = 18.89, $P < 0.01$.
†Chi-square = 19.55, $P < 0.01$.

Table 3 presents frequencies of students who had no preference on one problem but did have some preference on the other problem. Among males, some preference was expressed more frequently on a personal than a vocational problem (chi-square = 14.53, $P < 0.01$). Among females, the same trend is evident, but the required level of significance was not reached (chi-square = 3.00, $P < 0.10$).

TABLE 3

PREFERENCE AND NO-PREFERENCE FREQUENCIES
OF NONCLIENT STUDENTS FOR COUNSELORS

Group	*Personal Problem*	*—Vocational Problem—* *Had Preference*	*No Preference*
Male*	Had Preference	131	34
	No Preference	9	45
Female†	Had Preference	24	18
	No Preference	9	15

*Chi-square = 14.53, $P < 0.01$. (Chi-square from McNemar's [*14, p. 229*] change test.)
†Not significant.

Comparison of Student Preferences for Confidantes and Counselors.—If we consider only male students, and compare their preferences for confidantes (Table 1) and for counselors (Table 2), we find that male students more frequently expressed some preference on a personal problem when choosing a professional counselor than when choosing a personal confidante and this preference is for a male counselor (chi-square = 17.66, $P < 0.01$). The preferences of female students for professional counselors and personal confidantes were not significantly different.

Client Preferences for Counselors.—A comparison of the preferences of clients for counselors by client sex and presenting problem is included in Table 4.

TABLE 4
PERCENTAGES OF CLIENTS EXPRESSING PREFERENCES FOR COUNSELORS

Group	*Presenting Problem*	*Prefer Male*	*Prefer Female*	*No Preference*	*N*	
Male	Educational	26.74	2.33	70.93	86	
	Vocational	46.85	0.00	53.15	143	
	Personal	50.98	2.00	47.10	51	
	Other*	33.33	0.93	65.74	108	
					Total	388
Female	Educational	20.00	2.50	77.50	40	
	Vocational	29.63	3.71	66.66	27	
	Personal	42.86	9.52	47.62	21	
	Other*	24.13	8.62	67.25	58	
					Total	146

*Includes test interpretations and ambiguous problems.

In contrast to non-clients, expected frequency of preference for female counselors among clients was too small to justify comparison of preferences by counselor sex despite an N of 534. It is apparent however that the previously observed preference of students for male counselors holds *a fortiori* among clients, and when we test this by rearranging the data into same-sex and other-sex preferences, a comparison between male and female clients indicates that males more frequently preferred male counselors than females preferred female counselors (chi-square = 126.11, $P < 0.01$).

Presence or absence of a preference was related to presenting problem (chi-square = 17.65, $P < 0.01$), some preference being expressed more frequently when the problem was personal than when it was not.

Comparison of Preferences of Clients and Non-Clients.—Preferences of clients with real vocational problems did not differ significantly from preferences of students presented with a hypothetical vocational problem either among males or females. However, female clients with real personal problems (Table 4) expressed preferences for male counselors more often and for female counselors less often than did non-client female students (Table 2) presented with a hypothetical personal problem (chi-square = 7.03, $P < 0.05$).

Changes in Preferences After Counseling.—Pre- and post-counseling preferences of 40 clients are summarized in Table 5.

TABLE 5
FREQUENCIES OF CLIENTS' PRE- AND POST-COUNSELING PREFERENCES REGARDING COUNSELOR SEX

	Pre-Counseling Preferences								
	Male Clients				*Female Clients*				
Post-Counseling Preferences	*Preferred Male*	*Preferred Female*	*No Preference*	*Total*	*Preferred Male*	*Preferred Female*	*No Preference*	*Total*	*Total*
Prefer Male	7	3	2	12	8	0	4	12	24
Prefer Female	0	1	0	1	0	2	1	3	4
No Preference	1	0	6	7	0	2	3	5	12
TOTAL	8	4	8	20	8	4	8	20	40

In this form, expected frequencies do not justify the use of chi-square to compare pre- and post-counseling preferences. However, if we rearrange the data, Fisher's exact test can be applied to compare clients who initially had a preference but changed preference, with clients who had a preference and did not change. Using this test, clients who initially preferred female counselors were more likely to change preferences than were those who initially preferred male counselors ($P < 0.01$) but there was no difference in frequency of change between male and female clients.

DISCUSSION

The findings that both males and females prefer male counselors more than they prefer female counselors and that preferences for male counselors are more stable than preferences for female counselors are not unexpected. Both boys and girls assign greater prestige value to the masculine than the feminine role [*1*]. Boys prefer boy playmates while girls seem evenly divided [*3*]. Girls express more negative attitudes toward their own sex with increasing age [*10, 11*] and older males attribute more unfavorable characteristics to women than any other age-sex group [*17*]. This pattern is apparently not peculiar to this culture. In a study of sex-dependent differences of national stereotypes [*19*], both men and women attributed more highly valued characteristics to men than they attributed to women.

Before jumping to any conclusions about the relative stimulus value of male and female counselors, it should be remembered that no relationship has been established between client preference or client assignment according to that preference and any counseling variables.

However, preference patterns may be of interest in designing research concerned with both client and counselor variables. For example, one client variable thought to be associated with counseling failure is ethnocentrism [*2*]. If we define ethnocentrism as an exaggerated tendency to prefer those of like persuasion, having a strong preference might be studied in relation to failure in counseling. Or, again, when client and counselor sex are of interest, simple balancing of male and female clients and male and female counselors might well result in more frequent opposite preference assignments for male clients, female counselors, and personal problem clients, than for female clients, male counselors, and vocational problem clients. In addition, although the preferences of vocational problem clients seemed similar to the preferences of students in the population from which the clients were drawn, the preferences of personal problem clients were apparently somewhat different from those of other students, so that findings regarding preferences of a student population are not very useful predictors of preferences of clients even in the same student body.

A considerable research effort has been devoted to discovering subtle similarities between clients and counselors, sometimes assuming that clients are not sufficiently sophisticated to know or describe what they want or need. By comparison, merely asking a client about his preferences and proceeding from there seems a simple-minded approach. However, clients may have preferences and perceptions regarding other counselor characteristics (age, educational background, experience, socio-economic status, etc.) which can be verbalized by them and investigated in relationship to counseling process and outcome.

Summary

Pre-counseling preferences regarding counselor sex were secured from 588 non-clients and 534 clients, and both pre- and post-counseling preferences from 40 of the clients.

Male non-clients preferred male counselors and confidantes more frequently and female counselors and confidantes less frequently than did females for both vocational and personal problems. Males expressed some preference more often on a personal than a vocational problem, and more often when choosing a counselor for a personal problem than when choosing a confidante.

Female clients with personal problems preferred male counselors more frequently than female non-clients. Clients who preferred female counselors before counseling were more likely to change preference after counseling than were clients who had preferred male counselors.

Although no relationship between preferences and any counseling variables has been established, the implications of this study for the design of research concerned with client and counselor variables were discussed.

References

1. Brown, D. G. "Sex Role Preference in Young Children." *Psychological Monographs,* 1956, *70,* No. 14 (Whole No. 421).

2. Brown, D. C. "Masculinity-Femininity Development in Children." *Journal of Consulting Psychology,* 1957, *21,* 197–202.

3. Campbell, Elsie H. "The Social-Sex Development of Children." *Genetic Psychology Monographs,* 1939, *21,* 461–552.

4. Curtis, H. S., & Wolf, B. "The Influence of the Sex of the Examiner on the Production of Sex Responses on the Rorschach." *American Psychologist,* 1951, *6,* 345–46.

5. Fiedler, F. E. "Quantitative Studies on the Role of Therapists' Feelings Toward Their Patients." In O. H. Mowrer, *Psychotherapy, Theory and Research.* New York: Ronald Press, 1953.

6. Gibby, R. G. "Examiner Influence on the Rorschach Inquiry." *Journal of Consulting Psychology,* 1952, 15, 449–465.

7. Gibby, R. G., Miller, D. R., & Walker, E. L. "The Examiner's Influence on the Rorschach Protocol." *Journal of Consulting Psychology,* 1953, *17,* 425–28.

8. Goodstein, L. D., & Grigg, A.E. "Client Satisfaction, Counselors, and the Counseling Process." *Personnel and Guidance Journal,* 1959, *38,* (1), 19–24.

9. Guilford, J. P. *Fundamental Statistics in Psychology and Education.* New York: McGraw-Hill, 1956.

10. Harris, D. G., & Tseng, S. C. "Children's Attitudes Towards Peers and Parents as Revealed by Sentence Completions." *Child Development,* 1957, *28,* 401–11.

11. Hawkes, G. R., Burchinal, L. G., & Gardner, B. "Preadolescents' View of

Some of Their Relations with Their Parents." *Child Development,* 1957, *28,* 387–99.

12. Hollingshead, A. B., & Redlich, F. "Social Stratification and Psychiatric Disorders." *American Sociological Review,* 1953, *18,* 163–69.

13. Koile, E. A., & Bird, Dorothy J. "Preferences for Counselor Help on Freshman Problems." *Journal of Counseling Psychology,* 1956, *3,* 97–106.

14. McNemar, Q. *Psychological Statistics.* New York: John Wiley, 1955.

15. Meyers, J. K., & Schafer, L. "Social Stratification and Psychiatric Practice: A Study of an Outpatient Clinic." *American Sociological Review,* 1954, *19,* 307–13.

16. Sanford, R. M. "Psychotherapy." In *Annual Review of Psychology.* Stanford: Stanford University Press, 1953.

17. Secord, P. F. "Facial Features and Inference Processes in Interpersonal Perception." In R. Tagiuri & L. Petrullo (eds.), *Person Perception and Interpersonal Behavior.* Stanford: Stanford University Press, 1958.

18. Smith, S. "Age and Sex Differences in Children's Opinions Concerning Sex Differences." *Journal of Genetic Psychology,* 1939, *54,* 17–25.

19. Sodhi, K. S., Bergues, R., & Holzkamp, K. "Geschlechtsabhangige Uterschiede Nationales Sterotypen." *J. Psychol,* 1956, *4,* 263–96. Cited in *Psychological Abstracts,* 1958.

20. Tougas, R. R. "Ethnocentrism as a Limiting Factor in Verbal Therapy." In C. R. Rogers & R. F. Dymond (eds.), *Psychotherapy and Personality Change.* University of Chicago Press, 1954.

21. Tyler, Leona E. *The Psychology of Human Differences.* New York: Appleton-Century-Crofts, 1947.

CLIENT PERCEPTIONS OF THERAPISTS: A STUDY OF THE THERAPEUTIC RELATION

MAURICE LORR

An important feature of the therapeutic relationship is the client's perception of and feeling toward the therapist. This aspect of the relationship has become identified with Freud's term "transference." However, in defining transference, some investigators such as Apfelbaum (1958) emphasize the clients' "strongly held expectations regarding the personalities of their prospective therapists" gained prior

*This article is reprinted from *Journal of Consulting Psychology,* 1964, *28,* 146–49, by permission of the publisher, the American Psychological Association, and the author.

to therapy. These expectations mould experience, creating misperceptions and inappropriate responses. Others like Snyder and Snyder (1961) regard transference simply as the character of the client's feeling and attitudes toward his therapist. The view taken by the writer is that the client brings to treatment certain well-established interpersonal reaction patterns. An individual's interpersonal behavior with significant others will be similar to the behavior he experienced in childhood, usually with his parents (Schutz, 1958, p. 196). When the client perceives his adult position in an interpersonal situation to be similar to his own position in his childhood relations, his adult behavior will be similar to his childhood behavior toward significant others. For example, the client may perceive and react to his therapist as though the latter were a rejecting parent, a competitive sibling, a nurturant protector, or a stern authority figure. The client's perception of his therapist will thus, at any stage of therapy, be a useful indicator of his interpersonal relation to his therapist.

In view of the importance of client perception of the therapist, it would be of considerable value to determine the major ways in which clients view their therapists. Accordingly, this study was designed to identify some of the principal dimensions of client perception of therapists. To this end eight constructs were hypothesized. Several concepts were drawn from Fiedler's (1950, 1953) conceptualizations of what constitutes a good therapeutic relationship. Other sources examined were Apfelbaum's *Q*-sort statements, as well as the concepts developed by Leary and his associates (Leary, 1957). The constructs postulated were the following: Directiveness, Nurturance, Understanding, Acceptance, Equalitarianism, Independence-Encouraging, Critical Detachment, and Hostile Rejection.

Method

An inventory of 65 statements was constructed and assembled. Each of the postulated constructs was defined by 4–10 statements descriptive of therapist behaviors. The patient indicated how often the therapist exhibited the behavior described (almost never, sometimes, usually, nearly always). The inventory was administered to 523 patients in individual psychotherapy in 43 veterans' clinics in connection with a larger study of the correlates of length of psychotherapy. All patients had been in treatment at least 3 months but not more than 10 years. Approximately 50 per cent of the sample were neurotics, 32 per cent psychotics, and the remainder, personality disorders and psychophysiological disturbances.

TABLE 1

CORRELATIONS OF PERCEIVED THERAPIST BEHAVIORS WITH FACTORS

	r_{tv}
Factor A: Understanding	
Seems to know exactly what I mean.	.66
Seems to understand how I feel.	.61
Realizes and understands how my experiences feel to me.	.60
Understands me even when I don't express myself well.	.59
Misses the point I am trying to get across.	—.48
Has a hard time seeing things as I do.	—.47
Has difficulty understanding what I am trying to express.	—.45
Is protective of and really concerned about my welfare.	.43
Makes comments that are right in line with what I am saying	.41
Factor B: Accepting	
Shows a real interest in me and my problems.	.66
Is easy to talk to.	.58
Acts as though we were co-workers on a common problem.	.54
Makes me feel that he is one person I can really trust.	.52
Is quick to praise and commend me when I am doing well.	.50
Gives generously of his time and energy to others.	.50
Understands my problems and worries.	.49
Shows a real liking and affection for me.	.47
Makes me feel free to say whatever I think.	.46
Seems to have a very real respect for me.	.45
Makes me feel better after talking about my worries with him.	.43
Relates to me as though I were a companion.	.43
Factor C: Authoritarian	
Is full of advice about everything I do.	.61
Tells me what to do when I have difficult decisions to make.	.59
Offers me advice on my everyday problems.	.54
Seems to try to get me to accept his standards.	.52
Expects me to accept his ideas and opinions.	.50
Tries to get me to think as he does.	.47
Makes me feel that I don't have to agree with him.	—.29
Tells me what I should talk about.	.28
Factor D: Independence-Encouraging	
Expects an individual to shoulder his own responsibilities.	.71
Thinks people should be able to help themselves.	.67
Encourages me to work on my own problems in my own way.	.51
Tries to get me to make my own decisions.	.47
Factor E: Critical-Hostile	
Becomes impatient when I make mistakes.	.46
Acts smug and superior as though he knew all the answers.	.45
Acts as though he were trying to outsmart me.	.41
Gives me the impression that he doesn't like me.	.37
Talks down to me as if I were a child.	.35
Ignores some of my feelings.	.32
Is critical and not easily impressed.	.32
Acts as though I were dull and uninteresting.	.29
Is a difficult person to warm up to.	.29
Seems glad to see the interview finished.	.28

TABLE 2

CORRELATIONS AMONG THERAPIST BEHAVIOR PATTERNS AS PERCEIVED BY CLIENTS

Therapist Behavior	*Factor*				
	A	*B*	*C*	*D*	*E*
Understanding (A)	—				
Accepting (B)	.23	—			
Authoritarian (C)	.29	.25	—		
Independence-Encouraging (D)	.02	—.14	—.05	—	
Critical-Hostile (E)	—.25	—.44	.14	.17	—

Responses to the statements were intercorrelated and ordered into a matrix on the basis of the hypothesized eight clusters. Examination revealed that three of the clusters were not distinguishable from the remaining five. As a consequence, the variables were reclustered entirely on the basis of their statistical properties. Five distinguishable orthogonal factors were extracted simultaneously by the multiple-group centroid method, with the highest correlation in a column as the communality estimate. The factor matrix was then transformed to oblique simple structure.

RESULTS

The results of the analysis are presented in Tables 1 and 2. The behaviors most substantially correlated with each factor are given in Table 1. Negative signs should be interpreted to mean that the behavior described occurred rarely.

Factor A, Understanding, is defined by behaviors that indicate the therapist understands what the patient is communicating and what he is feeling. The factor corresponds closely to Roger's (1957) postulated requirement for effective therapy. Factor B is the broadest of the five factors isolated. Interest, Nurturance, and Equalitarianism appear to play equal roles in definition of this factor, which is tentatively called Accepting.

In Factor C may be found those behaviors of the therapist relating to control. The client perceives the therapist as offering advice, direction, and assistance in reaching decisions. It should be noted that nurturant and supportive items correlate with Factor B and not with Factor C, which is labeled Authoritarian. The fourth factor, D, is relatively small but sharply defined. The pattern describes the postulated Independence-Encouraging construct. Every statement allocated to D correlated significantly only on D as predicted. The fifth factor, E, is labeled Critical-Hostile. The client perceives his therapist as critical, cold, impatient, even competitive and disapproving.

The correlations among the factors (Table 2) indicate that on the whole the five factors are relatively independent. The small positive intercorrelations among factors Understanding, Accepting, and Authoritarian imply that a higher order factor common to the three could be demonstrated.

Discussion

Rausch and Bordin (1957) in their discussion of the concept of therapist warmth present it as divisible into three more elementary notions called commitment, understanding, and spontaneity. Commitment refers to the degree to which the therapist seems willing to devote and lend himself to what the patient lacks. The concept of commitment appears to correspond closely to the factor of Accepting. Their concept of understanding refers to the therapist's effort to understand how the patient experiences himself and the world around him and appears to correspond to Factor A. The third element, spontaneity, is not clearly defined and appears not to have a correlative factor in the present study.

Fiedler (1950) envisages three dimensions in the therapeutic relationship. One is the therapist's ability to communicate with and to understand the patient. This variable is confirmed in Factor A, Understanding. The emotional distance which the therapist maintains toward the patient (close versus far), Fiedler's second variable, appears to be represented both by Critical-Hostility and Acceptance. The third Fiedler variable, the status of the therapist in relation to the patient (superior, equal, or subordinate), appears to be a composite variable. The attitude of superiority is reflected to some extent in the Authoritarian factor. The equalitarian tendencies are absorbed in Accepting, Factor B.

Apfelbaum (1958) in constructing his *Q*-sort items attempted to maximize intersorter variance. He constructed statements which were ambiguous enough to make the meaning given them a source of differentiating power. However, by and large, the items covered a wide variety of interpersonal expectations relevant to the psychotherapeutic situation. His procedures permitted him to discover only the principal themes that created difference among his three patient clusters, as he did not factor his *Q*-sort items. The themes suggested by the discriminating items were: warmth-nurturance versus coldness-indifference; directiveness versus nondirectiveness, i.e., independence-encouraging. The first theme may be seen to resemble the Accepting and Critical-Hostile factors. The second theme is represented by Authoritarian and Independence-Encouraging factors.

The factors identified thus correspond fairly well to those described by Rausch and Bordin, Fiedler, and Apfelbaum. But, do the dimensions isolated represent observed therapist behaviors or the expectations and distortions of the patient who made the ratings? The data do not permit such a question to be answered. The situation itself suggests the rating constitutes a complex amalgam of both sources of variance. However, it seems likely that the same dimensions are involved in either case. Dimensions of patient expectations will correspond fairly well to observed therapist behavior dimensions in therapy. Indirect support for this hypothesis is the *Q*-sort findings of Apfelbaum previously cited.

TABLE 3
RELATIONS BETWEEN CLIENT AND THERAPIST RATINGS AND PERCEIVED THERAPIST BEHAVIORS

	Improvement Rating		*Judged Client*
Therapist Behavior	*Client*	*Therapist*	*Satisfaction*
Understanding	.31	.19	.30
Accepting	.24	.16	.24
Authoritarian	—.16	—.03	—.19
Independence-Encouraging	.13	.08	.09
Critical-Hostile	—.19	—.06	—.08

Note.—Correlations greater than .13 are significant, $p < .02$.

Of some interest are the relations of three ratings, obtained from patients and their therapists at the time of the completion of the inventory, to the inventory scores. As Table 3 shows, patient ratings of overall improvement and therapist judgments of patient satisfaction with treatment are positively correlated with the same factors. Patient ratings of therapist Understanding and Accepting are significantly associated with these two judgments. To a lesser extent the therapist improvement ratings are also associated with favorable perceptions of the patient. The results thus support the hypothesized importance of client views of their therapists.

REFERENCES

Apfelbaum, B. *Dimensions of Transference in Psychotherapy.* Berkeley: University of California Publications, 1958.

Fiedler, F. E. "The Concept of an Ideal Therapeutic Relationship." *Journal of Consulting Psychology,* 1950, *14,* 239–45.

Fiedler, F. E. "Quantitative Studies on the Role of Therapists' Feelings Toward Their Patients." In O. H. Mowrer (ed.), *Psychotherapy Theory and Research.* New York: Ronald Press, 1953.

Leary, T. *Interpersonal Diagnosis of Personality*. New York: Ronald Press, 1957.

Rausch, H. L., & Bordin, E. S. "Warmth in Personality Development and in Psychotherapy." *Psychiatry,* 1957, *20,* 351–63.

Rogers, C. R. "The Necessary and Sufficient Conditions of Therapeutic Personality Change." *Journal of Consulting Psychology,* 1957, *21,* 95–103.

Schutz, W. C. *FIRO: A Three-Dimensional Theory of Interpersonal Behavior*. New York: Rinehart, 1958.

Snyder, W. J., & Snyder, B. June. *The Psychotherapy Relationship.* New York: Macmillan, 1961.

COUNSELOR NEEDS FOR AFFILIATION AND NURTURANCE AS RELATED TO LIKING FOR CLIENTS AND COUNSELING PROCESS[1]

DAVID H. MILLS
NORMAN ABELES

Most writers who concern themselves with counseling make the assumption, either explicit or implied, that the counselor must have a need to help and to be with others. Rogers (1959) stressed such counselor traits, primarily in his discussion of positive regard (which includes such counselor characteristics as warmth, liking, respect for the client, sympathy and acceptance), and its corollary, unconditional positive regard. In another, less formal presentation, Grater, Kell, and Morse (1959), have addressed themselves to what they call "the social service need" which seems essentially the need to

*This article is reprinted from *Journal of Counseling Psychology,* 1965, *12,* 353–58, by permission of the publisher, the American Psychological Association, and the authors.

[1]Based in part on an unpublished doctoral dissertation of the first author at Michigan State University. This study was in part supported by a National Institute of Mental Health Post-Doctoral Research Grant, 1-F2-MH-23, 027-01 taken at the University of Illinois. The authors are greatly indebted to John Hartzell who collected some of the data.

help clients and, therefore, to be with them. They have called this need to help "almost a prerequisite and probably a necessity for job satisfaction" as a counselor (p. 10). This seems to be the general trend throughout the literature. One possible exception might be classic psychoanalytic theory which would, in its "purest" form, demand of the counselor that he ". . . put aside all his own feelings, including that of human sympathy, and concentrate his mind on one single purpose, that of performing (the counseling) as skillfully as possible" (Freud, 1912, p. 327). However, most current analytic thinking has deviated from the above dictum and will allow the counselor his own feelings and satisfactions from the counseling (e.g., Reich, 1951; Menninger, 1958). Indeed, a careful reading of Freud's published case histories will suggest that Freud allowed himself this very freedom.

However, despite the general agreement concerning the importance of the therapist's need to help and to be with others (hereafter, called the needs for nurturance and for affiliation), there has been only a limited amount of research in this area. Abeles (1964) in a study relating "liking" for clients to therapists' personality found an inverse relationship between "liking" and therapists' projection of hostility and anxiety on a projective test. This study also suggested an inverse relationship between accuracy of form perception (of therapists) and liking for clients. The author speculated that "those therapists who are able to like clients who are on an objective basis rather unlikeable, set aside a certain amount of perceptual accuracy in order to facilitate therapeutic movement."

Other studies (Stoler, 1963; Caracena, 1963; Strupp, 1960) suggest that a counselor's positive feelings about a client (he likes the client, and presumably desires to be with him and to help him) would predict successful therapeutic outcomes, longer counseling, or, in the absence of outcome measures, a favorably rated prognosis. These findings have implications that the counselor's need for nurturance and affiliation has important bearing on counseling.

Method

SUBJECTS

The subjects in this study were all either staff members, interns, or practicum students at the Michigan State University Counseling Center. The sample consisted of 13 full-time staff members (all with doctoral degrees in either clinical or counseling psychology), 14 interns all of whom were advanced doctoral students in either clinical or counseling psychology working a minimum of 20 hours weekly at the Counseling Center (most of this time being spent in doing individual counseling), and ten beginning practicum students who were seeing their first clients in counseling.

Nurturant and Affiliative Needs.—The dependent variables in this study are the needs for nurturance and for affiliation as measured on the Edwards Personal Preference Schedule (Edwards, 1953).

The Independent Variables.—The independent variables in this study are twofold. First, each participating therapist contributed a tape-recorded fifth counseling interview with a client coming for personal counseling or therapy. For the senior staff and intern groups, these tapes were obtained from the Counseling Center tape library and are presumably randomly selected clients. The practicum students contributed their tapes directly. Each tape ($N = 37$) was then scored contentually, using a system reported by Winder, Ahmad, and Rau (1960), yielding two content scores for each therapist, the per cent of times he approached his client's dependency bids and the per cent he approached the client's hostility statements. Reliability of the scoring, established using an independent scorer for 33 of the 37 tapes, was .9435 (product-moment) for the approach to dependency, and .8872 for the approach to hostility.

The second independent variable was "liking for clients" as a counselor trait. This was established using the semantic differential (Osgood, Suci, and Tannenbaum, 1957). "Liking" was operationally defined for each participating therapist as the average deviation between his responses to a semantic differential, the stimulus for which was "the kind of client with whom I like to work" and his responses to five identical semantic differentials, the stimulus for each being the client in five typescripts of actual counseling sessions (which the counselor was furnished but heretofore unfamiliar with). Two "liking" scores were thusly derived, one the raw mean deviation between the two sets of responses (called "Raw Liking"), and the second being the "Raw Liking" score corrected for the rater/counselor's central tendency style (and called "Corrected Liking").

HYPOTHESES

Four hypotheses were advanced. The first was that a counselor's need for nurturance and his liking for clients would be positively related. Similar to the first, the second hypothesis was that the need for affiliation would relate positively to liking for clients. These hypotheses are in the main derived primarily from Edwards' (1953) description of the two need areas, i.e., need for nurturance being defined (in part) as being the need to help others, to treat them with kindness and sympathy, to show affection towards them, and to like to have others confide in you. The need for affiliation is likewise in part described as the need to do things for friends, to form new relationships, to make as many friends as possible, to form strong attachments. These descriptions also led to the other two hypotheses, i.e., that there will be a positive relationship between the therapist's needs for nurturance and for affiliation and his approaches to hostility and dependency. Essentially, these latter two hypotheses are that high affiliative and nurturant needs in therapists will cause them to approach both dependency and hostility in their clients; in Rogerian terms, nurturant, affiliative therapists, by their high approach rates, should help the client ". . . feel more acceptance (from the counselor) of all his own experiences, and this makes him more acceptant of all his own experiences, and this makes him more of a whole or congruent person, able to function effectively" (Rogers, 1959, p. 208).

With regard to counselors' approach to hostility, there seems to be considerable agreement that hostility needs to be dealt with in order for counseling to be successful. Fromm-Reichmann (1950) puts it this way:

> I am not in agreement with the teachings of classical analysis, according to which people are born to be hostile and aggressive. . . . In this hostile world of ours, however, every person . . . has sufficient reason for learning to develop reactions of hostility. . . . Furthermore, they interpret the therapist's behavior and communications along the lines of their unfavorable past experience with other people. Hence, it follows that every mental patient will have to express a marked degree of hostility in the course of his interpersonal dealings with the therapist. This being so, psychotherapy can be successful only if the psychiatrist is secure enough himself so that he will be able to deal adequately with the hostile reactions of his patients (p. 22).

While Fromm-Reichmann is talking here about mental patients, it is the authors' contention that to some extent this is equally applicable to the counseling situation with less severely disturbed individuals.

Results and Discussion

"Liking" and the Needs for Affiliation and Nurturance.—Table 1 reflects the relationship between the needs for nurturance and for

TABLE 1
CORRELATION BETWEEN COUNSELORS' LIKING FOR CLIENTS AND THEIR NEEDS FOR AFFILIATION AND FOR NURTURANCE

Liking Score	*Need for Nurturance*	*Need for Affiliation*
RAW LIKING		
All Counselors $N = 37$	.089	.143
Senior staff $N = 13$	.298	.256
Interns $N = 14$	—.130	—.146
Practicum $N = 10$	.695*	.670*
CORRECTED LIKING		
All Counselors	.133	.180
Senior Staff	.245	.435
Interns	—.076	—.262
Practicum	.799†	.898‡

*$p < .05$.
†$p < .01$.
‡$p < .001$.

affiliation and the counselors' liking for clients. A significant relationship between the need for nurturance and liking was found only for the practicum students. For the other two groups, the relationship was not significant though it was in the predicted direction for the senior staff. As Grater, Kell, and Morse (1961) have discussed, the area of counseling attracts people with initially high nurturant needs (hence the high relationship between need for nurturance and liking —the beginning therapist needs to nurture and to like people). However, with increasing experience, the counselor is faced with a paradox—he chose to do counseling in part presumably because of this need to take care of and to like people and yet he is forced "to limit the expression of his own needs and to derive his satisfactions essentially from meeting the needs of others rather than expressing his own except for nurturance . . . but his professional role limits how freely he may express his nurturant need lest he establish an unhealthy relationship" (Grater, *et al.*, p. 10). So with increasing experience in doing therapy, the counselor is forced to forego the satisfaction of his own nurturant need in part in order to enhance the well-being and protection of his client. The data suggest, though the entire trend is not significant statistically, that the beginning counselor expects to (and probably does) nurture clients whom he likes. With experience, however, he soon learns that too much nurturance is not good as he is exposed to "transference cures" (clients looking better only because of their relationship to the counselor) or, for the Rogerian or existentialist counselor, to the stifling of the client's self-actualization because of too much dependency upon the therapist. At a middle point in experience (i.e., for the present sample, during the internship), the therapist foregoes much of his need for nurturance with clients whom he likes. There then occur as mentioned above, trends in the data which suggest that once the intern is "over the hump," he again with increasing experience is able to satisfy his needs for nurturance with clients whom he likes (though not to the degree he had in his initial stages of training).

The relationship between the need for affiliation and the liking scores is essentially the same as that for nurturance and liking, i.e., for practicum students, the need is significantly and positively related with liking; for interns, the relationship is negative but non-significant; and for senior staff members, the relationship is again positive but not quite significant. The similarity between the results for practicum students for nurturance and for affiliation when compared with the liking scores is not surprising since, as reflected in Table 2, the two needs correlate for that group .69. Such a relationship is suggested in the Grater paper which indicates that counseling is chosen to satisfy a need to take care of and to be close to other people but once the profession is chosen it is found to be a "rather lonely kind of work . . . basically unilateral and not reciprocal" (p. 10). It is not surprising to see further in Table 2 that with experience in doing

TABLE 2

CORRELATIONS BETWEEN NEED FOR NURTURANCE AND NEED FOR AFFILIATION ACROSS EXPERIENCE LEVELS

Group	*Correlation*
Total Sample $N = 37$	.247
Senior Staff $N = 13$	—.234
Interns $N = 14$	—.260
Practicum $N = 10$	.690*
Edwards Normative Sample	.460

*$p < .05$

counseling, the needs for affiliation and for nurturance become quite disassociated, the correlations between the two needs for the interns and senior staff members are negative and non-significant. The present data then suggest that (in doing counseling) counselors beyond the beginning stages of training do not reflect a significant relationship between liking and the need for affiliation. As Grater, *et al.* (1961) would predict, experienced counselors do not systematically satisfy their needs to be with people simply because they have high liking scores. This is true only for the practicum students who ostensibly have not yet learned that therapy is a "rather lonely kind of work" and has to be that way.

Approaches to Dependency and Hostility and Counselors' Needs for Nurturance and Affiliation.—The results of the two hypotheses relating the two need areas to the counselors' approach to hostility and dependency in an actual counseling situation are somewhat puzzling (as seen in Table 3).

TABLE 3
CORRELATIONS BETWEEN COUNSELORS' NEEDS FOR NURTURANCE AND FOR AFFILIATION AND THEIR APPROACH TO HOSTILITY AND TO DEPENDENCY

	All Counselors	*Senior Staff*	*Intern*	*Practicum*
Approach to Hostility with				
Need for Nurturance	.366*	.491*	—.039	.752†
Need for Affiliation	.397*	.130	.495*	.625*
Approach to Dependency with				
Need for Nurturance	—.119	—.240	—.160	.044
Need for Affiliation	.093	—.035	—.096	.189

*$p < .05$.
†$p < .01$.

The need for nurturance significantly related to the approach to hostility for the senior staff and practicum groups. No relationship, however, between the need for nurturance and the approach to dependency was found. Likewise, the need for affiliation related positively for the practicum and intern groups to the approach to hostility, but for none of the groups, to the approach to dependency. The immediate question which is raised is: why do presumably nurturant (and affiliative) counselors not approach dependency more often than less nurturant counselors? Also, why do these counselors approach hostility more than dependency? It must be remembered that the interviews from which the approach percentages were obtained were fifth interviews and, since the stress at the MSU Counseling Center is toward an intensive, relationship-oriented counseling, the quality of the relationships was likely strong enough to permit more approaches to client hostility. Initial dependency bids had presumably been met by the nurturant/affiliative counselors, and the quick drop-outs from counseling had already occurred. The approach to hostility percentage was rising from the level where it had been in the first interviews (Kopplin, 1963); the approach to dependency is, nonetheless, stable across interviews (Caracena, 1963; Schuldt, 1964) and, hence, relatively speaking there was more approach to hostility as compared to the approach to dependency in fifth interviews than in earlier ones.

Actually as has been suggested above, counselors may well have to bridle the expression of the nurturant and affiliative needs in order to meet the demands of the counseling situation and of the clients appropriately. That this may be the case is also suggested by Snyder (1963) who writes:

> Since the counselor is assuming in this situation a role much like that of a parent, he must be careful to avoid repeating the errors that the real parent has made in producing the excessive dependency of the client . . . when the client finds "leaning on the counselor" too comfortable, the counselor will need to push him to make some efforts of his own. The counselor must re-condition this dependency into a striving to do things himself (p. 6).

In other words, it may make sense, after counseling has started, to find that nurturant counselors begin to train the client for independent functioning rather than reinforce his present dependency. This could account for the present results.

As predicted, the need for nurturance and for affiliation in general related positively to the approach to hostility. This adds support to Muncie (1959) who stated that apart from being nurturant one of the counselor's needs must be "the need to uncover the damaging personality aspects in the actual workings, thereby generating additional suffering as guilt, anxiety, and hostility directed against us or against self" (p. 1325).

Then, as therapy progresses (at least until the fifth interview) this need to uncover apparently also increases, thus generating hostility toward the counselor and toward the self. The present data reflect that high-nurturant practicum students and senior staff members are able to tolerate (i.e., approach) this hostility. The intern group, as has been noted elsewhere (Mills, 1964), appears to be in a state of flux where the interns' intense concentration on counseling and their learning of the danger of satisfying their own nurturant needs too much in counseling has meant a withdrawal of the direct satisfaction of this need in counseling. The practicum students have yet to be exposed to this difficulty, and the senior staff apparently have resolved it. The situation is somewhat different in looking at the need for affiliation. Here, only the practicum and intern groups reflect significant relationships between the need and the approach to hostility. This is quite congruent with the discussion of Grater, *et al.* (1961) who posit for beginning counselors a high need to be with people (i.e., for affiliation) which is progressively frustrated in the actual "lonely kind of work" of doing counseling. Hence, the relationship between the need for affiliation and the approach to hostility decreases as experience increases.

References

Abeles, N. "Liking for Clients—Its Relationship to Therapist's Personality and Empathic Understanding." Paper presented at American Psychological Association, Los Angeles, 1964.

Caracena, P. F. "Verbal Reinforcement of Client Dependency in the Initial Stage of Psychotherapy." Unpublished doctoral dissertation, Michigan State University, 1963.

Edwards, A. L. *Manual for the Personal Preference Scale.* New York: Norton, 1953.

Freud, S. "Recommendations for Physicians on the Psychoanalytic Method of Treatment (1912)." In *Collected Papers,* Vol. 2, New York: Basic Books, 1959.

Fromm-Reichmann, F. *Principles of Intensive Psychotherapy.* Chicago: University of Chicago Press, 1950.

Grater, H. A., Kell, B. L., & Morse, Josephine. "The Social Service Interest: Roadblock and Road to Creativity." *Journal of Counseling Psychology,* 1961, *8,* 9–12.

Kopplin, D. A. "Hostility of Patients and Psychotherapists' Approach-Avoidance Responses in the Initial Stage of Psychotherapy." Unpublished master's thesis, Michigan State University, 1963.

Menninger, K. *Theory of Psychoanalytic Technique.* New York: Basic Books, 1958.

Mills, D. H. "Liking as a Therapist Variable in the Psychotherapeutic Interaction." Unpublished doctoral dissertation, Michigan State University, 1964.

Muncie, W. "The Psychobiological Approach." In S. Arieti (ed.) *American Handbook of Psychiatry.* New York: Basic Books, 1959.

Osgood, C. E., Suci, G. J., & Tannenbaum, P. H. *The Measurement of Meaning.* Urbana: University of Illinois Press, 1957.

Reich, Annie. "On Counter-Transference." *International Journal of Psycho-Analysis,* 1951, *32,* 25–31.

Rogers, C. R. "A Theory of Therapy, Personality and Interpersonal Relations, as developed in the Client-centered Framework." In S. Koch (ed.), *Psychology: A Study of a Science,* III, 184–256. New York: McGraw-Hill, 1959.

Schuldt, W. J. "Psychotherapists' Approach-Avoidance Reactions and Clients' Expressions of Dependency: A Longitudinal Analysis." Unpublished doctoral dissertation, Michigan State University, 1964.

Snyder, W. U. *Dependency in Psychotherapy.* New York: Macmillan, 1963.

Stoler, N. "Client Likability as a Variable in the Study of Psychotherapy." *Journal of Consulting Psychology,* 1963, *27,* 175–178.

Strupp, H. H. *Psychotherapists in Action.* New York: Grune & Stratton, 1960.

Winder, C. L., Ahmad, F. Z., & Rau, Lucy. "Dependency of Patients, Psychoterapists' Responses, and Aspects of Psychotherapy." *Journal of Consulting Psychology,* 1962, *26,* 129–34.

*

LIKING FOR CLIENTS—ITS RELATIONSHIP TO THERAPIST'S PERSONALITY: UNEXPECTED FINDINGS

NORMAN ABELES

Both analytic and client centered therapists recognize the importance of the therapist's personal reactions to his clients. Freud (1910) discussed these personal reactions as "the result of the patient's influence on his (the analyst's) unconscious feelings." Freud concluded, "We have noticed that every analyst's achievement is limited by what his own complexes and resistances permit."

In the client centered view (Rogers, 1959), the therapist's personal reaction (unconditional positive regard) is a key construct. It includes warmth, liking, respect, sympathy and acceptance.

The present investigation focuses on a particular personal reaction of the therapist, that of *liking* for clients. (1) An analytically oriented question might be: Is liking as a global, personal reaction of the therapist related to accuracy of perception? (2) Liking represents a kind of empathic identification, according to client centered theory. Klopfer (1954) suggests that an empathic identification exists when a human figure exists and is then endowed with attributes of movement. There ought to be a positive relationship between liking and the projection of human movement. (3) Finally, client centered theory would suggest that therapists who are able to like ("prize") their clients would have a lesser degree of incongruence with respect to their own experience.

From these considerations it was hypothesized that:

---

*This article is reprinted from *Psychotherapy: Theory, Research and Practice,* 1967, *4,* 19–21, by permission of the publisher and author.

1. There is a positive relationship between liking for clients and the form appropriateness of the therapists' projections.

2. There is a positive relationship between liking for clients and the projection of human movement.

3. There is an inverse relationship between liking for clients and the projection of anxiety and hostility.

Method

The experimental variables were derived from subject's responses to the Holtzman inkblot technique (Holtzman, 1961).

This technique consists of 45 inkblots which are presented to the subject one at a time. The subject associates to the blot, giving only one response for each blot. An inquiry, from which the determinants, location and associational content are determined, follows the administration of each blot.

The Holtzman was employed as the research instrument because, while it approximates the unstructured projective character of Rorschach materials, control of productivity (one response per card) standardizes inter-subject analyses and permits comparison with a single normative reference group.

In addition, the instrument was to be administered to advanced clinical students who were using the Rorschach in their own clinical work.

With regard to movement scores, Holtzman assumes a static-dynamic continuum of movement and weights are assigned according to the intensity of the projected movement. For purposes of this study, only movement responses involving human content were utilized.

For purposes of this study the blots were scored only for Movement (M); Human Content (H); Anxiety (Ax); Hostility (Hs); and Form Appropriateness (FA). Form appropriateness is the counterpart to form level in Rorschach methodology. Scoring of all variables followed Holtzman.

The second instrument consisted of a rating scale designed to assess the "ease of liking" for clients. Subjects used the rating scale in reacting to typescripted interview excerpts of therapy sessions. An example of the liking scale is given below.

Client preference scale (circle one) This client is:

A	B	C	D
difficult for me to like	less likable than many of my clients	more likable than many of my clients	easy for me to like

SUBJECTS AND PROCEDURES

The 28 subjects were currently enrolled Ph.D. candidates at Michigan State University.

The sample consisted of six clinical and seven counseling psychology students who were completing internships at the Counseling Center and ten clinical and five counseling psychology students in an advanced practicum. The Counseling Center serves as the primary agency on campus for undergraduate and graduate students who seek counseling and psychotherapy.

The Holtzman Inkblot Technique was administered to each of the subjects by a single administrator, and all protocols were scored at another University by a single scorer.

Subjects tape-recorded a fifth interview of one of their therapy cases. Typescripts of two five-minute portions of each of these interviews were then coded, randomized, and returned to the subjects along with a copy of the rating scale.

It can be seen from this procedure that the participants acted both as subjects and judges. That is, each subject judged the therapy behavior of all other subjects, and his own behavior was in turn described by all other subjects. It is the author's impression that this procedure resulted in a considerable amount of involvement in the task on the part of the subjects.

Statistical Analysis.—Nonparametric methods of statistical analysis were employed in this study because of the relatively small sample size and the lack of knowledge about the underlying distribution of the study variables.

The 28 subjects' scores on the liking scale were rank ordered. (A rank of 1 always indicated the lowest score.)

The subjects' scores on the Holtzman variables of human movement, form appropriateness, anxiety and hostility were similarly ranked. (A rank of 1 reflected the least human movement, poorest form level, greatest anxiety and most hostility.)

RESULTS AND DISCUSSION

Table 1 reports the Spearman rank order correlation coefficients obtained between liking, hostility, anxiety, movement, and form appropriateness (opposite from the predicted direction). Therapists who "like" their clients tend to show significantly *more* anxiety and hostility on this projective test. If one speculates that therapist's anxiety and hostility tends to interfere with therapeutic progress (a speculation which may be open to question, particularly if there is but a moderate proportion of anxiety and hostility present) then "liking" would be associated with qualities undesirable for a therapeutic relationship.

TABLE 1

CORRELATIONS* BETWEEN LIKING FOR CLIENTS AND SELECTED HOLTZMAN VARIABLES

	Liking	*Anxiety*	*Hostility*	*Human Movement*	*Form Appropriateness*
Liking	—	—.41†	—.36†	.23	—.39†
Anxiety	—	—	.68‡	.11	.10
Hostility	—	—	—	.34	—.09
Movement	—	—	—	—	.11
Form appropriateness	—	—	—	—	—

*Correlations reported as rank order correlation coefficients.
†Significant at or beyond the .05 level.
‡Significant at or beyond the .01 level.

The negative relationship between "liking" and form appropriateness (also opposite from predicted direction) adds an interesting and surprising note. One possible explanation is that these young therapists represent the top end of the continuum of those expected and expecting to "like" emotionally upset and needy people. Perhaps it is only among such a top end group, that those who are less rigid and conventional, more anxious, hostile and emotional do more liking. Nevertheless, the inverse nature of the relationship would lend some weight to an analytic position that an unconditional acceptance of the client may also mean a less accurate perception in general and perhaps also of the client and his world.

Tagiuri (1958), working in the area of interpersonal perception goes so far as to suggest that "certain forms of accuracy may be *negatively* related to certain forms of 'interpersonal effectiveness'." He suggests that the popular notion that being accurate in judging others makes one effective in interpersonal relations needs to be reexamined. A recently completed study by Mills and Abeles (1966) attempts to deal with some of these issues by relating liking to process variables in psychotherapy.

A somewhat unexpected finding is the high correlation between the projection of anxiety and hostility in this population. While Holtzman (1961) does report a relationship between these two variables in his normative data, no correlations of this magnitude are evident. Perhaps, when dealing with one's own hostility and the hostility of others is a problem, it makes therapists more anxious than it does others.

References

Alexander, F. *The Scope of Psychoanalysis.* New York: Basic Books, 1961.
Freud, S. "The Future Prospects of Psychoanalytic Therapy." *Collected Papers.* Vol. 1. London: Hogarth, 1950.
Holtzman, W. *Holtzman Inkblot Technique.* New York: The Psychological Corporation, 1961.
Klopper, B., Ainsworth, M., Klopper, W., & Holt, R. *Developments in the Rorschach Technique.* Yonkers: World Book Co., 1954.
Mills, D., & Abeles, N. "Counselor Needs for Affiliation and Nurturance as Related to Liking for Clients and Counseling Process." *Journal of Counseling Psychology,* 1965, *12,* 353–58.
Mueller, W. & Abeles, N. "The Components of Empathy and Their Relationship to the Projection of Human Movement Responses." *Journal of Projective Techniques & Personality Assessment,* 1964, *38,* 322–30.
Reich, A. "On Counter-Transference." *International Journal of Psychoanalysis,* 1951, *32,* 25–31.
Rogers, C. "A Theory of Therapy. Personality and Interpersonal Relationships, as Developed in the Client-centered Framework." In S. Koch (ed.), *Psychology: A Study of a Science.* New York: McGraw-Hill, 1959. Pp. 184–256.
Tagiuri, R. & Petrullo, L. (eds.), *Person Perception and Interpersonal Behavior.* Stanford: Stanford University Press, 1958.

*

RELATIONSHIP OF DOGMATISM AND PREJUDICE TO COUNSELING EFFECTIVENESS

ROBERT L. MILLIKEN
JOHN J. PATERSON

Counselors must respond to the challenge that the integration of schools has presented to all educators. The stress is particularly acute for counselors since their work implies many individual face-to-face contacts with students, and the contacts between white counselors and Negro students will become even more commonplace.

*This article is reprinted from *Counselor Education and Supervision,* 1967, *6,* 125–29, by permission of the publisher and authors.

Counselors have a professional obligation to be empathic, understanding, friendly, tolerant, accepting, and respectful toward their counselees [*3*, *9*]. Therefore, by definition, they should be non-prejudicial toward their counselees. The counseling process would probably suffer deleterious results from the affects of prejudiced counselors.

The "effect" of prejudice has great impact on our society—since we all attempt to perceive how others feel toward us. Of importance to counselors is Newcomb's postulation [*7*] that minority group members are skilled at detecting signs of prejudice. If so, prejudiced counselors may have great difficulty concealing their true feelings. Also of importance to counselors is the contention by Phillips [*8*] that white counselors have great difficulty in understanding Negroes and consequently have reduced effectiveness in counseling them. The prejudiced counselor appears to be deficient in some of the positive characteristics to which he is professionally obliged. Can the counselor's prejudice toward a Negro be detected by the Negro and thereby influence the counseling relationship? Kemp [*4*] demonstrated that the open-minded counselor tended to be more permissive, understanding, and supportive than the dogmatic counselor. The purpose of the present exploratory study is to measure the extent to which both prejudice and dogmatism affect perceived effectiveness of counselors. It is based on prior research evidence of an inverse relationship between prejudice and counseling effectiveness. [*5*]

Procedure

During their practicum each of the thirty 1963-64 NDEA Guidance and Counseling Institute enrollees at Purdue University agreed to counsel one person in addition to their regular practicum load. It was stipulated that they would be supervised during this period (i.e., viewed through a one-way vision screen and tape recorded) and that an appointment would be made with each counselor candidate to discuss the "case." Approximately one week before his "counseling," each trainee completed the Bogardus Ethnic Distance Scale (EDS) and the Rokeach Dogmatism Scale (RDS). He was not informed that these scales were part of the present research.

A Negro was employed as a coached counselee to be counseled by each trainee. He portrayed a college sophomore who had problems with his grades and his obstreperous roommate. After each interview both the coached client and the supervisor assessed the effectiveness of the enrollee's counseling by completing an experimental 16-item Counselor Effectiveness Scale (CES). Two separate scores were derived from the scale: (a) a global rating of the counselor's effectiveness, and (b) a composite effectiveness rating accumulated from 16 items purporting to measure the counselee's feelings toward the counselor. The directions on the CES were, "To what extent do the following statements describe the counselor?" For each item a five-point rating was devised ranging from "very well" (scored five) to "very poorly" (scored one). After completing his interview, each counselor was asked not to divulge the type of client counseled or the content of the interview. Each interview lasted approximately 45 minutes.

The Mann-Whitney U was used to test the differences on the ranks of the dogmatism scores between the "good" and "poor" counselors. The Mann-Whitney U was also employed to test the differences on the ranks of the EDS scores between the "good" and "poor" counselors. Four separate U's were computed for each of the prejudice measures (RDS and EDS), one for the global rating and one for the composite score, for each of two evaluators.

It was hypothesized that the "good" counselors would have the lower rankings on prejudice and dogmatism.

Results

The findings of this exploratory study were that the "good" counselors did have the lower rankings on all four tests of EDS ranks and on three of four tests of RDS ranks. The only statistically significant U test, however, was the test of the ranks on the RDS between "good" and "poor" counselors when these categories were defined by the supervisor's composite score.

When the categories were defined by the *coached client's global rating*, the "good" counselors had a mean EDS rank of 11.7, and the "poor" counselors had a mean rank of 12.6. When the categories were defined by the *supervisor's global rating*, the "good" counselors had a mean EDS rank of 8.3, and the "poor" counselors had a mean rank of 10.3. When they were defined by the *coached client's composite score*, the "good" counselors had a mean EDS rank of 9.2, and the "poor" counselors had a mean rank of 10.9. The *supervisor's composite score* of the "good" counselors had a mean EDS rank of 8.4, and the "poor" counselors had a mean rank of 11.2.

When the categories were defined by the *coached client's global rating*, the "good" counselors had a mean RDS rank of 12.4, and the "poor" counselors had a mean rank of 11.2. This is the only test in which the "poor" counselors had the lower mean rank. When the categories were defined by the *supervisor's global rating*, the "good' counselors had a mean RDS rank of 7.4, and the "poor" counselors had a mean rank of 10.8. When they were defined by the *coached client's composite score*, the "good" counselors had a mean RDS rank of 9.9, and the "poor" counselors had a mean rank of 11.2. The *supervisor's composite score* of the "good" counselors had a mean RDS rank of 7.4, and the "poor" counselors had a mean rank of 12.6. This is the only test in which the rank of the "good" counselors was significantly different from the rank of the "poor" counselors. (Mann Whitney $U = 23$, and the critical value of U at the 5 per cent significance level is $U = 26$.)

Discussion

Only one of the eight analyses statistically supported the authors' hypothesis. However, six of the remaining seven analyses were in the hypothesized direction. Although the findings do not statistically support the authors' postulation, the fact that seven of the eight differences were in the hypothesized direction still allows one to conjecture that both dogmatism and prejudice may be factors in the successful counseling relationship.

Several questions for future investigations were suggested by this research and the interpretation of these results.

1. Could counselor effectiveness with Negro clients be increased by the use of contact with Negro clients during the preparation period? The counselors' prejudicial attitudes which could potentially impair counseling might be ameliorated through counseling and through discussions with their supervisors.

2. Could the effectiveness of "prejudiced" counselors be related to the amount of experience of the counselors? It is expected that the experienced counselor would be more capable of controlling his prejudicial feelings than the neophyte counselor.

3. Are counselors better classified as to whether they are "effective" or "ineffective" by the clients or by the counseling supervisors after counseling with the coached client? In this study the categories defined by the supervisor's composite score most clearly separated the counselors with high prejudice from those with low prejudice and also the counselors with high and low dogmatism. These results may have occurred because the supervisor is more cognitively aware of qualities in counselors which affect the counseling relationship and thus is able to make a "better" discrimination among counselors. The client may mistake kindness for competence and judge the counselor high on all aspects of the relationship.

4. Would the effectiveness of the "prejudiced" counselor be related to the type of problem presented by the client? In this study, the coached client portrayed a gentle Negro with some typical college

problems. A more aggressive, hostile Negro may have elicited more negative feelings.

Summary

The results of this study failed to show statistically that the "good" counselors did have lower rankings on prejudice and dogmatism than did the "poor" counselors. The only significant difference was on the rank on the Rokeach Dogmatism Scale when the "good" and "poor" counselors were defined from the supervisor's composite score. However, six of the other seven differences were in the hypothesized direction. Further research is needed to ascertain if there is a true relationship between counseling and prejudice and discrimination. This question may be helpful in delineating some of the problems which need to be tested.

References

1. Allport, Gordon. *The Nature of Prejudice.* Garden City, New York: Addison-Wesley, 1954.
2. Barron, Milton L. *American Minorities.* New York: Alfred A. Knopf, 1957.
3. Brammer, Lawrence & Shostrom, Everett. *Therapeutic Psychology.* Englewood Cliffs, N. J.: Prentice-Hall, 1960.
4. Kemp, C. Gratton. "Influence of Dogmatism on the Training of Counselors." *Journal of Counseling Psychology,* 1962, *9,* 155–57.
5. Milliken, Robert L. "The Relationship Between Prejudice and Counseling Effectiveness." *Personnel and Guidance Journal,* 1965, *43,* 710–12.
6. Myrdal, Gunnar. *An American Dilemma.* New York: Harper, 1944.
7. Newcomb, Theodore. *Social Psychology.* New York: Dryden Press, 1950.
8. Phillips, Waldo B. "Counseling Negro Students: An Educational Dilemma." *California Journal of Educational Research,* 1959, *19,* 185–89.
9. Tyler, Leona E. *The Work of the Counselor.* New York: Appleton-Century–Crofts, 1961.

2

Group and Multiple Counseling

It has been estimated that by 1970 there will be a shortage of 40,000 counselors in the United States. This includes vacancies in schools, colleges, employment offices, rehabilitation agencies, and counselors employed in various phases of such federal antipoverty programs as the job corps, neighborhood youth corps, etc. Existing counselor-education programs cannot be expected to prepare enough counselors to meet the demand.

This problem would seem to indicate at least two possible solutions. The first would involve the expansion of existing counselor-education programs and the development of new programs. The major difficulty in this solution lies in finding enough qualified counselor educators to fill faculty positions. This becomes increasingly important in light of the movement toward accreditation of counselor-education programs, and the recommended two-year minimal training for counselors. If these movements become a reality, it is likely that the numbers of counselors being prepared will decrease rather than increase.

A second solution would involve a rethinking of counseling as being primarily a one-to-one relationship. As the population increases, the number of those who could benefit from counseling also increases. Despite improvement in the recommended ratios of counselors to counselees, and the values associated with counseling in a one-to-one relationship, it seems likely that we shall see development in the field of group counseling as a means of helping more people with fewer counselors.

In addition to the hoped-for benefits in increasing the ability of counselors to serve more people, group techniques introduce additional sources of therapeutic influence. Often problems of individuals are related to the social existence of these people. Group counseling provides an opportunity for social experience during therapy. Reinforcement by the social group becomes a significant variable in the counseling relationship. The therapeutic relationship becomes a multiple one, thus the counselor shares significance with other participants in a group.

Despite the differences between individual and group counseling, the latter often rests on theoretical frameworks closely resembling those underlying the former. The relationship between a counselor and a group of counselees remains at least as difficult, and probably becomes even more difficult, to examine. As one reviews the literature, several questions seem to emerge. They point up some of the unknown quantities in group counseling. These are the questions:

1) Are there significant differences in results obtained through the variety of approaches which include group guidance, group counseling, group therapy, and sensitivity groups?
2) On what basis should participants be placed in groups?
3) What are the variables that define the optimum size of groups?
4) Should group sessions be subject to the same rules and/or limits as are individual sessions?
5) How persistent are the effects of group counseling?

The articles selected for inclusion in this chapter attempt to deal with certain facets of the above questions. The first four articles deal with some general characteristics of the group-counseling relationship. The next article deals with group counseling with socially maladjusted individuals. The last three are concerned with group approaches to helping test-anxious or underachieving students.

The Branan article is concerned with a common problem in individual counseling, i.e., when, if ever, to use self-experience to facilitate the counseling process. This study provides evidence that self-experience is not helpful, and may be harmful, in fostering a counseling environment when used in a group-counseling situation. However, the subjects were all graduate students, and results might differ with groups of younger persons.

The Gutsch and Bellamy study attempted to isolate the effects of group work with problematic students, but is weakened by the smallness of the groups and the brevity of the time span. The lack of specific detail in the article leaves the reader wondering exactly what is meant by "attitudinal group approach." It seems to be a compromise between a group-guidance and group-counseling procedure. The findings of the study suggest rather strongly that attention, even if just testing, has a beneficial effect on students. Group activities may result in a Hawthorne Effect if they are presented as an effort to help.

The Zimpfer article describes a group-counseling approach with high school students. It represents an interesting effort to relate warmth, hostility, and flight to acceptance by peers as measured by the succorance scale of the Syracuse Scales of Social Relations. The Baymur *Q*-sort was used for self-evaluation by the participants. Despite the lack of clear-cut findings, it presents interesting possibilities for further research.

The Spaights study was designed to test some of the techniques used in behavioral counseling. He used group counseling, individual counseling, and a control group—all with undergraduate college students—to test social reinforcement as a method of changing personal adjustment scores as measured by the California Test of Personality (CTP) and self-ratings by the counselees.

McDavid's work was done with institutionalized juvenile delinquents. He found that social reinforcement was effective in increasing the amount of assimilation of approval statements on the Social Reinforcement Interpretation Test (SRIT) when measured immediately after group therapy. When measured after a week, the scores were significantly lower; the author assumes therefore that long-term effects are nil. It would be interesting to revisit the groups after the passage of several years to investigate the effect of long-term treatment on the SRIT scores of the participants.

The study by Katahn, *et al.* was done with college students selected through use of the Test Anxiety Scale (TAS). The authors describe conditioning as "systematic desensitization" and counseling as "suggestion and advice." The treatment group emphasized relaxation procedures during the group sessions. The control group included both volunteers who were assigned to the control group, and a group of test-anxious students who did not volunteer. The treatment group changed significantly. Their grades went up and self-reported test anxiety went down.

Gilbreath compared leader-structured groups, group-structured groups, and a control group for their effect on college male underachieving volunteers. The leader structured method of group counseling seemed superior in rate of change of grade-point average and gains in ego strength as measured by selected scales on the Stern Activities Index (SAI) and the Minnesota Multiphasic Personality Inventory (MMPI).

The Bosdell and Tiegland article seems to lend support to the conjecture that counseling can only be individual. Although not stated specifically, their study apparently used underachieving adolescents in a group-counseling situation. The findings seem to indicate that adolescents will not expose themselves in a group, and thus that group counseling may have a built-in safety device preventing overexposure of personal problems in an environment that may become hostile outside of the group.

The final study in the chapter is an original paper by Orsburn investigating the use of some techniques derived from the procedure variously described as T-groups or sensitivity training. While it is pointed out that the procedure used was an adaptation to high school student groups of the techniques more precisely delineated by the National Training Laboratories (NTL), some remarkable results are obtained. Not only does the group provided with the modified treatment exceed the control group in the criteria dimensions, it also exceeds another treatment group that gets significant attention but different treatment. Further, the beneficial effect of the experimental treatment continues to develop for a period of time after the termination of treatment.

The research designs in the investigations bear marked similarities. There is a preference for experimental designs that utilize treatment and control groups and then present findings based upon analysis of variance. A few studies used correlations and differences in means as the basis for statistical analyses. Only in two studies were nonparametric techniques used to test for significance of differences (Bosdell and Teigland, and Orsburn).

Most of the data were derived from standardized tests, gradepoint averages, *Q*-sorts and rating scales that would permit reporting of data in a form that would seem to justify the use of parametric statistics. There were no investigations based on case studies or other subjective approaches to understanding group counseling.

In all instances in which a control group was used, the control group was provided with no comparable attention. It may well be that, except in the instances where several different treatments were used (Spaights, Bosdell and Teigland, and Gilbreath), the advantage of the experimental over control group was a reflection of attention versus no attention rather than support for a particular approach to group therapy. The use of placebo activities with control groups may serve to diminish the suspicion that the Hawthorne

Effect rather than group counseling is achieving the positive results.

One final observation relative to the research is the short-time span encompassed by the investigations intended to measure client change. The longest investigation of a longitudinal nature includes 180 days with a treatment period of 60 days (Gutsch and Bellamy). The short-time periods probably reflect a number of limiting factors. Among these is the fact that much of the research is carried out by graduate students as part of their doctoral requirements. These students frequently are pressed for time. Further, it is extremely difficult to maintain continuity with a group of participants and counselors. There is a great deal of mobility among both clients and professional staff which necessitates that an investigation that extends beyond a year carry a very large *N* to assure that enough subjects will remain after three or four years to provide tests of significance.

Lack of long-term designs results in lack of data about the effects of longer treatment and also the persistence of the changes that occur during treatment. The Orsburn study and that of Gutsch and Bellamy both suggest that the effects of group work continue and even intensify following treatment. If efficiency of effect is a criterion for consideration in the selection of group counseling, then a tendency toward persistence and perhaps even intensification of the positive effects of group treatment are worthy of study.

*

CLIENT REACTION TO COUNSELOR'S USE OF SELF-EXPERIENCE

JOHN M. BRANAN

There are several indications from writings in the literature that the counselor's use of his own experiences may have value in the counseling relationship. Rogers (1961) states, "To withhold one's self as a person and to deal with the other person as an object does not have a high probability of being helpful." Jourard (1964) writes, "It is my growing opinion, somewhat buttressed by accumulating experience in my own therapeutic work, that valued change—growth—in patients is fostered when the therapist is a rather free individual functioning as a person with all of his feelings and fantasies as well as his wits. . . . I have come to recognize, too, that those who habitually withhold their real selves from others, and instead strive to manipulate them in one way or another, do violence to their own integrity as well as to that of their victim. . . . I don't see how we can reacquaint our patients with their real selves by striving to subject them to subtle manipulations and thus to withhold our real selves from them."

Information regarding counselor use of self-experience is extremely limited both in terms of theoretical basis and in regard to the actual state of its use by counselors. Use of self-experience is a question that confronts counselors-in-preparation, counselor educators, and practicing counselors. This research was undertaken to augment the meager literature on the use of counselor's self-experience in counseling and to provide a framework for further research in this area.

*This article is reprinted from *Personnel and Guidance Journal,* 1967, *45,* 568–72, by permission of the publisher, the American Personnel and Guidance Association, and the author.

Hypotheses

The following hypotheses were developed from the rationale:

1. Use of self-experience in counseling relationships will result in greater self-disclosure than in counseling situations where the counselor does not disclose his own similar experiences.
2. Use of self-experience in counseling relationships will result in greater self-confidence than in counseling situations where the counselor does not disclose his own similar experiences.
3. Use of self-experience in counseling relationships will result in a greater atmosphere of genuineness than in counseling situations where self-experience is not used.
4. Use of self-experience in counseling relationships will result in client's perceiving a greater sense of empathic understanding than in counseling situations where the counselor does not disclose his own relevant experiences.

Methods and Procedures

The participants for this study were all registered as graduate students in the College of Education at the University of Florida during the winter trimester of 1965. They were all volunteers who were interested in participating in a series of group-counseling sessions structured around problems of the graduate student. There were 30 participants in this group, 15 males and 15 females. They were placed in six groups of five each on the basis of available time for counseling sessions and to provide for a balance of men and women. These six groups were randomly divided into three experimental and three control groups.

In obtaining volunteers interested in participating in this study, the researcher contacted 17 different graduate classes in education offered during the winter trimester of 1965 at the University of Florida. These graduate classes were in the divisions of General Education, Educational Administration, Elementary Education, Foundations of Education, Personnel Services, Secondary Education, and Vocational Agriculture.

Each of the groups met at a regularly scheduled time each week. All groups met for five one-hour sessions scheduled one week apart. All sessions were tape recorded. The researcher served as counselor for all groups, both experimental and control. This had the advantage of controlling the personality variable of the counselor. All sessions were conducted in the same manner except for the variable of counselor use of self-experience. In the experimental groups, counselor self-experience examples were used extensively; in the control groups, self-experience examples were not used.

Two questionnaires were given before the counseling sessions began and again at the end of the counseling sessions to all members of the control and experimental groups. One questionnaire was concerned with self-disclosure regarding academic situations and the other with self-confidence in graduate work.

Tape recordings of the counseling sessions were reviewed by two independent raters who had been trained by the researcher in the identification of counselor use of self-experience and client self-disclosure. Ratings of self-disclosure were made to compare the actual amount of self-disclosure between the control and experimental groups.

At the end of the counseling sessions each participant was interviewed by a certified psychologist trained at the doctoral level and experienced in interviewing and counseling. These interviews were concerned with the participants' perception of the counselor's behavior as it related to the genuineness of the counseling relationship and to their feelings of being understood. A five-point, precoded schedule was used to quantify the degrees of genuineness perceived and the extent that participants felt understood. Interviews were tape recorded. Two independent raters listened to the tape recordings of the interviews and also rated the responses as a check on interviewer reliability.

Being graduate students, the counselees were more mature and were better able to articulate their feelings and thinking than younger students with less educational background.

Treatment of Data

Statistical comparisons were made of the results of the questionnaires before and after counseling for both control and experimental groups. Statistical comparisons were also made between control and experimental groups on quantitative data from the post-counseling interviews and ratings of actual self-disclosure in the sessions. Analysis of variance was used in these statistical comparisons. In addition a subjective analysis was made of clients' reactions from the post-counseling interviews and the counseling sessions themselves.

In neither the experimental nor the control groups did counseling result in significant changes in self-disclosure as measured by the self-disclosure questionnaire. As there was no significant change in either group, there was no evidence to support *hypothesis one*, that the use of self-experience in counseling would result in greater self-disclosure than in counseling situations where the counselor did not disclose his own experiences. In Table 1 analysis of variance data on the self-disclosure questionnaire are presented for the experimental group. In Table 2 analysis of variance data on the self-disclosure questionnaire are presented for the control group.

TABLE 1

ANALYSIS OF VARIANCE DATA FOR THE EXPERIMENTAL GROUP ON THE SELF-DISCLOSURE QUESTIONNAIRE (PRE- AND POST-COUNSELING)

Source	*Sum of Squares*	*df*	*Mean Square*	*F Ratio*	*p*
Between people	1264.9	12			
Within people	197.0	13			
Treatment	3.9	1	3.9	.24	.99*
Residual	193.1	12	16.1		
Total	1461.9	13			

*No significant differences were found.

TABLE 2

ANALYSIS OF VARIANCE DATA FOR THE CONTROL GROUP ON THE SELF-DISCLOSURE QUESTIONNAIRE (PRE- AND POST-COUNSELING)

Source	*Sum of Squares*	*df*	*Mean Square*	*F Ratio*	*p*
Between people	2839.4	12			
Within people	530.0	13			
Treatment	97.8	1	97.8	2.71	.25*
Residual	432.2	12	36.0		
Total	3369.4	25			

*No significant differences were found.

To obtain a measure of actual self-disclosure in the counseling sessions, tape recordings were made of all sessions. Two independent raters who had been trained in the identification of self-disclosure by the researcher tallied self-disclosures from the recordings. Their ratings of self-disclosure were highly reliable with a reliability coefficient between the two raters of .94. The mean self-disclosure scores of the raters for the experimental and control groups were analyzed using analysis of variance. There were no significant differences between the control group and experimental group on the total amount of self-disclosure within the counseling sessions.

In Table 3 analysis of variance data are presented on self-disclosure within the counseling sessions. These data do not support the first hypothesis that self-disclosure would be greater in those counseling situations where the counselor used his own self-experiences.

TABLE 3
ANALYSIS OF VARIANCE DATA FOR THE EXPERIMENTAL AND CONTROL GROUPS ON SELF-DISCLOSURE WITHIN THE SESSIONS

Source	*Sum of Squares*	*df*	*Mean Square*	*F Ratio*	*p*
Treatment	7.9	1	7.9	.016	.90*
Error	13,208.3	27	489.2		
Total	13,216.2	28			

*No significant differences were found.

To test *hypothesis two* (use of self-experience in counseling relationships will result in greater self-confidence than in counseling situations where the counselor does not disclose his relevant experiences), a self-confidence questionnaire was administered before and after counseling to the control group and experimental group. Differences in pre- and post-counseling responses were analyzed using analysis of variance. There were no significant changes in self-confidence in either the experimental or control group. As there were no significant changes in either group, there was no evidence to support the second hypothesis. In Table 4 analysis of variance data on self-confidence are presented for the experimental group, and in Table 5 analysis of variance data on self-confidence are presented for the control group.

TABLE 4
ANALYSIS OF VARIANCE DATA (PRE- AND POST-COUNSELING) FOR THE EXPERIMENTAL GROUP ON SELF-CONFIDENCE

Source	*Sum of Squares*	*df*	*Mean Square*	*F Ratio*	*p*
Between people	24.62	12			
Within people	8.00	13			
Treatment	.62	1	.62	1.00	.50*
Residual	7.38	12	.62		
Total	32.62	25			

*No significant differences were found.

TABLE 5

ANALYSIS OF VARIANCE DATA (PRE- AND POST-COUNSELING) FOR THE CONTROL GROUP ON SELF-CONFIDENCE

Source	*Sum of Squares*	*df*	*Mean Square*	*F Ratio*	*p*
Between people	36.5	12			
Within people	20.5	13			
Treatment	3.2	1	3.20	2.22	.25*
Residual	17.3	12	1.44		
Total	57.0	25			

*No significant differences were found.

To test the third and fourth hypotheses, the participants were interviewed at the end of the counseling sessions by a certified psychologist regarding their perceptions of the genuineness of the counseling relationship and the degree to which they felt understood. A five-point, precoded schedule was used for each of the above ratings to quantify the interview information regarding the two hypotheses. Interviews were tape recorded and two independent raters rated the same responses as the interviewer. The interview was a highly reliable measure as the two raters achieved a 1.0 correlation between themselves and the rater. Differences between experimental and control groups were analyzed using analysis of variance.

In Table 6 analysis of variance data are presented regarding perceived genuineness of the counseling relationship. The *third hypothesis* (use of self-experience in counseling relationships will result in a greater atmosphere of genuineness than in counseling situations where self-experience is not used) was refuted as there was significant difference between experimental and control groups in the direction of greater perceived genuineness by the control group. This was the reverse of the third hypothesis. This difference exceeded the .01 level of confidence.

TABLE 6

ANALYSIS OF VARIANCE DATA FOR THE EXPERIMENTAL AND CONTROL GROUPS ON PERCEIVED GENUINENESS

Source	*Sum of Squares*	*df*	*Mean Square*	*F Ratio*	*p*
Treatment	13.9	1	13.9	30.89	.0005*
Error	10.8	24	.45		
Total	24.7	25			

*Statistically significant difference beyond the .01 level. The control group perceived the relationship as significantly more genuine than the experimental group.

In Table 7 analysis of variance data are presented regarding the degree that the counselees felt understood. The *fourth hypothesis* (use of self-experience in counseling relationships will result in clients' perceiving a greater sense of empathic understanding than in counseling situations where the counselor does not disclose his own relevant experiences) was not supported as there were no significant differences between experimental and control groups on perceived empathic understanding. Although the difference was not significant, it was in the direction of greater perceived empathic understanding by the control group rather than the experimental group.

TABLE 7

ANALYSIS OF VARIANCE DATA FOR THE EXPERIMENTAL AND CONTROL GROUPS ON PERCEIVED EMPATHIC UNDERSTANDING

Source	*Sum of Squares*	*df*	*Mean Square*	*F Ratio*	*p*
Treatment	5.5	1	5.5	4.23	.10*
Error	31.1	24	1.3		
Total	36.6	25			

*No significant differences were found.

DISCUSSION

The results of this study do not support the use of self-experience in group counseling relationships. There are no demonstrated advantages and one significant disadvantage. The counseling atmosphere was perceived as less genuine when self-experience was used than in similar counseling situations where it was not used. Although Rogers (1951, 1961), Combs (1959), and Parloff (1961) all emphasize the importance of perceived genuineness in the counseling relationships, this research contraindicates the use of self-disclosure by the counselor as a means of increasing perceived genuineness.

However, this study raises several questions which have implications for further research. When a counselor uses a self-experience example in a group setting, it may be applicable to some members of the group but not to others. This may result in individuals reacting negatively to the use of self-experience examples that do not relate specifically to their experiences and needs. In individual counseling it would be easier to use self-experiences that are particularly relevant to the individual. It is more difficult to use self-experiences that have value for several persons. A study designed so that comparable groups could receive individual counseling from the same counselor rather than group counseling would add important data to the question of the value of using self-experience in counseling.

There is also a question of whether other groups of individuals would react to the use of self-experiences as did graduate students in education at the University of Florida. There is a possibility that the similar educational backgrounds of these students may have predisposed them to perceive the counseling relationship in a certain way. For instance, all graduate students in education at the University of Florida are exposed primarily to a phenomenological view of behavior, and emphasis is placed on a client-centered approach in helping relationships. Would undergraduate students, students in other graduate programs, or high school students perceive the counseling relationship differently from these graduate students?

References

Combs, A. W., & Snygg, D. *Individual Behavior.* (Rev. ed.) New York: Harper, 1959.

Jourard, S. M. *The Transparent Self.* Princeton, N. J.: Van Nostrand, 1964.

Parloff, M. B. "Therapist-Patient Relationships and Outcome of Psychotherapy." *Journal of Consulting Psychology,* 1961, *25,* 29–38.

Rogers, C. R. *Client-Centered Therapy.* Boston: Houghton Mifflin, 1951.

Rogers, C. R. *On Becoming a Person.* Boston: Houghton Mifflin, 1961.

*

EFFECTIVENESS OF AN ATTITUDINAL GROUP APPROACH AS A BEHAVIOR DETERMINANT

KENNETH U. GUTSCH
WILLIAM D. BELLAMY

Group guidance is usually thought of as an auxiliary educational function within and beyond the curriculum, designed to provide a personal service to a group of individuals having common or similar problems in vocational, educational, and personal-social areas.

Although group guidance, as a part of the total school program, has become an accepted auxiliary function, the evaluation of the effectiveness of such a service has been a continual challenge. If we assume that group guidance is capable of producing a change in the behavior of the individual receiving these services, then these changes in behavior must, in some way, lend themselves to an appropriate means of evaluation. Relative to such a proposition, this study sought to determine (1) what change, if any, occurs when problematic students become part of an attitudinal group setting and (2) whether or not such change, if it does occur, is attributable to the group guidance setting and not some other factors.

PROCEDURE

This study was implemented at the D. U. Maddox Junior High School in Laurel, Mississippi, during the school year 1963–1964. The participants consisted of 16 male students between the ages of 12 and 16. Participants were divided into two groups, i.e., an experi-

*This article is reprinted from *The School Counselor,* 1966, *14,* 40–43, by permission of the publisher, the American School Counselor Association, and the authors.

mental group, Group E, and a control group, Group C. Each group contained eight students and both groups were approximately matched in terms of age, number of offenses, and socio-economic status. The members for each group were randomly selected from among the total group of matched pairs.

In an effort to determine the influence of such variables as the artifact of testing, the passage of time, and the effects of anticipated group guidance services upon members of the group, Groups E and C were divided into smaller groups. Group E was divided into two smaller groups of four members each, i.e., Group E_1 and E_2, and Group C was divided into two smaller groups of four members each, i.e., Groups C_1 and C_2.

The study covered three consecutive periods, each 60 days in length. The first period was known as the Pre-wait Period and referred to a period of time immediately preceding an attitudinal group guidance setting. The second period was called the Action Period and referred to a 60-day period of time immediately following the Pre-wait Period, during which specific participants in this study were engaged in 24 systematically scheduled attitudinal group guidance settings, each 50 minutes in length.

The third period was known as the Post-wait Period and referred to a 60-day period of time immediately following the attitudinal group guidance setting. To observe within and between group movements before, during, and after group-guidance services, four testing periods were established, and a battery of evaluative instruments was administered to C_2 and E_2 participants at matched time intervals. The testing periods were referred to as T_1, T_2, T_3, and T_4. The testing period which took place at the beginning of the Pre-wait Period was referred to as T_1. The testing period which took place at the end of the Pre-wait Period was referred to as T_2. T_3 was used to represent the testing period which took place at the end of the Action Period, and T_4 was used to designate the testing period which took place at the end of the Post-wait Period. Evaluative instruments utilized during this study were the Behavior Preference Record, Form B; the California Test of Personality, Form AA; and the SRA Youth Inventory, Form A.

A guidance committee consisting of four faculty members who were familiar with the participants of both the experimental group and the control group were asked to rate participants through the use of the SAQS Chicago *Q*-sort technique. In order to determine the consistency of ratings by members of the guidance committee, each member of the committee was asked to rate an ideal self-concept at the beginning of the Pre-wait Period and again 180 days later or at the end of the Post-wait Period. It was believed that if such ratings lacked consistency or were not highly similar when correlated that the rater could not be used since his own concept was subject to considerable modification. With the establishment of an ideal self-concept formulated by each member of the guidance committee, it was possible for members of the committee to rate participants of Groups E and C at T_1, T_2, T_3, and T_4 periods and thus provide information which made it possible to determine, through Pearson Product Moment Correlation techniques, whether participants of Groups E and C were moving toward or away from the ideal self-concept held by each respective rater.

In addition to the evaluative instruments utilized to obtain objective information relative to group movements, such movements were also studied through an analysis of grade point averages, citizenship grades, and number of disciplinary offenses committed during the Pre-wait, Action, and Post-wait Periods.

Results

Great emphasis was placed on an analysis of data for each specific period of time with the focus of attention always directed toward the influence of such variable factors as the passage of time, the artifact of testing, and the effect of anticipated group-guidance services. Through proper within- and between-group comparisons, it was possible to isolate and compare group movements.

PRE-WAIT PERIOD

From a study of data reflecting the Pre-wait Period, it appeared that some movement took place within both the experimental and the control groups. The Behavior Preference Record revealed that, while the experimental group moved away from the ideal behavior pattern during this 60-day period, the control group moved toward an ideal behavior pattern, thus producing performance scores between Groups E and C at the beginning of the Action Period which reflected a significant difference beyond the .01 level of confidence. It was also observed that the within-group movements of the experimental group away from the ideal behavior pattern was significant beyond the .10 level of confidence.

Results from the California Test of Personality and from the SRA Youth Inventory during this Pre-wait Period did not reveal any statistically significant difference,

Q-sort results indicated that the experimental group remained unchanged during the 60-day Pre-wait period while the control group appeared to regress slightly.

There were no disciplinary offenses reported against the experimental group during this period, although seven offenses were reported against the control group. Within-group comparison, i.e., E_1, E_2, C_1, C_2, revealed a significant difference in grade-point average between the T_1, T_2, testing periods for E_1 and C_2 groups. The T_1–T_2 difference for the E_1 group was significant at the .05 level of confidence and for the C_2 group at the .10 level of confidence. A further analysis of these four groups, i.e., E_1, E_2, C_1, and C_2, indicated that all four groups moved and that all movements were away from a better grade-point average.

ACTION PERIOD

It was during the 60-day T_2–T_3 Action Period that the attitudinal group-guidance services were initiated. Results from the Behavior Preference Record, the California Test of Personality, and the SRA Youth Inventory revealed no statistically significant movement in either group during this period of time. However, a further analysis of data revealed that those movements which did take place as indicated by the Behavior Preference Record and the California Test of Personality were in a positive direction for the experimental group and in a negative direction for the control group.

At the end of the Action Period, the guidance committee was again asked to rate the participants of both the experimental and control groups using the *Q*-sort Technique. T_2–T_3 comparisons indicated the beginning of a pattern of movement for both the experimental and control groups during this period of time The experimental group formed a pattern of movement which reflected a consistent movement toward an ideal self-concept, while the control group formed a pattern of movement which reflected a consistent movement away from an ideal self-concept.

During this 60-day Action Period, no disciplinary offenses were reported against the experimental group and three offenses were reported against the control group.

Within-group comparisons of E_1, E_2, C_1, and C_2 groups during the Action Period revealed that both the E_1 and E_2 groups moved toward a better grade-point average and that for the E_1 group this movement was significant at the .10 level of confidence. The C_1 and C_2 groups moved away from a better grade-point average but the movement was not significant.

An analysis of movement relative to citizenship revealed that movements were not significant at or beyond the .10 level of confidence.

POST-WAIT PERIOD

The T_3–T_4, Post-wait 60-day period provided an opportunity for a longitudinal view of the study from its inception as well as the movement within the 60-day period itself. An examination of results from the Behavior Preference Record, the California Test of Personality, and the SRA Youth Inventory did not reveal any results which were statistically significant at or beyond the .10 level of confidence during this period.

An analysis of *Q*-sort ratings by guidance committee members indicated that, while the experimental group was continuing to move in a positive direction, the control group continued to move in a negative direction. One instance of objectionable behavior was reported against the experimental group, and three instances of objectionable behavior were reported against the control group.

No significant movements were found relative to citizenship.

Discussion

Although every effort was made to equate the two groups, the mean IQ scores favored the control group by 14 points. In an effort to gain maximum effectiveness in such a study, it appears that the study might best be implemented within a setting which would produce a large enough sample of problematic students to afford one the opportunity to produce groups that more closely parallel each other. It also appears that instruments which are more sensitive to change should be utilized in making objective evaluations and that the Post-wait Period should be extended in an effort to show more adequately the long-range effects of such attitudinal group guidance services as were experienced in this study. A final observation, although seemingly not of much consequence from an objective point of view, is the fact that the school used in this study became guidance conscious, and as a result of this study has extended efforts to assist students who are socially or educationally disadvantaged.

Conclusions

From an analysis of the data yielded and the comparisons made, it now appears that the artifact of testing had a beneficial effect on participants in the E_2 and C_2 groups and that, although not always significant, such improvements as were revealed did reflect an improved pattern of behavior. It is also concluded that testing had a stabilizing influence on those participants tested, as compared with those participants who were not tested. Further observation of the data seems to indicate that an attitudinal group guidance setting was instrumental in maintaining a pattern of movement which reflected stability among the experimental group participants during the Post-wait Period. With regard to grade-point average, it appears from evidence revealed within the confines of this study that, when testing and group guidance services were combined, there was continued academic improvement as evidenced by the movement of the experimental group toward a higher grade-point average.

*

EXPRESSION OF FEELINGS IN GROUP COUNSELING

DAVID G. ZIMPFER

This paper presents a process analysis of the feelings expressed by high school students in group counseling. As data were analyzed for a larger project (Zimpfer, 1964), the following question was asked: To what extent is the nature of feeling interaction in group counseling related to measured changes in counselees' self-evaluation and to changes in evaluations by peers?

Few studies have been undertaken to explore the relationship between the process of group counseling and its outcomes. Ohlsen and Oelke (1962), using categories of verbal content, found no clear relationship between counselee growth and such variables as topic discussed, self-talk, and amount of talk. Wigell (1960), after a content analysis of tape-recorded group sessions, found little support for his hypotheses about the relationship between counselees' expression of affect and their dealing with or solving problems. The findings of Katz, Ohlsen, and Proff (1959) are counter to what one might expect. Their results, in a study of nonverbal behavior in a

*This article is reprinted from *Personnel and Guidance Journal,* 1967, *45,* 703–8, by permission of the publisher, the American Personnel and Guidance Association, and the author.

counseling group, show that the two members who had negative influence on the therapeutic movement of the group were the only two who had made significant growth.

The difficulties encountered in earlier studies may have been artifacts of the procedures used. Thus, nonsignificant or unexpected findings may be attributed to limitations in the system of categories (for instance, concentration on topic or content), or in the behavior studied (for instance, restriction to the nonverbal), or in the method (for instance, using a recording without visual cues to assist in classification). It is the intention of this study to make a genotypical process analysis of counseling in groups, to relate process findings to outcomes, and to deal with problems such as are presented above.

Joel and Shapiro (1949) have proposed that attention to the feelings underlying overt behavior will serve to provide a clearer basis for analyzing client attitude than will content analysis. Their analysis system is adaptable to both verbal and nonverbal behavior. It stresses the interpersonal manifestation of feeling as the most significant element to study in group behavior. Their categories follow Horney (1945), and are intended to be exhaustive of the range of interpersonal expression of feeling. They are: warmth (movement toward others), hostility (movement against others), and flight (movement away from others). Process was analyzed in this study according to the Joel and Shapiro categories.The analysis was performed by observers, who classified both verbal and nonverbal behavior on the spot as it occurred, in terms of the feelings underlying counselees' interpersonal expressions.

Hypotheses

In the present study the outcomes of counseling were assessed in two ways: acceptance of self, expressed as the degree of congruence between reported self-perception and ideal self-perception; and acceptance by others, expressed as the combined rating received from the rest of the members of the counseling group, reflecting their perception of their willingness to approach the subject for help with their problems.

The hypotheses expressed relationships between changes in the affective behavior of counselees in groups and the measured outcomes of the counseling experience:

1a. There is a positive relationship between change in expression of warmth during counseling and change in congruence between real and ideal self.

1b. There is a positive relationship between change in expression of warmth during counseling and change in degree of acceptance by others.

2a. There is a negative relationship between change in expression of hostility during counseling and change in congruence between real and ideal self.

2b. There is a negative relationship between change in expression of hostility during counseling and change in degree of acceptance by others.

3a. There is a negative relationship between change in expression of flight during counseling and change in congruence between real and ideal self.

3b. There is a negative relationship between change in expression of flight during counseling and change in degree of acceptance by others.

Procedures

Seventy high school students in nine groups were referred for counseling because they exhibited behavior that did not correspond to school expectations in some respect, such as conduct, attitude, or achievement. The goals of the experience were directed primarily at self-understanding and more complete personal functioning, based essentially on the model of self-theory. The counseling style of the nine counselors, all of whom had completed specific preparation for group counseling at the same graduate institution, was generally client-centered. Details of selection of subjects, formation of the groups, and organizational procedures have been discussed elsewhere (Zimpfer, 1964). Twelve counseling sessions of 45 minutes each, twice a week, were conducted with each group. Three nonparticipant observers attended session 2, 3, 11, and 12, and made a written record of the effective interaction according to the Joel-Shapiro categories. This provided early and late indexes of affective behavior. Inter-observer reliabilities were obtained by intraclass correlation. By the end of a training period the *R* among ratings was .94 for warmth, .93 for hostility and .91 for flight, based on a simultaneous observation by the raters of a group counseling session similar to those actually conducted in the study.

The *Q*-sort developed by Baymur was used as the self-evaluative outcome instrument (Baymur and Patterson, 1960). It seemed appropriate because its 45 items had been selected as having relevance to students who were having problems in school. Peer evaluation was measured by the succorance scale of the Syracuse Scales of Social Relations. This scale seemed relevant for group counseling since it indicates the extent to which one is solicited as a helping agent by others who know him. Both outcome instruments were administered as pre- and post-counseling tests.

In order to test the hypotheses, the differences between pre- and post-counseling scores or tallies on the three-process and two-outcome dimensions were calculated. Product-moment correlations were computed between arrays of difference scores.

Results

Table 1 presents the correlations between the affective process variables and the outcomes, representing the tests of the six hypotheses.

TABLE 1
CORRELATIONS BETWEEN CHANGE SCORES FOR PROCESS AND OUTCOME VARIABLES

	Process		
Outcome	*Warmth Change*	*Hostility Change*	*Flight Change*
Q-sort change	—.05	—.02	—.09
Succorance change	.20*	.11	—.23*

*Significant at .05 level.

These findings were made: Increase in expression of warmth was not related to increase in reported self-ideal congruence. However, as a counselee showed more warmth, he tended to be seen as more acceptable by his peers. Reduction in hostility expression did not accompany increased self-acceptance nor increased acceptability to peers. As an individual reduced his flight responses, his level of self-acceptance did not change significantly. Finally, and in the strongest correlation, as the frequency of counselee refusals to become involved with the group diminished, he became more acceptable to the other members of his group.

For this study, the .01 level was chosen as the index of significance, because the subjects had not been selected at random from a population of referrals, nor had they been assigned randomly to groups. (The fact that the groups were located in eight different schools precluded randomization.) None of the correlations is significant at the level chosen; however, two are significant at the .05 level (with 69 degrees of freedom in a one-tailed test). In general, the process variables correlate more closely (either positively or negatively) with peer evaluation than with self-report.

It may be noted that only the dimension of flight predicts the outcomes consistently in the desired and same direction. It may be that change in flight behavior, where noted, may be a reliable indicator of movement in the self-concept.

It is possible that the pooling of data from the nine groups may have reduced the possibility of more significant findings. Ohlsen and Oelke (1962) have suggested that "data from individual sessions not be combined. . . . The emotional climate within a group of young adolescents is very sensitive to changes in individual clients. . . ." One-way analyses of variance and covariance were used to test the differences among group means to determine whether there were differing rates or kinds of behavior among the several groups.

The means on the outcome variables were not statistically different from group to group, either for post-counseling means or adjusted post-counseling means. Nor were differences among regression coefficients significantly different. (These data are treated more fully in the study previously cited.) However, similar analyses of the process variables show great divergence among the groups. Table 2 shows significant differences both on pre-, post- and adjusted-post-counseling means. Even the assumption of homogeneity of post-counseling means is violated in each case. The greatest between-group mean discrepancies appear on the warmth dimension. When the standard deviations and variances of the process variables were examined, great dissimilarity was noted here, also.

TABLE 2

RESULTS OF TESTS FOR MEAN DIFFERENCES ON PROCESS VARIABLES AMONG THE NINE COUNSELED GROUPS, BY ANALYSIS OF VARIANCE AND ANALYSIS OF COVARIANCE

		Process		
Test	*df*	*Warmth Obtained*	*Hostility Obtained*	*Flight Obtained*
F for pre-counseling means	8,61	6.98*	4.26*	3.20*
F For post-counseling means	8,61	21.41*	8.98*	6.11*
X^2 for homogeneity of variance of post-counseling means	8	49.78*	81.65*	32.76*
F for group regression coefficients	8,52	2.51	<.01	<.01
F for adjusted post-counseling means	8,60	18.31*	6.48*	6.24*

*Significant at the .01 level.

The data were explored further in order to learn more about the affective factors. Table 3 presents relevant findings.

TABLE 3

PRE-, POST-, AND CROSS-CORRELATIONS AMONG THE PROCESS VARIABLES: WARMTH, HOSTILITY, AND FLIGHT

	Pre-test			*Post-test*			*Pre-test*		
	H	*F*		*H*	*F*		*W*	*H*	*F*
Pre-test			*Post-test*			*Post-test*			
W	.78	.03	W	.65	.07	W	.50	.41	—.13
H	. .	.23	H	. .	.46	H	.74	.80	.16
F	. .	. .	F	. .	. .	F	.38	.47	.41

A strong relationship between warmth and hostility was discovered. These two dimensions correlated .78 on the pre-counseling test and .65 on the post-counseling test. These are disappointingly high for variables that were expected to predict in opposite directions. Either of two situations may have occurred: First, both dimensions may be more a measure of verbal productivity—talkativeness—than discriminators between kinds of affect. A rather voluble counselee may express both warmth and hostility, reacting more to the momentary situation than out of an internalized attitude toward self and others. This may be an illustration of what Ohlsen and Oelke found: That adolescents do seem to talk more on impersonal topics than do adults. Or one might infer the worst: That the counseling groups were not engaging in psyche process, that deeply personal levels of feelings were not being tapped.

An alternative explanation is that the observers, despite high level of agreement on classifications, may not have distinguished sharply enough between interactions of warmth and hostility. The more ambiguous the interaction, the more blurred the distinction between ratings might become. As Cohn, Ohlsen, and Proff (1960) suggested, for example, hostility may have positive as well as negative qualities.

Pre-, post- and cross-correlations were calculated on the other process variables. Flight correlates more closely with hostility (.23, pre; .46, post) than with warmth (.03, pre; .07, post). This is in keeping with the rationale that underlies both flight and hostility as negative predictors in the hypotheses.

Flight behavior seems to have undergone the most change of the three affective dimensions during counseling. The cross-correlation on this dimension is the lowest, .41. This suggests that the greatest movement among counselees occurred on this dimension, even though the mean change between pre- and post-counseling tests was nonsignificant.

The test of the fourth hypothesis found an unexpected positive relationship between hostility change and succorance change. This is borne out further by their pre-test correlation, .31, and may be a function of the dynamics of group counseling. The first counseling meeting, during which much hostility is typically vented, had been allowed to pass by before the succorance scale was administered, in order to give all counselees an opportunity to become acquainted and appraise each other. If the ventilation had been directed at teachers, parents, and other authority figures, such expression may have strengthened a counselee's popularity and acceptability to his peers. However, since this seems an unwise way for one to judge another's potential for helpfulness, it may be inferred that group counseling had not yet proceeded to the point of bringing the counselees to use those criteria for evaluating each other that would be considered appropriate in counseling. Peer evaluation may not be free from contamination as an evaluative criterion early in group counseling.

Discussion

The results have suggested that change in affective interaction is more strongly correlated with degree of peer acceptance than with self-evaluation. The relative strength of the affect-peer acceptance correlations suggests that more accurate assessments of changes in attitude of an individual may be made from his interactional behavior than from his self-report of progress. This parallels Bales, who wrote in reference to group situations: "The best method we have for understanding what goes on *inside* the individual is the model of what goes on *between* individuals. . . ." (1950, p. 62).

The affect-peer judgment relationship may be noted especially in the results for the last hypothesis, in which the correlation between reduction in flight behavior and improved peer evaluation approaches significance at the .01 level. This has implications for dealing with silent members of groups. Members apparently are willing to reward other members with acknowledgment of the others' approachableness only if they reduce the number of their escaping, dodging behaviors. (Reduction of such behaviors might imply concomitant increase in warmth behavior, or the "confessing" of one's own problems, either of which might also enhance his acceptability to others. However, since these relationships were not studied, fuller implications cannot be drawn from the findings.)

The lack of consistency in process findings from group to group suggests a new area for research in group counseling. It has often been said that mean scores on given variables among the several groups in a research are likely to vary, and that the pooling of results may cancel out significant findings in individual groups. Even more is implied here. Great discrepancies in standard deviations (and variances) may suggest that quite different processes were operating, even when means among groups are statistically similar. Thus, in this study it is to be noted that the assumption of homogeneity of variance (on which the means tests were based) was violated in each case (Table 2). These findings suggest that such variables as counselor competence and personality, as well as cohesiveness and other aspects that flow from the composition of a group, need more careful consideration in group counseling research. The distribution of scores are as important as the means.

The results may be compared to previously reported research. Ohlsen and Oelke, and also Wigell (1960), found that expression of affect occurs irregularly from session to session. This was particularly true when there were differences in membership, such as when a productive or hostile member was absent one time but present another. In this study, interpersonal affective activity appeared to be quite constant as long as the same members were present. The correlations between sessions 2 and 3 was .82, and between 11 and 12 was .91 for the total affective interaction of members. This suggests that while a long-range change of interpersonal affect expression may be expected, there is considerable similarity from one session to the next.

Both Wigell (1960) and Wigell and Ohlsen (1962) hypothesized that members' interaction over the course of counseling would reflect less negative and more positive affect. Their results did not bear this out, except in those instances (Wigell and Ohlsen) where members were discussing authority figures. In the present study the overall frequency of hostility decreased over the counseling series, as was desired. If hostility can be inferred to be a primarily negative affect, these results tend to contradict the findings of the two cited studies. Further, the increase in warmth that was expected did tend to occur. Neither of the other studies had similar findings, except again in the case of authority figures.

Wigell and Ohlsen (1962) found that negative affect was the most common feeling expressed. Again assuming hostility to be primarily negatively motivated (against others), the finding here is similar: hostility was the chief affect expressed by the counselees.

Hostility was reduced somewhat by the end of counseling. However, the fact that it still was so high at the end would seem to indicate that counseling had not yet achieved its purposes. This is consonant with the finding of Wigell and Ohlsen 1962), who felt that the high incidence of hostility at the end of their counseling series may indicate that counseling ended too soon. Under the assumption that the treatment was correct and that the problem was only in the brevity of the experience, that inference may be true. Broedel, who also had similar findings, provided a tentative explanation. He expressed the possibility that the counselees were in the process of re-evaluating themselves and were just beginning to learn to live with their new selves (Broedel, Ohlsen, Proff, and Southard, 1960). Hoch's findings apply here (1950). He found that when therapy was continued for its full course, negative feelings, after reaching a peak in the middle sessions, decreased markedly. Toward the end of the series they constituted only a small portion of the total number of client statements. The implication for group counseling is that it ought, if conducted effectively and for a sufficient period of time, to evoke a similar pattern in regard to feeling expression.

The conclusion one might draw from the tests of the hypotheses is that the selected outcomes of counseling are not predictable from an analysis of overt affective interaction. It is certainly true that no predictions for individuals could be made based on the correlations derived from this study. However, even with methodological problems, some of which have been discussed here, the signs for the correlations testing four of the six hypotheses were in the desired direction, and the movement between pre- and post-counseling for four of the five variables studied was appropriate for counseling. It seems that there is fertile ground here for further study of the relationship between process and outcome in group counseling.

References

Bales, R. F. *Interaction Process Analysis: A Method for the Study of Small Groups.* Reading, Mass.: Addison-Wesley, 1950.

Baymur, Feriha B., & Patterson, C. H. "A Comparison of Three Methods of Assisting Underachieving High School Students." *Journal of Counseling Psychology,* 1960, *7,* 83–90.

Broedel, J., Ohlsen, M., Proff, F., & Southard, C. "The Effects of Group Counseling on Gifted Underachieving Adolescents." *Journal of Counseling Psychology,* 1960, *7,* 163–70.

Cohn, B., Ohlsen, M., & Proff, F. "Roles Played by Adolescents in an Unproductive Counseling Group." *Personnel and Guidance Journal,* 1960, *38,* 724–31.

Hoch, E. "The Nature of the Group Process in Non-Directive Group Psychotherapy." Unpublished doctoral dissertation, Teachers College, Columbia University, 1950.

Horney, Karen. *Our Inner Conflicts.* New York: Norton, 1945.

Joel, W., & Shapiro, D. "A Genotypical Approach to the Analysis of Personal Interaction." *Journal of Psychology,* 1949, *28,* 9–17.

Katz, Evelyn W., Ohlsen, M. M., & Proff, F. C. "An Analysis Through the

Use of Kinescopes of the Interpersonal Behavior of Adolescents in Group Counseling." *Journal of College Student Personnel,* 1959, *1*(2), 2–10.

Ohlsen, M., & Oelke, M. "An Evaluation of Discussion Topics in Group Counseling." *Journal of Clinical Psychology,* 1962, *18,* 317–22.

Wigell, W. "A Content Analysis of Tape Recordings of Group Counseling Sessions with Gifted Underachieving Ninth Grade Students." Unpublished doctoral dissertation, University of Illinois, 1960.

Wigell, W., & Ohlsen, M. "To What Extent Is Affect a Function of Topic and Referent in Group Counseling? *American Journal of Orthopsychiatry,* 1962, *32,* 728–35.

Zimpfer, D. "The Relationship of Self-Concept to Certain Affective Dimensions in Multiple Counseling." Unpublished doctoral dissertation, State University of New York at Buffalo, 1964.

EFFECTS OF SOCIAL REINFORCEMENT AS A TECHNIQUE IN COUNSELING

ERNEST SPAIGHTS

Sufficient evidence exists to support the notion that social reinforcement can influence verbal behavior. NcNair (1957) studied the effect of a bell-tone, defined by instructions as signifying approval, on rate of verbalization in an 18-person discussion group. In the study, subjects were shown pictures depicting interpersonal situations and were instructed to talk about them. Results indicated that the rate of verbalization was influenced by the reinforcer and varied as a function of the schedule of reinforcement.

Nonverbal gestures were used by Cieutat (1959) to influence the verbal behavior of students in a seminar situation. Positive reinforcement consisted of attention directed toward the subject; that is, he was looked at and given occasional nods. Negative reinforcement

*This article is reprinted from *The Journal of College Student Personnel,* 1967, *8,* 116–20, by permission of the publisher and author.

consisted of inattention. Cieutat found that the amount of time during which a subject spoke was positively associated with attention and negatively associated with inattention.

There is little doubt that the two studies cited provided some of the foundation for behavioral counseling, but it was not until the last few years that social reinforcement was incorporated directly into counseling techniques. Perhaps one of the most revealing studies concerned with the effectiveness of social reinforcement in counseling was conducted by Ryan and Krumboltz (1964). By systematically reinforcing "deliberation" responses during the interview, the counselor increased the extent to which the client continued to deliberate. They showed that both "deliberation" and "decision" statements could be increased during counseling interviews in as little as 6 to 10 minutes, and that, in the case of the group reinforced for "decision" responses, a tendency to make decisions could be detected later in a projective type of problem test in a classroom setting.

The purposes of this study are to determine: (1) the effects of social reinforcement as a technique in counseling (both individual and group settings) versus no counseling, on personal adjustment scores of college students, and (2) the effects of individual and group counseling versus no counseling on the accuracy of self-estimated personal adjustment. Personal adjustment was assessed by use of the Personal Adjustment subtest of the California Test of Personality (CTP). More specifically, this study seeks to test the following four null hypotheses:

I. There will be no significant difference between pre-counseling and post-counseling mean personal adjustment scores for each group.

II. There will be no significant differences in post-counseling mean gain scores in personal adjustment among the three groups.

III. There will be no significant difference between pre-counseling and post-counseling accuracy of self-estimated personal adjustment for each group.

IV. There will be no significant differences among groups in the accuracy of self-estimated personal adjustment at the post-counseling stage.

Method

Subjects

The subjects for this study were students enrolled in the course, Introduction to the Study of Education, during the autumn quarter of the 1964-65 academic year. The total study group, randomly selected from a universe of 640 students available, was composed of

78 students. Twenty-six students were assigned to each of the groups, which received individual counseling, group counseling, and no counseling. The 26 students designated to receive group counseling were then randomly subdivided into counseling groups of 6 or 7 students. Each person of the individual counseling group and each subgroup of the group counseling group were counseled for four sessions. The investigator acted as counselor for individual as well as group counseling groups.

TREATMENT

After the subjects had been assigned to groups for individual and group counseling, a structuring statement was made to each of the four group counseling subgroups and to each person who participated in individual counseling. The statement was as follows:

> These sessions have two main purposes. First, it is hoped that you will begin to identify those characteristics and attitudes possessed by good teachers. It is hoped secondly that you will be able to assess yourself in relation to the desired characteristics identified by you during our sessions together. During our sessions I would like for you to do most of the talking. Lastly, express your ideas and thoughts freely. From time to time, I might clarify a point or initiate a statement. You are free to take issue with me (or anyone else) during our sessions. I would like to begin by asking this question: What kind of people should teachers be?

The investigator carefully listened during each of the counseling sessions for responses that he judged to be examples of insight regarding adjusted personal behavior. When such a response was made by a subject, the counselor provided a verbal reinforcement. The following statement is representative of the kind that was reinforced by the investigator:

> I believe that a person should live according to ideals set by himself, although he might not always voice those ideals.

Only statements relating to personal adjustment were positively reinforced. Other statements, unrelated to the selected criterion, received neutral responses from the counselor. Such verbal reinforcers as "Good" or "Yes, that is a most perceptive idea," were the most frequent comments made by the investigator, although an occasional comment such as "Mm-hmm" was used to encourage continuation of an idea expressed by a student.

PROCEDURES

Phase 1.—Upon completion of the Personal Adjustment subtest of the CTP by all study group members, mean scores were calculated for each of the three groups. A procedure was employed that was designed to test the significance of the difference between means obtained from the same test administered to the same group upon two different occasions (Garrett, 1962). In order to determine whether the groups were equal at the pre-counseling stage, mean scores were compared by analysis of variance. The variance ratio did not reach the .05 level; therefore, the investigator assumed that members of the three groups were assigned strictly on a random basis. Variance analysis was again employed to analyze mean gain scores at the .01 level. Subsequent use of the t-test was necessary in order to ascertain where differences between mean gain scores lay.

Phase 2.—In the pre-counseling stage each student was asked to indicate the quartile in which he ranked himself in relation to other members of his beginning education class in the area of personal adjustment. A Student Self-Rating Sheet (SSRS) was used for this purpose. The number circled by the student became his personal adjustment self-rating score. Students' earned scores on the CTP were placed in numerical order (descending) and divided into quartiles. Thus, if a student received a CTP score that fell into the highest quartile, he was assigned a score of one. Other ranks were assigned (two, three, or four), depending on the quartile in which the student scored on the subtest. Each student's self-rating score was placed beside his earned score. The scores were analyzed by Guilford's product-moment correlation for original measures. This procedure was used before and after the experimental period. In order to determine whether or not differences between correlation coefficients were significant, the investigator converted the coefficients into Fisher's z functions and tested for significance.

RESULTS

Hypothesis I (There will be no significant differences between pre-counseling and post-counseling mean personal adjustment scores for each group).—Table 1 shows the means and standard deviations for each group before and after counseling. It can be seen that both group and individually counseled students made significantly (.01 level) higher scores at the end of the experimental period than at the beginning of counseling. The control group also evidenced a slight gain during the experimental period; however, the gain was not significant. In light of the data in Table 1, Hypothesis I cannot be supported for the group and individually counseled student. The data do support this hypothesis for the control group.

TABLE 1

MEANS AND STANDARD DEVIATIONS OF PRE-COUNSELING AND POST-COUNSELING CTP (PERSONAL ADJUSTMENT) SCORES FOR THREE GROUPS.

	Pre-Counseling		*Post-Counseling*				
Groups	*Mean*	*SD*	*Mean*	*SD*	*Gain*	*SE*D	*t*
Multiple N = 26	66.5	18.7	77.2	19.7	10.7	3.1	3.45*
Individual N = 26	69.2	19.2	78.1	19.1	8.9	2.7	3.29*
Control N = 26	65.4	18.3	66.6	18.7	1.2	1.4	.85

*Significant at .01 level.

Hypothesis II (There will be no significant difference in post-counseling mean gain scores in personal adjustment among the three groups).—Table 2 shows the mean gain scores for each group. It can be seen that students who were counseled in a group setting had the highest mean gain score, approximately nine times larger than that of the no-counseling group. The difference between the mean gain scores of the group counseling and the no-counseling groups was significant at the .01 level. The mean gain score difference between the group counseled and the individually counseled groups was not significant. Students counseled individually had a mean gain score over seven times larger than that of the control group. Such a difference represents a significant difference at the .01 level. In light of these data, Hypothesis II can be rejected.

Hypothesis III (There will be no significant difference between

TABLE 2

DIFFERENCES BETWEEN POST-COUNSELING MEAN GAIN SCORES ON THE CTP (PERSONAL ADJUSTMENT)

Post-Counseling	*Gain*	*Post-Counseling*	*Gain*	*Difference*	*t*
Multiple N = 26	10.7	Control N = 26	1.2	9.5	4.69*
Individual N = 26	8.9	Control N = 26	1.2	7.7	3.72*
Multiple N = 26	10.7	Indvidual N = 26	8.9	1.8	1.96 NS

*Significant at .01 level.

pre-counseling and post-counseling accuracy of self-estimated personal adjustment for each group).—Table 3 shows the means and standard deviations of self-estimated and actual levels of personal adjustment for each group at the pre- and post-counseling stages. It can be seen that mean self-rating scores before and after counseling are quite similar for each group. This is also true for earned scores for each group. What is not obvious in Table 3 is that members of the two counseling groups shifted (in both negative and positive directions) their self-ratings after the experimental period in greater numbers than did members of the control group.

TABLE 3

MEANS AND STANDARD DEVIATIONS OF SELF-RATING AND EARNED SCORES ON THE CTP (PERSONAL ADJUSTMENT) AT THE POST-COUNSELING STAGE

	Pre-Counseling				*Post-Counseling*			
Groups	*SR*	*SD*	*ES*	*SD*	*SR*	*SD*	*ES*	*SD*
Multiple N = 26	3.4	1.6	2.5	1.2	3.5	1.6	2.5	1.2
Individual N = 26	3.3	1.7	2.5	1.2	3.3	1.6	2.5	1.2
Control N = 26	3.6	1.5	2.5	1.2	3.5	1.5	2.5	1.2

Pre- and post-counseling self-rating and earned scores were correlated, and the significance of differences was determined between paired pre- and post-counseling correlations. Table 4 shows the t-ratios resulting from an analysis of the difference between z functions for each of the three groups under study. Each of the three groups evidenced an increase in the relationship of self-estimated and earned scores, but the correlation coefficients that expressed the relationships do not change significantly from pre- to post-counseling. Although not significant, it is noteworthy that the two experimental groups had a greater gain in z points than did the control group. In light of data contained in Table 4, Hypothesis III cannot be rejected.

Hypothesis IV (There will be no significant difference among groups in the accuracy of self-estimated level of personal adjustment at the post-counseling stage).—Table 5 shows the mean gain scores (z scores) for students who participated in group, individual, and no counseling. Both the group counseled and individually counseled student obtained z points that were approximately three times larger than the control group, but the differences were not large enough to be significant at the .05 level. These data, then, do not provide a foundation for the rejection of Hypothesis IV.

TABLE 4

DIFFERENCES BETWEEN PRE- AND POST-COUNSELING CORRELATION COEFFICIENTS OF SELF-RATING AND EARNED SCORES ON THE CTP (PERSONAL ADJUSTMENT)

Groups	*Pre-Counseling* *r*	*(z functions)*	*Post-Counseling* *r*	*(z functions)*	*Difference Between z's*	*t*
Multiple N = 26	.38	.40	.63	.74	.34	1.13NS
Individual N = 26	.38	.40	.67	.81	.41	1.36NS
Control N = 26	.41	.44	.52	.58	.14	.47NS

TABLE 5

DIFFERENCES BETWEEN POST-COUNSELING CORRELATION COEFFICIENTS OF SELF-RATING AND EARNED SCORES ON THE CTP (PERSONAL ADJUSTMENT)

Post-Counseling	*Gain Scores (z functions)*	*Post-Counseling*	*Gain Scores (z functions)*	*Difference*	*t*
Multiple N = 26	.34	Control N = 26	.14	.20	.67
Individual N = 26	.41	Control N = 26	.14	.27	.90
Individual N = 26	.41	Multiple N = 26	.34	.7	.02

DISCUSSION

There are some factors that should be considered in evaluating the results of this study. First, there existed the possibility that the investigator, serving as counselor, might have been biased in favor of one approach. However, if bias existed the counselor was not aware of it, for no preconceived notions concerning the relative effectiveness of social reinforcement in group and individual settings were harbored. The purposes of the investigation were exploratory. Second, it was difficult to implement the social reinforcement schedule in a similar fashion for both groups. On several occasions during the group counseling sessions, members of the group interrupted before the full reinforcement was given. This was not so in the individual counseling sessions. Third, the fact that the Personal Adjustment subtest of the California Test of Personality measures perceptions of internal feelings and not actual behavior might be a limiting factor. The fact that a student might score higher on the instrument as a result of counseling does not guarantee that his behavior will change accordingly, although the assumption made here is that the behavior will change. A follow-up study of the subjects using behavior changes as the major criteria would provide some valuable information about the adequacy of the instrument employed.

Summary and Conclusions

Seventy-eight beginning education students enrolled in the course Introduction to the Study of Education at the Ohio State University were randomly divided into three groups that received individual counseling, group counseling, and no counseling for four sessions. Before counseling all students were asked to complete the Personal Adjustment subtest of the California Test of Personality and the Student Self-Rating Sheet.

The results of the study lend support to the conclusions that follow:

1. There was a tendency for group and individually counseled students to manifest more growth in personal adjustment as evidenced by the CTP than students who received no counseling.
2. Social reinforcement as a technique in counseling was equally effective for producing a change in personal adjustment scores of college students in both treatment modes. However, it might be mentioned that one setting might prove superior to the other if the number of counseling sessions exceeded the four sessions involved in this study.
3. There is no evidence that social reinforcement as a technique in counseling is effective in increasing students' accuracy of self-estimation in the area of personal adjustment, although there was a tendency for the counseled groups to evidence greater accuracy at the end of the experimental period than the control group.

References

Cieutat, V. J. "Surreptitious Modification of Verbal Behavior During Class Discussion." *Psychological Reports,* 1959, *5,* 648.

Garrett, H. E. *Statistics in Psychology and Education.* New York: David McKay, 1962.

McNair, D. M. "Reinforcement of Verbal Behavior." *Journal of Experimental Psychology,* 1957, *53,* 40–46.

Ryan, T. A., & Krumboltz, J. D. "Effect of Planned Reinforcement Counseling on Client Decision-Making Behavior." *Journal of Counseling Psychology,* 1964, *11,* 315–23.

*

IMMEDIATE EFFECTS OF GROUP THERAPY UPON RESPONSE TO SOCIAL REINFORCEMENT AMONG JUVENILE DELINQUENTS[1]

JOHN W. McDAVID

The practice of group therapy with institutionalized juvenile delinquents is widespread and increasing. At least two general considerations make the group approach to therapy well suited to such settings. With a severe shortage of trained personnel for handling therapy among such populations, some economy may be gained by enabling the therapist to deal with a group of individuals rather than single individuals. Furthermore, to the extent that juvenile delinquency may be interpreted as a consequence of the failure of social controls (Riess, 1951), the group setting provides for realistic retraining and controlled experience in interpersonal relations. It is likely that the first consideration may lead to the use of didactic therapist-centered techniques, while the latter consideration may more often lead to the use of nondidactic group-centered techniques. Both Slavson (1948) and Gersten (1952) have reported encouraging evidence of the efficacy of relatively nondidactic group therapy with juvenile delinquents.

The study described here, unlike most evaluative studies of thera-

*This article is reprinted from *Journal of Consulting Psychology,* 1964, *28,* 409-12, by permission of the publisher, The American Psychological Association, and the author.

[1]The research described here was executed while the author was a member of the faculty of the Iowa Child Welfare Research Station, State University of Iowa, and was supported by that agency.

The cooperation of Ernst Schmidhofer and his associates at the Training School for Boys, Eldora, Iowa, and of the Iowa Board of Control of State Institutions is appreciatively acknowledged.

peutic techniques, is concerned with *immediate* rather than *lasting* or long-range effects of experience in a therapeutic group. Only one kind of effect of the group experience is investigated: That upon the degree of effective assimilation of interpersonal approval and disapproval as reward and punishment events. The research is entirely serendipitous, in that the design was a fortuitous product of circumstances in arranging to administer a battery of psychological evaluation instruments to a sample of delinquents. Thus, while the overall design is imperfect, the observations made here are sufficiently provocative to merit their report.

A paper-and-pencil group test has been designed to gauge the individual's assimilative recognition of events of interpersonal praise as rewarding (enhancing self-evaluation) or events of interpersonal criticism as punishing (decreasing self-evaluation). This instrument represents modification and extension of a similar device utilized in earlier research (McDavid, 1959; McDavid and Schroder, 1957; Schroder and Hunt, 1957). An earlier investigation (McDavid and Schroder, 1957) demonstrated that delinquent adolescents score significantly lower on this measure than non-delinquent adolescents, and this finding has been replicated subsequently using the revised form of the test.

Presumably, controlled and optimized social interaction (both with the adult therapist and with peer members of the group) in therapy groups may lead to increased effectiveness of interpersonal approval and disapproval events as rewards and punishments for members of the group. That is, to the extent that the practice of group therapy involves the establishment of a warm, permissive, but realistic interpersonal relationship with an adult (therapist) as well as catalyzed and controlled interaction with peers in the group, the therapy group may be thought of as a potential training situation with respect to the individual's reactions to such interpersonal events as approval and disapproval. Thus, assimilative reactions to verbal praise and criticism should be fostered, while denial or indifferent reactions should tend to be extinguished.

Method

Social Reinforcement Interpretation Test (SRIT).— The assessment device utilized in this study was an elaborated revision of an instrument utilized in earlier research (McDavid and Schroder, 1957; Schroder and Hunt, 1957). It contained 20 items depicting hypothetical situations in which a verbal statement of approval or disapproval is delivered by either an adult or a peer. Within the 5 items representing each of the possible combinations of these factors, one described a work situation (part-time job), one a social situation (dating behavior or table manners), one a hobby situation (unspecified hobby activity), and two describe academic situations (grade report cards and a homework assignment). Subjects were instructed to imagine that they are engaged in the activity described, and to indicate their reaction to the approval or disapproval statement by selecting one of two alternative responses. One alternative was designed to indicate *assimilation* of the event (recognition of its reward properties, as indicated by increased self-evaluation following praise or decreased self-evaluation following criticism), and the other to indicate *denial* or indifference to the event. No items were repeated, and the subjects were urged to read each item carefully but to report their first reaction after clearly understanding the situation.

Subjects.—Subjects for this investigation included 89 boys between the ages of 13 years, 4 months, and 18 years, 5 months, with a median age of 16 years, 11 months. All were institutionalized at a State Training School for Boys in the Midwest. Bases for commitment ranged from conviction for forgery, extortion, assault, and larceny, to parental declarations of incorrigibility and transfer from the State Home for Dependent and Neglected Children. However, the vast majority of the boys were committed by direct court action as a consequence of actual criminal behavior.

Group Therapy Variable.—All of the 89 subjects were participants in a newly organized program of group therapy which had been in effect at the institution for approximately 7 weeks at the time of testing with the SRIT. Consequently, long-range or lasting effects of group therapy would be expected to be constant for all subjects. Arrangements for conducting group therapy were such that boys were randomly assigned to one of three therapists (two males and one female) in a ratio of 2:1:1. Each therapist conducted group-therapy sessions at two appointed hours on a given day, with boys randomly assigned to one of the two hours. Thus, it was possible to administer the SRIT during a 1-hour interval between the two scheduled sessions. As a result, all subjects were tested simultaneously, but one group (designated *Post-Therapy*) was tested immediately following a 1-hour session of group therapy, and the other (designated *Pre-Therapy)* was tested immediately preceding their scheduled group therapy session. For the latter group, the interval following their last experience in the therapeutic group, then, was exactly 1 week.

Because of the schedule for testing, the Post-Therapy group includes slightly less than half the number of subjects ($n = 25$) in the Pre-Therapy group ($n = 64$). Of the 25 Post-Therapy subjects, 12 were assigned to Therapist A (male), 7 to Therapist B (male), and 6 to Therapist C (female). Although no explicit procedures were employed for one-to-one matching of the two samples, comparison on (*a*) basis for commitment to the institution, (*b*) duration of stay at institution, (*c*) scores on an abbreviated verbal intelligence scale (Thorndike, 1942), (*d*) age, and (*e*) school grade revealed no differences between the Pre-Therapy and Post-Therapy groups, or among the subjects assigned to each of the three therapists.

It is difficult to determine precisely the nature of the variable or variables operative during group therapy which might produce effects upon an individual's response to social interaction in general or upon his reactions to interpersonal approval and disapproval in specific. Responses of each therapist to a questionnaire concerning his practices in group therapy indicated that all three attempted to create a "controlled but accepting atmosphere," to be "warm" but yet "firm" in interacting with the boys, and to make explicit use of interpersonal approval and disapproval in responding to the boys' behavior during the therapy session. Therapist A characterized his approach as clearly more authoritarian and didactic than did Therapists B and C, and the degree of interaction among members of the group permitted or fostered by the therapist was clearly greater for Therapist C than for Therapists A and B. While no well-defined assessments of the therapists' actual practice were made, it appears that the three therapists range from A to B to C along a continuum from "didactic therapist-centered" practice to "nondidactic group-centered" practice. All three, however, appear to employ at least moderately firm control over the group and to maximize therapist-client interaction while minimizing client-client interaction. No further attempt was made to specify the variables which might operate during the therapy session. It was merely assumed that intensive interaction with peers and an adult under conditions designed to optimize the nature of social interaction might lead to immediate (even if temporary) increase in the effective recognition of interpersonal approval and disapproval as reinforcing events.

Results and Discussion

A mixed-design analysis of variance of SRIT scores for the two groups, with the Pre- or Post-Therapy condition operating between subjects and the Source (Adult-Peer) and Direction (Positive-Negative) factors operating within subjects, was carried out. The results of this analysis, summarized in Table 1, indicate that the Pre- and Post-Therapy conditions differed significantly ($p < .025$), and reveal that the effects of the within subjects factors parallel those found with a nondelinquent high school male sample. That is, the Source effect was nonsignificant, and the Direction effect was significant ($p < .001$), with positive reinforcers (approval) being assimilated more readily than negative reinforcers (disapproval). The Source by Direction interaction was also significant ($p < .001$), with the difference between assimilation scores for positive and negative reinforcement from adults being greater than that between positive and negative reinforcement from peers. None of the interactions between therapy condition and the SRIT factors was significant.

TABLE 1

ANALYSIS OF VARIANCE OF SRIT SCORES FOR PRE-THERAPY AND POST-THERAPY GROUPS

Variable	*df*	*MS*	*F*
Between subjects	88		
Therapy conditions (A)	1	29.940	5.696*
error (b)	87	5.256	
Within subjects	267		
Source (B)	1	2.363	2.404
Direction (C)	1	60.700	40.602†
B×C	1	10.451	14.657*
B×A	1	0.333	—
C×A	1	0.006	—
B×C×A	1	0.233	—
error (w)	261		
$error_1$ (w)‡	87	0.983	
$error_2$ (w)§	87	1.495	
$error_3$ (w)#	87	0.713	
Total	355		

*$p < .025$.
†$p < .001$.
‡Used to test B and B×A.
§Used to test C and C×A.
#Used to test B×C and B×C×A.

An additional mixed-design analysis of variance of SRIT scores was executed for the Post-Therapy group to determine what, if any, differences might occur among the three therapists. For this analysis, the Therapist (A, B, or C) factor operated between subjects, and the SRIT Source and Direction factors operated within subjects. No significant differences among the three therapists, either in terms of simple effects or of interactions with the SRIT Source and Direction factors, were observed.

Scores on the four basic subscales of the SRIT (Adult-Positive, Adult-Negative, Peer-Positive, and Peer-Negative) and on combined subscales (Adult Sources, Peer Sources, Positive (Approval) Events, and Negative (Disapproval) Events, and Total Event Assimilation Scores) for the Pre-Therapy and Post-Therapy groups were compared and the differences tested by the Cochran-Cox test (Cochran and Cox, 1950). The Post-Therapy group was found to score significantly higher on the Adult-Positive scale ($p < .01$) and on the Peer-Positive scale ($p < .05$), and on all of the combined subscales ($p <$ .05 or less). Scores for each group are reported in Table 2.

TABLE 2
SRIT SCORES FOR PRE-THERAPY AND POST-THERAPY GROUPS

SRIT Scale	*MS*		*t Ratio of Difference*
	Pre-Therapy	*Post-Therapy*	
Adult-Positive	3.59	4.36	2.956†
Adult-Negative	3.14	3.80	1.921
Peer-Positive	3.84	4.36	2,159*
Peer-Negative	2.64	3.28	1.727
Adult-Sources	6.73	8.16	2.737*
Peer sources	6.48	7.64	2.312*
Positive reinforcers	7.44	8.72	2.843†
Negative reinforcers	5.78	7.08	2.085*
Total reinforcer assimilation	13.22	15.80	2.817†

*$p < .05$ (Cochran-Cox test).
†$p < .01$ (Cochran-Cox test).

These data suggest that whatever the variable or variables which operate during group therapy may be, they appear to bring about an immediate but apparently transitory enhancement in the effective recognition of interpersonal approval statements as rewards. While SRIT reinforcer assimilation scores were higher on all subscales for the Post-Therapy group than for the Pre-Therapy group, the only statistically significant differences on primary subscales occurred on the same two subscales (Adult-Positive and Peer-Positive) on which delinquent and nondelinquent male adolescents were found to differ significantly in a related unpublished investigation.

In spite of the fact that the three therapists conducting the groups studied here appear superficially to differ slightly in their approaches to therapy, no significant differences among the three were observed with respect to the effects of group therapy on SRIT scores. It is interesting to note that social reinforcer assimilation scores on all four of the SRIT primary subscales (Adult-Positive, Peer-Positive, Adult-Negative, and Peer-Negative) were largest for the seven Post-

Therapy subjects under Therapist C, who was descriptively characterized as the most permissive, least authoritarian, and least didactic, of the three therapists. These score differences, however, were not statistically significant.

Thus, there is evidence of a directly relevant therapeutic effect as a consequence of the use of group therapy with institutionalized delinquents. This effect, however, appears to be only immediate and temporary, since both groups of subjects were participants in identical group therapy programs. The only difference between the two groups was that of recency of experience in the therapy group: for one group, the last experience in the therapy group occurred immediately prior to testing, and for the other group, the last such experience occurred exactly 1 week earlier. While the specific nature of variables which may operate during group therapy to produce this increase in effective recognition of the reward properties of social reinforcers is not determined, these findings suggest that controlled social interaction under optimal conditions may provide beneficial experience in learning the incentive and reinforcement value of social reinforcers.

References

Cochran, W. G., & Cox, G. M. *Experimental Designs.* New York: Wiley, 1950.

Gersten, C. "Group Therapy with Institutionalized Delinquents." *Journal of Genetic Psychology,* 1952, *80,* 35–64.

McDavid, J. W. "Some Relationships Between Social Reinforcement and Academic Achievement." *Journal of Consulting Psychology,* 1959, *23,* 151–54.

McDavid, J. W., & Schroder, H. M. "The Interpretation of Approval and Disapproval by Delinquent and Nondelinquent Adolescents." *Journal of Personality,* 1957, *25,* 539–49.

Reiss, A. J. "Delinquency as the Failure of Personal and Social Controls." *American Sociological Review,* 1951, *16,* 196–207.

Schroder, H. M., & Hunt, D. E. "Failure-Avoidance in Situational Interpretation and Problem Solving." *Psychological Monographs,* 1957, *71*(3, Whole Number 432).

Slavson, S. R. "Group Therapy in Child Care and Child Guidance." *Jewish Social Service Quarterly,* 1948, *25,* 203–13.

*

GROUP COUNSELING AND BEHAVIOR THERAPY WITH TEST-ANXIOUS COLLEGE STUDENTS[1]

MARTIN KATAHN
STUART STRENGER
NANCY CHERRY

While test anxiety seems to be fairly widespread among college students, the magnitude of the problem together with the lack of clear-cut therapeutic procedures has discouraged the development of regular continuing programs for test-anxious students on most college campuses. Wolpe's (1958) procedures for systematic desensitization seem to be especially well suited to this problem in terms of both their reported effectiveness in reducing anxiety (Eysenck and Rachman, 1965; Grossberg, 1964) and their efficiency in time and personnel. Lazarus (1961) has reported success using desensitization with phobic reactions in a group setting, which further increases the economy of the procedures. While not specifically aimed at the problem of test anxiety, work done by Spielberger and Weitz (1964) indicates that group-counseling procedures may be effective in improving the grades of generally anxious, underachieving college students. Only a limited number of students, however, benefited from the counseling procedures without desensitization, and a number of other factors interfered with the program's overall effectiveness. Nevertheless, this program of counseling is one of but 2 out of 15

---

*This article is reprinted from *Journal of Consulting Psychology,* 1966, *30,* 544–49, by permission of the publisher, the American Psychological Association, and the authors.

[1]This research was supported by Grant No. MH–11149–01 from the National Institute of Health.

studies mentioned by Chestnut (1965) in which group counseling had any effect on the academic achievement of underachieving college students. Similarly, Chestnut's results, while encouraging, seem ambiguous since changes due to counseling were manifested only in differences in regression coefficients among treatment and control groups. These regression coefficients related pre- and post-counseling grade-point averages (GPA's). Significant pre- and post-counseling changes in GPA's themselves were not obtained.

This paper describes a group-behavior therapy approach to the treatment of test anxiety which combines systematic desensitization and counseling procedures. The aim of these therapy groups was to change directly behaviors which are maladjustive in the academic setting. Systematic desensitization was used to bring the students' anxiety within manageable limits and counseling (suggestion and advice) was used to help the students develop the necessary skills for improved academic performance.

Method

Participants.—The 45 students involved in this study were Vanderbilt University undergraduates enrolled in one or more psychology courses during the fall and spring semesters of the 1964-65 academic year. A group program for test-anxious students was described in four second-year psychology classes during regular class periods by the senior author. Following the program's description, students were given a questionnaire containing 8-point scales on which they rated their tension, excitement, and feelings of unpleasantness before, during, and after examinations. Students wishing to participate in one of the test-anxiety groups so indicated at the end of the questionnaire. Scores on a 16-item true-false version of the Test Anxiety Scale (TAS) (Sarason, 1958) were available for all students from previous testing earlier in the semester.

Forty-five students obtained scores of 10 or more on the TAS (the upper 25 per cent of the distribution). Of these, 22 indicated a desire to participate in the program; 16 of these were initially selected for the program simply because their schedules permitted them to attend the meetings; the other 6 had conflicting schedules and comprised a volunteer control group. All remaining students with TAS scores over 10 comprised a nonvolunteer control group. The first group of 8 students (4 males and 4 females) began meeting in October, 1964, and the second group (4 males, 4 females) began meeting in February, 1965. Two of the 8 students in the second group, both males, felt that the group might not be suited to their particular problems at the end of the first group meeting and decided not to participate. Data for these two subjects are not included in any of the analyses (their mean GPA decreased by .06 of a point during the period of this investigation).

In addition to changes in TAS scores, results were assessed on the basis of any differences in cumulative GPA before the semester of counseling and (*a*) for the fall group, the average of the two semesters following counseling, and (*b*) for the spring group the semester following counseling. GPA's at Vanderbilt are a weighted average in which 3 points are credited for each hour of A, 2 for B, 1 for C, and 0 for D and F. (Differences in hours credited for graduation requirements for D and F grades are irrelevant for GPA computations in this study.) A 1.00 average is required of students in order to remain in good standing, and a 2.00 average (honor roll) is obtained by about 15 per cent of the student body.

Procedure.—Space limitations naturally preclude detailed presentation of the procedures and the content of group discussions.[2] In brief, groups met with a leader and coleader (the senior author and one or the other of the junior authors) for a total of eight sessions, each approximately one hour in length. The senior author would be considered psychoanalytically oriented by previous training, and the coleaders were advanced graduate students who had participated in other forms of group therapy prior to this study. The meetings were held in a psychology department seminar room, with members seated in lightly padded armchairs around a long table.

The first session began with general introductions of the students to each other. The leader stated the purpose of the group, emphasizing that the members shared common reasons for their participation. He explained the theoretical orientation under which he would operate (Wolpe, 1958), with examples of how anxiety may be acquired and how it might be reduced. The group members then discussed their own particular problems, with the leaders themselves contributing examples from their own personal experience. Students found that certain types of experiences were likely to elicit a great

[2]A manual used by the counselors in the training of deep muscle relaxation in the groups is available upon request from the first author of the paper, together with transcribed excerpts taken from tape recordings of ongoing groups, which convey something of the mood and nature of the group meetings. Sections of the recorded interviews are now being analyzed according to three content analysis methods (Jaffe, 1961; Laffal, 1960; Lennard and Bernstein, 1960). The authors would like to thank three of the counselors now active in the test-anxiety programs, Norman E. Wheeler, C. Warren Thompson, and Leighton J. Cunningham, for their invaluable assistance in this project. Copies of the sections of the tapes which were analyzed, together with the results are also available upon request.

deal of anxiety in everyone, for example, waiting for the professor to hand out the test 5 minutes before the examination or taking out their notes to study the night before the test. They also found that their anxiety could be manifested in idiosyncratic ways, for example, becoming anxious as they found that they could not keep up with the professor while taking notes during classes, feeling their hands cramp up while writing answers to the test, or just taking out their books to study the material before a regular class period. Most students felt some degree of anxiety when they were faced with telling their parents about their grades. This discussion lasted approximately 25 minutes.

At that point the leader explained the procedure for constructing an anxiety hierarchy (Wolpe, 1958). Students were asked to list 10 experiences which elicited various amounts of anxiety. They then ranked these experiences in the order of increasing anxiety from 1 to 10 so that 1 was the experience which elicited the least anxiety and 10 was the experience which elicited the greatest amount of anxiety. A typical hierarchy is as follows: (1) going into a regularly scheduled class period, (2) going into a regularly scheduled class in which the professor asks the students to participate, (3) sitting down to study before a regularly scheduled class, (4) having a test returned, (5) studying for a class in which I am scared of the professor, (6) seeing a test question and not being sure of the answer, (7) studying for a test the night before, (8) waiting to enter the room where a test is to be given, (9) being called on to answer a question in class by a professor who scares me, and (10) being in the class waiting for the examination to be handed out. After approximately 10 minutes of work on the anxiety hierarchies, the leader interrupted, asking the students to consider their experiences during the coming week, so that they would be able to complete their hierarchies at the next session. The remaining 15 minutes were devoted to the first steps in relaxation training.

The procedures followed in relaxation training were an adaptation of those used by Wolpe (1958). The role of the skeletal muscle system in the feeling of anxiety was explained. As an example, the leader and coleader demonstrated the feeling of tension in the arms by circulating around the room holding the students' wrists and asking them to push and pull as hard as they could against the stabilizing pressure exerted by their leader and coleader. Each student was then asked to pull as hard as he could against the pressure exerted by the leader (or coleader) for about 5 seconds. Then he was instructed to relax slowly and to let his arm fall onto the arm of his chair or into his lap. This procedure was repeated with each arm, with the leader and coleader checking to be sure that each student was able to achieve a satisfactory degree of relaxation. (In this and the following session one student was unable to learn the relaxation procedures in the group setting. Two private meetings were held with the leader in order to train him in the relaxation procedures. He was able to learn them in these two meetings, and his progress in the group was satisfactory.) The first meeting ended with this preliminary demonstration of the relaxation procedures. Students were told that the relaxation procedures would be completed at the next meeting and reminded to keep track of their anxiety experiences during the following week so that they would be able to complete their anxiety hierarchies at the second session.

The second session and the sessions thereafter began with the leaders asking one or the other of the following questions: "How have things been going this week?" or "What kinds of experiences have you been having this past week?" Whenever possible the leaders made definite suggestions for the handling of certain problems. For example, if a student had trouble organizing himself for studying before a test or before a class, he was encouraged to set himself a minimum goal that he could be quite sure of reaching and then, over time, to increase the requirement he set for himself. Many students seemed to be so anxious about their course work that just the thought of studying before a class elicited enough anxiety to prevent them from sitting down and working. By the third or fourth session, after they had had practice in relaxation, they were instructed in how to use these procedures to reduce their tension before studying, while at the same time setting for themselves a reasonable period of time for working.

Some students reported feeling guilty about not working hard enough, no matter how long they studied. This led to discussions over the role of work and play in their education and of ways of planning each day's work so that reasonable amounts of time were spent in both activities. Since most of the test-anxious students felt that grades were terribly important, some time was spent discussing the aims of education, professors' attitudes towards grades, and what professors themselves might find rewarding about teaching. Ways of studying and of rehearsing the material in lectures and texts were discussed.

Sometime during the second meeting it was suggested that students buy a book entitled *On Becoming an Educated Person* by Virginia Voeks (1964). This book discusses a number of problems faced by students during their college careers and makes certain suggestions for overcoming them. The leaders suggested that students read this book, paying special attention to anything that was personally relevant and perhaps bringing in their thoughts and questions for discussion by the group. No attempt was made by the leaders to refer to anything specific in this book.

After approximately 20 minutes of discussion at the start of this second meeting, another 10 to 15 minutes were spent in completing the anxiety hierarchies. The leaders helped by giving examples of the kinds of experiences students in general might have with respect to academic anxieties. The students were encouraged to make their anxiety hierarchies as specific as possible so that with each item an actual scene could be visualized during the desensitization procedures which were to follow. The remaining 25 minutes were devoted to completing the relaxation training. In contrast to Wolpe's procedure, training proceeded from the toes to the head. Select muscle groups were chosen for tensing and relaxing and the leaders circulated around the room holding ankles, knees, etc., in order to illustrate the difference in feeling between tension and relaxation.

Students were asked to practice their relaxation procedures preferably twice but at least once a day for 15 minutes. In the remaining sessions, approximately 40 minutes were devoted to group discussion and the remaining 20 minutes to systematic desensitization. During systematic desensitization students were asked to pick three items from their hierarchies, starting with the item which elicited the least amount of anxiety. Systematic desensitization began in the third session with each scene envisioned three times for 5 to 10 seconds. While anxiety was occasionally not completely extinguished to a particular scene before going on to the next, it was, in these groups, invariably reduced from the first presentation to the third. During remaining sessions, students were asked to pick up where they left off, beginning with the last scene to which they had been able to completely extinguish anxiety and going on with two more for that particular session. Occasionally a student would report that certain of the items on his list, which he had not yet worked on, were no longer very anxiety-producing, but that certain things had happened to him during the week which did cause considerable anxiety. He was encouraged to delete irrelevant items and to substitute these new items at their appropriate place. As early as the fourth session, students began to report signs of improvement, for example, sleeping better before a test than they ever had before and no longer getting writer's cramps while they were taking notes in class or in writing answers to test questions.

Students were encouraged to attempt to generalize the results of their relaxation training to other situations which might cause them to feel some anxiety. Special emphasis was placed on the role of breathing as an aid to relaxation. Students were told that with practice they would soon learn to substitute a relaxation response in every anxiety-producing situation by simply "letting go" in the tense part of their bodies after taking a deep breath and exhaling. As the sessions progressed, students reported increasing ability to do this.

Results and Discussion

Mean GPA's before and after the group program are presented in Table 1. For Treatment Group 1 (TG 1) the "after" average is the mean of the first and second semester during and after participation in the program. For Treatment Group 2 (TG 2) the "after" average is for the semester in which the students completed the program. Averages for control subjects obtained from the fall semester are averaged in a way similar to that used for TG 1. Averages for controls obtained during the spring semester are averaged in a way similar to that for TG 2. It can be seen from Table 1 that the mean GPA of the treatment groups increased from 1.28 to 1.63, while the mean of the control groups increased from 1.30 to 1.36. Since results did not appear to differ between treatment groups or between types of controls, for statistical comparison, TGs 1 and 2 are combined into a single treatment group while volunteer and nonvolunteer control groups are combined into a single control group. Comparing GPA's before and after the program, the interaction of groups by grades before and after was significant, $F = 4.42$, $p < .05$ [Lindquist (1953) Type I analysis of variance]. A *t*-test directly comparing the grades of the treatment group before and after was significant at the .01 level ($t = 3.46$). The small change in the control group mean was not significant. Thus, the group program had a significant effect on the academic achievement of the students who participated.

TABLE 1
GRADE POINT AVERAGES BEFORE AND AFTER THE GROUP TEST-ANXIETY PROGRAM FOR TREATMENT AND CONTROL GROUPS

	Before	*After*
Treatment Group I ($N = 8$)	1.42	1.74
Treatment Group II ($N = 6$)	1.11	1.46
Mean of treatment groups	1.28	1.63
Volunteer controls ($N = 6$)	1.24	1.24
Nonvolunteer controls ($N = 23$)	1.31	1.39
Mean of control groups	1.30	1.36

A question might be raised concerning the duration of the program's effects. This can be partly answered by looking at the GPA's for TG 1 alone since this group was started in the fall semester and students completed six of the eight sessions before their final examinations in that semester. Their mean GPA increased from 1.42 to 1.72 during the first semester of their participation. The program ended for this group during the second week of the second semester. Their average for that semester remained higher than that before treatment—1.75.

Results for individuals in the group program indicate that 11 of the 14 students increased their GPA after participation. Of the 3 who did not, 2 were failing to maintain satisfactory grades before the program. One of these, a draft-eligible male, decided during the program to go into the Army at the end of that semester. His average fell from .88 to .53. The other, a girl, decided to transfer to another school. Her average fell from .73 to .60. The third, another girl, had a decrease of .02 points in a GPA which was 1.96 to begin with. Among the 11 students who increased their GPA, 3 had unsatisfactory averages before group participation (.81, .97, and .90). These averages increased to 1.00, 1.38, and 1.20, respectively, after group participation. Whereas only 1 student was on the honor roll before the group program, 6 made 2.00 averages after participation. In view of the borderline and conditional nature of changes reported by other investigators (Chestnut, 1965; Spielberger and Weitz, 1964) and the general failure of most programs designed to influence academic achievement, these results seem striking indeed. Further evidence of the value of combined behavior therapy and counseling has recently been reported by Paul and Shannon (1966). After participation in a group program similar to that presented here, students suffering from interpersonal performance anxiety in a public speaking course showed significantly higher overall academic achievement. Test anxiety was treated as a subsidiary problem in Paul and Shannon's groups.

The effects of the present group program were not dependent upon the sex of the participants. Males and females showed almost identical increases—females from 1.36 to 1.70, males from 1.18 to 1.53. The higher overall average for females is consistent with a university-wide tendency and is probably due to the fact that admission requirements are much more stringent for females than for males at Vanderbilt.[3]

---

[3]Latest GPA including fall 1965 indicate that for seven students still in college, average posttreatment GPAs are 1.56 compared with 1.31 prior to

TAS scores for the treatment groups decreased from an average of 12.4 before treatment to 7.1 after completing the program ($t = 8.60$, $p < .01$). It was possible to get an "on-the-spot" evaluation of the treatment's effect on TAS scores for the first group at the conclusion of their final psychology examination and to compare their changes with that of eight control *S*'s who happened to be in one particular course. It will be recalled that students had had six of eight scheduled meetings up to that time. The students involved were given the TAS immediately after finishing the final exam, just before handing in their completed papers. The eight treatment *S*'s had a TAS score of 11.6 prior to treatment. They obtained a score of 9.2 at the time of this exam. Eight control *S*'s in this class decreased from 11.2 to 10.4. While the interaction, Groups $\times$ Ratings, just failed to reach significance ($F = 4.17$, with 4.60 needed for $p = .05$), it was felt that a direct *t* test of the differences was in order because of the specific predictions made for the treatment group. For the treated group, a test of the difference in TAS scores resulted in a *t* value of 4.00, $p < .01$, while a test of the difference for the control *S*'s was not significant ($t = 1.08$, $p < .30$). Thus, after six sessions, it appears that the program was having an ameliorative effect on self-reported test anxiety.

While it is difficult to define the exact nature of the factors producing GPA gains and the changes in TAS scores, the general theoretical orientation of the test-anxiety program is that students with a high degree of anxiety associated with taking tests have somehow learned patterns of behavior which are essentially maladaptive in the academic setting. Therapy took the form of eliminating some of the old responses and of teaching new responses which were more adaptive. Little or no attention was focused on how the old habits were acquired or upon any underlying personality problems. Wolpe's (1958) procedures for systematic desensitization were applied to decondition some of the anxiety experienced by group members. After the conclusion of the group program, all members reported that the relaxation procedures were helpful in alleviating some of the physical symptoms accompanying their anxiety, for example, general tension, difficulty in sleeping the night before an examination, intestinal problems, and in one case a skin rash. In the case of the girl with the skin rash, there was no appearance of this symptom during final-examination week following her participation

---

participation. This offers further evidence regarding the permanency of the results. (Of the 14 original students, 2 left as indicated above, 3 graduated, 1 left following her marriage, and 1 transferred to a school closer to home following the death of her father.)

in the group. While the relaxation procedures and the desensitization process seemed important to the students, they *invariably* felt (in response to a questionnaire item at the conclusion of the program) that the most important aspects of the program were just being able to talk about their problems with other students, finding out that there were others having similar experiences, and learning how to organize their study habits. Several of the students commented that it was very helpful getting to know a professor better and becoming acquainted with a teacher's point of view. Thus, from the students' standpoints, changes in their approaches to studying and in their attitudes toward education were more responsible for their increased academic effectiveness than were the desensitization procedures. While these comments add little to its resolution, they serve to highlight the significance of the recent controversy between Breger and McGaugh (1965, 1966) and Rachman and Eysenck (1966) concerning the exact nature of the changes which take place in behavior-oriented therapy and the factors responsible for such changes. Since the counseling procedures were combined with systematic desensitization in the present study, it is impossible to determine which aspect of the program was, in fact, more important. Working within a behavior therapy conceptualization, Lazarus (1961) has suggested that the medium of verbal interchange within the interviewing situation may itself bring about the incidental or nonspecific reciprocal inhibition of neurotic responses. At the present time a program is under way comparing the effects of the counseling procedure alone, systematic desensitization alone, and the combination as reported in this paper. Prestige of the therapist is also being controlled by using both advanced graduate students and full time faculty as leaders.

It seems worth pointing out that while the groups were unconcerned with any fundamental personality change, many members expressed increased satisfaction with themselves in general as well as greater comfort in the academic environment. The effects of the combination of counseling and behavior therapy seemed to generalize to other situations. For example, one student, a musician, reported feeling much more relaxed when he performed in public and very happy over that development since he did not come into the group with that goal in mind.

While the results of this study strongly indicate that systematic desensitization coupled with behavior-oriented discussion in a group setting is an effective and economical approach to the treatment of test anxiety, a number of other factors may have influenced the outcome of the program. First of all, the participating students were highly motivated volunteers who entered the program with a specific purpose in mind, which contrasts with the orientation of the usual counseling program for underachieving students. Secondly, all participants were in some nonintroductory level psychology course, which reflects an interest in psychological processes. Thirdly, the groups were led by a full-time professor in the department who indicated to the group that he had a research interest in the proceedings. Finally, no controls for placebo effects, prestige of the therapist or therapist-differences were contained in the present design. It goes almost without saying that these variables should be examined in future research.

References

Berger, L., & McGaugh, J. L. "Critique and Reformulation of Learning-Theory Approaches to Psychotherapy and Neurosis." *Psychological Bulletin,* 1965, *63,* 338–58.

Berger, L., & McGaugh, J. L. "Learning Theory and Behavior Therapy: A Reply to Rachman and Eysenck." *Psychological Bulletin,* 1966, *65,* 170–73.

Chestnut, W. J. "The Effects of Structured and Unstructured Group Counseling on Male College Students' Underachievement." *Journal of Counseling Psychology,* 1965, *12,* 388–94.

Eysenck, H. J., & Rachman, S. *The Causes and Curse of Neurosis.* San Diego: Knapp, 1965.

Grossberg, J. M. "Behavior Therapy: A Review." *Psychological Bulletin,* 1964, *62,* 73–88.

Jaffe, J. "Dyadic Analysis of Two Psychotherapeutic Interviews." In L. A. Gottschalk (ed.), *Comparative Psycholinguistic Analysis of Two Psychotherapeutic Interviews.* New York: International Universities Press, 1961.

Laffal, J. "The Contextual Associates of Sun and God in Schreber's Autobiography." *Journal of Abnormal and Social Psychology,* 1960, *61,* 474–79.

Lazarus, A. A. "Group Therapy of Phobic Disorders by Systematic Desensitization." *Journal of Abnormal and Social Psychology,* 1961, *63,* 504–10.

Lennard, H. J., & Bernstein, A. *The Anatomy of Psychotherapy.* New York: Columbia University Press, 1960.

Paul, G. L., & Shannon, D. T. "Treatment of Anxiety Through Systematic Desensitization in Therapy Groups." *Journal of Abnormal Psychology,* 1966, *71,* 124–35.

Rachman, S., & Eysenck, H. J. "Reply to a Critique and Reformulation of Behavior Therapy." *Psychological Bulletin,* 1966, *65,* 165–69.

Sarason, I. G. "Interrelationships Among Individual Difference Variables, Behavior in Psychotherapy, and Verbal Conditioning." *Journal of Abnormal and Social Psychology,* 1958, *56,* 339–51.

Spielberger, C. D., & Weitz, H. "Improving the Academic Performance of Anxious College Freshmen: A Group Counseling Approach to the Prevention of Underachievement." *Psychological Monographs,* 1964, *78*(13, Whole No. 590).

Voeks, V. *On Becoming an Educated Person.* Philadelphia: Saunders, 1964.

Wolpe, J. *Psychotherapy by Reciprocal Inhibition.* Stanford: Stanford University Press, 1958.

*

GROUP COUNSELING, DEPENDENCE, AND COLLEGE MALE UNDERACHIEVEMENT

STUART H. GILBREATH

Previous studies in teaching methods (McKeachie, 1951, 1958) indicate that the effectiveness of the method is dependent on the personality characteristics of the learner. In these studies some students were placed in lecture or recitation sections of a highly structured nature in which course requirements were carefully and precisely made known, while others were placed in highly unstructured sections in which the students were allowed to determine their own goals, discussion topics, and course requirements.

It was discovered that some students, characterized as emotionally insecure and dependent, could not progress satisfactorily unless they were participants in the highly structured learning situation.

Wispe (1951) indicates why the insecure and dependent student may have difficulty in the unstructured setting:

> The behavior of the want-more-D (direction) student . . . becomes clearer as a manifestation of two of the cardinal signs of personal insecurity. In the first place, this insecurity demands an abnormal amount of structuring of the situation, so that tensions arising out of the fear of doing the wrong thing can be reduced, and so that the responsibility for one's intellectual success can be put upon another person. In the second place, this insecurity is manifested in a kind of egocentric intropunitiveness, where the person tends to blame

*This article is reprinted from *Journal of Counseling Psychology,* 1967, *14,* 449–53, by permission of the publisher, the American Psychological Association, and the author.

himself for whatever goes wrong. When this kind of student, who is disposed towards a highly dependent type of education system, with desires for direction that cannot be met by any "normal" amount of instructor-structuring of the situation, is placed in a permissive section, the real conflict comes to the fore. Being intensely frustrated, and lacking the personal security to make the best of a bad situation, this student becomes rigid, intropunitive and vindictive in his evaluation of sections and instructors. To this student the permissive section meetings are "absolutely worthless," a place where intellectual confusion is heaped upon personal anxiety (p. 176–177).

Grimes and Allinsmith (1961) analyzed the interaction of both structured and unstructured methods of teaching children how to read and the personality characteristics of the students. They found that the condition of structure was so important that it had a significant beneficial effect upon the achievement of the anxious child, even though personal relationships and support from the teacher did not exist, and the emotional support for such children was of little avail in the absence of structure. The authors concluded:

. . . the feeling the teacher imparts to the child is evidently not so influential as the extent to which the teacher lets the child know exactly what is expected and structures the learning in simple, logically ordered steps (p. 262).

Problem

In recent years many investigators have studied the effect of group counseling on male academic underachievement without significant changes occurring either in the various personality dimensions under study or in academic achievement (Gilbreath, 1967). In spite of the fact that most of the studies failed to achieve the desired results, the majority of them indicate that some of the participants improved in GPA while others in the same group either remained at the same GPA level or became worse.

A possible explanation for the results of previous research based upon the conclusions of McKeachie (1951, 1958), Wispe (1951), and Grimes and Allinsmith (1961) is that group methods (most often nondirective or unstructured in nature) were conducive to some students, alleviated dysfunctional anxiety, and allowed them to achieve more academically, while for others the same group atmosphere was dysfunctional, not in harmony with their particular personality needs and, as a result, created a level of anxiety that actually interfered with the desired academic improvement. It would therefore be important to discover whether or not an interaction exists between the degree of structure in group counseling, academic improvement, and the personality characteristics of the participants.

In recent studies by Chestnut (1965) and Gilbreath (1967), investigations were made of the effects of two different methods of group counseling on the male college underachiever. The directive leader-structured (LS) method of group counseling was designed to focus specifically on the underlying personality dimensions that theoretically lead to low academic performance, while the nondirective group-structured (GS) method was designed to allow the group to have as much freedom as possible in determining the topic for discussion.

Method

POPULATION

A male underachiever was defined as a freshman or sophomore student who scored at the 50th percentile or higher on the College Qualification Test (CQT) and whose cumulative GPA at the end of the fall term was below 2.00 (2.00 is a C or passing average on a 4.00 grading scale).

SELECTION AND ASSIGNMENT

Of 683 male students who were classified as academic underachievers, 96 responded to a mailed invitation to participate in the program and were separated into 12 groups on the basis of common times available for meetings. Four groups were then randomly selected to serve as a no-treatment control group, while the remaining eight groups were randomly divided into those who would experience the LS method of group counseling and those who would experience the GS method. Two counselors were then assigned to two groups within each treatment cell on a random basis (by flip of a coin) in order to obtain replication within the design.

SAMPLE

Eight 1.5–2 hour sessions of group counseling were conducted during the academic term. Of the 96 students who participated in the study, 15 were not included in the final analysis due to illness or failure to attend the minimum number of five sessions of group counseling. Consequently, 81 students (LS = 22, GS = 26, control = 33) were left for statistical analysis at the conclusion of the experiment.

TREATMENT

The LS method of group counseling placed emphasis on topics that relate to the underlying emotional patterns in the underachiever as discussed in the recent descriptive and theoretical literature (Berger and Sulker, 1956); Farquhar, 1963; Gebhart and Hoyt, 1958; Kirk, 1952; McClelland, Atkinson, Clark, and Dowel, 1953; McKenzie, 1964; Roth and Meyersburg, 1963; Taylor, 1964)—a strong need for dependent relationships; a concept of self that is inadequate and inferior; a high degree of anxiety and depression; an inability to overtly express feelings of anger; an overall weakness in ego strength; and ambiguous or unrealistic purposes, goals, and values.

At each LS group session the counselor presented to the group one of the topics concerning the dynamics of underachievement and gave a realistic example of how this particular facet of personality could affect academic behavior. The group was then given the opportunity to freely discuss their feelings and experiences as they related to the particular topic under discussion. Throughout each session the group counselor would actively relate personality patterns to scholastic skills in order to hasten group movement and increase awareness.

The GS method of group counseling placed emphasis on topics which spontaneously originated within the group. The group counselor was an active participant in the group discussion, but the examination of what seemed to be a significant area for exploration, the frequency and degree of digression, and the time spent on particular problems were all determined by the group rather than by the group counselor.

In order to determine whether the two methods of group counseling were perceived differently by the respective groups, a questionnaire was prepared and administered to all groups just prior to the last session. The questionnaire was composed of 24 items designed to discriminate between the two methods of treatment. For example, the subjects were asked to determine whether the leader or the group initiated and directed the topics for discussion, who determined the amount of time spent on a particular problem, who controlled the overall pace of the group, etc.

A statistical analysis (*t*-test) of the results of the questionnaire supported the contention (at the .01 level) that the two counselors were consistent in maintaining the difference between the leader-structured and group-structured methods throughout the experimental period.

INSTRUMENT

At the conclusion of the experiment all students were administered the Stern Activities Index (SAI). The SAI is composed of 30 subscales with 10 items in each scale. Subjects are required to respond to these items by indicating their preference or rejection of the activity mentioned.

From the original 30 subscales, 12 personality factors have been extracted in a principal-components Equamax analysis devised by Saunders (Stern, 1963). The matrix of intercorrelations between these factors was then refactored in order to obtain a clearer picture of the basic structure of the SAI. This analysis yielded three second-order personality factors labeled Intellectual Orientation, Dependency Needs, and Emotional Expression.

RESULTS

An analysis of variance revealed no significant differences between the LS, GS, and control groups in either the winter or spring GPA. Although an analysis of co-variance was computed, it could not be completed because the slopes of the regression lines were not parallel. The regression coefficients were found to be significantly different; it was concluded that at the end of the winter term the men in the LS group had a significantly higher rate of change than did men in either the GS or the control group and, at the end of the spring term, a significantly higher rate of change than men in the control group only. (For tables and further elaboration of these results refer to Chestnut, 1965, and Gilbreath, 1967).

As a result of the research of Grimes and Allinsmith (1961), McKeachie (1951), and Wispe (1951), a decision was made to analyze the differences between those students whose GPA's improved by .5 or better and those whose did not so improve and discern whether any interaction existed between the degree of structure in group counseling, academic improvement, and the personality characteristics of the underachiever as measured by the SAI.

An analysis of variance of the SAI, GPA, and LS, GS, and control groups was therefore computed. The results are presented in Table 1.

There were three main effects. Only C, the SAI factor, was significant, and, as the factor scores were not in standardized form, this was to be expected.

The AB interaction was significant ($p < .05$) and indicates that men in the LS group whose GPA's increased .5 or better scored

TABLE 1
ANALYSIS OF VARIANCE OF THE STERN ACTIVITIES INDEX, GPA, AND LEADER-STRUCTURED, GROUP STRUCTURED, AND CONTROL GROUPS

Source	*SS*	*df*	*MS*	*F*
GPA increase vs. nonincrease (A)	82.9554	1	82.9554	2.4755
GS, LS, & C groups (B)	11.5482	2	5.7741	<1
SAI factors (C)	13,906.6877	14	993.3348	29.6426†
AB	217.5451	2	108.7725	3.2459*
AC	337.1198	14	24.0799	<1
BC	2,829.0420	28	101.0372	3.0151†
ABC	7,267.4574	28	259.5520	7.7454†
Within cell	37,699.12	1,125	33.5103	

*$p < .05$.
†$p < .01$.

higher on all the scales combined than did the LS men who did not improve; men in the GS group who improved .5 or better showed lower overall scores on the SAI than men who did not improve.

The BC interaction was significant ($p < .01$) and indicates that the overall patterns of the LS, GS, and control groups on the three second-order factors of Intellectual Orientation, Dependency Needs, and Emotional Expression were significantly different from each other.

The ABC interaction was also significant ($p < .01$) and indicates that the characteristic personality pattern of students in the LS group whose GPA's improved was different from the pattern of students who improved in the GS or control group. It also indicates the possibility of significant differences between improvers and non-improvers on the several personality dimensions within each of the experimental groups. Therefore, the ABC interaction was analyzed in an effort to determine whether the men whose GPA's improved .5 or better differed significantly from each other across groups on any personality dimension and whether, within each group, those who improved were significantly different from those who did not improve.

An analysis of the second-order factor Intellectual Orientation (defined as measuring intellectual interests, achievement motiavation, and a high level of intellectual and social aggressiveness) revealed no differences between the LS, GS, and control groups.

An analysis of the second-order factor Dependency Needs (defined as measuring dependent, submissive, and socially controlled behavior) revealed that LS students whose GPA's improved .5 or better were significantly different from and higher than the LS men who did not improve ($p < .001$). It was also found that GS men who improved .5 or better were significantly different from but lower in dependency than the GS men who did not improve ($p < .002$).

An analysis of the interaction between the different counseling methods, grade improvement, and dependency scores also revealed a significant difference ($p < .001$). Thus, the second-order factor Dependency Needs was separately analyzed in order to determine what specific personality dimensions were associated with success or failure in positive GPA change and its relation to the structured or unstructured method of group counseling.

The first-order factors of the SAI measuring dependence are: Applied Interests—the degree of interest in achieving success in concrete, tangible, and socially acceptable activities; Constraint-Expressiveness—the degree of guardedness and emotional constriction; Diffidence-Egoism—preoccupation with the self as the source of gratification; Orderliness—personal organization, deliberativeness, maintenance of ritual and routine, and avoidance of impulsive behavior; Submissiveness—the level of emotional control which is based on social conformity, deference, and other-directedness; Timidity-Audacity—the degree of concern for any risk or danger to the self, whether physical, psychological, or social; and Closeness—the need for warmth and emotional supportiveness.

Significant interaction effects were found on Constraint-Expressiveness ($p < .02$), Diffidence ($p < .05$), Orderliness ($p < .01$), and Submissiveness ($p < .05$) but not on Timidity-Audacity or Closeness, although the LS students whose GPA's improved were found to be significantly different from and higher in their need for closeness than the LS students who did not improve ($p < .01$).

The analysis of the interaction effects between counseling method, grade improvement, and the second-order factor of Emotional Expression revealed no significant differences, although an analysis of the factor and grade improvement alone did reveal that GS men whose GPA's improved were significantly different from and higher in emotional expression than GS men who did not improve ($p < .001$).

Discussion

The analysis of the interaction between the two different methods of group counseling, academic improvement, and scores on the SAI lead to the conclusion that male underachievers who have strong dependent needs and are described as guarded, emotionally constricted, submissive, orderly, and deliberate are more likely to improve in GPA if they are participants in a high authority, leader-structured method of group counseling and less likely to improve in GPA if they participate in a low authority, nondirective method of group counseling. Conversely, underachieving men who are more autonomous and independent, who express their emotions more spontaneously, and who avoid deliberativeness and routine procedures in organization are more likely to improve in GPA if they participate in the unstructured, low authority method of group counseling and less likely to improve if they participate in the leader-structured, high authority method of group counseling.

It is possible that the same effect occurs in settings other than the group counseling situation. For instance, the professor who tries to teach in an unstructured manner may create a classroom atmosphere that is dysfunctional to the dependent underachiever and significantly hinders his ability to perform adequately, while the same atmosphere may facilitate the ability of the independent underachiever to achieve academically.

The level of structure may also be an important aspect of the residence hall and fraternity. For example, a residence hall with clearly designated study areas and specific and enforced rules for study may be most appropriate for the dependent underachiever and, yet, inappropriate for the more autonomous student who would experience the highly structured environment as restrictive and incompatible with his underlying needs.

The college counselor and student adviser, as a result of the present study and its implications, ought to be aware of the personality characteristics of the male underachievers with whom they counsel, noting especially their needs for dependence or autonomy and the atmosphere of the environment into which the students are placed. If both of these variables are taken into account it may effectively reduce the incidence of underachievement and, consequently, reduce the need for group counseling.

References

Berger, I. L., & Sulker, A. R. "The Relationship of Emotional Adjustment and Intellectual Capacity to the Academic Achievement of College Students." *Mental Hygiene,* 1956, *40,* 56–77.

Chestnut, W. "The Effects of Structured and Unstructured Group Counseling on Male College Students' Underachievement." *Journal of Counseling Psychology,* 1965, *12,* 388–94.

Farquhar, W. W. "Motivation Factors Related to Academic Achievement." Cooperative Research Project No. 846, Michigan State University, College of Education, Office of Research and Publications, January 1963.

Gebhart, G. G., & Hoyt, D. P. "Personality Needs of Under- and Overachieving Freshmen." *Journal of Applied Psychology,* 1958, *42,* 125–28.

Gilbreath, S. H. "Group Counseling with Male Underachieving College Volunteers." *Personnel and Guidance Journal,* 1967, *45,* 469–76.

Grimes, J. W., & Allinsmith, W. "Compulsivity, Anxiety and School Achievement." *Merrill-Palmer Quarterly,* 1961, *7,* 247–71.

Kirk, B. "Test Versus Academic Performance in Malfunctioning Students." *Journal of Consulting Psychology,* 1952, *16,* 213–16.

McClelland, D. C., Atkinson, J. W., Clark, R. A., & Dowell, E. L. *The Achievement Motive.* New York: Appleton-Century-Crofts, 1953.

McKeachie, W. J. "Anxiety in the College Classroom." *Journal of Educational Research,* 1951, *45,* 153–60.

McKeachie, W. J. "Students, Groups, and Teaching Methods." *American Psychologist,* 1958, *13,* 580–84.

McKenzie, J. D., Jr. "The Dynamics of Deviant Achievement." *Personnel and Guidance Journal,* 1964, *42,* 683–86.

Roth, R. M., & Meyersburg, H. A. "The Nonachievement Syndrome." *Personnel and Guidance Journal,* 1963, *41,* 535–46.

Stern, G. G. *Scoring Instructions and College Norms.* Syracuse: Psychological Research Center, 1963.

Taylor, R. G. "Personality Traits and Discrepant Achievement: A Review." *Journal of Counseling Psychology,* 1964, *11,* 76–82.

Wispe, L. G. "Evaluating Section Teaching Methods in the Introductory Course." *Journal of Educational Research,* 1951, *45,* 161–86.

PROBLEMS DISCUSSED BY UNDERACHIEVERS IN DIFFERENT TREATMENT GROUPS

BETTY J. BOSDELL
JOHN TEIGLAND

Adolescence is usually described as a period with unique problems resulting from the physical changes of puberty, the increased expectations and different demands placed upon the adolescent and

*This article is reprinted from *The School Counselor,* 1965, *12,* 222-27, by permission of the publisher, the American School Counselor Association, and the authors.

This research was supported through the Cooperative Research Program of the Office of Education, U.S. Department of Health, Education, and Welfare. The authors are indebted to Mary Nichols and Ronald Winkler who assisted in the tape analyses. This study is one part of a research program on counseling with underachievers, Cooperative Research Project, 1263. A microfilm of the total project is available from the Photoduplication Center, Library of Congress.

his actions by society, as well as the adolescent's changing expectations of himself.

Problems of adolescence are frequently seen as typical or idiosyncratic. Gardner suggests that the majority of the problems of adolescents are normal reactions or phases without any serious emotional maladjustment arising from the problem situation. These normal problems faced by all adolescents in their striving for adult status provide a basis for observation of the specific adolescent's problems.

Bell [*1*] in one of the early studies on adolescent problems reported that young people not attending school viewed economic security, educational, vocational, home, personal, and social problems as being important.

Carlson and Sullenger [*3*] and Garrison and Cunningham [*5*] among others have found that problems concerning school, future plans, home life, social relations, boy-girl relations, health, and religion were of importance to high school students.

Frankel [*4*] and Phelps [*9*] in their study of high ability high school boys found that the underachievers were less interested in school, had fewer problems in the social relations area, and were less active and less interested in future educational plans. Bressee [2] reported that underachievers manifested greater feelings of insecurity, expressed greater hostility, and were more concerned with physical characteristics. Kimball [*6*] and Morrow and Wilson [*8*] studied the home atmosphere of underachievers. Kimball found that underachievers often had negative relationships with their fathers. Morrow and Wilson suggested that the home atmosphere of underachievers did not foster academic achievement.

In terms of self-perception, Shaw, Edson, and Bell [*11*] found differences in self-concept between achievers and underachievers. Male underachievers had more negative feelings about themselves while female underachievers tended to have ambivalent feelings about themselves.

The identification of the concerns of underachievers in the above studies was approached through studying their responses to personality instruments and questionnaires.

This study was concerned with ascertaining the types of problems that underachievers discussed in interview situations. Statistical comparisons were utilized to determine: (1) if different types of problems were discussed in different treatments (individual counseling, group counseling, and study skills groups) and, (2) if the frequency with which problems were discussed differed between treatments.

Procedure

For this study tapes were randomly selected from a pool of tapes. They were analyzed for five males and five females who had received individual counseling, three counseling groups, and three study skill groups. Individual counseling sessions were 25 to 30 minutes long. Group counseling and study skill sessions were for 55 minutes, the length of the class period. Eighteen interview hours were analyzed for each treatment: individual (boys), individual (girls), group counseling, and study skills instruction. The results of this study are based on 72 hours of tape analysis. For each counseling group and for each study skills group an average of 6 tapes was analyzed; for individual clients an average of 7 tapes was analyzed.

Ten different counselors served as the counselors for the individual and group sessions with eight of these counselors having both individual and group sessions.

Judges (project research assistants who had had secondary school counseling experience) listened to the tapes. When a problem was discussed by the student, whether it was introduced by him initially or whether it followed a counselor lead which the student picked up and discussed, the problem was listed by the judge. After all tapes had been analyzed in this fashion, the problems were tallied according to their area and specific subtopic. The frequency of a specific problem was determined by the number of times that problem was brought up in the treatment condition. The categories used for classification were ascertained from the tapes and the related research. The Mooney Problem Checklist [7] and the SRA Youth Inventory [*10*] served as guidelines for the classification of problems. The classification system used for the problems of underachievers is as follows:

I. *School Problems*
   1. Teachers
   2. Other Students
   3. Course Work
   4. Tests
   5. Grades
   6. Studying Habits
   7. School Activities
   8. Problems with Memory
   9. Interest and Motivation
   10. School Regulations

II. *Family Relations*
   1. Father

2. Mother
3. Siblings
4. Home Environment
5. Parental Control

III. *Relationship with Others*
1. Peers
2. Adults
3. Popularity
4. Social Impressions
5. Relatives
6. Dating and Sex Problems

IV. *Personal Problems*
1. Insecure and Nervous
2. Unhappy
3. Behavior Problems
4. Self-concept
5. Lazy
6. Shyness
7. Physical Appearance

V. *Future Problems*
1. College
2. Vocational Choice
3. Service (Military)
4. Marriage
5. General Outlook
6. Uncertainty of Future

VI. *Activity Problems*
1. Car
2. Social Activities
3. Working
4. Having Money

RESULTS

The results of the analysis of tapes for problem areas and frequency with which the problems were discussed was analyzed using chi-square [Table 1]. The chi-squares for each treatment across all problems are found in Table 2.

The significance of the main chi-square indicates that the types and numbers of problems brought up is significantly different (P .001) for the various treatment conditions.

Individual chi-square analyses were conducted for each treatment across all problems involving school experience with some discussion of problems related to future plans. It was the only experimental treatment condition in which students did not discuss problems relating to activities.

TABLE 1
FREQUENCY OF PROBLEMS WITHIN TREATMENTS

	*Problem Categories**									
Treatment	*SP*	*FR*	*RO*	*PP*	*FP*	*AP*	*TOT.*		*df*	*P*
Study Skills	49	5	0	0	18	0	72	157.16	5	.001
Group Counseling	63	8	5	2	14	14	106	171.23	5	.001
Individual Girls	33	25	16	17	13	13	117	24.44	5	.001
Individual Boys	52	16	12	20	20	20	140	42.27	5	.001
Total†	197	54	33	39	65	47	435			

**SP*—School Problems; *FR*—Family Relations; *RO* Relationships with Others; *PP*—Personal Problems; *FP*—Future Problems; *AP*—Activity Problems.

†Total = 100.31 with 15 df, P .001

TABLE 2
FREQUENCY OF PROBLEMS ACROSS TREATMENTS

	*Treatment Conditions**							
Problem Categories	*GC*	*SS*	*IG*	*IB*	*TOT.*	χ^2	*df*	*P*
School Problems	49	63	33	52	197	9.36	3	.05
Family Relationships	5	8	25	16	54	17.85	3	.001
Others—Relationships	0	5	16	12	33	18.51	3	.001
Personal Problems	0	2	17	20	39	32.07	3	.001
Future Problems	18	14	13	20	65	2.01	3	.80
Activity Problems	0	14	13	20	47	37.78	3	.001
Total	72	106	117	140	435			

**GC*—Group Counseling; SS—Study Skills; *IG*—Individual Counseling (Girls); *IB*—Individual Counseling (Boys).

Similarly, those underachieving adolescents in group counseling spent the majority of their time discussing school problems. Future problems and activity problems were secondary problems, with problems in other areas being discussed infrequently.

The types of problems discussed in individual counseling by the underachieving girls were more evenly distributed, although the results were still significant. School problems arose most frequently, followed by family relationships. Personal problems and relationships with others were discussed slightly more frequently than were future problems and activity problems.

Boys in individual counseling stressed their school problems, discussing with less frequency their problems related to personal matters, the future, and activities. Relationship problems with family or others received less emphasis than other problem categories.

The chi-square analyses for each problem area across all treatment groups indicated some significant differences.

Future problems were considered to the same extent by counselees in all treatment conditions. Although school problems were discussed significantly more than any other category of problems by all counselees, it was considered to a slightly greater extent by those in the group treatments (counseling and study skills) than by those in individual counseling.

Problems in family relationships were considered proportionately more times by the individual counselees, particularly by the girls, with group treatment counselees discussing this problem area with less frequency.

Greatest concern in the area of problems with relationships with others was shown by the girls in individual counseling. The study skills group did not discuss problems in this area.

Personal problems were discussed frequently by the individual counselees and rarely by those students in the group treatments.

Problems relating to working, social activities, having a car and money were discussed more frequently by boys in individual counseling than by students in the other treatment conditions.

Discussion

It is quite apparent on the basis of the chi-square analyses that students participating in different treatments discuss different kinds of problems. Whether it can be assumed that the treatment condition evoked different responses is not determinable from the data. However, the data do indicate that students in the counseling treatments discussed problems that were of a more personal nature than did students in the study skills groups. The goals of study skills groups, whether a class or a small group, usually tend to be oriented toward educational and vocational goals related to the present and future. This would probably account for the lack of the "personal orientation" in the study skills groups and for the concentration on problems relating to school and future plans. Although there is an element of personal investment in these topics, discussion of them tends to be more topic oriented.

Students in group counseling tended to resemble more closely students in study skills groups than students in individual counseling. Although problems of the more personal nature were discussed, it was not with the same frequency as in individual counseling. It would appear that the underachievers in group counseling were reticent to discuss personal problems. From the tape analysis it can be postulated that the different levels of readiness on the part of the clients, as well as the proficiency of the counselors, were partially responsible for the topical emphasis in the counseling groups. Many references can be found concerning the values of group counseling in helping adolescents to discuss their personal problems; however, the present study would raise a question as to whether this might be from a more topical frame of reference than from an intrapersonal one.

Problems concerning school, teachers, grades, and other facets of the educational setting were the most predominant topic of discussion for all the treatments. The emphasis in these discussions usually was more "What's wrong with them?" than "How am I responsible for these school difficulties?" Since the students were told initially that the school felt they could be doing better in their school work, this undoubtedly influenced the preponderance of school problems discussion. However, since other problem topics were discussed in initial interviews and the students, not the counselors, usually initiated the topics relating to school problems, the investigators felt the results reflected a real concern on the part of the underachievers. Specific topics such as "lazy teachers' unfairness to individual students," "tests not covering material we had in class," "dull classes," and "subjects not related to my plans," were frequently discussed. The manuals and norm tables of the two inventories revealed that the majority of senior high school youth did not consider such things as predominant problems. The underachievers in this study reflected much greater concern with such topics.

Problems relating to future plans, checked frequently by the inventory's norm groups, were also of concern to the underachievers. The specific emphasis, however, differs somewhat with the underachiever's major concern being his ability to get into college, and finding a suitable vocation while the norm groups indicated concern with need for actual information concerning their future plans.

From the review of the literature and the data obtained in the present study it would appear that although underachievers have the same types of problems as other adolescents, they differ from other adolescents in intensity and emphasis.

Summary

An analysis was made of a random sampling of tapes representing group counseling, study skills instruction, individual counseling (boys) and individual counseling (girls) to ascertain the type of problems and frequency with which these problems were discussed.

Chi-square analyses of the data indicated a significant difference (P .001) in the types of problems and frequency with which they were discussed between the various conditions. Individual chi-square analyses for all treatment groups across all problems were significant beyond the .001 level. Chi-square analyses also showed significant differences for the frequency with which problems in the areas of family relationships, relationships with others, personal problems and problems relating to activities were discussed in the different treatments.

Problems of a personal orientation were discussed more frequently by students in the counseling treatments as compared to study skills and more so by those in individual counseling than in group counseling.

The investigators concluded that although types of problems are common for all adolescents, the underachiever differs in the intensity and emphasis with which he views some of these problems.

References

1. Bell, H. M. "Youth Tell Their Own Story." Washington, D. C.: *American Council of Education,* 1938, 249–55.

2. Bresee, C. W. "Affective Factors Associated with Acadamic Underachievement in High School Students." *Dissertation Abstracts,* 1957, *17,* 90.

3. Clarson, M. B., & Sullenger, T. E. "A Study of Certain Areas in which High School Youth Desire Counseling." *Journal of Educational Sociology,* 1958, *31,* 179–82.

4. Frankel, E. "A Comparative Study of Achieving and Underachieving High School Boys of High Intellectual Ability." *Journal of Educational Research,* 1960, *53,* 172–80.

5. Garrison, K. C., & Cunningham, B. W. "Personal Problems of Ninth Grade Pupils." *School Review,* 1952, *60,* 30–33.

6. Kimball, B. "Completion Technique in a Study of Scholastic Underachievement." *Journal of Consulting Psychology,* 1952, *26,* 353–58.

7. Mooney, R. L., & Gordon, L. V. *Mooney Problem Check List.* New York: Psychological Corporation, 1950.

8. Morrow, W. R., & Wilson, R. C. "Family Relations of Bright High-Achieving and Under-Achieving High School Boys." *Child Development,* 1961, *32,* 501–10.

9. Phelps, M. O. "An Analysis of Certain Factors Associated with Underachievement among High School Students." *Dissertation Abstracts,* 1957, *17,* 306–7.

10. Remmers, H. H., Shimberg, B., & Drucker, A. J. *Examiner Manual, SRA Youth Inventory.* Chicago: Science Research Associates Inc., 1953.

11. Shaw, M. C., Edson, K., & Bell, H. M. "The Self-Concept of Bright Underachieving High School Students as Revealed by an Adjective Check List." *Personnel and Guidance Journal,* 1960, *39,* 193–96.

*

SENSITIVITY TRAINING WITH HIGH SCHOOL STUDENTS

JACK D. ORSBURN

Although definitions of a specific role for the school counselor differ, the task of helping students to understand themselves better and to become aware of the possibility of behavior modification appears in some form in most statements of role. School counselors also have come to realize that practices believed to be an important part of a program of developmental guidance are more readily accepted if they can be employed immediately to correct crisis situations. The student who is a "behavior problem" presents such a crisis situation to most principals and teachers. Sensitivity training is based on the premise that group-membership skills are learned and, thus, can be modified. It seemed appropriate that such techniques be introduced as a method to influence behavior change with those students whom the staff perceived as needing a change in behavior.

Purpose and Design of the Study

The purpose of this study was to determine whether different group procedures were related to improved classroom behavior, as judged by classroom teachers, and/or changed real-self–ideal-self congruence, as determined by change in the students' distribution of fifty self-referent items on a *Q*-sort.

The persons involved in this study were sophomore high school students judged by their teachers as being in the bottom one-third of their class in the dimension of classroom behavior. This selection procedure did not require that the students had been involved in disciplinary situations with school or community authorities. As it

*This article is an original paper, printed here by permission of the author.

developed, however, the vast majority of the participants had been involved in formal disciplinary action. The sex ratio of the selected sample was 39 girls and 45 boys. The community in which the students lived was suburban and agricultural. The socio-economic status of the families ranged from upper-lower to lower-upper, with a preponderance of lower-middle.

Procedure

The procedure involved the random assignment of the 84 students to three separate groups, each group consisting of two subgroups of 14 students. Group A participated in eight weeks of group work described as sensitivity training, meeting in groups of 14 for 45-minute periods three times weekly. The same trainer conducted all of the sessions. Group B attended lecture sessions for eight weeks, meeting in groups of 14 once weekly for a 45-minute period. School and community leaders conducted the lecture series, the topics being generally related to causes and effects of undesirable behavior. Group C was assigned as a control group. They met on only three occasions for the purpose of completing the *Q*-sort.

Data of the study were obtained through the use of the locally devised Behavior Rating Scale. The scale was to provide a quantitative value to teacher-perceived classroom behavior. An adaptation of the Page and Pettinato *Q*-sort (1963) was used to determine correlation between real self and ideal self at a given time. These data were gathered on three occasions: Immediately before the commencement of the group procedures, the day after the completion of the eight weeks of group procedures, and as a follow-up eight weeks later.

The statistical procedures used in this study were the Sign Test for within-group changes and the Mann-Whitney Test for between-group changes. A .05 level of confidence, using a two-tailed test, was used. Null hypotheses concerning change, both in perceived classroom behavior and in real-self congruence, were proposed within and among all groups.

SENSITIVITY TRAINING

Sensitivity training is not a recent innovation in the area of group procedures despite the fact that it has only recently gained wide recognition and acceptance. The principle underlying the procedure was born in 1947 as the result of what Benne (1964) described as an accident of circumstances. Early recognition of the value of the principle and foresight on the part of the original participants led to the formation of a group dedicated to research into theoretical foundations and applications of the process. From this group evolved the National Training Laboratory (NTL), an organization which serves as research laboratory, training facility, and clearing house of information for those actively involved in group procedures.

Variations of the training-group principle appeared as different persons adapted the basic theory to their own setting and their own unique background of training. These variations have been identified by many titles such as T-Group (Training Group), and Group Dynamics, Human Relations Laboratory, Sensitivity Training, or Basic Encounter Group, to name a few of the more popular designations. In addition to the proliferation of titles that have appeared over the years, the several trainers (leaders, facilitators, participant-observers, etc.) operating under the same group designation may employ what appear to be quite different techniques.

There is, however, a central principle discernable throughout most sensitivity-training groups. That is, a norm is established whereby the here-and-now behavior of group members (the process) becomes the subject of concern and examination (the content) of the sessions. A union of the affective and the cognitive domains is accomplished as interpersonal skills are examined cognitively and practiced affectively. The purpose of the group is to help each member to determine whether his intentions are congruent with his actions. Historical reasons for behavior are irrelevant, but giving and receiving of feedback concerning perceptions of behavior is crucial.

The here-and-now emphasis of sensitivity training does not negate the possibility of coping with an individual's "external" problems within the group setting. Rather, once provisional tries at new behavior have been attempted and a climate of trust has been established, members feel quite free to try the open sharing of difficulties as another way of presenting self. The major factor is that this comes about as such norms are knowingly established by the participants. The presentation of this aspect of self seems to arise out of an expectation of understanding and usable feedback rather than out of conformity to an imposed norm. The problem is usually examined by other members as an understandable and alterable flaw in interpersonal relationships rather than as a flaw in personality.

It is not possible in this presentation to dwell at length on either the theory or the procedure of sensitivity training. For those who are totally uninitiated, Luft (1963) presents a succinct exposition of the theory of the group-process approach. For those who have grasped the procedure only intellectually, books by Miles (1959) and by Bradford, Gibb, and Benne (1965) should prove very helpful to further cognitive exposure. Only participation in a sensitivity-training group can afford full flavor of the experience.

Results of the Study

Results of the statistical tests of the hypotheses revealed that the sensitivity-training group's teacher-perceived classroom behavior and real-self congruence changed an amount significant at the .01 level. This significance was found both within the group and between the sensitivity-training group and each of the other two groups. Results immediately following the eight weeks of training showed significantly improved behavior and a tendency toward improved real-self–ideal-self congruence. The follow-up study indicated that improvement in both variables not only lasted, but continued after the termination of the training session. Both objectives of the study were achieved by the sensitivity-training group.

Results immediately following the eight weeks of lectures showed that the lecture group had shown improved teacher-perceived classroom behavior, both within-group and between the lecture and the control group. However, the final check on results of the eight-week follow-up, showed that the behavior had regressed to where it only approached significance, and the decrease in congruence had rebounded to where it was only a tendency. Neither of the objectives of the study was achieved lastingly by the lecture group.

No significant within-group change in measure of either variable was noted for the control group at either stage of the study. The only significant difference among groups involving the control group was in the variable of real-self–ideal-self congruence between the lecture group and the control group. Examination of the data indicated that this was attributed to a decrease in congruence by the lecture group.

Conclusions

Results of this study justify the following conclusions about the group procedures employed:

1. Sensitivity training was more effective than either lecture sessions or no treatment for improving classroom behavior.

2. Both sensitivity training and lecture sessions were more effective means of improving behavior than was no treatment.

3. Sensitivity training was more effective than either lecture sessions or no treatment for influencing improved congruence.

4. Lectures had the temporary effect of improving behavior and decreasing congruence.

5. Both sensitivity-training sessions and lecture sessions resulted in immediate change in behavior, but the sensitivity-training group continued to improve after the action phase of the study while the lecture group regressed, resulting in significant long-range change for the sensitivity-training group and no significant long-range change for the lecture group.

6. Improved congruence did not necessarily precede or accompany initial indications of improved behavior, but the evidence is strong that improvement in congruence is associated with the permanence of improvement in behavior.

Discussion

Both group membership skills and interpersonal skills can be learned and/or improved. Statements of the broad goals of many schools include "the nurturing of the whole student" and "preparation for responsible citizenship in the community." The possibility of consciously providing the opportunity to acquire or improve interpersonal and group membership skills, however, has been largely ignored in the curriculum of the schools. The reason for this inconsistency in philosophy and practice can be hypothesized—either (1) it is assumed that these social goals are natural by-products of didactic course work, or (2) the administrators and curriculum supervisors are unaware of the methods now available to actively promote these goals.

An increasingly definable experience just as important as a course in chemistry or in shorthand is available for inclusion in the school program. A quick calculation shows that one skilled trainer, operating within the schedule of the school day, could offer sensitivity training to 500 students per year by devoting only four periods a day to the project. Twenty-four hours of the student's time could well be devoted to developing or improving skills which could possibly help to create a more satisfying and productive relationship with other persons.

In listing "target populations for laboratory training," Bradford, *et al.* (1965) cite children, youth, and college students as a recent addition to the list. Glanz (1962) suggests the sensitivity-training approach as a method for promoting increased understanding of the effects of individual behavior. These authors have suggested the inclusion of some kind of human-relations training in the schools. It is hoped that this study has provided an opportunity to examine the possibility of adapting the sensitivity-training approach to use with adolescents in the schools. It now seems reasonable to believe that adolescents can benefit from an experience formerly reserved for high-status adults.

References

Benne, K. D. "From Polarization to Paradox." In L. P. Bradford, J. R. Gibb, & K. D. Benne (eds.), *T-Group Theory and Laboratory Method.* New York: Wiley, 1965. Pp. 216–57.

Bradford, L. P., Gibb, J. R., & Benne, K. D. "Two Educational Innovations." In L. P. Bradford, J. R. Gibb, & K. D. Benne (eds.), *T-Group Theory and Laboratory Method.* New York: Wiley, 1965. Pp. 1–14.

Glanz, E. C. *Groups in Guidance.* Boston: Allyn & Bacon, 1962.

Luft, Joseph. *Group Processes: An Introduction to Group Dynamics.* Palo Alto: The National Press, 1963.

Miles, M. B. *Learning To Work in Groups.* New York: Teachers College Press, 1959.

3
Vocational and Educational Counseling

A survey of the literature in counseling suggests that while counseling may be a technique of significance in the area of personal concerns, the primary counselor activities in solving problems of an educational and vocational nature seem to be testing, giving information and arranging placement. Despite this apparent separation, counselors in schools and colleges have long recognized that it is impossible to differentiate among vocational, educational, and personal concerns.

Vocational counseling has received emphasis today in the development of programs designed to meet the needs of the terminal high school student, technical school student, workers unemployed because of technological changes, and minority groups for whom new job opportunities exist. Public and private employment agencies in the past have been in the forefront of vocational counseling theory and practice. However, today the spread and development of vocational and technical schools has resulted in increasing attention being paid by counselor educators to the task of the vocational counselor. The problems in this area are unique because not only must the counselor possess the skills of the counselor dealing with personal concerns, but he must also possess technical skills and knowledge peculiar to the provision of assistance in entering and progressing in a career.

The articles included in this chapter deal with a number of important elements in vocational and educational counseling. Included are studies utilizing different groups, different methods, and different emphases on specific job skills and/or personality characteristics.

Since the passage of the Vocational Education Act of 1963, there has been an increase in the development of area or regional vocational schools. The Waters and Zenger article presents a status report related to guidance and counseling in such schools. It has value in reporting the present role and function of counselors in a number of vocational schools. The findings suggest that vocational school counselors are assigned roles that may indicate need for specialized training beyond or different from that generally provided most school counselors.

The study by Pool investigates the relationship between counseling and the reality of vocational choices of clients who received and did not receive counseling. The experimental group was provided with counseling while those who did not receive counseling were placed on a "wait" status. His experimental and control groups each consisted of 25 white male patients in a Veterans Administration Hospital. Utilizing the Edwards Personal Preference Schedule (EPPS), an attempt was made to relate personality needs to the effectiveness of vocational counseling as indicated by changes in the appropriateness of vocational choices. His experimental group showed significantly greater reality of vocational choice than his control group with clinical judgment used as the criterion of reality choice. He also found that certain needs identified by the EPPS differentiated between clients who did and did not improve in the reality of their choices after counseling.

The Andersen and Heimann article describes an investigation of the effectiveness of vocational counseling with eighth-grade girls. The experimental group was exposed to six individual counseling sessions of a highly structured nature. Eighteen weeks after the termination of counseling, scores were obtained for both the experimental and control groups utilizing the Vocational Maturity Scale (VMS), the Occupational Information Test (OIT), and self-ratings of ability, interest, aptitude, and achievement. The results indicate that eighth-grade girls may be assisted to become somewhat better prepared for vocational planning through even a short period of structured counseling or interviewing of the type described in the study.

The study by Wall, *et al.* tests Holland's theory of vocational choice by using the groupings of occupations provided on the Strong Vocational Interest Blank (SVIB). The subjects selected were male college freshmen to whom the SVIB was administered during freshman orientation. The categorization into the Holland personality types was accomplished by a self-rating of the subjects. The results indicate a relationship between SVIB scores and Holland classifications. It is concluded that Holland's theory has use in understanding the relationship between a person's self-rating based on the theory and his vocational choice.

The Watley article is based on the premise that a counselor who can accurately predict academic success will be a more effective educational-vocational counselor. In addition, it examined the relationship between counselor prediction and the amount of information available. This would seem to indicate that those counselors who emphasize the gathering of a great deal of test and case material in working with a counselee may be wasting their time if accuracy of prediction is a criterion of success. The findings also suggest that even the best counselor predictors are only capable of accurate prediction of academic success about half the time.

The Leubling article is unique in that it is one of the few found in a review of the literature that examines the dropout and the culturally disadvantaged youth in the sixteen-eighteen age range. The results presented deal with the findings on a selected group. A control group was also identified, but the data were unavailable at publication time. The study is useful in presenting a descriptive picture of a group of dropouts, their belief patterns as revealed by projective instruments, their personality characteristics as reported by counselors, the types of problems they present in counseling, and some outcomes of one approach to helping such youth. Much of the descriptive data related to these dropouts is similar to the data presented by Combs in his work with underachieving boys with an IQ of 115 or above.

It should be noted that the group in the Leubling study was provided not only with counseling, but also social casework, remedial education, pre-vocational training, and job placement. It is also important to note that despite the comprehensive program offered the experimental group, the results were quite modest. It is apparent that the problems that are related to the lack of social and personal success experienced by the subjects in this investigation will require a great deal of attention. Later data describing the control group must be studied to determine if the approach described will point a way.

The Combs study examined achievers and underachievers among 50 high school junior boys who had obtained an IQ of 115 or higher on the Wechsler Adult Intelligence Scale (WAIS). He compared the self-perception of the two groups as indicated by selected segments of the Thematic Apperception Test (TAT) and the Combs School Apperception Test (CSAT). The article should be of great value in assisting counselors to understand an important aspect of the personality organization of underachievers. It may provide rather specific direction for the function of the counselor as he attempts to help such youth.

Most of the studies in the present chapter were investigations of a status-type. The topics of concern were addressed to such questions as the role of the vocational counselor (Waters and Zenger), the relationship between academic achievement and self-concept (Combs), the relationship between vocational adjustment and self-concept (Leubling), vocational interests as indicated on the SVIB related to Holland's theory of vocational choice (Wall, *et al.*) and the relationship between counselor effectiveness and the counselor's ability to predict academic success and major field of the client (Watley).

Three studies dealt with the effectiveness of a particular kind of treatment over a period of time. The longest specified time was six weeks (Andersen and Heimann). No marked effects of treatment were observed in any of the studies although a number of the findings did provide statistically significant changes in the direction anticipated. These studies as well as those reported in other chapters suggest the need for more prolonged efforts if the effects of counseling are to be dramatically illustrated.

The statistical treatment of data ranged from reporting of frequency percentages resulting from a survey through both nonparametric and parametric tests of differences or relationship.

Most of the investigations provide results that indicate further need for study before clear conclusions may be drawn. The studies by Combs and Leubling strongly support one another in suggesting that the nature of a male's self-concept may be extremely significant in determining his level of performance. It would seem that an advocate of a learning theory approach to counseling would have a strong basis for applying his methodology to a group of underachieving counselees.

*

GUIDANCE PERSONNEL IN AREA VOCATIONAL-TECHNICAL SCHOOLS

HARRY J. WATERS
WELDON F. ZENGER

Scientific and technological advancements have made the expansion and flexibility of post high school programs imperative in every field of vocational education. The newly created area vocational-technical schools are a part of the answer to this challenge.

Area vocational-technical schools are designed to meet the vocational training needs of all age groups in given geographic areas. The teaching personnel of these schools are equipped to increase the student's knowledge of new materials and processes. It would be most unfortunate, both economically and to the people involved, if expensive equipment and highly trained personnel were used to train people not suited for the training. Therefore, the guidance and counseling of the school's applicants is extremely important.

Because of the newness of the area vocational-technical schools, studies pertaining to their guidance and counseling services are almost nonexistent. This survey was completed in January of 1965 and its purpose was to determine (1) the title given to the person responsible for guidance and counseling services in area vocational-technical schools; (2) the duties and responsibilities of that person; and (3) the extent to which guidance services were being used by students, instructors, administrators, and prospective community employers.

*This article is reprinted from *Vocational Guidance Quarterly,* 1966, *14,* 278–82, by permission of the publisher and authors.

Methods and Procedures

Questionnaires were sent to all area vocational-technical schools (74) in a five-state area. States were chosen from as many different areas of the United States as possible to obtain a cross-section picture. The entire United States could not be covered because some sections have not started area schools. The five states surveyed were Connecticut, Minnesota, North Carolina, Ohio, and Washington. Since 15 of Washington's 25 vocational-technical schools were located in colleges, those 15 were not included in this study.

The questionnaire was constructed so that the questions could be answered by making a check mark; however, there was considerable room provided for writing in additional information deemed important.

Results

A total of 69, or 93.5 per cent, of the 74 questionnaires sent out were returned. There were 18 area schools that reported they did not even have a guidance counselor on the staff; therefore, all percentages throughout this analysis were based on the 51 schools that did employ counselors.

It might be noted that almost every school that did not have a counselor was still in the formative stage; and almost without exception, they indicated that a guidance counselor would be employed as soon as possible. Minnesota, where area vocational-technical schools are just being formed, had 11 of the 18 schools without a counselor. North Carolina and Connecticut employed counselors in all of their schools.

As shown by Table 1, the titles of the persons responsible for the guidance and counseling services in area schools were many and varied. However, five titles accounted for all but a few schools which seemed to have their own individual titles. Guidance Counselor was the most commonly used by nearly one-fourth of the schools. Counselor, Guidance Coordinator, Director of Student Personnel, and Pupil Personnel Director were all widely used but considerably less than Guidance Counselor.

Table 2 shows that the guidance counselor was in charge of or helped with every item listed on the questionnaire in almost every school surveyed. He was in charge of 9 of the 15 activities asked in 50 per cent or more of the schools, and was in charge of 3 more activities in just under 50 per cent of the schools. If not in charge,

TABLE 1

TITLES OF PERSONS RESPONSIBLE FOR GUIDANCE AND COUNSELING SERVICES

Title	*Total Number Checked*	*Number*	*Per Cent*
Guidance Counselor	50	12	24
Counselor	50	8	16
Guidance Coordinator	50	7	14
Director of Student Personnel	50	7	14
Pupil Personnel Director	50	5	10
Student Personnel Director	50	2	4
Guidance Counselor and Placement Officer	50	1	2
Coordinator of Guidance Counseling and Testing	50	1	2
Coordinator of Student Services	50	1	2
Occupational Research and Guidance Director	50	1	2
Coordinator of Miscellaneous Trades	50	1	2
Director of Vocational and Adult Education	50	1	2
Dean of Students	50	1	2
Associate Dean, Student Services	50	1	2
Supervisor	50	1	2

the guidance counselor helped with all 12 of these activities except in a very few schools.

As might be expected, the guidance counselor was in charge of the testing program in almost 90 per cent of the schools. There were two schools where testing was done by the state employment office; the counselor helped with the testing program in four other schools where some person such as a pupil personnel director was in charge.

Item 12, Provision for Information about the Vocational Program to Area Schools, was not considered by the authors to be a primary responsibility of the guidance counselor; however, over half, 55.1 per cent, reported that the counselor was in charge of providing information to the schools. Other fields in which the guidance counselor helped that were not directly connected with guidance were public relations, publicity, and studying employment opportunities, trends, and training demands. All but a few of the directors reported that the counselors helped in these fields; some reported he was in charge of these activities.

Placement of graduates and maintenance of records not included in the cumulative folder were the only two items that the counselor had nothing to do with in enough schools to be of any importance, and this occurred in only 19.6 and 18 per cent of the schools respectively.

TABLE 2

THE AMOUNT OF RESPONSIBILITY GIVEN THE GUDIANCE COUNSELOR FOR GUIDANCE FUNCTIONS

Function	*Total Number Marked*	*In Charge —Of—*		*Helps With*		*Nothing To Do With It*		*It Is Not Done*	
		No.	*%*	*No.*	*%*	*No.*	*%*	*No.*	*%*
1. Testing program	51	45	88.2	4	7.8	2	3.9		
2. Selection of students	50	29	58	20	40	1	2		
3. Admission of students	51	27	52.9	22	43.1	2	3.9		
4. Transfer of students in and out of program	50	27	54	23	46				
5. Counseling in matters of training and employment	51	30	58.8	16	31.4	4	7.8	1	2
6. In school follow-up progress of students	50	27	54	20	40	1	2	2	4
7. Orientation of students to the school	51	21	42	28	54.9	2	3.9		
8. Placement of graduates	51	15	29.4	26	51	10	19.6		
9. Follow-up of graduates	51	22	43.1	22	43.1	4	7.8	3	5.9
10. Dropout contract and counseling	51	33	64.7	16	31.4			2	3.9
11. Maintenance of records not included in cumulative folder	50	27	54	14	28	9	18		
12. Provision for information about the vocational program to area schools	49	27	55.1	19	38.8	3	6.1		
13. Public relations with community	51	4	7.8	44	86.3	2	3.9	1	2
14. Publicity activities	50	4	8	42	84	3	6	1	2
15. Studying employment opportunities, trends and training demands	51	4	7.8	41	80.4	3	5.9	3	5.9

TABLE 3

STUDENT UTILIZATION OF GUIDANCE AND COUNSELING SERVICES

Utilization of Services	*Total Number Marked*	*All Students*		*Most Students*		*Some Students*		*Few Students*		*No Students*	
		No.	*%*	*No.*	*%*	*No.*	*%*	*No.*	*%*	*No.*	*%*
1. Utilization of guidance and counseling services by	51	14	27.5	26	51	9	17.6	2	3.9		
2. Utilization of guidance and counseling services by the instructor for	51	8	15.7	18	35.3	23	46	2	3.9		
3. Utilization of guidance and counseling services by the administration for	51	16	31.4	19	37.3	15	29.4	1	2		
4. Utilization of guidance and counseling services by the prospective employers of the community for	50	6	12	15	30	19	38	9	18	1	2

As shown by Table 3, the largest number of schools reported that the guidance and counseling services were utilized by and for most of the students. About the same number of schools indicated the services were utilized by and for all the students as by and for just some of the students. Utilization of guidance and counseling services by the prospective employers of the community was the only item in which enough schools reported that the services were used by just a few students to merit consideration; this occurred in only 18 per cent of the schools.

Summary and Conclusions

In summary, it was found that Guidance Counselor was the title most often given to the person responsible for guidance and counseling services in area vocational-technical schools. The guidance counselor was responsible, in most of the schools, for anything that had to do with testing, selecting, and counseling students. He was responsible in over half the schools surveyed for getting information about their program out to the feed-in high schools. The counselor helped with public relations, publicity, and studying employment opportunities in almost every school. The guidance and counseling services were used by all or most of the students, by instructors and administrators for all or most of the students, and by prospective community employers for most or some of the students.

The only area schools not employing guidance personnel were those still in the formative stage. Many area school directors commented on the importance and necessity of guidance and counseling services. One such comment was, "We have found increasing need to divide some of the aforementioned responsibilities as our enrollment increased (presently 644). Adequate counseling service is considered important and we are implementing this phase of our program at a rapid rate." Another summed it up this way: "I feel a 'new breed' of counselor is required in our Area Voc-Tech School. Specifically well prepared in occupational information, and closely associated with industry."

References

1. American Vocational Association Inc. *Area Vocational Education Programs.* Washington, D.C.: American Vocational Association, 1964.

2. State Board for Vocational Education. *Proposed Guidance Functions and Standards.* Kansas: State Board for Vocational Education, 1964.

3. State Department of Education. *Nebraska Vocational Technical School.* Nebraska: State Department of Education, *5*, 1964–66.

4. State Department of Education. *New Horizons for the Future Ohio Vocational Educational Program.* Ohio: State Department of Education, 1964.
5. State Department of Education. *Program Practices in Connecticut Vocational-Technical Schools.* Connecticut: State Department of Education, 1964.

*

THE RELATION OF PERSONALITY NEEDS TO VOCATIONAL COUNSELING OUTCOME

DONALD A. POOL[1]

Vocational counseling has advanced from a narrow approach which stressed accumulating and transmitting educational and occupational information to a broader approach which not only includes these data but also places greater emphasis on dealing with the individual's subjective reaction to the information. Counselors began to be aware that many clients made unrealistic vocational choices no matter how much information was available to them. Consequently many counselors began to shift their attention and emphasis from the information they could give their clients to an understanding of the client's aspirations and needs. Bordin (1955) points out that today, to an increasing degree, counselors are examining their clients' efforts to solve vocational problems with a view toward understanding what there is about an individual's personality that makes these problems difficult for him to solve.

Research findings also emphasize the importance of personality factors to the outcome of vocational counseling. Ward (1951) evaluated the effectiveness of vocational counseling in the Vocational

*This article is reprinted from *Journal of Counseling Psychology,* 1965, *12,* 23–27, by permission of the publisher, the American Psychological Association, and the author.

[1]This article is based upon the author's doctoral dissertation completed at the University of Texas under the chairmanship of Gordon V. Anderson. It was a paper presented at the meeting of the American Psychological Association, Philadelphia, Pennsylvania, August 30, 1963.

Rehabilitation and Education program of the Veterans Administration and emphasized the lack of adjustment of clients as one of the causes of failure in vocational counseling. Carmichael (1949) found that 19.7 per cent of a group of World War II veterans discontinued their training because of personal, social and home conditions.

Thus the vocational counselor is faced with a situation in which he recognizes the existence of emotional factors that hamper or interfere with the selection of realistic vocational goals, but there is little research data to which he can turn for clarification and understanding of the important personality variables involved. There have been studies which have attempted to evaluate the effectiveness of vocational counseling (Apostal, 1960; Biersdorf, 1958; Bilovsky, 1953; Hoyt, 1955), but they did not relate personality variables to success or failure in evolving realistic vocational goals.

This study was designed to identify some of the personality variables related to vocational counseling outcome. Specifically, the problem was to study the relation of personality need variables to changes in reality of vocational choice as the result of vocational counseling.

Hypotheses

Two hypotheses were formulated in connection with this study:

(1) Participation in vocational counseling will result in more realistic vocational choices.

(2) Individuals whose vocational choices become more realistic with vocational counseling will be different on measures of needs than those whose choices do not become more realistic or become less realistic.

Procedure

Subjects.—The subjects were 50 hospitalized patients in the Veterans Administration Hospital, Houston, Texas. All white, male patients referred from the Neuropsychiatric, Physical Medicine and Rehabilitation, and Tuberculosis services were accepted as subjects until 50 such referrals had been received.

Method.—Alternating assignments were made to two groups: 25 experimental subjects who were to participate in vocational counseling immediately, and 25 wait-control subjects who were not to participate in vocational counseling until a two-week period had elapsed (all 50 patients eventually received vocational counseling). The treatment for the experimental subjects consisted of individual vocational counseling conducted according to the following general procedure: (a) initial interview, (b) administration of tests, (c) test interpretation and discussion of goals and (d) final interview. The experimental subjects were asked to name their vocational choice before and after counseling, and the control subjects were asked for their choice before and after the two-week wait period. In the experimental group there were 14 patients who were emotionally handicapped and 11 who were physically handicapped. The control group included 10 patients with emotional handicaps and 15 with physical handicaps. Thus neither group had a disproportionate number of emotionally or physically handicapped patients. No significant differences were found between the two groups on age, years of education, or intellectual level.

The clinical judgments of experienced vocational counselors were used as the criteria in determining the reality of the vocational choices. All three judges had Ph.D.'s in Counseling Psychology and had had several years of experience as vocational counselors. The counselors were provided with case folders in which test results and pertinent information were detailed. The judges did not know if they were judging an experimental or a control subject, and they did not know which choice represented the pretest and which represented the posttest. No judge rated his own former counselee.

Using a modification of a counselor rating scale of reality of vocational choice developed by Chernow (1955), each of the following ten items was evaluated on a scale of values ranging from one to five: (1) intellectual and academic abilities, (2) vocational aptitudes and skills, (3) measured interests, (4) previous education and training, (5) previous work experience, (6) previously demonstrated interests, (7) family background, (8) employment opportunities, (9) physical qualities and (10) personality traits. Reality discrepancy scores were then computed by subtracting the assigned value from the maximum value of five. A total discrepancy score was obtained by summing all the discrepancies for the ten items. The vocational choices given pre- and post-experimental period for all subjects were rated by this method. It was assumed that a low total reality deviation score would indicate a relatively high degree of reality of vocational choice, and that conversely, a high total reality discrepancy score would denote a high degree of unreality of vocational choice.

In order to determine the reliability of the Rating Scale of Reality of Vocational Choice, 32 vocational choices were rated independently by all three judges.[2] The product-moment method was utilized to

[2]Appreciation is expressed to Derwood Carnes, Phil Hanson and Monroe Ledyard, who made the various ratings of reality of vocational choice.

determine the extent of agreement between the three independent raters. Interjudge reliabilities were .76, .77, and .77. Intrajudge reliabilities after an interval of one month were .84, .89, and .90.

The subjects were divided into (1) "effective" and (2) "not-effective" groups on the basis of whether their choices (1) became more realistic with vocational counseling or (2) did not change or became less realistic. The personality needs of these groups as measured by the Edwards Personal Preference Schedule were compared.

Results

The reality of the vocational choices of the experimental and control groups prior to the experimental period was compared. This comparison is presented in Table 1. The *t* of .29 is not statistically significant for the difference between means. The two groups, therefore, were not significantly different in relation to reality of vocational choice prior to the experimental period.

TABLE 1
Comparison of Reality Discrepancy Scores Between the Experimental and Control Groups Prior to the Experimental Period

E Pre-Counseling		*C Pre-Wait*		*t*
Mean	S.D.	Mean	S.D.	
14.76	6.16	13.80	6.12	.29

An analysis of variance technique was used in order to test for the effect of vocational counseling on reality of vocational choice. The means for the experimental group pre- and post-counseling were 14.8 and 12.0 with standard deviations of 6.16 and 5.86. The control group means were 13.8 and 14.3 with standard deviations of 6.12 and 6.06. Since some of the variables are correlated, the Type 1 mixed design described by Lindquist (1953) was used. The results are presented in Table 2. These results indicate that vocational counseling produced a significant change toward greater reality of vocational choice in the experimental group.

The second hypothesis was concerned with comparing the needs of clients whose vocational choices became more realistic after vocational counseling with those whose choices did not become more realistic or became less realistic.

Table 3 presents a comparison of the needs of these two groups on the EPPS. Three of the comparisons reached an acceptable level of significance (.05 level) and one was significant at the .10 level. The not-effective group indicated lower need for Intraception and Endurance and higher need for Succorance and Autonomy.

TABLE 2

ANALYSIS OF VARIANCE OF PRE- TO POST-REALITY DEVIATION SCORES FOR THE EXPERIMENTAL AND CONTROL GROUPS

Source	*df*	*Sum of Squares*	*Mean Square*	*F*
Between Subjects	49	3221.24		
Groups	1	11.56	11.56	
Error Between	48	3209.68	66.86	
Within Subjects	50	402.00		
Scales	1	31.36	31.36	4.91*
Scale X Groups	1	64.00	64.00	10.02†
Error (Within)	48	306.64	6.39	
Total	99	3623.24		

*$p < .05$.
†$p < .01$.

TABLE 3

COMPARISON OF NEEDS OF EFFECTIVE AND NON-EFFECTIVE COUNSELING-OUTCOME SUBJECTS ON THE EPPS

	Effective Group ($N = 26$)		*Not-Effective Group* ($N = 24$)		
Need	*Mean*	*S.D.*	*Mean*	*S.D.*	*t*
Ach	16.00	4.77	16.46	3.75	.38
Def	14.73	4.14	14.73	3.50	.44
Ord	14.81	4.46	14.79	4.82	.02
Exh	12.85	3.95	13.00	3.26	.15
Aut	11.46	4.68	14.17	4.81	2.02*
Aff	14.65	4.83	13.12	4.79	1.12
Int	16.12	4.60	12.92	4.28	2.54*
Suc	9.50	3.79	11.38	3.46	1.83‡
Dom	14.00	4.53	14.96	5.11	.70
Aba	16.96	4.51	14.67	5.02	1.70
Nur	15.62	4.46	15.00	3.61	.54
Chg	12.65	4.56	14.38	4.68	1.32
End	20.15	3.62	17.13	5.53	2.30*
Het	10.69	6.85	12.46	6.92	.91
Agg	11.19	5.02	12.71	4.53	1.12

*$p < .05$.
‡$p < .10$.

DISCUSSION

After vocational counseling, the experimental subjects made vocational choices which were judged to be more realistic than their choices before counseling. In general the present study seems to support comparable studies (Gonyea, 1962; Hoyt, 1955; Stone, 1945) in their findings that when clients are asked to state their vocational choices immediately after counseling, these choices are more realistic than the ones stated before vocational counseling. In addition the subjects whose choices became more realistic with vocational counseling indicated different needs on the EPPS than those whose choices did not become more realistic with counseling.

The above findings suggest that the veteran with whom counseling is not effective is an individual who seeks solutions to his adjustment problems in dependency relationships with others and in trying to avoid responsibilities and obligations. He lacks persistence to accomplish his goals and needs help and support from others. He has little interest in analyzing his own motives and limitations, and when he fails, he tends to blame others for not giving him enough help. Possibly in these circumstances the individual limits self-awareness in order to avoid becoming aware that his adjustment is based on such immature mechanisms. Thus, in the vocational counseling process he is less likely to accept new information about himself than the more self-reliant and intraceptive client with whom vocational counseling is effective.

That personality needs have an important role in the making of vocational choices restates what counselors have long realized: vocational choices are often based on emotional needs rather than on a realistic basis. All this points to the desirability for counselors to have means for identifying and working with the personality needs of their clients. The findings are sufficiently encouraging to warrant further research with the EPPS as an instrument to elicit and evaluate personality needs and to help identify clients who are unlikely to profit from vocational counseling. The delineation of the importance of such personality dynamics in vocational counseling should further the ability to evaluate the counseling process and lead to more effective counseling.

References

Apostal, R. A. "Two Methods of Evaluating Vocational Counseling." *Journal of Counseling Psychology,* 1960, *7,* 171–75.

Biersdorf, K. R. "The Effectiveness of Two Group Vocational Guidance Treatments." *Dissertation Abstracts,* 1958, *19,* 163–64.

Bilovsky, D., McMaster, W., Shorr, J. E., & Singer, S. L. "Individual and Group Counseling." *Personnel and Guidance Journal,* 1953, *31,* 363–65.

Bordin, E. "A Theory of Vocational Interests as a Dynamic Phenomena." *Educational and Psychological Measurement,* 1943, *3,* 49–66.

Carmichael, L. "Review and Summary of a Study Evaluating the Veterans Administration Advisement and Guidance Program in New England." *Information Bulletin* 7–10. Vocational Rehabilitation and Education Service, Veterans Administration, Washington 25, D.C., September 30, 1949.

Chernow, H. M. "The Effects of Personal Adjustment Counseling Upon the Reality of Vocational Choice." Unpublished doctoral dissertation, New York University, 1956.

Gonyea, G. G. "Appropriateness-of-Vocational-Choice as a Criterion of Counseling Outcome." *Journal of Counseling Psychology,* 1962, *9,* 213–19.

Hoyt, D. P. "An Evaluation of Group and Individual Programs in Vocational Guidance." *Journal of Applied Psychology,* 1955, *39,* 26–30.

Lindquist, E. F. *Design and Analysis of Experiments.* Boston: Houghton Mifflin, 1953.

Stone, C. H. "Are Vocational Orientation Courses Worth Their Salt? *Educational and Psychological Measurement,* 1948, *8,* 161–81.

Ward, C. E. "Evaluating Counseling in the Vocational Rehabilitation Program Administered by the Veterans Administration. *Educational and Psychological Measurement,* 1951, *2,* 409–18.

*

VOCATIONAL MATURITY OF JUNIOR HIGH SCHOOL GIRLS

DALE G. ANDERSEN
ROBERT A. HEIMANN

Career development studies of adolescent girls are uncommon; yet predictions from the United States Department of Labor [*5*] project the increasing importance of the female worker and forecast a total of 30 million women workers by 1970. Many of the attitudes toward women workers which have shaped their vocational role expectations in our culture in the past are undergoing a liberalizing process with the result that there are expanding educational and occupational opportunities for women [*6*]. By 1980 we may look with bewilderment upon the 1966 attitude that women are restricted in their occupational choice because they are women [*10*].

---

*This article is reprinted from *Vocational Guidance Quarterly,* 1967, *15,* 191–95, by permission of the publisher and authors.

One outcome of the growing manpower needs of the nation and the expanding role of women in the labor market has been to produce a complex of problems for the young female who is entering early stages of vocational planning. In addition to her need for occupational information, decision-making experiences, and a setting in which to examine her feelings and needs, the adolescent girl is also faced with such problems as her emerging life plans of marriage and/or career, cultural biases against women in some occupations regarded as not feminine, and an understanding of herself in relation to these forces [*3*, *6*, *7*].

The Problems and Procedures

This study was designed to test the supposition that short term, vocational counseling would contribute to the career development and vocational maturation of junior high school girls to a measurable degree. Vocational maturity measures used in this study were: (A) Verbal expressions concerning approaches to planning for vocational choice, degree of awareness of training, need for making a choice, assumption of responsibility for making a choice, and (B) knowledge of self and of occupations.

Data concerning "A" were solicited in a structured interview schedule which was a further revision of the Vocational Maturity Scales of Super [*8*] modified by Jessee [*4*]. Estimates for the second area were obtained with a revised test of knowledge of the world of work and a self-discrepancy scale based on differences between scores on 36 measures and self-estimates of these scores [*1*].

The sample used in this study consisted of 60 eighth-grade girls drawn randomly from two schools in a single school district in metropolitan Phoenix, Arizona. These two groups of 30 each were designated experimental and control. Each member of the experimental group was involved in six individual counseling sessions in the last six weeks of the spring semester prior to graduation. The counseling was conducted by two male third-year graduate students in guidance and counseling. The counseling sessions, which averaged 35 minutes in length, were conducted in empty classrooms in the subjects' school and all interviews were tape-recorded.

The counseling was highly structured and the "leads" designed to encourage the subjects to think about career choice as well as occupations and concepts of self. Within this structure free interchange between counselor and client was encouraged, particularly in terms of reflection of feeling and clarification by the counselor. The general outline of these six sessions was as follows:

STRUCTURE OF INDIVIDUAL INTERVIEWS
(WITH SAMPLE "LEADS")

1. The first interview was pointed toward expressed and manifest interests in terms of ultimately making vocational choices. The emphasis was placed upon taking into consideration things which the subject liked to do. Some time was spent on verbalizing perceptions of family influences, parental attitudes, role models, and attitudes toward work.

Sample "leads":

"Some girls belong to clubs or take dancing or piano or something like that outside of school. Do you do anything like this?"

"Do you often find yourself making most of the plans when you are in a group?"

"I suppose girls dream like boys and adults do, maybe some think of being the first woman President or the first lady astronaut or perhaps of being a movie star; what do you daydream about when you just let yourself go?"

2. The second interview was directed toward discussion of total assets and barriers including aptitudes, health, attitudes, desires and expectations. Attempts were made to have the subject recognize these as factors in making vocational choices. The first portion of the interview was devoted to an interpretation of D. A. T. scores.

Sample "leads":

"Do you see yourself as having any health problems or physical impairments that might interfere with your choosing some types of occupation?"

"What types of things such as school subjects, sports, or pastimes do you feel you do especially well?"

"How will you pay for the training or the schooling involved with your future?"

"Is there agreement among your father, mother and yourself as to the subjects you will take next year in high school? Whether you go to college or not?"

"Do you feel there are some types of occupations that you would feel uncomfortable to be in? (If question—airline hostess because you are meeting many people and don't get to know any of them very well; waitress because of the physical strain of being on your feet all the time; or secretary because you are under close supervision of your boss all the time)."

3. The third interview was devoted to a clarification of counselee

perceptions regarding things to consider in making vocational choices, the need to ultimately make vocational choices, the location of resources of occupational information, and an attempt to bring the subject to an awareness of some of the factors involved in success or failure in any occupation.

Sample "leads":

"What do you think you will be doing ten years from now?"

"What are some things you would want to know about a job before you took it?"

"How do you see your ability or aptitudes in comparison to other boys and girls?"

"Where do you look in your classroom when you want some information on a specific occupation?"

"If someone asked you to describe an occupation for them what are the types of things that you would tell them about?"

4. During the fourth, fifth, and sixth weeks the subjects were asked to complete an Occupational Work Sheet [*1*] consisting of two pages. The first page required general occupational information on a specific occupation. The second page was an instrument designed to stimulate the subject to evaluate her own chances of getting into and succeeding at the occupation investigated and to think about the degree to which she felt the occupation would meet her aspirations for satisfaction. The subject was free to choose any occupation she wished or to leave the work sheet blank if she wished. She could write as much or as little as she chose. The interview during each of these three weeks was taken in going over the work sheet, getting the subject to verbalize on how she felt about various aspects of the occupation on which she had written, pointing out or getting the subject's views on how the occupation she had chosen related to others, looking for common aspects among the occupations chosen and clarifying as the situation developed. The objective of these three weeks was to aid the subject in relating self to various aspects of the world of work, in examining self-feelings about the world of work and in increasing the subject's knowledge of some specific occupations.

The regular program of the schools included no provisions for the study of occupations or for counseling services. An assumption was made that the controls would not have had a similar set of experiences within the framework of the school. A follow-up of all 60 subjects was made in the fall following their graduation from elementary school and criterion measures were gathered prior to any contacts by the high school counseling department.

FINDINGS

Vocational Maturity Scale (VMS) scores were obtained on all 60 subjects in the fall through interviews conducted by two male doctoral students in counseling who had no previous contacts with the subjects and were unfamiliar with the design or hypothesis of the research. The VMS was developed as an adaptation of the scales utilized by Super and Overstreet [*8*]. Interjudge reliability estimates were found to be 0.95 based on an analysis of variance technique [*9*] on the 50 items finally selected. The total score on the VMS was used as one criterion measure.

An achievement test of occupational information, called the Occupational Information Test (OIT), which was a revision of a test developed by Jessee [*4*], was used as a second criterion measure. This measure was administered to all 60 subjects in the fall.

The third criterion measure was a self-estimate technique in which each subject was asked to estimate her relative score on 36 scales of ability, interest, aptitude and achievement. Differences between estimated scores and obtained scores were summed to yield an overall deviation score. In this case the lower score indicated less deviation and possibly more self-insight. This technique was used with the 57 subjects who had taken the complete battery of standardized tests given routinely to all entering ninth-grade students in the local school district.[1]

MEANS, STANDARD DEVIATIONS, AND
F VALUES FOR EXPERIMENTAL AND CONTROL GROUPS

Measure	*Experimental*	*Control*	*Statistical Technique*	*Result of Comparison*	*Significance Level*
VMS	M. 76.1	M. 64.4	ANOVA	F = 4.38	.05
(*N* = 60)	S.D. 18.4	S.D. 24.1			
OIT	M. 43.7	M. 40.1	ANOVA	F = 2.91	ns
(*N* = 60)	S.D. 8.7	S.D. 7.5			
*Self-	M. 55.0	M. 58.6	†Kruskal-Wallis	H = 2.59	ns
Estimates	S.D. 10.2	S.D. 11.7	ANOVA by Rank		
(*N* = 57)					

*Lower scores indicate more agreement between estimates and actual scores.
†Since an assumption of normality of this distribution was unlikely, a non-parametric test, the Kruskal-Wallis analysis of variance by rank, was used.

Analysis of results indicated the experimental subjects had more favorable scores in the predicted direction than did the controls in

[1]Test data for 3 subjects were incomplete.

every case. However, when subjected to a series of analysis of variance tests, only differences on the VMS reached the 0.05 level of significance.

Discussion

The finding of a significant difference between the groups on the Vocational Maturity Scales criterion measure indicates that the experimental treatment was effective in increasing the measured vocational maturity of the subjects as here defined. Among the implications of this finding is that girls at the eighth-grade level are developmentally ready for preliminary career planning activities. Given the opportunity to sit down with a counselor at regular intervals and think about and discuss themselves, the world of work, and their perceptions of their vocational future, they will benefit significantly by becoming more vocationally mature as reflected by their increased scores on the VMS. To the extent that increased vocational maturity is regarded as a suitable objective of our educational system, the present findings provide one justification of short term, vocational counseling at the eighth-grade level with girls as a regular school activity.

While the differences between the groups were not large enough to be statistically significant in the case of knowledge of occupational information and self-estimating capability, both measures were in favor of the counseled group and thus were seen as encouraging further research in these areas.

In the case of knowledge of occupational information, the experimental treatment provided structure for investigation of only three careers. Perhaps this was too restricted to expect significant differences on a test covering a broad scope of careers. The data do not disprove the possibility that the subjects retained only that information which concerned occupations which they saw as tentative or potential choices for themselves.

The ability to estimate self impinged not only upon the self-knowledge of the subject but also upon the accuracy of the standardized instrument scores and teacher grades. Interest inventories and teacher grades are known to have questionable reliability and validity. It may be that factors such as these caused the results in this area to be less than significant.

Summary

This study assessed the effects of short term, individual, vocational counseling with eighth-grade girls on their vocational maturity, knowledge of occupational information, and ability to do self-estimates. The measurement of these criteria was made as the girls were in the ninth grade, approximately eighteen weeks after the termination of counseling.

An experimental design which was basically one involving differential treatment of equivalent groups was employed. Collection and treatment of data showed a significant difference between scores of the experimental and control groups on one of three criteria, the VMS. This indicated that the experimental treatment, counseling, did have a significant effect on measured vocational maturity.

References

1. Andersen, D. G. *The Effects of Short Term, Individual Vocational Counseling with Eighth Grade Girls.* Unpublished doctoral dissertation, Arizona State University, 1964.

2. Commission on the Status of Women. *American Women.* Report of the President's Commission on the Status of Women, Washington, D. C., 1963.

3. Havighurst, R. J. "Counseling Adolescent Girls in the 1960's." *The Vocational Guidance Quarterly,* 1965, *13,* 153–60.

4. Jessee, B. E., and Heimann, R. A. "The Effects of Counseling and Group Guidance on the Vocational Maturity of Ninth-Grade Boys." *Journal of Educational Research,* 1965, *59,* 68–72.

5. U. S. Department of Labor. *Manpower, Challenge of the 1960's.* Washington, D. C.

6. Matthews, Esther. "Career Development of Girls." *Vocational Guidance Quarterly,* 1963, *11,* 273–77.

7. Miller, C. H. "Vocational Guidance in the Perspective of Cultural Change." In H. Borow (ed.), *Man in a World at Work.* Boston: Houghton Mifflin, 1964.

8. Super, D. E., & Overstreet, P. *The Vocational Maturity of Ninth-Grade Boys.* New York: Bureau of Publications, Teachers' College, Columbia University, 1960.

9. Winer, B. J. *Statistical Principles in Experimental Design.* New York: McGraw-Hill, 1962.

10. Wrenn, C. Gilbert. *The Counselor in a Changing World.* Washington, D.C.: American Personnel and Guidance Association, 1962.

*

SVIB SCORES, OCCUPATIONAL CHOICES, AND HOLLAND'S PERSONALITY TYPES

HARVEY W. WALL
SAMUEL H. OSIPOW
JEFFERSON D. ASHBY

Holland [*1*, *2*] has recently developed a theory of personality with ramifications for vocational choice. The theory proposes that people behave in accordance with the characteristics of one of six major personality styles, and that these styles influence, among other behaviors, their vocational decisions.

Thus, people following the *Realistic* (R) style, characterized by aggressive masculinity, would be likely to select careers in such fields as engineering, forestry, mechanical trades, or agriculture. The *Intellectual* (I) individual, thoughtful, asocial, and intraceptive, would be likely to choose a scientific career. The *Social* (S) type, interested in satisfying his oral dependent needs, needing attention, and behaving in a sociable, responsible manner, would be likely to select a helping profession such as teaching, social work, or clinical psychology. The *Conventional* (C) type, preferring structure and subordinate roles, is likely to choose accounting or library work. The *Enterprising* (E) style is illustrated by lawyers, salesmen, and small businessmen and is characterized by oral aggression, verbal domination, and manipulation of others. Finally, the *Artistic* (A) mode of behavior is typified by a strong need for individual expression, asocial behavior, and intraceptiveness, and is likely to lead to careers in art and music education, journalism, and the fine and applied arts.

---

*This article is reprinted from *Vocational Guidance Quarterly*, 1967, *15*, 201–5, by permission of the publisher and authors.

In developing this theory, Holland [*3*] pointed out that these modal orientations may be inferred from typical vocational interest inventories, such as the SVIB, though it is not necessary to do so to implement his theory. Although Holland's theory assumes a relationship, no direct test of the correlation between SVIB scores and major personal orientations has been conducted. Some relationships should be expected between (1) the personality styles in Holland's theory and SVIB scores, and (2) categories of actual occupational choice and SVIB scores. The present study was designed to investigate the following questions:

1. Does the expected relationship proposed by Holland's theory between an individual's major Holland personality style and SVIB group scores hold?
2. Are occupational choices in Holland categories related to highest SVIB group scores?

Method

SAMPLE

The *S*'s were 186 male freshmen at the Pennsylvania State University. They were selected in two ways. During the fall orientation program, a period of time is devoted to the experimental testing of freshmen aimed at developing new tests. Freshmen are assigned to participate in this testing program according to the alphabetic order of their last name. Three testing sessions in the fall of 1964 chosen at random resulted in 81 *S*'s. The remaining 105 *S*'s represented all the male freshmen beginning their college studies in the Division of Counseling at Penn State in the summer and fall terms of 1964. The Division of Counseling represents an administrative academic unit equivalent to a college with the difference being that it offers no courses but is designed to provide an exploratory period for college students having difficulty deciding on educational-vocational questions.

PROCEDURES

Certain data are routinely collected on all Penn State freshmen at the time of their admission to the University. Of that pool of information, the Strong Vocational Interest Blank (SVIB) and several items asking students to indicate their first through fifth vocational choices on the Personal Information Blank (PIB) were used in this study.

Data concerning Holland personality types were collected either in the special testing sessions mentioned above, or during the Division of Counseling orientation meetings prior to the academic term. The students were presented with descriptions of each of the six personality types and were instructed to rank the descriptions according to the order in which they described themselves [*4*]. Following the ranking, the S's were instructed to rate each description on a one-to-five scale according to how well it described them. This combination of ranking and rating procedures was introduced to permit *S*'s to express the degree to which the descriptions were accurate in addition to ordering them, since the ordering procedure might be insensitive to the fact that the *S*'s could feel that no description was accurate.

The first vocational choice of each subject, as expressed on the PIB, was classified into one of Holland's six categories. These classifications were made according to examples of careers relevant to the various types that Holland gives. While occasionally occupational choices were difficult to classify, generally the occupations fit relatively clearly into one of the six categories.

The SVIB group scores were developed by taking the letter scores and converting them to numbers which approximated the raw scores. A mean score was computed for each of the seven occupational groups on the male form of the SVIB. Thus, an A score became 5.75; B+ was 3.25; B 2.75; B− 2.25; C+ 1.75; and C 0.75). Group I of the SVIB is composed of the General Professional occupations (biological scientist, doctor, dentist, veterinarian, clinical psychologist, architect, and artist), Group II is Science and Engineering (chemist-physicist, engineer, mathematician, and experimental psychologist), Group III is called the Practical (farmer, carpenter, forest service man, and math-physical science teacher), Group IV is Social Service (social science teacher, YMCA physical director, personnel manager, public administrator, YMCA secretary, guidance counselor, and minister), Group V is Business (accountant, office worker, purchasing agent, banker, industrial relations, and pharmacist), Group VI is Sales (sales manager, life insurance sales, and real estate sales), and Group VII is Literary (advertising, author-journalist, and lawyer).

Results

Table 1 shows the results of the analyses comparing the SVIB group scores according to the first ranked personality type. It can be seen that with the exception of Group VII of the SVIB, the scores earned on the SVIB groups differed according to the first personality rank of the *S*. Not only do the personality types differ in their SVIB group scores, but in many cases the personality types have high group scores where they would be expected, and low ones where low scores would be expected. For example, most of the occupations that R-types would be predicted to select are found in SVIB Groups II and III. Table 1 reflects the finding that the R-group scored its highest SVIB scores in Groups II and III. The R-group also had its lowest scores on SVIB Groups IV, VI, and VII, which would include occupations requiring considerable interaction with people and ideas and little to do with the real, concrete world.

TABLE 1
MEAN SVIB GROUP SCORES ACCORDING TO FIRST PERSONALITY RANK AND SUMMARY OF ANALYSIS OF VARIANCE

SVIB	*First Personality Rank*						
Group	*R*	*I*	*S*	*C*	*E*	*A*	*F*
I	2.32	2.24	2.36	1.97	1.64	2.20	5.17†
II	3.54	3.31	2.66	2.82	2.07	2.50	7.68†
III	3.49	2.91	3.13	2.86	2.48	2.22	2.44*
IV	1.66	1.86	2.58	1.81	2.49	2.55	5.52†
V	2.27	2.27	2.46	2.61	2.82	2.25	3.07*
VI	1.61	1.89	2.23	2.03	2.53	2.04	3.40†
VII	1.72	2.06	1.17	1.71	1.90	2.37	1.04

df = 5 and 180.
* = $p < 0.05$.
† = $p < 0.01$.

In Table 2, which represents the relationship between the SVIB group scores and the categories of the actual choice of the *S*'s, the situation is even clearer. Here it can be seen that *S*'s choosing occupations in the R-category scored their highest SVIB scores in

TABLE 2
MEAN SVIB GROUP SCORES FOR SIX OCCUPATIONAL CHOICE CATEGORIES AND SUMMARY OF ANALYSIS OF VARIANCE

SVIB	*Occupational Choice Category*						
Group	*R*	*I*	*S*	*C*	*E*	*A*	*F*
I	2.20	2.15	1.54	1.64	1.29	1.81	6.36†
II	3.48	2.76	1.84	2.47	1.24	2.63	12.06†
III	3.40	2.60	2.27	3.19	1.61	2.23	9.25†
IV	1.87	1.98	2.74	2.30	2.97	1.87	5.83†
V	2.38	2.44	2.44	3.67	3.19	2.31	4.90†
VI	1.69	2.17	2.27	2.29	3.29	2.25	8.16†
VII	1.63	1.96	2.00	1.33	2.62	2.19	4.21†

df = 5 and 177.
† $p = < 0.01$.

Groups II and III, *S*'s in the S-category scored highest in Group IV, C-*S*'s scored highest in Group V, and E-*S*'s highest in Group VI. Only the I- and A-*S*'s present mixed pictures on the SVIB, and this is likely to be the result of more diffuse occupational possibilities for these people.

The results of discriminant analysis between the SVIB group scores and first personality rank resulted in a Wilks lambda of 0.68 ($p < 0.001$) and the discriminant analysis between the SVIB group scores and category of first occupational choice resulted in a Wilks lambda of 0.518 ($p < 0.001$). These indicate that distinct differences in SVIB group scores exist for the *S*'s who (1) ranked themselves first on different personality types and (2) chose careers falling into different occupational categories.

The next question to be assessed was the relationship between the personality ratings and the SVIB group scores. These results are summarized in Table 3. Most of the resulting correlations are small, although several of them reach significance at the 0.01 or 0.05 levels of confidence.

TABLE 3

CORRELATIONS BETWEEN SVIB GROUP SCORES AND PERSONALITY RATINGS

SVIB Group	*Personality Ratings*					
	R	*I*	*S*	*C*	*E*	*A*
I	0.20†	0.10	0.06	0.08	—0.13	0.13
II	0.20†	0.01	—0.05	0.06	—0.26†	0.02
III	0.27†	—0.12	—0.02	0.07	—0.12	—0.05
IV	—0.09	0.05	0.14	—0.14	0.22†	0.02
V	—0.05	—0.08	0.01	0.05	0.08	—0.16*
VI	—0.16*	0.02	0.02	—0.08	0.19†	—0.07
VII	—0.18*	0.14	—0.07	—0.11	0.05	0.14

df = 184.
* = $p < 0.05$.
† = $p < 0.01$.

DISCUSSION

The expected relationships, according to Holland's theory, between the SVIB group scores and the personality types appear to exist. Even more impressive are the relationships between the SVIB group scores and choice categories. The relationship between Holland's categories and the SVIB provides considerable face and construct validity for Holland's theory. Table 2 clearly reflects the fact that the choices are related to SVIB scores. Thus, the *S*'s making Realistic choices are highest in SVIB Groups II and III (science-engineering and practical, respectively), which include the engineering, scientific, and technical occupations that would be located in the Realistic category. Similarly, the Social chooser tends to score highest in Group IV of the SVIB, social service; the Conforming chooser scores high on Group V, business; the Enterprising chooser scores high on Group VI, sales. Only the Intellectual and Artistic choosers do not appear to have clear SVIB patterns that are consistent with their choices. These latter two types contain a variety of occupations which fall into several of the SVIB groups.

The correlations between the personality ratings and the SVIB group scores support Holland's position. The slightly positive relationships between the R-ratings and Groups I, II, and III, and the negative relationships between R and Groups VI and VII are consistent with the characteristics of R-people and the respective SVIB groups. Similarly, for the E-ratings, the negative relationship found with Group II and positive relationships between Groups IV and VI are as would be expected from people of the E-type and occupations in SVIB Groups II, IV, and VI. Although expectations are not as clear for the A-group, the negative relationship between the A-ratings and Group V is not surprising. What is somewhat surprising is the lack of relationships to SVIB groups of any significant degree for the I-, S-, and C-ratings.

The characteristics of the sample studied may have increased the applicability of the findings to vocational and career counseling. Since the sample included a substantial number of students who were quite undecided about their vocational and educational objectives, it has much in common with the counselor's typical case load which is usually comprised of many vocationally undecided students. Thus, counselors may find the results of practical use in understanding and identifying appropriate educational and vocational careers for undecided students.

In general, the findings indicate that Holland's theory possesses considerable construct validity with respect to SVIB scores and vocational choices of college students. SVIB group scores were high in areas consistent with personality ratings, and occupational preferences coded in Holland's terms were very consistent with SVIB group scores.

References

1. Holland, J. L. "A Theory of Vocational Choice." *Journal of Counseling Psychology,* 1959, *6,* 35–45.

2. Holland, J. L. "Some Explorations of a Theory of Vocational Choice: I. One- and Two-Year Longitudinal Studies." *Psychological Monographs,* 1962, *76,* 26 (whole No. 545).

3. Holland, J. L. "Exploration of a Theory of Vocational Choice and Achievement: II. A Four-Year Prediction Study." *Psychological Reports 5,* 1963, *12,* 547–94.

4. Osipow, S. H., Ashby, J. D., & Wall, H. W. "Personality Types and Vocational Choice: A Test of Holland's Theory." *Harvard Studies in Career Development, Number 37.* Cambridge, Massachusetts: Center for Research in Careers, Harvard Graduate School of Education, 1965.

*

COUNSELOR PREDICTIVE SKILL AND RATED COUNSELOR EFFECTIVENESS

DONIVAN J. WATLEY

Much has been written in the counseling literature emphasizing the counselor's role as a predictor (e.g., Strang, 1937; Williamson, 1939; Meehl, 1954; Pepinsky and Pepinsky, 1954; Super, *et al.,* 1957; Goldman, 1961). However, it has been generally concluded from research assessing the accuracy of clinical predictions that the prognoses of the average clinical judge are none too accurate (Meehl, 1954; Meehl, 1956; Gough, 1962). Tyler (1961, p. 209) stated that counselor prognoses of success for clients are not sufficiently accurate to safely base decisions on them. This presents a rather confusing situation to the practicing counselor as well as the counselor-in-training. While counselors maintain that prediction is a fundamental part of counseling, little experimental evidence supports the counselor's role as a prediction maker.

In assessing the predictive skills of clinical judges, little attention has been given to the variability that exists among counselors in their ability to predict accurately. For example, the clinical versus

*This article is reprinted from *Personnel and Guidance Journal,* 1967, *45,* 579–84, by permission of the publisher, the American Personnel and Guidance Association, and the author.

statistical prediction research has placed most emphasis upon the predictive abilities of the *average* judge (e.g., Sarbin, 1942; Kelly and Fiske, 1950), or upon the predictions of a few individual judges. Watley and Vance (1964) conducted a study designed explicitly to assess the differences among counselors in their ability to predict accurately. Predictions of scholastic achievement were made by 66 counselors who normally worked in three different educational settings. Not only were there significant differences among the predictions of the *average* judge from the counselor groups, but individual counselors varied markedly in their ability to predict this criterion. Some of the judges predicted grades equally as efficiently as the statistical equation normally used to predict achievement for the sample of students studied. Although neither the clinical nor the statistical prediction method has yet reached a respectable level of accuracy, the fact that some counselors consistently predict more accurately than others should be recognized.

While counselors differ in their ability to predict accurately, there is no evidence that those who predict most accurately do the best job of counseling. Prediction making is largely an intellectual process and it cannot be assumed that the ability to predict accurately automatically makes one a "good" counselor. Since prediction is of basic importance for effective educational and vocational counseling, it can be argued, however, that the ability to predict accurately is important toward being a "good" or effective counselor. The purpose of this study was to investigate the relationship between counselor predictive ability and counseling effectiveness as judged by counselor supervisors.

METHOD

Judges.—The clinical judges were 14 counselors (or advisors) in the Advisors Office of the College of Liberal Arts at the University of Minnesota. At the time of this study, one had a Ph.D. in educational psychology and the others were graduate students at Minnesota. Five had career plans in counseling or closely related fields (e.g., child development), and four others had formal graduate coursework in counseling or psychology. Eleven had completed graduate courses in measurement or statistics. All of the counselors participated in a continuing in-service training program conducted by the supervisors. Although some of them had worked only on a part-time basis, they had on the average 2.4 years of counseling experience, some of which had been gained in positions such as residence hall counseling. As Arts College counselors, their primary responsibilities were to assist freshmen and sophomores in making educational and vocational plans and to help them in planning their course programs. They had direct contact with the type of student (Arts College freshman males) for whom predictions were made in this study.

Prediction Sample.—The sample consisted of 100 freshman males who entered the Liberal Arts College at the University of Minnesota in the fall quarter of 1959. These students were randomly selected from among the entire entering class of freshman males, but final inclusion of each student was based upon whether all of the desired information described below could be obtained and whether each student graduated from a Minnesota high school during the spring of 1959 and spent at least one quarter in the Arts College.

Predictions.—The judges predicted whether students would persist and be academically successful in the educational programs they selected at the time of admission to college. The accuracy of predictions was assessed on the basis of the number of hits recorded for each judge. A hit was defined as a correct prediction for a student to remain or not ("yes" or "no") in the "major" program selected upon college admission, and whether the student would graduate from college. That is, a judge was required to correctly predict academic success in addition to the "major" prediction before a hit was recorded for a given student. If a student withdrew from college he was considered to have been unsuccessful in completing a degree program. Of the 100 students included in the sample for which predictions were made, 53 did not finish (or were about to finish) any four-year academic program successfully at Minnesota. However, of the 53 who dropped out, 43 had less than a C average at the time of the withdrawal. A change of educational major was primarily determined by a student's transfer to a different college at the University of Minnesota or to a different department within the same college in which he was initially registered, but the student's ultimate vocational goal (as indicated on an admission form) was also considered in determining change of major. This prediction attempted to assess whether there were observable differences among counselors in their knowledge of constructs associated with success in the various educational programs. This investigation was conducted four years after these students initially enrolled in the Arts College, thus making it possible to determine the academic performance of each student in the sample.

Conditions.—The judges made predictions for the same sample of 100 students in each of three conditions, although they were not informed that repeated judgments were being made for the same students. The three conditions differed in the amount and type of case information given in the case folders.

Condition I included information related to scholastic aptitude and past academic achievement. This consisted of the name of the high school from which the student graduated and his relative high school percentile rank (HSR); test scores for the Minnesota Scholastic Aptitude Test (MSAT); the Cooperative English Test (CET); and the Social Studies Test of the Sequential Tests of Educational Progress (STEP) battery; the last high school grade earned in the areas of mathematics, English, social studies, and natural science; and the student's educational major plans for college.

The Condition II case folders included all of the information presented in Condition I plus the Strong Vocational Interest Blank (SVIB) and the Minnesota Multiphasic Personality Inventory (MMPI).

The Condition III folders contained all of the data provided in the Condition II folders plus considerable biographic information given on the Minnesota College Admission Form and the Personal Inventory for Entering Students. Three kinds of statistical data were also given in this condition that could have been used to predict academic achievement in the Arts College. This included grade expectancy tables for HSR and the MSAT; zero-order correlations and multiple correlations between freshman grades and HSR, MSAT and CET; and a regression equation that included prediction coefficients for the high school grades of mathematics, English, social studies, and natural science.

Ratings of Counselor Effectiveness.—The 14 counselors were rated on their general counseling effectiveness by three supervisors. Supervisor ratings were based primarily on an evaluation of each counselor's overall effectiveness in helping students plan educational and vocational objectives, and assisting them in selecting course programs to fulfill these objectives. Two of the supervisors had Ph.D.'s in counseling psychology. The other supervisor had no formal counselor training. However, each of the three had direct association with the Arts College Advisors Office for at least six years, and each supervisor had the opportunity to observe and work with each of the counselors for whom ratings were made.

Ratings of counselor effectiveness were made independently by each supervisor. Each supervisor ranked the counselors from 1 to 14 on their general effectiveness. A coefficient of concordance (Siegel, 1956, p. 229) was computed and the obtained chi-square of 31.59 (with 13 degrees of freedom) was significant at beyond the .01 level of probability. This finding suggested that considerable agreement existed among the ratings of the supervisors, and suggested that they were using essentially the same standard in ranking the counselors.

The three rankings received by each counselor were combined and the counselors then re-ranked from 1 to 14. Except in the case where one counselor received a rank of 6, the supervisors agreed about the five most effective counselors. These five composed the "most" effective counselor group. The supervisors also agreed about the four least effective counselors, and these four comprised the "least" effective group. The largest disagreements occurred for the counselors who received a combined ranking of 6 to 10. These five were placed in the moderately effective group. These three groups were compared on the mean number of hits recorded.

The supervisors were not aware that their ratings were made in relation to an assessment of counselor predictive skill; and prior to making their effectiveness ratings, they received no information from the investigator about the predictive abilities of individual counselors.

Results

The mean number of hits obtained by the three "effectiveness" groups of counselors are given in Table 1. These means were based on the number of correct predictions made by judges from the 100 cases presented in each condition. An analysis of variance was computed on these data using the procedure described by Walker and Lev (1953, p. 381) for unequal subclass frequencies.

TABLE 1
SUMMARY DATA FOR HITS FOR THE
THREE "EFFECTIVENESS" GROUPS OF COUNSELORS

Effectiveness	*Conditions*							
	I		*II*		*III*		*Total*	
Groups	*Mn*	*SD*	*Mn*	*SD*	*Mn*	*SD*	*Mn*	*SD*
Most	52.80	6.08	51.60	4.88	50.80	7.25	51.73	6.20
Moderate	46.80	7.76	47.00	7.21	44.40	10.63	46.07	8.74
Least	39.50	10.14	43.25	6.26	43.25	11.32	42.00	9.65
Total	46.86	9.60	47.57	7.04	46.36	10.34		

The obtained F for assessing the differences among the means for the counseling effectiveness groups was 3.95 and was significant at beyond the .05 level of probability. This suggested that there were differences among these groups in predicting whether a student would graduate and whether he would remain in the "major'" educational program he selected at the time of admission to college.

The F ratio for comparing the differences among the means for the conditions under which predictions were made was < 1 and was not significant at the .05 level. Table 1 shows that the total mean number of hits obtained by the "effectiveness" groups was similar for all three conditions. This indicates that the predictive efficiency of the counselors was not significantly affected by the increased amount of case data available in the second and third conditions. That is, the availability of the SVIB, the MMPI, the biographical data, and the other information did not result in increasing or decreasing the accuracy of counselor judgments over the level of accuracy achieved from using only the scholastic aptitude scores and high school grade records given in the first condition. The interaction term for conditions and groups also was not significant at the .05 level.

Since the mean number of hits for the "effectiveness" groups was quite similar across the three conditions, the "total" means and standard deviations (Table 1) were used to compare between-group differences on the number of hits recorded. The "total" mean number of hits for the "most" effective counselors was significantly greater than the mean for the "least" effective group at beyond the .01 level of probability, and significantly greater than the mean for the "moderate" group at the .05 level. The difference between the means for the "moderate" and "least" effective groups was not significant at the .05 level.

Discussion

Prediction is basic to effective educational and vocational counseling. If prediction is important, logically, then, a counselor should be able to predict relatively accurately before he is an "effective" counselor. There is general agreement that while the power of decision remains with the student, the professional responsibility for accurate interpretation of test scores and other case information is largely the counselor's, regardless of his particular philosophical point of view. Yet, since prediction is primarily an intellectual process, the ability to predict relatively accurately does not alone make a counselor "effective" in his work with students. The results of this study provided evidence that counselors rated most effective in their work with students also tended to predict more accurately than the counselors rated less effective. Why?

This difference in predictive skill *cannot* be attributed to amount of counselor training or amount of experience. There was no difference in the amount of formal training received by the counselors rated most or least effective, and they all participated in the in-service training program provided by the Lower Division Advisors

Office. Although some counselors had professional goals in fields other than counseling, the career choices of these Arts College counselors were not related to their ability to predict accurately. The counselors comprising the "least" effective group had on the average about six months *more* experience than the counselors in the "most" effective group.

Perhaps interest in their jobs and the desire to help students make "good" decisions were reasons some counselors were considered by their supervisors to be more effective than others. Perhaps these were also important reasons why the most effective counselors became more accurate predictors than the counselors considered less effective. Since prediction was routinely of considerable importance in their work with students, the accumulation of knowledge of factors related to the criterion constructs (different "major" choices) with which they were concerned was crucial. Recognizing the importance of prediction, perhaps the better counselors were more curious and persistent in their attempts to learn about the students and the alternatives from which the students could choose.

In making their counselor evaluations, the supervisors no doubt also took into account the counselor's knowledge of content information related to the educational programs available to students. While the supervisors had no empirical evidence about the counselors' predictive skills or objective data about their knowledge of content information, subjective appraisals no doubt were made in their supervisory work with the counselors. This suggests that although the supervisors were unaware that their counselor ratings would be associated with counselor predictive accuracy, a subjective assessment of the counselor's ability to predict was a factor that entered into the supervisors' ratings.

While rated counseling effectiveness was positively related to predictive accuracy for this group of counselors, it is important to recognize that the *level* of accuracy achieved was far from perfect. But it should also be noted that this was an extremely difficult prediction for the counselors to make. Not only did they have to correctly predict whether a student would graduate, but they also had to predict whether the student would persist in his original "major" choice before a hit was recorded. Although the graduation-nongraduation base rate for the sample of students studied was 47–53, and 53 hits would be recorded if all students were predicted *not* to graduate, this does not take into account the additional "major" prediction made by the counselors. Still, the most effective group of counselors got on the average only about 52 out of every 100 predictions correct. This suggested that although counselor predictive efficiency is related to counselor effectiveness, the *level* of accuracy for all counselors needs to be improved considerably. There still is considerable error in the predictions of all counselors regardless of their present level of accuracy.

The accuracy of the counselors' predictions was not significantly affected by the increased amounts of case data available in the second and third conditions. That is, about the same number of hits were recorded on the average from using only ability test scores and high school grades as were made when the SVIB, MMPI, and other data were also available. Inspection of the hit records of the counselors revealed that the variability in their predictive skills was primarily related to the *graduation* prediction, which correlates highest with the type of data provided in Condition I. While an instrument such as the SVIB could be useful to the counselors in discussing alternative programs with students, the additional interest, personality, and biographical information did not increase the counselors' ability to predict accurately.

References

Goldman, L. *Using Tests in Counseling.* New York: Appleton-Century-Crofts, 1961.

Gough, H. G. "Clinical Versus Statistical Prediction in Psychology." In L. J. Postman (ed.), *Psychology in the Making.* New York: Alfred A. Knopf, 1962.

Kelly, E. L., & Fiske, D. W. "The Prediction of Success in the VA Training Program in Clinical Psychology." *American Psychologist,* 1950, *5,* 395–406.

Meehl, P. E. *Clinical Versus Statistical Prediction.* Minneapolis: University of Minnesota Press, 1954.

Meehl, P. E. "Clinical Versus Actuarial Prediction." In *Proceedings, 1955 Invitational Conference on Testing Problems.* Princeton, N.J.: Educational Testing Service, 1956. Pp. 136–41.

Pepinsky, H. B., & Pepinsky, Pauline N. *Counseling: Theory and Practice.* New York: Ronald Press, 1954.

Sarbin, T. R. "A Contribution to the Study of Actuarial and Individual Methods of Prediction." *American Journal of Sociology,* 1942, *48,* 593–602.

Siegel, S. *Nonparametric Statistics for the Behavioral Sciences.* New York: McGraw-Hill, 1956.

Strang, Ruth. *Counselor Techniques in College and Secondary Schools.* New York: Harper, 1937.

Super, D. E., Crites, J. D., Hummel, R. C., Moser, H. P., Overstreet, Phoebe L., & Warnath, C. F. *Vocational Development: A Framework for Research.* New York: Bureau of Publications, Teachers College, Columbia University, 1957.

Tyler, Leona E. *The Work of the Counselor.* New York: Appleton-Century-Crofts, 1961.

Walker, Helen M., & Lev, J. *Statistical Inference.* New York: Holt, Rinehart, & Winston, 1953.

Watley, D. J., & Vance, F. L. "Clinical Versus Actuarial Prediction of College

Achievement and Leadership Activity." Final report, Project No. 2202, Cooperative Research Program, Office of Education, U.S. Dept. of Health, Education, and Welfare, 1964.
Williamson, E. G. *How To Counsel Students.* New York: McGraw-Hill, 1939.

COUNSELING WITH DROPOUTS: A THREE-YEAR STUDY

HARRY E. LEUBLING

In an effort to bridge the gap between the dropout's unsuccessful school experience and his subsequent attempts to find a place for himself in the world of work, the Vocational Advisory Service (VAS) initiated a three-year Youth and Work Program in May 1962 on Manhattan's Upper West Side. The program was sponsored by the New York State Division for Youth in cooperation with the New York City Youth Board and New York State Employment Service. The primary goal was to enhance the employability and vocational adjustment of sixteen- to eighteen-year-old school dropouts by means of individual counseling and ancillary services. Applicants were assigned on a random basis to an experimental group and a control group. The services available to the experimental group consisted of counseling, social casework, pre-vocational training, remedial education, and job placement. The control group received only job placement assistance. Since control group data were collected independently by the Division for Youth and are not yet available, the relative effectiveness of these two approaches cannot be evaluated until a later date. In the meantime, however, it seems profitable to examine some of the findings available on the experimental group.

Client Characteristics

Over 75 per cent of the 463 clients in the experimental group were

*This article is reprinted from *Vocational Guidance Quarterly,* 1967, *15,* 173–80, by permission of the publisher and author.

sixteen- and seventeen-year-olds. Boys outnumbered girls 3 to 1. The ethnic distribution was Puerto Rican (45 per cent), Negro (35 per cent), and white (20 per cent). Level of education ranged from 3rd grade to 11th grade with a median of 8.9. Table 1 presents a comparison of the levels of education attained by the white, Negro, and Puerto Rican clients.

TABLE 1
LEVEL OF EDUCATION BY ETHNIC GROUP

Grade Level Completed	*White (N = 94) Per Cent*	*Negro (N = 160) Per Cent*	*Puerto Rican (N = 209) Per Cent*	*Total (N = 463) Per Cent*
11th	18	8	2	8
10th	26	22	16	20
9th	35	48	40	41
8th	18	17	26	21
7th	0	2	10	5
6th	1	1	1	1
5th	1	0	1	1
4th	1	0	1	1
3rd	0	2	3	2
Total	100	100	100	100

Forty-four per cent of the whites had completed at least the 10th grade as against only 30 per cent of the Negroes and 18 per cent of the Puerto Ricans. Assessment of socio-economic level was carried out by means of a modification of Hamburger's *Revised Occupational Scale for Rating Socio-Economic Class* [2]. This scale, as modified, runs from Level 1 (highest) to Level 9 (lowest). Levels 8 and 9 consist of families dependent partially and wholly on public assistance, respectively. Table 2 presents the socio-economic classification of the entire experimental group and affords comparisons along ethnic lines.

Fifty per cent of the white clients came from the four lowest socio-economic levels as against 83 per cent of the Negroes and 89 per cent of the Puerto Ricans. The percentages of whites, Negroes and Puerto Ricans from families dependent wholly or partially on public assistance were 3 per cent, 22 per cent, and 34 per cent, respectively. These findings on socio-economic level and level of education lend support to the assertions of Puerto Rican leaders in New York City [3] that Puerto Ricans are even more disadvantaged than are Negroes. Some of the factors that may play a role in this are suggested by the psychological test data obtained.

TABLE 2
SOCIO-ECONOMIC LEVEL BY ETHNIC GROUP

Socio-Economic Level	*White (N = 94) Per Cent*	*Negro (N = 160) Per Cent*	*Puerto Rican (N = 209) Per Cent*	*Total (N = 463) Per Cent*
1	2	0	0	0.5
2	2	0	0	0.5
3	4	0	0	1
4	20	7	5	9
5	22	10	6	10
6	40	45	49	45
7	7	16	6	10
8	1	9	12	9
9	2	13	22	15
Total	100	100	100	100

PSYCHOLOGICAL TEST FINDINGS

Psychological tests were administered to 263 of the 463 clients in the experimental group. Those not tested consisted mainly of the following: (1) clients whose cultural and language handicaps were such that standard psychological tests were not suitable; (2) clients who were extremely resistant to testing, possibly because of previous school failures.

The Wechsler Adult Intelligence Scale (WAIS) was administered to 218 of the clients tested. Table 3 presents the intelligence test data obtained on these clients and affords a comparison with the classification of intelligence for the general population.

TABLE 3
INTELLIGENCE CLASSIFICATION OF YOUTH AND WORK CLIENTS
COMPARED WITH THE GENERAL POPULATION

IQ Interval	*Intelligence Classification*	*Percentage in Each IQ Category*	
		General Population	*Youth and Work Clients*
130 and above	Very Superior	2.2	0
120-129	Superior	6.7	.9
110-119	Bright Normal	16.1	4.1
90-109	Average	50.0	50.5
80-89	Dull Normal	16.1	29.8
70-79	Borderline	6.7	12.8
69 and below	Defective	2.2	1.9
		100.0	100.0

Approximately 50 per cent of the clients who were tested scored in the average category of intelligence. This proportion is identical with the classification of intelligence for the general population [6]. Here is where the resemblance ends, however. Only 5 per cent of the clients scored above average in intelligence as against 25 per cent for the general population. Only 15 per cent of the group, however, could be considered as seriously limited in intelligence and even here the findings have to be interpreted with caution since educational, cultural, and language factors may have affected their functioning. In any event, 85 per cent of the clients tested ranged from slightly below average to above average in intelligence. The implication of this is that—given the necessary vocational and educational assistance—these youngsters would seem to have the potential ability to make a satisfactory vocational adjustment in their adult lives. A comparison of intelligence by ethnic group is presented in Table 4.

TABLE 4
LEVEL OF INTELLIGENCE BY ETHNIC GROUP

IQ Interval	*Intelligence Classification*	*Percentage in Each IQ Category* *White (N = 43)*	*Negro (N = 71)*	*Puerto Rican (N = 104)*
130 and above	Very Superior	0	0	0
120-129	Superior	4	0	0
110-119	Bright Normal	14	1	1
90-109	Average	64	62	41
80-89	Dull Normal	14	27	38
70-79	Borderline	4	9	17
69 and below	Defective	0	1	3
		100	100	100

Only 18 per cent of the white clients scored below average in intelligence as against 37 per cent of the Negroes and 58 per cent of the Puerto Ricans. These differences in intellectual functioning may be related to the previously noted differences in educational attainment which in turn may be related to socio-economic, cultural, and language factors. It should also be noted that the WAIS is not a culture-free test of intelligence as certain parts of this test presuppose a familiarity with the American culture. There are also aspects of the test which are dependent on knowledge and proficiency in school subject matter, notably vocabulary and arithmetic. In these areas Negro and Puerto Rican clients were at a greater disadvantage than white clients: only 25 per cent of the white clients scored below the 4th-grade level in reading compared with 39 per cent of the Negro clients and 49 per cent of the Puerto Rican clients. Similarly, although none of the white clients scored below the 4th-grade level in arithmetic ability, 11 per cent of the Negroes and 21 per cent of the Puerto Ricans were unable to achieve beyond this level. The crucial role played by education seems clear.

The Thematic Apperception Test (TAT) was administered to about 10 per cent of the client population (N = 47). Many of the behavior patterns exhibited by these clients, however, were also manifested by a considerable number of the other clients. Among these were the following:

1. *Difficulty in Coping With Reality Factors.*—This pattern seemed to be composed of a constellation of psychological attributes such as low frustration tolerance, inability to postpone immediate gratification of needs, a pessimistic outlook, and conflict between environmental demands and personal desires.

2. *Inadequate Self-Awareness.*—Self-concepts lacked clarity and were pervaded by feelings of inferiority, lack of confidence in coping with demands and responsibilities, and uncertainty of the role to be played and its requirements.

3. *Impaired Interpersonal Relationships.*—Difficulties seemed to occur primarily in relation to adult authority figures. When TAT responses were synthesized with case history material, the possible antecedents often appeared to be rejection and frustration in childhood, coupled in some cases with outright abuse or abandonment. This seemed to lead to a generalized view of adults as representing parent surrogates at whose hands one could expect only further punishment and disappointment.

4. *Immaturity and Dependency.*—Psychosocial development frequently appeared to have been arrested at a childhood level. As a probable consequence, there was the above mentioned tendency toward the immediate satisfaction of needs that one would expect of a young child.

5. *Ambivalence, Negative Attitudes, and Antisocial Tendencies.*—Few clients showed serious antisocial inclinations, but virtually all manifested negative or ambivalent attitudes toward the larger society. Their case histories suggested that these attitudes stemmed from the early alienation or indifference they experienced within their families. That these attitudes should have generalized to the larger community is not difficult to understand. The indoctrination of the child into the community and his socialization within it is brought about largely through the school, and it is here these youngsters experienced much of their failure, frustration and rejection. When it is realized that similar negative experiences followed their attempts to find a place for themselves in the world of work, the basis of their hostility becomes even more apparent. As Erikson [*1*]

has pointed out, ". . . it is primarily the inability to settle on an occupational identity which disturbs young people."

The Counseling Approach

A basic premise of the entire program was that of working with the client in those problem areas in which he felt ready to accept assistance. In effect, the counselor was required not only to try to determine the client's basic difficulty but to ask himself, "What are the immediate problems facing this person? How ready is he to work on his problem? How much responsibility is he able to take right now?" and "How much responsibility can he learn to take?" This also meant recognizing that individuals vary in their readiness to face their problems and that emotional factors cannot be overlooked in the vocational decision-making process. [5]

Flexibility was another keynote of the program. Experience in working with these relatively nonverbal clients revealed the need for modification of traditional counseling methods which rely mainly on verbal communication and are aimed at the development of long-range objectives. These clients not only were unaccustomed to verbalizing, but they found it difficult to plan toward goals which they perceived as attainable only in the distant future, if at all. Consequently, it was necessary to focus on relatively short-range goals and on helping the client to find solutions to his more pressing immediate problems. It was also necessary to develop concrete activities in which the client could try himself out and experience a measure of success. The prevocational workshop and the remedial program were direct outgrowths of this experience.

Counselor Observations

The VAS Youth and Work counseling staff was asked to describe their experiences in working with the experimental client group in terms of client characteristics, attitudes, and values, and in terms of the problems with which clients needed assistance. The following is a summary of what the counselors reported:

CLIENT CHARACTERISTICS, ATTITUDES AND VALUES

1. Distrust and Suspicion of Authority Figures.—This characteristic manifested itself mainly in the initial interview, although with some youngsters several interviews were needed to win their confidence. "But once they did trust you, they wanted to tell you everything. It seemed that some of them never ever had anyone before in whom they could confide without fear of being criticized or judged."

2. *Unrealistic Aspirations and Work Attitudes.*—Most of the clients had a limited knowledge of the world of work. Equally limited was their appraisal of their abilities and aptitudes. Some aspired beyond their level, while others underestimated their ability to learn. Considerable ego-involvement was seen in those who over-aspired which no doubt was due to unmet emotional needs. Those who underaspired seemed to have been conditioned to failure.

3. *Hypersensitivity to Criticism or Rejection.*—Many clients failed to keep appointments. Interestingly, however, they often walked in on their own a day or two later. In this and in other areas, such as their need to confide about past misbehaviors, it seemed that they had a strong need to be accepted on their own terms and that they used broken appointments as a means of testing the counselor's acceptance of them.

4. *Facade of "Toughness."*—This characteristic seemed to be a carryover from their behavior in their peer group where it was often a prerequisite for acceptance. In view of their strong need for acceptance, it was not surprising that this type of behavior should appear in the counseling relationship. This facade was abandoned, however, once they found that their acceptance did not depend on it.

5. *Dependency Needs.*—Dependency needs seemed to be strongest among clients whose family history revealed chronic dependence on public assistance. Dependency seemed to have become a way of life. On the other hand, clients whose families had been on public assistance only a short time, usually desired to become self-supporting as soon as possible. Another form of dependency was also seen which was not related to public assistance. This was the dependency on others to make one's decisions. Although difficulty in decision-making is found among clients on all socio-economic levels, in a dropout population this is further aggravated by their deep-seated fear of failure and their feelings of inadequacy. Moreover, these clients often have urgent problems requiring immediate decisions. The counselor faced a particularly difficult dilemma here. If he made the decision for the client because the client was not yet ready to make his own decision, the immediate problem may have been solved—but the client may have been made that much more dependent. On the other hand, if he refused to do this and concentrated instead on helping the client to find his own solution, he may have contributed to the client's future problem-solving ability—provided the client did not break contact first because he did not receive immediate concrete assistance.

6. Impaired and Confused Self-Concepts.—In order to function effectively, each person needs to know who he is; he needs to have an image or concept of himself. Nowhere was the confusion of these youngsters more apparent than in the vagueness of the images they had of themselves. Many came from families on public assistance and families where employment and income were both marginal and sporadic. Many, too, came from broken homes and homes where there had never been even a semblance of stable family relationships. In the absence of appropriate role models, these clients were unable to determine what their own role in life should be.

7. Rejection of Social Values.—There was little evidence that the clients had any life goals beyond the moment. Many came from homes where they had ample opportunity to see the seedier side of life, where out-of-wedlock relationships were common, where they saw their mothers living with a succession of different men, none of whom lingered long enough to assume any responsibility. From what the clients told their counselors, it seems that for most of them the values of our society were alien to their backgrounds and, consequently, they found it difficult to make them a part of their own value system.

TYPES OF PROBLEMS ON WHICH CLIENTS NEEDED ASSISTANCE

1. Employment Problems.—Almost every client gave this as his main reason for applying to the program. Some were able to accept help only in this area. For others, however, when this was approached on more than a superficial level, it was found that most of them felt vocationally unprepared and had little or no conception of their interests. The desire for an immediate job often stemmed from family pressure, the Department of Welfare, or a probation officer. Many doubted their ability to hold down a job or to even obtain a job. In general, they had a bleak outlook on their vocational future.

2. Family Relationships.—Most of the youngsters spoke of the indifference of their families, the discord in the home, their inability to get along with their mothers or—more frequently—their "stepfathers." Some had no idea who their real fathers were and knew nothing of their whereabouts. Some even told of having been put out of their homes to fend for themselves. As counseling progressed and plans for training were made, quite a few told of being under pressure from their families to obtain a job immediately.

3. Health Concerns.—One out of every three clients expressed concern about his health. Through a health examination, some were found to have such serious health problems as epilepsy, tuberculosis, or rheumatic heart disease.

4. *School-Related Difficulties.*—Most of the clients had no desire to return to school. To them school had meant only failure and frustration. They knew that the better jobs went to those with education and training, and yet they could not retrace their steps.

5. *Concern About Personal Problems.*—Some youngsters reported being worried about inner anxieties, tensions, and "nervousness." Others were troubled by their feelings of hostility, their tendency to act on impulse, their inability to control their tempers. Still others were depressed or uncertain of their ability to handle their lives successfully.

6. *Responsibilities of Raising Children.*—About 10 per cent of the clients, none of whom were over eighteen, were mothers and fathers themselves. The girls reported feeling inadequate in their role as a mother. They seemed to feel they could function better as a wage-earner with the care of their child taken over by their own mothers, a relative, or a day nursery, yet they did not want to give up their children. The boys, too, felt inadequate in their roles as fathers, largely because of their employment difficulties. They were virtually unanimous, however, in asserting that they wanted to assume their responsibilities. This is especially noteworthy in view of the fact that the families of these clients had not provided them with responsible role models to emulate. What this client behavior means is not entirely clear. It may represent a reaction to the neglect these clients experienced in their own childhood and a consequent rejection of their parents as desirable role models. There is also the interesting possibility that—through a process of identification with their counselors—these clients may have undergone a change in values and attitudes.

Some Preliminary Results

Job Placement.—When job placement was attempted at the initial stage of the youngster's contact with the program, it frequently was not successful. There were many instances in which clients who were referred to a job opening did not report to the employer. Follow-up often revealed that the youngster simply did not have sufficient confidence and had already concluded that he would not be hired. There were also instances in which a client was hired but did not report to work. Here, too, the youngster often reported later that he did not think he would be able to perform the work and was afraid he would be fired after a few days.

The vast majority had had little or no previous work experience—and what little they did have was unsuccessful. Many were illiterate to the point of being unable to fill out an employment application. That pre-vocational training and remedial education was of value is suggested by the fact that many of the youngsters who dropped out of the program returned when they could not obtain employment. With additional preparation, most of them were subsequently placed.

Altogether 338 clients were referred to job openings and of this number, 252 (75 per cent) were hired. What seems significant is that most of these clients either had not been able to secure employment previously or had been able to hold a job for only a few days. Thirty-two per cent of the placements lasted at least one month, 15 per cent lasted from one to two months, 11 per cent from two to six months, and 6 per cent from six months to over one year. Since control group data are not yet available, there is no way of knowing what the employment data would have been in the absence of the services provided by the program. However, if past performance is any predictor, it seems safe to assume that few of these youngsters would have been any more successful than they had been previously.

Resumption of Education.—Sixty-nine of the clients (15 per cent) have resumed their education. Although this may seem like a small number, it is nonetheless noteworthy when one considers the fact that virtually all of them initially had expressed negative feelings toward school and had been almost unanimous in declaring they had not wished to return to school. Since many of them showed potential for a higher level of education than they had attained, counseling was aimed at helping them to overcome their fear of failure and develop more positive self-concepts. In this area, too, remedial education was of value in that learning to read not only gave them a feeling of accomplishment but opened doors that previously had been closed.

Conclusions

Many of the counseling problems encountered are not unique to this type of client population. Many vocational counseling clients from higher socio-economic levels exhibit similar problems, such as difficulty in decision-making, vocational immaturity, impaired family relationships, and inadequate motivation. What may distinguish the economically disadvantaged are the multiplicity of complicating problems along with a serious difficulty in coping with reality factors. This is often accompanied by an attitude of hopelessness and a depressed outlook on life. As Super [*4*] has pointed out, ". . . the high school dropout who never did well in his studies, who was never accepted by his classmates, and who was fired from the job that he finally got only after a number of rejections, finds the occupational translation of his self-concept as ne'er-do-well confirmed and implemented." Remedial education, pre-vocational and vocational training, and job placement can do much to improve the dropout's self-confidence. However, the problem is not merely one of developing job skills, especially when it is considered that the rate of technological change is such that narrow skills may well become obsolete within a reasonably short time after their acquisition. Moreover, counseling that is focused exclusively on the vocational area overlooks the important area of attitudes and values. The dropout is basically a person who is alienated from himself and society. A broad spectrum of counseling is needed to help him develop a more positive self-concept and a closer integration with the larger society.

References

1. Erikson, E. H. "Identity and the Life Cycle." *Psychological Issues,* New York: International University Press, 1959.
2. Hamburger, M. *Realism and Consistency in Early Adolescent Aspirations and Expectations.* Unpublished doctoral dissertation, Teachers College, Columbia University, 1958.
3. Puerto Rican Forum. *Proposal: A Comprehensive Program To Service 2,500 Disadvantaged Youth in New York City by Building Career and Leadership Opportunities.* New York: Puerto Rican Forum, Inc., March 10, 1965.
4. Super, D. E. "Self-Concepts in Vocational Development." In D. E. Super, R. Starishevsky, N. Matlin, & J. P. Jordaan. *Career Development: Self-Concept Theory,* Research Monograph No. 4. New York: College Entrance Examination Board, 1963.
5. Thompson, A. S. "Decision-Making in the Counseling Process." In A. Jacobs, J. P. Jordaan, & S. G. DiMichael (eds.), *Counseling in the Rehabilitation Process.* New York: Teachers College, Columbia University, Bureau of Publications, 1961.
6. Wechsler, D. *The Measurement and Appraisal of Adult Intelligence* (4th ed.). Baltimore: The Williams & Wilkins Co., 1958.

*

PERCEPTION OF SELF AND SCHOLASTIC UNDERACHIEVEMENT IN THE ACADEMICALLY CAPABLE

CHARLES F. COMBS

The present study examined the proposition that academically capable, underachieving high school boys tended to see themselves and their relationship with others in certain ways that were quite unlike those who were making a more happy and successful adjustment to the scholastic situation.

Subjects

The subjects participating in this study were selected from the 11th grade of the high schools in adjacent suburban communities in Westchester County, New York. The experimental group was composed of 25 underachieving boys, while 25 achieving boys comprised the control group. The groups were comparable with respect to sex, race, nationality, age, grade, socio-economic status and intelligence.

Procedure

The three high schools involved sent all of their high school juniors each year to the Guidance Center of the Board of Cooperative Educational Services in Bedford Hills, New York. (This is a cooperative project of eight school districts in Northern Westchester County.) All of these students were administered the Wechsler Adult Intelligence Scale. If a student obtained a Full Scale IQ of 115 or better,

*This article is reprinted from *Personnel and Guidance Journal,* 1964, *43,* 47–51, by permission of the publisher, the American Personnel and Guidance Association, and the author.

his cumulative grade-point average was computed. If this average fell below the first quartile in scholastic achievement for his grade, he was defined as an underachiever; if the average was above the median for his grade, he was considered an achiever.

As the subjects were identified as underachievers (experimental group) or achievers (control group), they were administered an apperceptive instrument consisting of four cards from the Thematic Apperception Test and four cards from the Combs School Apperception Test. The responses were recorded on magnetic tape. Both the tape recorder and the microphone were concealed from the subject in order to avoid any inhibition in the subject's response.

Each subject's protocols were identified only by a code number so that neither the subject, the group, nor the school could be identified by the experimenter. All protocols were individually judged in terms of six perceptual continua which had been developed to evaluate the perceptions revealed in the apperceptive device. These continua were:

1. Sees self as adequate to inadequate
2. Sees self as acceptable to unacceptable
3. Sees peers as acceptable to unacceptable
4. Sees adults as acceptable to unacceptable
5. Approach to problems is positive to negative
6. Freedom of emotional expression is positive to negative

Five ratings were possible in each continuum. Each story was judged in its entirety and then given a rating in a specific continuum.

A sample of 10 per cent of the protocols was drawn and scored by the experimenter and after a period of three weeks the stories were again rescored by the experimenter and the results were compared by a series of Pearson product moment correlation coefficients (*see* Table 1).

TABLE 1
AGREEMENT DATA FOR JUDGMENTS ON SAMPLE PROTOCOLS OF PERCEPTUAL CONTINUA

	Self-Adequacy	*Self-Acceptance*	*Acceptance of Peers*	*Acceptance of Adults*	*Approach to Problems*	*Freedom of Expression*	*Overall*
Self-Self	0.98	0.99	0.96	0.99	0.93	0.95	0.97
Self-Judge A	0.89	0.96	0.95	0.94	0.97	0.80	0.93
Self-Judge B	0.90	0.96	0.98	0.98	0.91	0.92	0.95
Judge A-Judge B	0.93	0.92	0.91	0.96	0.84	0.82	0.91
Average r_{11}	0.94	0.97	0.96	0.97	0.92	0.89	0.94

The protocols to be judged were randomly selected from the total of 400 stories, and each such protocol was coded so that neither the school nor the group nor the identity of the subject could be determined.

These stories were also judged by two other counselor-psychologists who had previously been trained by the writer to use the scoring continua. Correlation coefficients were computed for the ratings of each story for each judge and for the experimenter (*see* Table 1). The agreement of the judgments of the criteria values assigned by the author and between the author and the other two judges and between the two judges is very high. The highest correlation coefficients were found in the "Acceptance of Adults" and "Feeling of Self-Acceptability" continua. The lowest coefficients of agreement seemed to be in the "Freedom of Expression" continuum. Agreement between the judges and between the experimenter and either judge or between the experimenter and himself over a period of time ran very high. For the purposes of this study it seemed reasonable to assume that judgments on all of the perceptual continua were quite consistent.

Results

The results are presented in terms of answering six major questions. The significance of the *t*-test of the differences between the means, and the median test (chi-square) upon which the answers to these questions were based is summarized in Table 2. All answers were strongly supported by the data.

TABLE 2

Comparison of the Scores Obtained by Achiever and Underachiever Groups on the Self-Perception Continua

Continuum	*F-test*	*t-test*	*P*	X^2	*P*
Self-adequacy	1.41	12.94	0.001	12.04	0.001
Self-acceptance	3.44	6.25	0.001	16.03	0.001
Acceptance of peers	1.02	5.35	0.001	7.95	0.010
Acceptance of adults	1.26	6.82	0.001	13.35	0.001
Approach to problems	1.00	5.69	0.001	10.24	0.001
Freedom of expression	2.77	8.54	0.001	12.96	0.001

Certain limitations were imposed on the distributions by the artifact of the five-point perceptual continua scales. An additional check upon the significance of the differences between the two groups was accomplished by the use of median tests (chi-square). On all of the variables, the differences between the two groups were found to be highly significant.

1. "*Do underachievers perceive themselves to be less adequate to solve their problems than do achievers?*" The underachiever group seemed to see themselves as inadequate and unable to successfully handle those problems that could occur in a school situation. They seemed to be much more constricted and were unable to "carry through" when faced with problems. They approached problems very fearfully and doubted their ability to overcome them. They lacked initiative and appeared to be quite helpless in the face of decisions. Achievers, on the other hand, seemed to feel much more adequate to deal with problems and more confident of their own abilities. They showed more initiative and spontaneity in pursuing their interests.

2. "*Do underachievers feel themselves to be less acceptable to others than do achievers?*" Underachievers often seemed to feel themselves not particularly liked or accepted by others and even threatened by the group. They felt that they had to defend themselves against others. Achievers, in contrast, seemed to feel well accepted and integrated, and very comfortable as members of the group. They seemed to experience a feeling of belonging, of togetherness.

3. "*Do underachievers seem less able to accept and trust their peers than do achievers?*" The underachiever group seemed to be threatened by others and to see them as people of little value. The achiever group seemed to regard their peers as acceptable, as people of dignity and integrity to a much greater extent than did the underachiever group. They saw their peers as persons who should be approached with sympathy and understanding. They seemed to lack the fearfulness and suspicion of others which apparently characterized the underachievers.

4. "*Do underachievers seem to be less able to accept and trust adults than do achievers?*" There was a significant difference between the achiever and underachiever groups in the way they perceived and reacted to adults. Achievers generally seemed to see adults as quite acceptable and as persons who were worthy of respect and understanding. Underachievers as a group, on the other hand, seemed to regard adults as being generally unacceptable and as persons whose motivations were somewhat questionable. They seemed to be threatened by adults and wanted to avoid contact with them.

5. "*Do underachievers seem to be less direct and efficient in approaching problems than do achievers?*" The underachievers seemed to be much more defensive and to use many more techniques of rebellion and oppositional types of behavior than did achievers. They seemed to see the environment as something very threatening to

themselves, against which they actively had to defend themselves. In contrast, the achievers seemed to utilize opportunities to gain direct satisfaction and were willing to accept reasonable limits.

6. "*Do underachievers have more difficulty in expressing their emotions directly and overtly than do achievers?*" The emotions of the underachiever group seemed to be blocked. Often, in their responses, there was torpor, apathy, exaggeration, or fear. The feelings expressed were often inappropriate or generalized or out of proportion to the objective stimulus. On the other hand, the achiever group's emotional expression seemed to be both adequate and direct. Whether positive or negative, the achievers seemed to be able to express their feelings, and this expression seemed more appropriate to the situations presented to them.

Implications

The underachiever cannot be treated in terms of any one facet of his problem. Underachievement must be understood to be a completely personal and consistent adaptation of the underachiever to his needs and capacities as he uniquely experiences them. It is because of this unique pattern of the perceptions that a basic reorganization of the self-concept must be effected if the underachiever is to be brought to the point where his perceptions can encompass success.

The basic thread running through this study is that a major determinant of how well one will be able to function is his feeling of capability of functioning. Many times for the underachiever educational experiences are perceived by him and are thus experienced by him as being largely non-facilitating experiences.

Pressure or stress techniques are often applied by teachers in order to bring about the behavior or learning they desire. It is only the adequate student who can truly benefit from such stress techniques. Many of these techniques have the effect of reducing feelings of personal adequacy, of inhibiting emotional responses, and of restricting the number of approaches to particular problems. These techniques often increase the distance between the underachiever and other pupils or between him and the teachers, or restrict communication with them.

The underachiever fails to achieve because he lacks a feeling of personal adequacy. He lacks the feeling that he is accepted either by his peers or by the adults with whom he deals. Because he feels unacceptable, he cannot invest in others or run the risk of failure. The underachiever, being under threat, is incapable of examining all of the data or evaluating the various techniques that he may apply to any problem. He cannot incorporate all the data and therefore he cannot adapt or effectively utilize his potential.

Summary

This study involves an exploration of the way underachievers see themselves and their relationships with others, in contrast to the perceptions of other students who are making a more successful and happy adjustment to the scholastic environment. Six general hypotheses were explored relating to views of self, views of others, and general behavioral and emotional efficiency. The study was concerned with high school junior boys of above average intelligence. It attempted to identify some of the specific factors which might have caused differences in academic proficiency.

Underachievers showed a significant and consistent difference from achievers in that they:

Saw themselves as less adequate;
Saw themselves as less acceptable to others;
Saw their peers as less acceptable;
Saw adults as less acceptable;
Showed an inefficient and less effective approach to problems; and showed less freedom and adequacy of emotional expression.

References

Combs, A. W. (ed.). "Perceiving, Behaving, Becoming: A New Focus for Education." *Yearbook Association Supervis. Curric. Develpm.* Washington: National Education Association, 1962.

Gowan, J. C. "The Underachieving Gifted Child—A Problem for Everyone." *Exceptional Children,* 1955, *21,* 247–49.

Miller, L. M. (ed.). *Guidance for the Underachiever with Superior Ability.* Washington: U. S. Department of Health, Education, and Welfare, 1961.

National Education Association. *The Identification and Education of the Academically Talented Student in the American Secondary School.* Washington: National Education Association, 1958.

Shaw, M. C., & McCuen, J. P. "The Onset of Academic Underachievement in Bright Children." *Journal of Educational Psychology,* 1960, *51,* 103–8.

Walsh, A. M. Self-Concepts of Bright Boys with Learning Difficulties." *Teachers College Studies in Education.* New York: Bureau of Publications, Teachers College, Columbia University, 1956.

Wolfle, D. L. *America's Resources of Specialized Talent.* New York: Harper, 1954.

Young, P. T. "Motivation." *Encyclopedia of Educational Research.* New York: Macmillan, 1950, 755–61.

4

Counseling Procedures and Techniques

A well-known problem in counseling supervision is the difficulty in assessing the relative merits of various counseling theories and techniques. Counselor educators face a similar problem: Should they teach the approach to counseling that reflects the orientation of the faculty or should they allow each counselor trainee to develop an approach to counseling that is unique to him? To a large extent this problem exists because there is little evidence to support a particular procedure or technique as being superior to other procedures and techniques. It is believed that answers to this and related questions must be approached through research into the effectiveness of various counseling techniques and procedures in different settings and with different groups of counselees. This type of research is the focus of the present chapter. The studies reported are encouraging attempts to provide empirical support for a variety of approaches to counseling.

In the present chapter articles have been included that involve relationships that are defined as counseling as well as some that are described as therapy. It is believed that much that exists in the relationship is common to both counseling and therapy. The attention of the reader is directed, however, to the differences in both the setting and the nature of the client. Procedures and techniques that may be effective in one setting and with one client may be quite inappropriate in other settings and with other clients. The authors of the articles have generally described the settings and clients with sufficient detail to provide the reader with the basic information needed for discrimination.

The Truax article is based on ratings by five clinical psychologists of specific segments of a long-term therapy case with Carl Rogers serving as the therapist. It attempts to explore the reinforcement-nonreinforcement controversy by examining Rogerian counseling. The findings suggest that Rogers utilizes reinforcement in counseling as a technique in controlling client behavior. The study would seem to indicate that nondirective counseling may be little more than a relative term, and that even the Rogerian counselor consciously or unconsciously manipulates the session by selective reinforcement of desired client behavior.

The Krueger study has implications both for counselor education and secondary-school counseling. The article deals with a comparison of client-centered and clinical or structured counseling in preventing counselee dropout among secondary school students. Based on the criterion of holding power, the study provides evidence to support a more clinical or structured approach to counseling. It is important to note the implicit relationship that exists between the counseling approach of the supervisor and the student counselors.

The next four articles deal with differences in counselor style and the effect on counselee responses (Heller, *et al*, Truax and Carkhuff, Holder, *et al*, and Carkhuff and Alexik). The study by Heller, *et al* found that "active" counselors, whether "friendly" or "hostile" were able to elicit more verbalization from their clients than passive counselors. To an extent, the findings of the Krueger article get support from the Heller study.

Three of these articles deal with the concept of "low-functioning" and "high-functioning" counselors. The articles all utilize four dimensions of counselor functioning as indicated by four scales developed by Truax. The scales are the Depth of Intrapersonal Exploration Scale, the Accurate Empathy Scale, the Unconditional Positive Regard Scale, and the Self-Congruence Scale. The scales have been effectively used to investigate several aspects and outcomes of both counselor and client behavior. The article by Truax and Carkhuff investigates the effect of high- and low-functioning therapist behavior upon three schizophrenic women patients. It was observed that the depth of self-exploration of the patient was affected by changes in accurate empathy and unconditional positive regard. To discover if the findings were appropriate only with seriously disturbed patients, the study by Holder, *et al* continued the Truax investigation. In this instance, clients were identified who were evaluated as high- and low-functioning in their work as counselors in training. The level of counselor functioning was varied during the session. The low-functioning clients responded to this manipulation in ways related to the Krueger study. The high-functioning clients did not respond significantly to changes in the counselor's level of functioning.

The Carkhuff and Alexik study investigates the effect of differential counselee behavior in a coached client and high- and low-functioning counselors. The low-functioning counselors responded with even lower levels of functioning with low-functioning clients, but high-functioning counselors did not lower their level of functioning to correspond with the functional level of the client. Gamsky and Farwell also subjected counselors to differential client behavior, in this instance friendly versus hostile expressions. Both client demeanor and sex affected the counseling behavior of counselors. The nature of the reaction was unrelated to either the counselor's sex or experience.

The final two articles (Gamsky and Farwell, and Holmes) are more technique-oriented. Holmes examines four different methods of providing test information to college freshmen. The findings suggest that the way test results are interpreted has an effect on the value students place on the results. There was definitely more perceived value by the student when the test results were interpreted personally than when the results were mailed with no personal contact.

Most of the research in the present chapter deals primarily with the effects of counselor or client behavior on the counseling relationship. The criteria measures include a variety of rating scales that are used to describe qualitatively or quantitatively the behavior of counselors. Of particular interest are the generally high levels of both inter-judge and intra-judge reliability that were obtained with the use of carefully designed scales and judges who had been instructed in the use of the scales.

Designs were primarily based upon an analysis of variance among types of treatment or among scale values assigned to client or counselor levels of functioning. One study consisted of an analysis of the behavior of one counselor and client during a series of counseling interviews (Truax).

The research that follows presents a number of approaches to investigation of that nebulous quality, the counseling relationship. While no absolute answers are provided to the question of what results in an effective relationship in terms of any global or ultimate counseling outcomes, the effects of a number of conditions, often defined in rather general terms, upon certain kinds of counselee behavior, also frequently defined in general terms, are investigated with sufficient clarity to provide the basis for judgments about counseling procedures and techniques. The findings seem to the writers to be sufficiently fruitful to encourage further effort to investigate the effect of procedures and techniques on both the counseling relationship and counseling outcomes.

REINFORCEMENT AND NONREINFORCEMENT IN ROGERIAN PSYCHOTHERAPY[1]

CHARLES B. TRUAX

The present study is aimed at exploring the possibility that important reinforcement effects occur within the transactions of nondirective therapy.

Client-centered theorists have specified the "therapeutic conditions" of empathic understanding and acceptance or unconditional positive regard as two main antecedents to constructive behavioral or personality change in the client (Dymond, 1949; Hobbs, 1962; Jourard, 1959; Rogers, 1951, 1957; Rogers and Truax, 1965; Truax, 1961; Truax and Carkhuff, 1963). Rogers, as the leading exponent of this viewpoint, holds that these "conditions" are primarily attitudinal in nature and are offered in a nonselective fashion to the patient: They are specifically not contingent upon the patients' ver-

*This article is reprinted from *Journal of Abnormal Psychology,* 1966, *71,* 1–9, by permission of the publisher, the American Psychological Association, and the author.

[1]Appreciation is gratefully extended to Carl R. Rogers for his freely given consent to the use of the completed successful counseling case recorded at the University of Chicago Counseling Center in 1955. This particular case is perhaps of special significance since it was heavily used by Rogers and others in the development of the "process conception of psychotherapy" and the "Process Scale" developed in 1957. Thanks are also due to James C. Baxter and Leon D. Silber for their critical comments. This work was supported in part by a grant from the Vocational Rehabilitation Administration, No. RD-906-PM.

balizations or behaviors. This viewpoint, in pure form, is incompatible with the behavioristic view of therapy and was one basis for the Rogers-Skinner debates (1956).

The basic difference between the views exemplified by Rogers and Skinner is that the latter holds that an effective therapist attempts to alter the patient's behavior while Rogers holds otherwise. Differential reinforcement is one of the procedures used in operant research *positions*. Thus, whether or not Rogers as a therapist uses differential reinforcement, thereby altering patient behavior, is a central question in the basic issue of control which philosophically differentiates the two positions.

The growing body of evidence indicates that the therapist's accurate empathy and unconditional positive regard are significant antecedents to therapeutic change (Rogers, 1962; Rogers, Kiesler, Gendlin and Truax, 1967). This evidence has been used both as support of Rogers' view and as an argument against the behavioristic views of psychotherapy typified by such theorists as Krasner (1962), Wolpe (1958), Eysenck (1952, 1960), and Bandura (1961). The evidence does suggest that when patients receive high levels of empathy and warmth there is significantly more constructive personality and behavioral change than when the patients receive relatively lower levels (Barrett-Lennard, 1962; Bergin and Solomon, 1963; Cartwright and Lerner, 1963; Dickenson and Truax, 1965; Halkides, 1958; Lesser, 1961; Rogers, 1962; Strupp, 1960; Truax, 1961a, 1961b, 1963; Truax and Carkhuff, 1964; Truax, Carkhuff and Kodman, in press; Truax, Wargo, and Silber, 1965; Wargo, 1962; and Whitehorn and Betz, 1954). None of the research just cited, however, *necessarily* argues against a behavioristic view of psychotherapy.

If, in contrast to Rogers' contention, the therapist does respond differentially to different patient behaviors (i.e., more accepting of and empathic to some patient behaviors but less accepting of and more directive in response to other patient behaviors) then a reinforcement view would not be inconsistent with the findings. It could be argued that if empathic understanding, warmth (and nondirectiveness) are therapeutic, then it may also be argued that these therapeutic conditions are reinforcing, rewarding, or somehow encouraging, and that the types of patient behavior (presumably more adaptive ones) that are followed by high levels of these therapeutic conditions will consequently increase during the course of therapy. For example, it may be that the "high conditions" therapist offers more intense levels of accurate empathy and unconditional warmth or acceptance on both a nonselective random basis at, say, a 40 per cent rate of reinforcement for all behaviors and, say, an 85 per cent rate for exploration of material relevant to the private self. By contrast the "low conditions" therapist may offer less intense levels of empathy and warmth, with only a 20 per cent rate of reinforcement for all behavior emitted and only a 40 per cent rate of reinforcement for the patient's explorations of private material.

Support for the position exemplified by Rogers, viewed from the findings on empathy and warmth, rests upon the assumption that the therapist offers levels of conditions that do not systematically covary with the verbalizations or behavior emitted by the patient. If this were true (if, say, the level of therapist empathy or warmth did not systematically covary with patient response classes) then differential reinforcement could not account for the research findings of relationships between therapist behavior and patient outcome. On the other hand, if the therapist, in this case Rogers, does systematically vary his level of warmth or his level of empathy depending on the behavior, then Rogers' position would not be supported.

In an attempt to add clarity to this theoretic controversy, an exploratory analysis of a single successful case handled by Rogers was aimed at determining whether or not important reinforcing effects are imbedded in the transactions of client-centered therapy.

Three qualities of the therapist's behavior were studied as potential reinforcers: (a) empathic understanding, (b) acceptance or unconditional positive regard, and (c) directiveness (a negative reinforcer). These therapist behaviors were examined in relation to nine classes of patient behavior in order to determine the presence or absence of differential therapist responding and any consequent changes in the patient behaviors.[2] The patient behaviors studied which might theoretically be of significance were: (a) degree of discrimination learnings by the patient, (b) ambiguity of patient's statements, (c) degree of insight development by the patient, (d) degree of similarity of patient's style of expression to that of the therapist, (e) problem orientation of the patient, (f) degree of patient catharsis, (g) degree of patient blocking, (h) degree of patient anxiety, and (i) degree of patient negative versus positive feeling expression.

Case Analysis Procedure

Five clinical psychologists rated an unbiased sample of 40 typewritten interaction units consisting of (a) a therapist statement, (b) a

---

[2]Thanks are due to Israel Goldiamond for critical and helpful questions which served as the stimulus for the analysis of change in patient behaviors over time.

succeeding patient statement, (c) the succeeding therapist statement. These interaction units (TPT, Therapist-Patient-Therapist) were designated by code numbers prior to the ratings, and were then assigned in random order to the five clinical psychologists who served as judges. Each judge rated separately each of the nine patient scales and the three therapist scales in different order, so as to minimize rating biases. The ratings were then decoded, and the ratings of the three classes of "reinforcers" were simply correlated separately with the nine classes of patient behavior under examination. The presence of significant correlations would then be positive evidence to indicate systematic, nonrandom use of these reinforcers with particular classes of patient behavior. Thus the question became, for example, "Does the therapist's degree of acceptance significantly covary with the patient's degree of discrimination learning?" If a positive correlation was found, this would indicate that the therapist systematically was most accepting and unconditionally warm when the patient was engaged in discrimination learning, and was least accepting and warm when the patient engaged in very little discrimination learning.

The Interaction Unit Sample.—The TPT interaction units were selected from the following interviews out of a total of 85 therapy sessions for the complete case, 1, 3, 5, 7, 10, 15, 20, 25, 30, 35, 40, 45, 50, 55, 60, 65, 70, 75, 80, and 85. Two intersection units were taken from each of the above 20 interviews for a total of 40 interaction units. Interviews from which the samples were drawn, with the exception of Numbers 3 and 7, which were added to give more weight to the earlier stages of therapy, were evenly spaced and should constitute an unbiased sample of interviews throughout the therapy case. The two interaction units from each interview were obtained by starting the playback of the recordings at approximately the end of the first and second one-third of the hour-long tape and then listening until the therapist made a statement. Transcriptions started at the therapist's first words and included the ensuing TPT interaction unit. As a result of this sampling procedure, the length of the therapist and the patient statements varied considerably. When measured to the nearest one-tenth of an 80-character type line the range was from 0.4 to 14.0 lines.

The Clinical Psychologists as Raters.—Of the five raters, none was trained in client-centered psychotherapy. One was trained in analytic therapy, while the remaining four clinicians described themselves as eclectic in orientation. All five judges had a minimum of 100 hours of supervised training as therapists, and 1,000 hours of experience as therapists. All post-doctoral clinical psychologists, the judges did not know the hypothesis being investigated. Further, they wrongly assumed that some of the more "nondirective" and "directive" statements could not have come from the same therapist.

The Rating Scales.—A set of graphic rating scales was prepared for each of the three therapist behaviors and nine patient behaviors, each having a brief statement of the variable to be rated and horizontal lines 170 millimeters long on which the rating was marked. The rating was made by simply placing an X along the line labeled "most," "very much," to "least," and "very little." The scales for each therapist and patient behavior class stated a bipolarity of the variable. The bipolar definitions for the three reinforcer variables were taken from Rogers' (1951) theoretic descriptions.

Although the actual therapy samples did not contain extreme examples of the scale values, examples from the present case should add meaning to the present study. Two examples of TPT samples, rated high on each of the three reinforcer variables, are presented below.

Therapist Acceptance or Unconditional Positive Regard.—The first example illustrates relatively high acceptance of the patient as he is feeling disappointed in the early results of therapy. This sample was rated relatively low on both empathy and directiveness:

T: There is nothing that I can do, but I can and do hope that the person will "lift" or something.

P: Yeh, but, well, for something to happen, or things to change, or me to change . . . inside, or . . . things to change outside, so I can change inside or something. Talking about it . . . doesn't really . . . seem to help, this kind of feeling. I mean, well . . . well, I don't know what I mean. I mean, I guess we're just talking about it. Well I don't know what I'm doing (he has been thumping on something—beating on the desk?—long, long pause) . . . I feel so tremendously self-conscious. I don't know, maybe it was the therapy session yesterday, and the other thing that happened yesterday, that has just thrown, so much on me, myself again. And dangerous, I don't know, not dangerous, but . . . I feel so un-free today. So . . . Hmm . . . (long pause) . . . Yeh, boy I really am self-conscious . . . sure tensed up inside.

T: I can't get the feel of what you mean by "self-conscious." It's very much aware of yourself? Or something, or generally embarrassed?

The second example illustrates relatively high acceptance of the patient's feelings of inadequacy and dependency. This sample was rated slightly above average on empathy but below average on directiveness.

T: I guess you're saying "I just can't trust those weak, and helpless, and inadequate parts of me. I have to have someone to . . ."

P: To really be me. (T: Mmm, mmm) Someone else, you know . . . that's so absurd . . . that would never work. It's the same thing as, as this, uh . . . being afraid of people. It ties in with being afraid. It's like . . . well, you can use any one of a number of examples. If you really want to be someone genuinely . . . or express something genuinely . . . then, all you have to do is feel the slightest tinge of fear and you won't be able to—really. And it's like that with myself. . . . It's kind of . . . when I am myself, it kind of echoes on me and makes me afraid. I suddenly hear myself saying that, and then know, "careful" (T: Mmm, mmm) "Hold on here! Lookout!" (T: Mmm, mmm) . . . like that. (T: Mmm, mmm) "You won't be allowed to live if you do that." (T: Mmm, mmm) "You won't be allowed to . . . *anything*" . . . just, "You'll be blown to smithereens if you try that kind of thing."

T: Mmm, So that if you sense yourself . . . being yourself . . . then my (P: I become afraid) Gosh! Lookout! You don't know what you're getting into—you'll be destroyed.

Therapist Directivenss.—The first example shows the therapist making a direct request to change the topic of discussion. This sample was rated slightly below average in empathy and low in acceptance:

T: Let's talk about something closer to you than that.

P: Or closer to you. I don't understand this at all, because I was really looking forward to this all the time, and now I just don't feel very good . . . about having harmed you.

T: You anticipated coming in, and now . . . today.

A second example of directiveness involves a more subtle "leading" of the patient. This sample was rated as average in empathy but above average in acceptance or unconditional positive regard:

T: It frightens you to even start to put it into words.

P: I guess I'll have to find it with someone else . . . first.

T: You feel that what would be demanded would be . . . put it in terms of "me" and, "you" . . . uh . . . make this the sort of thing you can sort of dimly visualize. I would need to want to really relate to that fine part of you, and find that so personally rewarding that, that in an attempt I would just . . . keep after it, or something. (P interjects: Yeh) One, one phrase that I . . . I'm bringing in my feelings rather than yours, but . . . ever read the poem "The Hound of Heaven"? It's kinda a weird thing, but, uh, the kind of persistent love of God is the whole theme, that, that won't let the person go . . . and, and, I think that's sort of what you're talking about.

Therapist Empathy.—The first example illustrates an excerpt in which the therapist attempts to verbalize what he senses is the client's uncertainty; this sample received an average rating on acceptance and a slightly above average rating on directiveness:

T: I've been trying to soak up that tone, uh, I'm not sure I'm right, but does it have some meaning like this, "What is it you want with me? I'm possibly willing to, to meet that, but I don't know what you want." Does that kinda describe it?
P: Yeh, I'm sympathetic, I'll try and do what I can. "Don't be this, and this, and this way to me." What is it? Yeh, that's it.
T: "So if you want me to get in with whatever it is you expect of me, just let me know."

The second example involves a moment when the therapist attempts to reflect the client's feelings and move one step beyond. This sample was rated average on directiveness and acceptance:

T: Seems as though all the dark things—hurting, and being hurt—and . . . decay, and corruption, ugliness, uhmmm, Death. It's all of those that (P: frightening) that you're afraid of.
P: Yeh . . . stink and corruption and . . . pus, and . . . There's just as. . . . It's something dark that ties them all together (T: Mmm, uhuh). Something putrid and (T: Mmm, mmm) . . . there are ten times the words (T: Mmm, mmm) for it . . . (laughs) it scares me.
T: Just to wander into that field verbally, and . . . and even name all these things that have to do with it . . . this dark side of hurting and rottenness . . . that's hurting in itself.

The patient scales measuring the degree of insight developed, the degree of similarity of the patient's style of expression to that of the therapist, the degree of problem orientation, the degree of catharsis, the degree of blocking in thought and feeling, the degree of anxiety present, and the degree of positive- versus negative-feeling expression were defined by the trained clinical psychologists who served as judges. Degree of ambiguity of the patient's statement was defined in terms of its clarity of meaning. The judges were asked to disregard speech disturbances and length of statement in rating ambiguity. Discrimination learning was defined as making new distinctions between old feelings or experiences, and thus included both cognitive and emotional discrimination learning.[3]

[3]Available from the author.

Findings and Discussion

QUALITATIVE ASPECTS

There are three qualitative aspects exemplified in this case which perhaps are worth noting. The first concerns the style of expression by the therapist: it was characteristic of the therapist to express, restate, or interpret what the patient has been saying by "quoting" what the patient *might well have said* in the first person singular—"In a sense I feel. . . ." Out of the 40 sampled interaction units, 23 involved first person singular quotes while an additional 5 (for a total of 28 out of 40) involved impersonal quotes of the type: "In a sense it's like feeling. . . ."

A second characteristic of this particular case was the almost total absence of psychological jargon. Few even semitechnical terms such as "anxious" or "hostile" were used by the therapist. Instead, the therapist relied heavily on everyday language that conveys affect. Thus instead of saying "depressed" the therapist says "hopeless badness." The third qualitative characteristic of this case is the tentative character of therapist statements. There is almost universal use of such prefacing remarks as "in a sense," "I guess," and "maybe." This tentative approach might tend to elicit less resistance from the patient so that actual confrontation might sound much like an attempt to agree with the patient.

THE QUESTION OF SELECTIVE RESPONDING

The reliability of each scale, which is given in parentheses under the scale label in Table 1, was estimated by the variance formula presented by Ebel (1951) for the intraclass correlation. As can be seen in Table 1, reliabilities range from .26 to .64 for the classes of patient behavior, and from .48 to .68 for levels of "reinforcement" offered by the therapist.

The low reliabilities obtained on certain classes of patient behavior would make it difficult to detect any but the strongest of relationships. For the present hypothesis of selective reinforcement the absence of particular relationships is not critical. Rather, the *presence* of selective responding (as indicated by some significant relationship between therapist and patient classes of behavior) would be evidence in support of the hypothesis.

The obtained average intercorrelations between the levels of therapist reinforcements and the levels of the selected patient behaviors are presented in Table 1. These average intercorrelations were obtained in the following manner. First a matrix of intercorrelations was generated for each of the five raters separately. The matrices were then inspected separately for correlations which were significant at or beyond the .05 level of significance. Average correlations for the five raters combined were then obtained for those intercorrelations that were significant in three out of five individual rater matrices. All other correlations were recorded as nonsignificant in the present study so that the reported correlations tend to minimize rather than maximize the possibility of obtaining significant relationships.

The significant intercorrelations presented in Table 1 show a quite different pattern than would be expected if therapist responses were not highly selective in client-centered psychotherapy. If there was no systematic selective use of empathy, acceptance, or directiveness, then all correlations would be nonsignificant and would approach zero. Such is not the case. The therapist significantly tended to respond selectively with differential levels of empathy, warmth, or directiveness to high and low levels of the following classes of patient behavior: (a) learning of discriminations about self and feelings, (b) a lack of patient ambiguity (patient clarity), (c) patient expressions of insight, (d) patient verbal expressions that were similar in style to the therapist's way of expressing himself, and (e) problem

TABLE 1

INTERRELATIONSHIPS BETWEEN THE LEVEL OF THERAPIST REINFORCEMENT AND LEVELS OF PATIENT BEHAVIORS

Classes of Patient Behavior	*Reinforcers* *Therapist Empathy* (*r* = .48)	*Therapist Acceptance UPR* (*r* = .59)	*Therapist Directiveness* (*r* = .68)
Patient learning of discriminations (*r* = .59)	.47	.37	*ns*
Patient ambiguity (*r* = .35)	—.35	—.38	.33
Patient insight (*r* = .32)	.46	.37	*ns*
Similarity of patient style of expression to that of the therapist (*r* = .57)	.48	.32	—.31
Problem orientation (*r* = .64)	*ns*	.35	*ns*
Catharsis (*r* = .44)	*ns*	*ns*	*ns*
Blocking (*r* = .54)	*ns*	*ns*	*ns*
Anxiety (*r* = .26	*ns*	*ns*	*ns*
Patient negative feeling expression (*r* = .29)	*ns*	*ns*	*ns*

orientation of the patient. Thus, when the patient expressed himself in a style similar to that of the therapist, the therapist was more empathic, more warm and accepting, and less directive. When the patient expressed himself in a style quite different from that of the therapist, the therapist tended to show significantly less empathy, less acceptance or warmth, and more directiveness.

No significant relationships were obtained between the therapist's use of empathy, acceptance, or directiveness, and patient behaviors described as blocking, anxiety, negative- versus positive-feeling expression, or catharsis. While it may be that the absence of these relationships might, in part, be accounted for by the relatively low reliabilities of measurement, it also seems likely that Rogers as a therapist does not tend to respond differentially to these classes of patient behavior. In particular, as a theoretician and therapist, Rogers (1957, 1961) has felt it important for the therapist *not* to respond selectively to negative- versus positive-feeling expression.

THE FURTHER QUESTION OF REINFORCEMENT

The above findings are consistent with, but not direct evidence for, the view that the therapist, in this case Rogers, is consciously or unconsciously using empathy, acceptance, and directiveness as reinforcers. The basic property of a reinforcer is that its use with specific classes of behavior leads to consequent changes in the probability of occurrence of these classes of behavior.

From Table 1, the nine classes of patient behavior can be ranked according to the degree of contingency between therapist "reinforcer" responses and patient responses. Now, if the therapist's systematic selective responding has the properties of reinforcement it would be predicted that, other things being equal, the five patient classes of behavior that were selectively "reinforced" would show increases over time in therapy, while the four classes of patient behavior not reinforced would show no such increase over time. Thus, for example, one would expect an increase over time in therapy of the "Similarity of the Patient's Style of Expression to that of the Therapist" and of "Patient-Learning Discriminations," and no such increase (or decrease) in patient "Blocking" or "Negative Feeling Expression."

To evaluate this the ratings of the 40 samples for each class of patient behavior were grouped into five blocks across time-in-therapy (five raters for eight samples per block or 40 ratings per block) and the Grant Orthogonal Polynomial Trend Test Analysis of Variance (Grant, 1956) was used to test for the significance of components of trend. Further, *t* tests were used to test for significance of differences between early and late in therapy on all nine patient behavior classes. These data are presented in Table 2.

TABLE 2

ANALYSIS OF CHANGES OVER TIME IN PATIENT RESPONSE CLASSES

Patient Response Classes	*Highest Single Correlation with Therapist "Reinforcer"*	*Grant Orthogonal Polynomial Analysis of Variance for Trend*			*t Test Between First and All Later Blocks*
		F Linear Trend	*F Quadratic Trend*	*F Cubic Trend*	
Similarity of patient style of expression to that of the therapist	.48	7.89‡	1.20	.85	2.84‡
Patient learning of discriminations	.47	3.10	.79	1.05	2.94‡
Patient insight	.46	4.73†	1.70	0.75	2.73‡
Patient ambiguity	—.38	3.04	1.50	0.91	1.35
Problem orientation	.35	3.28*	1.61	2.10	1.76†
Catharsis	*ns*	6.10†	2.13	1.20	2.03†
Blocking	*ns*	1.50	6.01*	1.50	1.29
Anxiety	*ns*	2.00	0.98	1.70	0.93
Patient negative-feeling expression	*ns*	1.17	0.65	0.89	0.75

*$p \leq .07$ for 1/39 *df* for trend.
†$p \leq .05$ for 1/39 *df* for trend or for 38 *df* for *t*.
‡$p \leq .01$ for 1/39 *df* for trend or for 38 *df* for *t*.

Of the classes of patient behavior to which the therapist selectively responded (i.e., reinforced), four out of five showed changes in patient behavior over time-in-therapy. Thus the data agree with the predictions in seven out of the nine classes of patient behaviors (78 per cent correct prediction).

Considering the probability that the therapist also used other types of rewards or reinforcers and also rewarded other related patient behavior classes, considering the unknown differential complexity levels of the patient response classes, and considering the crudity of measurement, the findings strongly suggest that important reinforcement effects do indeed occur even in client-centered therapy.

TOWARD EVALUATING THE VALIDITY OF THE FINDINGS

There are, of course, some difficulties in interpreting the intercorrelation matrix. One might argue that these are simply interrelationships in the "heads" of the raters, as the raters might have known what the "X" value was when they rated a sample on "Y." However, each of the 12 variables was rated separately and they were rated in different orders. One would think it difficult to recall the X value of a given unit when the rating of the other units intervened between the X value and its corresponding Y value (an average of 240 ratings intervening between corresponding X and Y values). It could be argued that some of this bias is removed by the procedure for averaging the five different raters, since the raters were unaware of the actual hypothesis under study.

Beyond the above considerations, tabulation of one well-known characteristic of the therapist's behavior also suggests selective differential responding. The use of "Uh huh" or "Mmm mmm" verbalizations has become, perhaps unfortunately, the hallmark of Rogerian psychotherapy. In the samples used in the present analysis, Mmm mmm's or Uh huh's occurred 23 times in a total of 12 of the 40 samples (in 30 per cent of the samples). The Mmm mmm occurred in 9 of the 12 samples (75 per cent of its occurrence) during high expression of negative feeling by the patient (all above the mean of ratings), while 0 per cent occurred during low "patient negative feeling expression." In the remaining three samples, they occurred during the patient's direct restatement of what the therapist had just said. This tabulation alone suggests conscious or unconscious selective responding by the therapist, and is consistent with the obtained findings based upon relationships between rated therapist and patient classes of behavior.[4]

Finally, and most importantly, the obtained data dealing with changes in patient-in-therapy behavior were consistent with the obtained findings based upon prediction from a reinforcement view. Since the raters had no knowledge of whether a given sample came from early- or late-in-therapy, those findings of a tendency for significant linear increases to occur over time in reinforced patient behaviors and not to occur in nonreinforced patient behaviors, would also argue strongly against the notion that the obtained intercorrelations were simply "in the heads" of the raters.

Implications

The present findings point to the presence of significant differential reinforcement effects imbedded in the transactions of client-centered psychotherapy. Since differential reinforcement is one of the procedures used in operant research to alter (or control) behavior, the

[4]It should be noted that the therapist's use of the "Uh huh reinforcer" is relatively ineffective since there is no increase over time in "patient negative feeling expression."

findings suggest that the therapist, in this case Rogers, implicitly alters (or controls) the patient's behavior in the therapeutic setting. To this extent, then, the evidence weighs in favor of the view proposed by Skinner rather than that of Rogers. The present findings are not consistent with Rogers' view that relatively *uniform conditions* which are globally "facilitative of personal growth and integration," are offered to patients in a manner not contingent upon the patient's behavior.

The present data, by demonstrating the role of empathy and warmth as positive reinforcers, suggest that the available evidence relating levels of these therapeutic conditions to patient outcome in therapy does not argue against a reinforcement interpretation of psychotherapy. On the contrary, the finding that empathy and warmth act as reinforcers suggests that the evidence relating empathy and warmth to patient outcome is open to a behavioristic interpretation, based in part on the therapist's use of differential reinforcement.

Recent studies have suggested that such humanistic qualities as empathy and warmth are antecedents to patient personality or behavioral change. In attempting to understand *how* such therapist qualities operate in producing therapeutic change, the present data suggest the potential value of studies utilizing behavioristic models. Since the available evidence relating empathy and warmth to patient outcome deals primarily with differences in *intensity levels* contaminated by differences in *rates* between therapists, it seems likely that additional and more precise understanding of the role of empathy (and hence more effective practice) might grow out of studies carried out from a reinforcement frame of reference. Considering only empathy as the type of reinforcer used in psychotherapy, it would be expected that successful and nonsuccessful therapists might differ in: (a) the particular patient behaviors chosen for differential reinforcement (say, self-concept statements versus historical-genetic statements); (b) the differential rate of reinforcement (say, 25 per cent versus 75 per cent for a specific class of patient behavior); (c) the intensity levels of the reinforcer used (say, the depth of empathy); and even the (d) scheduling of reinforcement (say, fixed ratio versus variable ratio).

Research aimed at identifying which patient behaviors, if reinforced at what intensity levels, etc., lead to positive therapeutic outcomes would provide more specific knowledge of how such positive human qualities as empathy and warmth operate to produce personality or behavioral change in the patient.

Such an approach aims toward more specific knowledge, but not at all toward more mechanical therapy. As the communication of any "reinforcing machine" qualities would by definition mean a low level of empathy and warmth, the present viewpoint is in full agreement with Schonbar's (1964) statement that "as a therapist I am no more a 'reinforcing machine' than my patient is a 'talking pigeon.' "

References

Bandura, A. "Psychotherapy as a Learning Process." *Psychological Bulletin,* 1961, *58,* 143–59.

Barrett-Lennard, G. T. "Dimensions of Therapist Response as Causal Factors in Therapeutic Change." *Psychological Monographs,* 1962, *76* (43, Whole No. 562).

Bergin, A. E., & Solomon, Sandra. "Personality and Performance Correlates of Empathic Understanding in Psychotherapy." Paper read at American Psychological Association, Philadelphia, September, 1963.

Cartwright, Rosalind D., & Lerner, Barbara. "Empathy: Need To Change and Improvement with Psychotherapy." *Journal of Consulting Psychology,* 1963, *27,* 138–44.

Dickenson, W. A., & Truax, C. B. "Group Counseling with College Underachievers: Comparisons with a Control Group and Relationship to Empathy, Warmth, and Genuineness." University of Kentucky and Kentucky Mental Health Institute, 1965.

Dymond, Rosalind. "A Scale for the Measurement of Empathic Ability." *Journal of Consulting Psychology,* 1949, *13,* 127–33.

Ebel, R. L. "Estimation of the Reliability of Ratings." *Psychometrika,* 1951, *16,* 407–24.

Eysenck, H. J. "The Effects of Psychotherapy: An Evaluation." *Journal of Consulting Psychology,* 1952, *16,* 319–24.

Eysenck, H. J. "The Effects of Psychotherapy." In H. J. Eysenck (ed.), *Handbook of Abnormal Psychology.* New York: Basic Books, 1960. Pp. 697–725.

Grant, David A. "Analysis of Variance Tests in the Analysis and Comparison of Curves." *Psychological Bulletin,* 1956, *53,* 141–54.

Halkides, Galatia. "An Investigation of Therapeutic Success as a Function of Four Variables." Unpublished doctoral dissertation, University of Chicago, 1958.

Hobbs, N. "Source of Gain in Psychotherapy." *American Psychologist,* 1962, *17,* 741–47.

Jourard, S. "I–thou Relationship Versus Manipulation in Counseling and Psychotherapy." *Journal of Individual Psychology,* 1959, *15,* 174–79.

Krasner, L. "The Therapist as a Social Reinforcement Machine." In H. H. Strupp & L. Luborsky (eds.), *Research in Psychotherapy.* Vol. II Washington, D. C.: American Psychological Association, 1962.

Lesser, W. M. "The Relationship Between Counseling Progress and Empathic Understanding." *Journal of Counseling Psychology,* 1961, *8,* 330–36.

Rogers, C. R. *Client Centered Therapy.* Cambridge, Mass.: Riverside Press, 1951. Pp. 73–74.

Rogers, C. R. "The Necessary and Sufficient Conditions of Therapeutic Personality Change." *Journal of Consulting Psychology,* 1957, *21,* 95–103.

Rogers, C. R. *On Becoming a Person.* Cambridge, Mass.: Riverside Press, 1961.

Rogers, C. R. "The Interpersonal Relationship: The Core of Guidance." *Harvard Educational Review,* 1962, *32,* 416–29.

Rogers, C. R., Kiesler, D., Gendlin, E. T., & Truax, C. B. *The Therapeutic Relationship and Its Impact: A Study of Psychotherapy with Schizophrenics.* Madison: University of Wisconsin Press, 1967.

Rogers, C. R., & Skinner, B. F. "Some Issues Concerning the Control of Human Behavior." *Science,* 1956, *124,* 1057–66.

Rogers, C. R., & Truax, C. B. "The Therapeutic Conditions Antecedent to Change: A Theoretical View." Chapter in *The Therapeutic Relationship and Its Impact: A Study of Psychotherapy with Schizophrenics.* University of Wisconsin Press, 1967.

Schonbar, Rosalea Ann. "A Practitioner's Critique of Psychotherapy Research." Paper read at American Psychological Association, Los Angeles, September, 1964.

Strupp, H. H. "Nature of Psychotherapists' Contribution to the Treatment Process." *Archives of General Psychiatry,* 1960, *3,* 219–31.

Truax, C. B. "Clinical Implementation of Therapeutic Conditions." In Carl R. Rogers (Chm.), *Therapeutic and Research Progress in a Program of Psychotherapy Research with Hospitalized Schizophrenics.* Symposium presented at the American Psychological Association, New York, September 1961, (a)

Truax, C. B. "The Process of Group Psychotherapy." *Psychological Monographs,* 1961, *75*(7, Whole No. 511). (b)

Truax, C. B. "Effective Ingredients in Psychotherapy: An Approach to Unraveling the Patient-Therapist Interaction." *Journal of Counseling Psychology,* 1963, *10,* 256–63.

Truax, C. B., & Carkhuff, R. R. "For Better or for Worse: The Process of Psychotherapeutic Personality Change." Chapter in, *Recent Advances in the Study of Behavioral Change.* Montreal: McGill University Press, 1963. Pp. 118–63.

Truax, C. B., & Carkhuff, R. R. "Significant Developments in Psychotherapy Research." In Abt & Riess (eds.), *Progress in Clinical Psychology.* New York: Grune & Stratton, 1964. Pp. 124–55.

Truax, C. B., Carkhuff, R. R., & Kodman, F., Jr. "Relationships Between Therapist-Offered Conditions and Patient Change in Group Psychotherapy." *Journal of Clinical Psychology,* in press.

Truax, C. B., Wargo, D. G., & Silber, L. D. *Effects of High Conditions Group Psychotherapy with Female Juvenile Delinquents.* University of Kentucky and Kentucky Mental Health Institute, 1965.

Wargo, D. G. "The Barron Ego Strength and LH4 Scales as Predictors and Indicators of Change in Psychotherapy." *Brief Research Reports,* 1962, *21.* (University of Wisconsin, Wisconsin Psychiatric Institute.)

Whitehorn, J. C., & Betz, Barbara J. "A Study of Psychotherapeutic Relationships Between Physicians and Schizophrenic Patients." *American Journal of Psychiatry,* 1954, *3,* 321–31.

Wolfe, J. *Psychotherapy by Reciprocal Inhibition.* Stanford: Stanford University Press, 1958.

*

COUNSELOR HOLDING POWER: CLINICAL vs. CLIENT-CENTERED

ALBERT H. KRUEGER

The following study was conducted at Arizona State University during the 1963–64 school year NDEA Guidance and Counseling Institute. The time of the study is limited to the last 12 weeks of the Institute program during which the trainees were engaged in a supervised counseling practicum experience. The 28 men and 2 women enrollees from 17 different states ranged in age from 23 to 37, all were married, and all had been teaching and/or counseling in secondary school during the previous year.

This study investigated the relationship between counseling method and counselee "drop out." It was hoped this study would contribute some new evidence to the old issue between clinical and client-centered counselors as to whether counselees are more faithful in keeping their appointments with a "clinically" oriented counselor than with a "client-centered" oriented counselor.

Methods and Procedures

During the last 12 weeks of the Institute, for counseling practicum purposes, the enrollees were split into six separate groups of five each with a different practicum supervisor. Three of the supervisors held doctor's degrees in guidance and counseling from different universities and three were graduate students completing their doctorate work in guidance and counseling at Arizona State University.

It was known in advance of this study that the theoretical orienta-

*This article is reprinted from *Personnel and Guidance Journal,* 1965, *43,* 981–84, by permission of the publisher, the American Personnel and Guidance Association, and the author.

tion of the supervisors differed, markedly in some respects. Five of the supervisors were on the client-centered side of the continuum, two of them being markedly so. The client-centered supervisors had their enrollees follow a relatively unstructured pattern. They were advised to follow the counselee's lead, to be nondirective, to use reflection and simple acceptance as the standard approach. The degree to which a client-centered technique was followed varied with the particular practicum supervisor.

The sixth supervisor adopted for purposes of this study a highly clinical, carefully structured approach. He insisted that the five enrollees under his supervision employ the following pattern: (1) At the first meeting with the counselee, the enrollee was to get acquainted with the counselee, establish rapport, and conduct a highly structured fact-finding interview seeking data which might prove helpful in subsequent educational and occupational decision-making processes. (2) The second session was devoted to interpretation of data in the school cumulative record and discussion of possible implications of these data for occupational-educational decision-making. (3) The third session was spent in consideration of one or two occupations that arose as likely possibilities as a result of the first two sessions. (4) The final session was devoted to consideration of institutions having programs for preparation in the occupation or occupations that were considered in the previous session. In addition, such things as scholarship assistance, loans, and other means of financial aid were considered. This pattern was used as a base by the counselor around which he could safely function and from which he could stray whenever the counselee indicated that he would like to deviate from the established pattern. The counselee was aware, however, that at all times he could return to the secure, highly structured home base of occupational-educational decision-making if and when he so desired.

The counseling practicum ran for a period of 12 weeks with four sessions a week. The counselees were recruited from a local high school, the majority coming from the sophomore, junior, and senior classes. Each counselee was scheduled for one hour per week until such time as he indicated that he would not return on the following week or until such time as he failed to meet his appointment. If he failed to return without notifying the counselor, he was considered a dropout and a new counselee was scheduled to replace him on the following week. It is with this dropout aspect of the 12-week counseling practicum that this study is primarily concerned.

Following the final week of the practicum experience, the 30 enrollees were asked to complete a questionnaire which was distributed to them in one of their classes. The questionnaire contained the following seven items to be completed:

1. Name of your practicum supervisor.__________________
2. Your supervisor's primary orientation in terms of counseling theory. (Check one)
   a. Clinical (Williamson)
   b. Client-centered (Rogerian)
3. Pattern of counseling recommended by your supervisor. (Check one)
   a. Structured
   b. Unstructured
4. Emphasis in your counseling sessions was placed on—(Check one)
   a. Educational-occupational problems
   b. Social-emotional problems
5. Give the total number of counselees that you worked with in the counseling practicum.__________________
6. Give the number of actual counseling contact hours that you had with counselees during the practicum.__________________
7. How many "dropouts" did you personally have among your counselees.__________________

The enrollees were given adequate time to complete carefully each of the items on the questionnaire and any questions which they had were carefully and completely answered. The idea of the continuum from "client centered" to "clinical" was stressed to them in regard to their responses to items No. 2, 3, and 4 in the questionnaire. It was felt that the responses to this questionnaire were as honest and sincere and probably as accurate as are ever received on a questionnaire study.

Findings

In general, the results of the questionnaire followed a rather definite pattern, the pattern of dropouts correlating highly with the counseling theory and technique employed by the enrollees.

A glance at Table 1 indicates quite clearly that the more client-centered and non-structured the counseling approach, the greater the number of dropouts. The number of dropouts incurred by the two groups of 10 enrollees who used an extreme client-centered, non-structured approach (supervisors No. 1 and No. 2) totaled more than the number incurred by the 20 enrollees in all of the other groups combined. It should be indicated, in all fairness to supervisor No. 6, that the one dropout included in the table did not really constitute a legitimate dropout since this individual called on the following day indicating that he had completely forgotten about his scheduled session and that he would appear to make up the missed session on the following week, which he did. So the dropout pattern may be even more pronounced than the table indicates with eight at the one extreme of the client-centered unstructured continuum and none at the other extreme of the clinical, highly structured end of the continuum.

TABLE 1
QUESTIONNAIRE RESULTS

Supervisor	*Clinical*	*Client-Centered*	*Structured*	*Unstructured*	*Educ.-Occup.*	*Social-Emotion.*	*No. of Counselees*	*Total No. of Counseling Hours*	*No. of dropouts*
1	...	5	...	5	1	4	14	41	8
2	...	5	...	5	1	4	13	46	5
3	1	4	1	4	1	4	12	40	4
4	1	4	1	4	1	4	10	52	1
5	2	3	...	5	3	2	11	44	4
6	5	...	5	...	5	...	15	56	1

Only the results of supervisor No. 5 disrupt the pattern. It should be noted from the table, however, that his five enrollees visualized him as "eclectic" in light of their responses to the "clinical, client-centered" and "Educational-Occupational, Social-Emotional" questions and yet they all felt that they were to follow an unstructured counseling approach. This apparent contradiction may have been due to a misunderstanding on the part of the enrollees. This misunderstanding and the partial feeling of uncertainty it might have created, might have been conveyed to the counselees, four of whom responded by dropping out. From the data on the table, this could appear to be a reasonable explanation.

Finally the data on the table under "Number of Counselees" and "Total Number of Counseling Hours" indicate that the group employing the highly structured, clinical approach not only saw a greater number of counselees during the practicum experience, but also experienced a greater number of counseling hours.

Implications

The results show quite clearly that there is a relationship between the incidence of counselee "no show" or dropout and the technique employed by the counselor. This finding would seem to suggest that with the average, normal, healthy, high school student a structured, clinical counseling approach is indicated if the counseling program is to be sensible and practical. The data imply that the counselor in secondary schools using a structured, clinical approach will see more students and will be able to spend a greater number of counseling hours with his students than will the client-centered counselor. He will be able to use his time more effectively in counseling since his program will be uninterrupted by troublesome dropouts who have been scheduled to appear for counseling but who for one reason or another fail to show.

An additional disadvantage of employing an extreme client-centered approach in secondary school counseling, not revealed by the findings above, is that it may create poor public relations with the high school student body and consequently with the parents and community, and thus discredit the whole guidance and counseling program. One actual instance will serve to illustrate this point. One of the counselees who met with an enrollee using an extreme client-centered approach indicated quite clearly why she had volunteered to participate in this counseling practicum and pointed out quite concretely what she expected to receive from it. This particular counselee requested specific help on college scholarship information. The counselor refused to supply this information but rather accepted and reflected for a period of 50 minutes. The counselee returned for a second session the following week. She again indicated her needs, the counselor again reflected and accepted. This continued for 15 minutes, after which time the counselee arose and said, "This is a complete waste of my time. I am getting nothing out of this," and she stomped out of the room in a huff and never returned. It is easy to imagine what her thoughts concerning counseling and the counseling profession must be. It is frightening to imagine what she will convey concerning counseling to her parents, to her fellow-students, and to other members of the community.

It would seem from this study that a most effective, most useful, most sensible approach to counseling in secondary schools is still the clinical, somewhat structured approach. It would seem also that although the highly client-centered, unstructured approach might do some good for some secondary school students, it will result also in counseling for a fewer number of students, in fewer number of actual counseling hours by the counselors, and in greater disruption of the counseling program as a result of dropouts on the counseling schedule. This, in addition to the possibility that it might create havoc in the public relations aspect of the counseling program, since it may lead students, faculty, administration, parents, and community to question the worthwhileness of a counseling program that, at least in their minds, accomplishes nothing, would lead one to believe that wholesale adoption of the client-centered approach could be harmful and possibly disastrous to the secondary school counseling profession.

*

THE EFFECTS OF INTERVIEWER STYLE IN A STANDARDIZED INTERVIEW[1]

KENNETH HELLER[2]

JOHN D. DAVIS

ROGER A. MYERS

There is reason to believe that interpersonal behavior can be represented, in large part, by the dimensions of control (activity-passivity) and affect (friendliness-hostility) (Adams, 1962; Borgatta, Cottrell, and Mann, 1958; Chance, Arnold, and Tyrrel, 1962; Foa, 1961; Leary, 1957; Shaefer, Bell, and Bayley, 1959). These variables, chosen for investigation in the present study, have also been considered as basic to the therapeutic endeavor. Early descriptions of therapy emphasized therapist passivity as a method of providing an unstructured atmosphere so that transference effects could be maximized. However, more recent evidence based on a small number of cases (Lennard and Berstein, 1960) suggests that therapist passivity is associated with decreased patient satisfaction as is evidenced by discontinuance of treatment, broken appointments, and patient complaints. Similarly, almost all descriptions of positive therapist personality characteristics emphasize "warmth" or friendliness. It has

---

*This article is reprinted from *Journal of Consulting Psychology,* 1966, *30,* 501–8, by permission of the publisher, the American Psychological Association, and the authors.

[1]This study was supported by Grant MH-07679-01 from the National Institute of Mental Health, United States Public Health Service, to the principal author. The results of the research have been reported in part at the 1963 American Psychological Association meetings in Philadelphia.

[2]The authors wish to thank Joel R. Davitz, Sanford J. Dean, Arnold P. Goldstein, and Sherman L. Guth for their helpful comments on this paper.

become almost axiomatic to describe good therapists by words such as: showing unconditional positive regard, tolerance, kindness, warmth, friendliness, etc. (Krasner, 1963). At the same time, hostility, disapproval, and open sarcasm are usually considered to have no place in the clinical consulting room, and if present, are a possible indication that the therapist himself is in need of treatment. When faced with a possible growing dislike of a particular aspect of his client's behavior, a therapist has the choice of referring his client elsewhere, analyzing his own motives and behavior, or openly discussing with his client the possible reasons for his dissatisfaction. Although research evidence is lacking concerning the desirability of each of these alternatives, therapists are being asked to consider the last choice with increasing frequency. For example, Rogers (1961), certainly an advocate of therapist friendliness (unconditional positive regard), has now moved to the position of stating:

> In my relationships with persons I have found that it does not help, in the long run, to act as though I were something that I am not. It does not help to act calm and pleasant when actually I am angry and critical (p. 16).

The purpose of this experiment was to examine the interaction of interviewer affect and activity level in a laboratory interview in which the behavior of the interviewer could be standardized and controlled.

Method

PREINTERVIEW PROCEDURE

Before entering the interview, 120 introductory psychology students, 69 males and 51 females, took a battery of personality tests and listened to a tape recording of a male college student seeking help for an unsolved problem, narrated in the first person. The purpose of the tape was to facilitate the subject's task of talking about himself while at the same time providing some indication of the type of material expected during the interview.

Before listening to the taped narrative and participating in the 15-minute interview, subjects were given the following instructions:

> The Psychology Department is interested in finding out how a client feels immediately after counseling and how different kinds of people would evaluate the counseling situation. Since it is very diffi-

cult to gain this information during counseling or to contact clients after counseling, you are asked to participate in a model counseling session. You will listen to a short taped example of a person talking about himself to give you information to discuss and to show what people might say in counseling. You will then be asked to talk to an interviewer for 15 minutes.

1. As a starter, for the *first five minutes* you should remember and report as much about the tape as you can.
2. For the *next five minutes* you should discuss how you would solve the situation on the tape.
3. For the *last five minutes* you should talk about yourself—about how you seem different from or like the person on the tape. Last and most important you will be asked to give your honest evaluation of the counseling situation and what went on there.

INDEPENDENT VARIABLES

Each interview immediately followed the subject's hearing of the taped narrative. The experimenter who had presented the preinterview materials led the subject to an adjacent room and introduced him to the interviewer. Interviewer roles were devised within the control and affect dimensions and graduate students in speech and theater were trained as interviewers. The general outline of these roles is described as follows.

Active-Friendly Interviewer (AF).—This interviewer led the interview by encouraging verbalization but did not direct the content of the discussion.[3] He was sympathetic, friendly, and considerate of the interviewee. He was supportive and helpful. He spoke often, tended to be verbose, and used nonverbal signs of approval.

Passive-Friendly Interviewer (PF).—This interviewer allowed the interviewee to lead the interview. He was agreeable, friendly, and interested. He was laconic, but agreed readily when he did speak. He used nonverbal signs of approval.

Active-Hostile Interviewer (AH).—This interviewer led the interview by requesting verbalization but did not direct the content of the discussion. Although not in extreme form, he showed disdain, disapproval, and lack of appreciation for the interviewee's approach to the task. He spoke often, tended to be verbose and used nonverbal signs of disapproval.

Passive-Hostile Interviewer (PH).—This interviewer allowed the interviewee to lead the interview. He was aloof and showed lack of interest. He was laconic, but voiced skepticism or disapproval when

---

[3]Unlike the typical verbal conditioning experiment, interviewers in all conditions were instructed not to reinforce specific verbal content.

he spoke. He used nonverbal signs of disapproval.

Silent Interviewer (*Sil.*).—This interviewer did not speak or communicate at any time either verbally or nonverbally. He attempted to maintain a neutral appearance, neither approving nor disapproving. Since this condition was so unlike normal social interaction, the subject was told before entering the interview that his interviewer would not speak or communicate with him in any way.

Twelve male interviewers, three per condition, were trained in each of the first four conditions, and each saw eight subjects in his condition. Originally, it had been planned that each interviewer would play all of the first four roles. However, a pilot study revealed that while an interviewer had no trouble playing the role which most closely matched his typical interpersonal style, he could not do as well and felt uncomfortable in other roles. Hence it was decided to train each interviewer for only one role, but to train several interviewers (three) for each role.

The fifth condition, silence, was not added until the experiment had started and new interviewers were not available. So it was decided to obtain pilot data concerning interviewer silence by having each of the 12 interviewers run two or more subjects in the silent conditions, after running his first eight subjects. This modification did not permit the inclusion of data from the silent condition in the nested-factor analyses (Winer, 1962) appropriate to the basic experimental design, but data for the silent group was included in subsequent analyses reported in Table 5.

DEPENDENT VARIABLES

Interview Reaction Checklist.—After completing the experimental interview, each subject was asked to complete an inventory stating his reaction to the interview, to his performance in the interview, and to the interviewer. This questionnaire was composed of 60 items scored in either a positive or negative direction. For 30 statements, agreement indicated a positive attitude, and for 30 statements a negative attitude.

Speaking Time.—For each minute of the interview, the time used by the subject for speaking was computed. Since the duration and frequency of interviewer remarks was not constant across conditions or even between time segments of a single interview, care was taken to insure that the speaking time measure was not confounded by differential interviewer speaking time. For this reason, the final speaking time score for each subject represented the subject's speaking time divided by the time available for the subject to speak.

Content Categories.—A content analysis was performed on the last five minutes of each interview which represented the portion of the interview in which the subject was asked to describe himself in terms of similarities with and differences from the tape narrator. The tape script was designed to cover many content areas, providing the subject freedom to choose some area in which he could identify with the tape narrator. However, there were two key problem areas on the tape, namely, family relations and sexual experiences. The tape narrator spoke about these problems at great length, indicating that they represented areas of continued and unresolved conflict for him. The selection of these particular content areas was motivated by the assumption that they would represent more difficult and anxiety arousing topics for the subjects. The following content scores were computed.

1. *Proportion of family words.* All words used in sentences descriptive of a family member or the subject's relationship with a family member were counted. To reduce possible bias which might result from individual differences in verbosity, a final score for each subject was computed by dividing family words by total number of words used during the last 5 minutes of the interview.
2. *Proportion of sex words.* All words used in sentences describing sex or a sexual relationship between the subject and another individual were counted. Words indicating a social, but not sexual, relationship were not included. The final score for each subject represented the number of sex words divided by the total number of words for the last 5 minutes of the interview.
3. *Proportion of problem words.* All words used in sentences which described a difficulty in living that the subject admitted was occurring in the present or had occurred in the past were counted. The final score for each subject represented the number of problem words divided by the total number of words for the last five minutes of the interview.

SUBJECT PERSONALITY SCORES

Before participating in the interview, each subject completed a battery of personality tests consisting of the Minnesota Multiphasic Personality Inventory (MMPI), Leary Interpersonal Checklist, and Mooney Problem Checklist. Product-moment correlation coefficients between subscales of these inventories and the dependent variables listed above were obtained for each experimental condition separately. In addition, a *pathology admission* score was computed for each subject. This score was the sum of the *T*-score values for the *F*, *Hs*, *D*, *Pd*, *Pa*, *Pt*, *Sc*, and *Si* subscales of the MMPI. For each condition, the ten subjects with the highest summed *T* score and the ten with the lowest summed *T* score were classified as high- or low-pathology admitters, respectively.

Results

INTERVIEWER CONSISTENCY

Since the interviewers could not be given scripts, it was important to know if they were able to maintain their role assignments through the experiment. In order to sample interviewer behavior, two master tapes were constructed each consisting of 12 randomly selected interviews. The 24 interviews were chosen so that each interviewer would be represented twice, with 1 interview from his first four and 1 from his last four subjects. The tapes were edited to exclude subject verbalization and only included interviewer remarks in sequence and without pauses for subject verbalization.

In order to judge the friendliness-hostility of the interviewers, the master tapes were given to two groups of judges each of which rated a different tape. In each group, the four judges, who did not know the nature of the study or that the interviewers were actors, were asked to rate each interviewer on a 9-point friendliness-hostility scale. The mean rated hostility for interviewers in the four responding conditions is presented in Table 1. With a rating of 1 representing the greatest friendliness and 9 greatest hostility, inspection of

TABLE 1

Mean Speaking Time and Rated Hostility for Interviewer Reliability

	AF	*AH*	*PF*	*PH*
Interviewer hostility (9-point rating scale)	1.66	7.75	3.58	5.21
Interviewer talk time (in seconds)	301.8	301.2	116.4	53.4

Note.—Hostility ratings are based on 6 interviews per condition, talk time means on 24 interviews per condition.

Table 1 reveals that for the active conditions, the impact of interviewer affect is clear. The distributions of friendly-hostile judgments were nonoverlapping in that no active-friendly interviewer was judged hostile and no active-hostile interviewer was judged friendly. However, for the passive conditions, affect rated from the master tapes was more ambiguous. The mean rating of passive-friendly interviewers was mildly friendly, but the mean rating was neutral for passive-hostile interviewers. Overlap in the distributions of judgments for the passive conditions was considerable. Thus the degree of affect of the passive interviewers could not be distinguished on the master tapes. However, this was not a completely unexpected finding and may not be a fair representation of the affect displayed by passive interviewers in the interview itself. Since these interviewers were laconic by definition, in order to convey affect they used largely nonverbal means which were not picked up on the tape (e,g., smiling or frowning, looking toward or away from the subject, acting interested, acting bored, etc.).

The appropriateness of interviewer activity-passivity was more simply assessed by using interviewer talk time as an index of interviewer activity level. Data on this variable were obtained for all interviews in the four responding conditions, and the means for each condition are also reported in Table 1. In keeping with the role definitions, interviewers talked longer in the active than in the passive conditions ($p < .01$). Interviewer friendliness-hostility did not affect interviewer talk time. However, there was a significant effect for interviewers nested within conditions ($p < .01$). Breakdown of this source of variance into its components showed the effect to be due entirely to interviewer differences within the active conditions. Interviewers differed in their activity levels within each of the active conditions, whereas the activity levels of passive interviewers were essentially equal.

DEPENDENT VARIABLES

Tables 2 and 3 represent summary tables for the means and analyses of variance, respectively. Analyses for nested factors (Winer, 1962) were performed for the four responding conditions since each interviewer was represented in only one responding condition.

TABLE 2

MEAN SCORES FOR CONDITIONS AND FOR PATHOLOGY ADMISSION ACROSS CONDITIONS

	Reaction Checklist	*Speaking Time*	*Sex Words*	*Family Words*	*Problem Words*
AF	31.75	9.91	.205	1.08	.694
AH	—0.87	9.93	.744	.81	.701
PF	16.29	9.20	.539	.67	.866
PH	—5.0	8.40	.802	1.10	.691
Sil.	4.36	8.02	.954	1.36	.827
High-pathology admission	2.12	8.70	.667	1.00	.845
Low-pathology admission	16.66	9.36	.572	1.00	.676

TABLE 3

SUMMARY TABLE FOR NESTED ANALYSES FOR THE DEPENDENT VARIABLES IN THE RESPONDING CONDITIONS

		Reaction Checklist		*Speaking Time*		*Sex Words*		*Family Words*		*Problem Words*	
	df	*MS*	*F*	*MS*	*F*	*MS*	*F*	*MS*	*F*	*MS*	*F*
Activity	1	2,301.04	3.42	27.57	9.69†	0.90	1.568	0.10	0.70	0.15	1.43
Friendliness	1	17,442.04	25.96†	4.25	1.49	3.78	6.57*	0.13	0.93	0.16	1.53
Activity × Friendliness	1	770.67	1.15	3.69	1.30	0.45	0.78	2.87	20.49†	0.19	1.86
Interviewers (within conditions)	8	617.73	0.92	3.72	1.31	1.57	2.73*	0.35	2.51*	0.05	0.43
Error	84	671.74		2.85		0.58		0.14		0.10	

* $p < .05$.
† $p < .01$.

Interview Reaction Checklist.—From Tables 2 and 3 it can be seen that subjects preferred friendly interviewers ($p < .01$). Active-friendly interviewers were best liked, while passive-hostile interviewers were least liked. There were no significant effects for interviewers within treatments. The mean preference scores for the silent group are between those of the hostile and friendly groups.

Speaking Time.—The proportions of subject speaking time to time available for each of the last five minutes of the interview were converted to arcsin equivalents and summed. These sums, reported in Table 2, reveal that subjects in the active conditions used the time available for speaking more than those in the passive conditions ($p < .01$). Subject talk time is lowest under interviewer silence. The speaking time variable produced no significant effects for interviewers within treatments.

Content Categories.—Inspection of Table 2 for the proportion of sex, family, and problem words used by subjects in the last five minutes of the interview, reported in arcsin equivalents, reveals that subjects in the hostile conditions used the greatest proportion of sex words ($p < .05$) while subjects in the active-friendly and passive-hostile conditions used the greatest proportion of family words ($p < .01$). However, interpretation of these effects must be guarded since considerable interviewer-within-treatment variance is also found for these variables. For both content variables the highest mean proportions occurred in the silent condition. No significant condition effects were found for the content variable dealing with the proportion of problem words.

PATHOLOGY ADMISSION

The matrices of correlations between personality inventory subscales and dependent variables, while suggestive for further research,[4] did not furnish sufficiently systematic results to justify discussion here. However, the most consistent effects are reflected in the analyses of pathology admission. Means for the ten highest and ten lowest pathology admitters within each condition were computed and are reported in Table 4. A condition by pathology admission analysis, performed for each dependent variable, is reported in Table 5.

TABLE 4
MEAN SCORES FOR PATHOLOGY ADMISSION WITHIN CONDITIONS

Pathology Admission	*Reaction Checklist*		*Speaking Time*		*Sex Words*		*Family Words*		*Problem Words*	
	High	*Low*	*High*	*Low*	*High*	*Low*	*High*	*Low*	*High*	*Low*
Conditions										
AF	33.8	29.7	10.1	10.1	.227	.034	1.107	1.140	.759	.643
AH	—8.6	9.5	8.7	10.5	.986	.644	.872	.801	.737	.643
PF	10.6	24.6	8.6	9.3	.363	.464	.718	.592	.938	.822
PH	—21.1	8.4	7.9	9.7	.615	.764	.990	1.154	.761	.606
Sil.	—4.1	11.1	8.2	7.2	1.144	.955	1.339	1.326	1.031	.668

TABLE 5
SUMMARY TABLE OF ANALYSIS OF VARIANCE
FOR CONDITIONS AND PATHOLOGY EFFECTS

		Reaction Checklist		*Speaking Time*		*Sex Words*		*Family Words*		*Problem Words*	
	df	*MS*	*F*	*MS*	*F*	*MS*	*F*	*MS*	*F*	*MS*	*F*
Conditions	4	4,684.69	9.637†	16.18	8.91†	2.55	4.39†	1.39	7.26	0.18	1.70
Pathology	1	5,285.29	10.957†	10.81	5.96*	0.22	0.38	0.00	0.00	0.71	6.61*
Conditions × Pathology	4	730.82	1.515	7.13	3.93*	0.22	0.38	0.00	0.33	0.42	3.93†
Error	90	482.38		1.82		0.58		0.19		0.11	

*$p < .05$.
†$p < .01$.

[4]Tables of correlations between personality inventory subscales and dependent variables have been deposited with the American Documentation Institute. Order Document No. 9031 from ADI Auxiliary Publications Project, Photoduplication Service, Library of Congress, Washington, D. C. 20540. Remit in advance $1.25 for microfilm or $1.25 for photocopies and make checks payable to: Chief, Photoduplication Service, Library of Congress.

A significant pathology-admission effect for the Interview Reaction Checklist indicates that high-pathology admitters reported less liking for their interviewers than low-pathology admitters regardless of condition ($p < .01$). The most negative reaction to the interviewers occurred for high-pathology admitters in the passive-hostile condition.

For speaking time, a significant effect for pathology admission was also found, with high-pathology admitters speaking less than low-pathology admitters ($p < .05$). For this variable, the interaction between pathology admission and conditions was significant ($p < .01$). High-pathology admitters spoke least in the passive-hostile condition. Low-pathology admitters spoke longest under active-hostility and least under interviewer silence.

A significant pathology-admission effect was found for only one content category. High-pathology admitters in all conditions used more problem words in the last 5 minutes of the interview than did low-pathology admitters ($p < .05$). The interaction between pathology admission and conditions was also significant for this variable ($p < .01$). Problem words were used most often by high-pathology admitters in the silent and the passive-friendly conditions. While low-pathology admitters used almost as many problem words in the passive-friendly condition, they used markedly fewer than high-pathology admitters in the silent condition.

Discussion

Perhaps the most noteworthy point in the results of the present experiment was that the only clear advantage of interviewer friendliness was that this condition was overwhelmingly preferred by subjects. Despite this preference there was no indication that verbal behavior during the interview changed in any way as a result of friendliness. If anything, there was evidence that subjects may have felt more pressure to discuss some possibly threatening topics (sex) with hostile interviewers. However, these findings may be true only of indiscriminate approval or disapproval since interviewers in this experiment continued to present the same role behavior regardless of what subjects said. Indiscriminate approval by an interviewer may be an inefficient method of inducing behavior change, because it retards the learning of new responses by rewarding erroneous as well as appropriate behavior.

The results of this experiment are to some extent inconsistent with predictions derived from studies of verbal conditioning, since it might be expected that indiscriminate friendliness would act as a generalized reinforcer, increasing the general verbal response level of the subject. Thus, in a verbal conditioning experiment, Reece and Whitman (1962) found that experimenter "warmth" increased verbalization, but did not change the rate of emission of the reinforced class of behavior. However, it should be noted that the experimenter in the Reece and Whitman study was extremely passive. Except for reading the instructions and saying "Mm-hmm" upon the emission of plural nouns by the subject, the experimenter was silent. The Reece and Whitman "warm" and "cold" experimenter might bear some resemblance to our passive-friendly and passive-hostile interviewers, and indeed in the present study there was a trend within the passive conditions for friendliness to induce higher verbalization rates than hostility. However, in the present experiment when activity level was varied as well as friendliness, it became clear that it was not friendliness but activity level that produced the greatest increases in verbalization.

The finding that greater interviewer activity produced higher proportions of subject verbalization supports the extensive research of Matarazzo and his associates. Matarazzo, Wiens, and Saslow (1965), summarizing this line of work, note that patients will verbalize actively in the presence of an active interviewer, a finding at variance with many texts on interview or therapy technique and with the nonresponding, noninteracting model presented by Freud and the early writings of Rogers. The importance of interviewer activity in sustaining the verbalization rate of interviewees is also supported in a clinical study by Lennard and Bernstein (1960). These investigators report that therapy dyads show the least amount of system strain (e.g., discontinuance of treatment, broken appointments, and patient complaints) when therapists are more active. Lennard and Bernstein suggest that this effect is due to the greater amount of orienting information that active therapists provide. They suggest that while therapist passivity may have been justified in traditional analytic theory as necessary to increase projection and transference, it also has definite deleterious effects. Passivity increases situational ambiguity and provides few orientation cues. The patient, being less sure of what is expected of him, becomes increasingly anxious and dissatisfied. It may be that the lack of structure associated with traditional psychotherapies is at least partly responsible for premature termination during the early stages of therapy.

Pathology admission, defined in this experiment as the sum of the *T* scores on eight clinical scales of the MMPI, should in no way be considered as reflecting actual pathology. While there are undoubtedly disturbed individuals in a population of 120 "normal" college students, they are not necessarily identified by high scores on the clinical scales of the MMPI. With these cautions in mind, it is still instructive to review the performance of pathology admitters in this experiment. In general, it would appear that as compared to low-pathology admitters, high-pathology admitters were most disturbed by the passive-hostile condition. Their subjective reaction to this condition was extremely negative, and they spoke less about themselves in this condition than any other. A possible determinant of this finding may be that in the passive-hostile condition, orientation cues are minimal and imply the interviewer's negative evaluation, but unlike the active-hostile condition, the nature of the dissatisfaction is never clearly stated, so that corrective action by the subject is difficult to initiate.

Finally, this study warns against a common practice in free-responding verbal conditioning studies of using interviewer silence to determine the operant level of the response to be conditioned. In these studies, the assumption is made that silence is neutral and is equivalent to "no-treatment." The results of the present study suggest that in an interview, silence on the part of one participant is far from representing a neutral condition against which the natural state of the other person can be measured. In the present experiment, silence was most verbally inhibiting in the sense of producing least subject talk time. If interviewer silence also decreases verbalization rates during the operant period of the typical verbal conditioning experiment, the cue value of the reinforcing stimulus during the conditioning phase of the experiment will be excessively enhanced. A better procedure for determining operant levels would be any schedule of interviewer responding that is noncontingent with the class of subject response to be subsequently reinforced. The results of free-responding verbal conditioning experiments without such a more natural method of obtaining operant levels should be interpreted with caution.

In conclusion, several cautions should be emphasized lest the results of the present laboratory interviews are generalized too far. The interviews were only 15 minutes in duration, and replication is needed with longer interviews and for interviews that form a series and are not restricted to a single occurrence. Such confirmation can already be found for interviewer activity but not for friendliness-hostility. The generality of the findings to other interview situations must also be tested, but more important, the interaction of different interviewer roles within the same interview dyad needs to be investigated. Normal interpersonal interactions do not rely on one type of role behavior applied indiscriminately as in the present experiment, but usually involve a series of reciprocally contingent interactions. This means that while an interviewer's behavior is determined by his prior conception of his role, it is also a function of his responding to the behavior exhibited by the other interview participant (Heller, 1963; Heller, Myers, and Kline, 1963). It is the belief of the present writers that such reciprocally contingent interactions can also be studied in the experimental laboratory.

References

Adams, H. B. "Toward a Comprehensive Classification of Adaptive and Maladaptive Human Conduct." Paper read at American Psychological Association, St. Louis, 1962.

Borgatta, E. F., Cottrell, L. S., Jr., & Mann, J. M. "The Spectrum of Individual Interaction Characteristics: An Interdimensional Analysis." *Psychological Reports,* 1958, *4,* 279–319.

Chance, E., Arnold, J., & Tyrrell, S. "Communality and Stability of Meaning in Clinical Case Description." *Journal of Abnormal and Social Psychology,* 1962, *64,* 389–406.

Foa, U. G. "Convergencies in the Analysis of the Structure of Interpersonal Behavior." *Psychological Review,* 1961, *68,* 341–53.

Heller, K. "Experimental Analogues of Psychotherapy: The Clinical Relevance of Laboratory Findings of Social Influence." *Journal of Nervous and Mental Disease,* 1963, *137,* 420–26.

Heller, K., Meyers, R. A., & Kline, L. V. "Interviewer Behavior as a Function of Standardized Client Roles." *Journal of Consulting Psychology,* 1963, *27,* 117–22.

Krasner, L. "The Therapist as a Social Reinforcer: Man or Machine." Paper read at American Psychological Association, Philadelphia, 1963.

Leary, T. *Interpersonal Diagnosis of Personality.* New York: Ronald Press, 1957.

Lennard, H., & Bernstein, A. *The Anatomy of Psychotherapy.* New York: Columbia University Press, 1960.

Matarazzo, J. D., Wiens, A. N., & Saslow, G. "Studies in Interview Speech Behavior." In L. Krasner & L. P. Ullmann (eds.), *Research in Behavior Modification.* New York: Holt, Rinehart and Winston, 1965. Pp. 179–210.

Reece, M. M., & Whitman, R. N. "Expressive Movements, Warmth, and Verbal Reinforcement." *Journal of Abnormal and Social Psychology,* 1962, *64,* 234–36.

Rogers, C. R. *On Becoming a Person.* Boston: Houghton Mifflin, 1961.

Shaefer, E. S., Bell, R. Q., & Bayley, N. "Development of a Maternal Behavior Research Instrument." *Journal of Genetic Psychology,* 1959, *95,* 83–104.

Winer, J. *Statistical Principles in Experimental Design.* New York: McGraw-Hill, 1962.

*

EXPERIMENTAL MANIPULATION OF THERAPEUTIC CONDITIONS[1]

CHARLES B. TRUAX
ROBERT R. CARKHUFF[2]

The present experimental research effort was an attempt to examine directly the nature of some of the aspects of the therapist-offered stimulus complex which might make for the "something more" attributed to the therapeutic relationship. Specifically, the purpose was to attack the potentially causal relationship between the therapist's level of accurate empathy and unconditional positive warmth, which are seen as critical aspects of the therapist's contribution to the therapeutic relationship, and the consequent patient engagement in intrapersonal exploration, a critical aspect of patient behavior in therapy, during initial psychotherapeutic interview.

Method

After establishing a level of patient depth of intrapersonal exploration during the first 20 minutes of an initial psychotherapeutic interview where relatively high conditions were present, the therapist deliberately experimentally introduced lowered levels of accurate

*This article is reprinted from *Journal of Consulting Psychology,* 1965, *29,* 119–24, by permission of the publisher, the American Psychological Association, and the authors.

[1]The findings are part of an ongoing research program supported by a grant from the Vocational Rehabilitation Administration, Number 906-PM, Department of Health, Education, and Welfare.

[2]The authors wish to acknowledge the helpful suggestions and critical comments of David A. Grant and Edward J. Murray and the able assistance in data analyses of Edward P. Williams.

Carkhuff's work with the Psychotherapy Research Group, University of Kentucky, was supported by Public Health Fellowship Number 7 F2-MH-19, 912-02 from the National Institute of Mental Health, Public Health Service.

empathic understanding and unconditional positive regard which were maintained for a 20-minute period. Finally, this was followed by a 20-minute period where the normally high conditions were re-established. The test of the hypothesis was simply an evaluation of the levels of patient depth of intrapersonal exploration or process to determine whether or not the lowered conditions indeed produced lowered levels of process in the patient.

The experiment was replicated on three different hospitalized patients. Finally, the experimental operations were checked by determining the levels of therapist accurate empathy and therapist unconditional positive regard offered throughout each of the psychotherapeutic interviews.

Patient Population.—The patients were three recent admissions to Mendota State Hospital, Madison, Wisconsin, with a tentative diagnosis of schizophrenic reaction.

Patient A was a white female, age fifty-five, the mother of four grown children. She was married at age fourteen when her husband was age twenty-two. She entered the hospital on court order. The reason given for hospitalization was that the patient threatened recently to kill her husband and burn her neighbor's house down. She had refused to eat or work about the house and spoke incessantly of delusional material. Her initial diagnosis was schizophrenic reaction which later was changed to psychosis with epilepsy.

Patient B was a twenty-one-year-old female, unmarried. She entered the hospital as a voluntary admission who was markedly depressed. During her junior year of high school she became concerned about her face, feeling that it was ugly, and began to avoid people and develop somatic complaints. She had been admitted previously to the psychiatric hospital and had been seen intensively for psychotherapy for over a year. The final diagnosis was schizophrenic reaction, chronic undifferentiated type.

Patient C was a twenty-two-year-old female, unmarried. This was her ninth admission to the hospital since the age of seventeen. She entered the hospital severely depressed and suicidal. She had had a long history of emotional upset and had given birth to an illegitimate child. Final diagnosis was schizophrenic reaction, chronic undifferentiated type.

Interview.—Each patient was seen for a one-hour initial psychotherapeutic interview. The therapist presented himself as a person who was trying to offer "as much help as possible in the time we have together," and began the sessions by inquiring how it was that the patient happened to be in the hospital. Thus, during the first 17–20 minute period the therapist attempted to be a helpful therapeutic person.

As a cover story for the therapist's intentional lowering of conditions (and as a breaking point for research design purposes), another person knocked at the door and the therapist left the room, and, upon returning to the room, the therapist said in audible tones to the second person, "Well, let me know as soon as you find out."

The therapist, it should be emphasized, was not visibly upset at any time during the interview and his voice in relating to the second person carried a concerned but matter-of-fact, business-like tone. The implicit cover story was used so that if one of the patients sensed a noticeable drop in "conditions," then there would be the implicit explanation that the therapist might be preoccupied. The therapist then endeavored to offer lowered conditions of accurate empathy and unconditional positive regard during the next 17–20-minute period. Conditions were not dropped precipitously. Thus, the therapist was not grossly nonempathic nor did he at any time show negative regard toward the patient.

The therapist experimentally lowered the conditions of accurate empathy and unconditional positive warmth not by being phony and manipulative, but by simply selectively withholding the "best" empathic and warm responses that automatically arose in him during that part of the therapeutic encounter. Thus, for example, the therapist was not deliberately appearing to misunderstand the patient when in fact he did understand. Instead, he simply selectively held back some of his better tentative "guesses" of what the patient was feeling or experiencing. It should be emphasized that the therapist was still actively attempting to be helpful and that the experimentally introduced "lowered conditions" were only moderately lower than usual. In addition, it was felt that any strong "about face" in the therapist behavior would mar and distort the therapeutic relationship. Thus, the therapist attempted to maintain his integrity, the oftmentioned self-congruence element throughout the therapeutic encounter.

At the end of the second 17–20-minute period, there was a knock at the door and the therapist left the room. Upon re-entering the room the therapist said in audible tones, "Well, I'm relieved to hear that (as part of the implicit cover story)." The therapist then endeavored to provide the usual level of moderately high therapeutic conditions for the final 17–20-minute period.

Measurement.—Excluding the initial and terminal statements and the time spent leaving the room, there were roughly 3 15-minute periods in the initial interviews with each of the three patients. These time periods were divided each into 5 3-minute time periods. These 3-minute time periods were re-recorded onto separate individual small spools of tape, providing 15 3-minute samples from each case or a total of 45 samples.

The 45 samples were then randomly assigned code numbers and randomly arranged for presentation to trained naive, lay raters. The randomly coded segments meant that the raters did not know whether a given sample came from the early, middle, or late phases of therapy nor did they know whether the sample was from the time period in which the therapist was attempting to offer high or lowered conditions. A total of four raters who had been previously trained in the use of the Truax Depth of Intrapersonal Exploration Scale rated each of the 45 3-minute samples. Three different raters who had previously been trained in the use of the Truax Accurate Empathy Scale were also presented with the 45 samples for rating. Three still different raters who had previously been trained on the Truax Unconditional Positive Regard Scale rated each of the 45 3-minute samples and, finally, three new raters who had been previously trained on the Truax Therapist Genuineness Scale rated each of the 45 samples (Truax, 1963; Truax and Carkhuff, 1964). At this point it is important to stress the independent training and rating of the raters. It should be emphasized that each rater was not measuring therapist empathy and then patient self-exploration.

The Depth of Intrapersonal Exploration Scale (DX) is a 10-point scale with a zero point to be used when no personally relevant material occurs and there is no opportunity for it to occur (as, for example, in a patient-therapist discussion of appointment hours, etc.). The reliability of all raters combined per segment was .78 as estimated by Ebel's (1951) formula for intraclass correlations. Some low and high examples of the stages are as follows:

Low. The patient actively evades personally relevant material (such as, by changing the subject, refusing to respond at all, etc.). . . . The patient does not respond to personally relevant material even when the therapist speaks of it.

High. The patient is . . . actively exploring his feelings, his values, his perceptions of others, his relationships, his fears, his turmoil, and his life choices.

The Accurate Empathy Scale is a 9-point scale attempting to specify stages along a continuum. The reliability of all raters combined per segment was .68. Some examples of the scale include the following:

Low. The therapist seems completely unaware of even the most conspicuous of the client's feelings. His responses are not appropriate to the mood and content of the client's statement and there is no determinable quality of empathy, hence no accuracy whatsoever.

High. The therapist . . . unerringly responds to the client's full range of feelings in their exact intensity. He expands the client's hint into a full-blown but tentative elaboration of feeling or experience with unerring sensitivity and accuracy. He is completely attuned to the client's shifting emotional content; he senses each of the client's feelings and reflects them in his word and voice.

The Unconditional Positive Regard Scale is a 5-point scale attempting to define five stages along the continuum of the therapist's nonpossessive warmth. The reliability of all raters combined per segment was .70. Some examples of the scale follow:

Low. The therapist . . . may be telling the patient what would be "best" for him, or maybe in other ways actively either approving or disapproving of his behavior. The therapist acts in such a way as to make himself the focus of evaluation and the therapist sees himself as responsible *for* the patient.

High. The therapist communicates unconditional positive regard without restriction. At this stage the patient is free to be himself even if this means that he is regressing, being defensive, or even disliking or rejecting the therapist himself. The only channeling by the therapist may be the demand that the patient communicate personally relevant material.

Finally, the therapist Self-Congruence Scale is a 5-point scale attempting to specify stages along a continuum of therapist genuineness. The reliability of all raters combined per segment was .83. Some examples of the scale follow:

Low. The therapist is clearly defensive in the interaction and there is explicit evidence of a very considerable discrepancy between his experiencing and his current verbalization. Thus, the therapist makes striking contradictions in his statements . . . or the therapist may contradict the content . . . with the voice qualities. . . .

High. The therapist is freely and deeply himself in the relationship. There is an openness to experiences and feeling by the therapist of all types—both pleasant and hurtful—without traces of defensiveness or retreat into professionalism.

Thus, every moment of the initial psychotherapeutic interviews (excluding the initial and terminal statements and the time immediately surrounding the door-opening events) was rated for each of the three patients on each of the four scales. The randomly coded segments meant that the raters did not know whether a given sample came from the early, middle, or late phases of therapy nor did they know whether it was from the time period in which the therapist was attempting to offer high or lowered conditions.

The test of the hypothesis simply involved the uncoding of the ratings and their examination to determine whether or not the experimentally induced drop in conditions resulted in a consequent drop in patient depth of intrapersonal exploration.

Results

The first step was the check on experimental operations to determine whether or not conditions were indeed lowered during the midsection of the first interview for each of the three patients. The averaged ratings from all raters on all segments on accurate empathy are presented in Figure 1. Here it can be easily seen that with all three patients the level of accurate empathy was clearly lowered during the middle experimental part of the therapy session. The differences in the predicted direction for levels of accurate empathy were significant ($p \leq .01$) using both a simple-randomized analysis of variance and the t-tests between means. It can be noted that with Patient C, accurate empathy, while noticeably lowered during the middle part of therapy, was not uniformly lower. That particular patient was quite upset prior to and during the therapeutic session so that the therapist could not in good conscience lower conditions markedly while the patient was acutely disturbed.

The data on unconditional positive regard show a similar pattern and are shown in Figure 2. Again, differences in the predicted direction were significant ($p \leq .01$) using both a simple-randomized analysis of variance and t-tests between means.

The objective data then indicate that the attempted experimental operations were to some degree successful and that the conditions were moderately high during the initial and terminal 15-minute time period and relatively low during the middle 15-minute time period.

Figure 3 displays the ratings of therapist congruence which was not to be intentionally lowered during the middle portions of the interview. Indeed, at some points the data show that the therapist actually "overcompensated" in his effort to remain genuine and congruent during the period of lowered conditions. Here, using both the variance ratio and the t-tests between means, the differences were significant ($p \leq .01$), indicating a *rise* in self-congruence during the period when the levels of accurate empathy and unconditional warmth were experimentally lowered.

Finally, the effects of the experimental operation on patient pro-

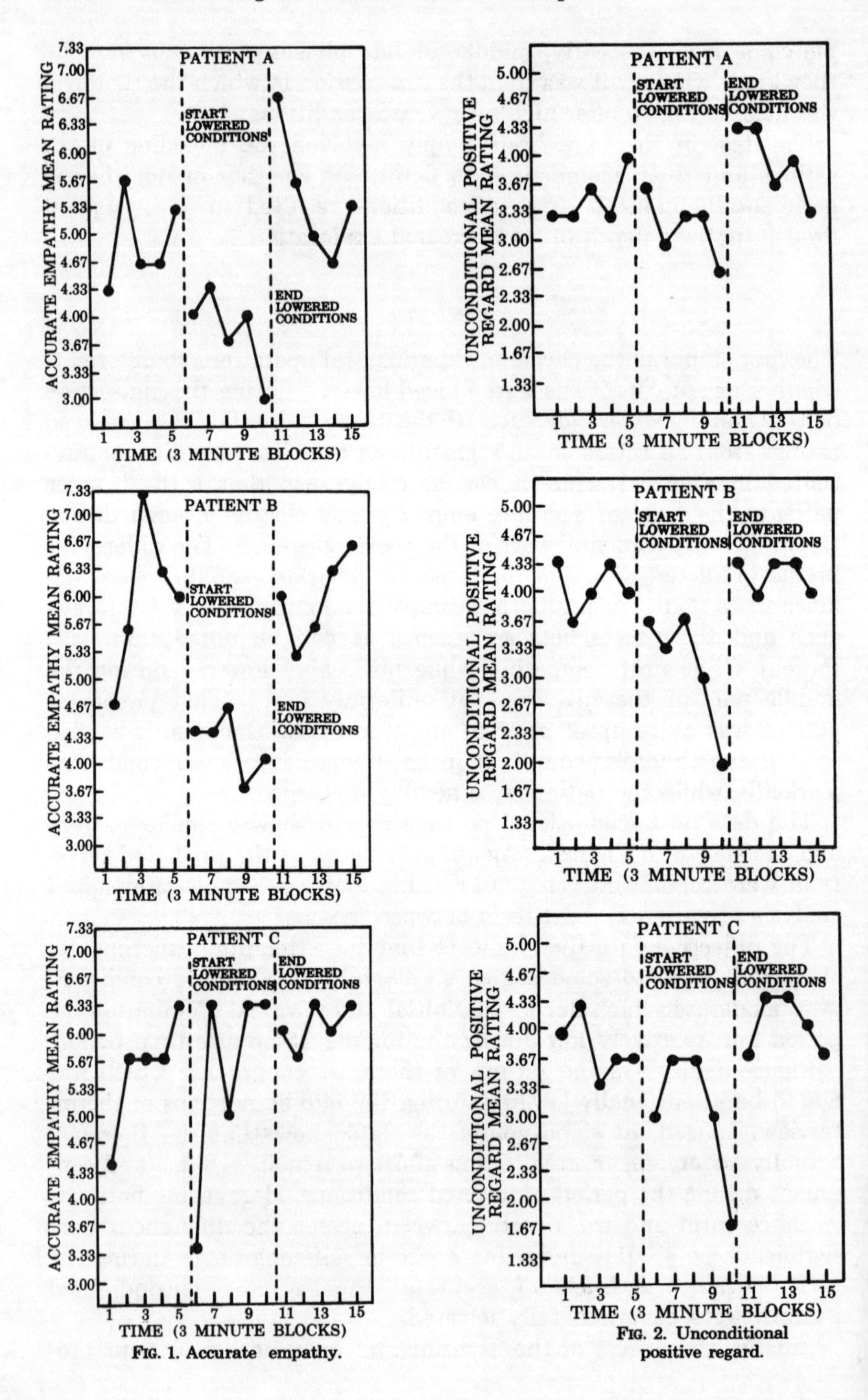

FIG. 1. Accurate empathy.

FIG. 2. Unconditional positive regard.

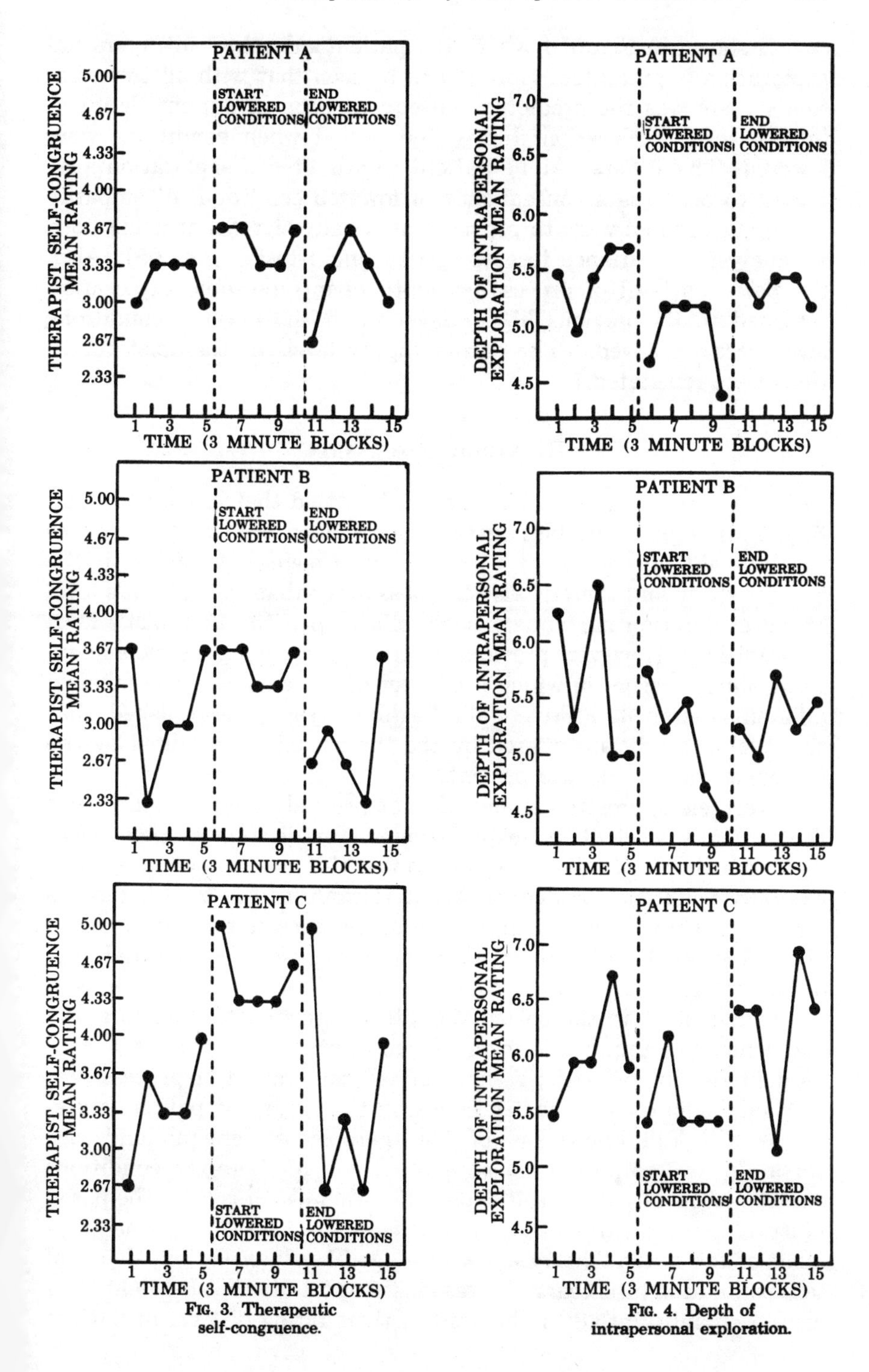

FIG. 3. Therapeutic self-congruence.

FIG. 4. Depth of intrapersonal exploration.

cess is shown in Figure 4 where the patient's depth of intrapersonal exploration is presented. Here it can be seen that with all three patients there was the predicted consequent drop in patient depth of intrapersonal exploration during the period when conditions were lowered. The differences in patient depth of self-exploration predicted to occur as a consequence of lowered conditions of empathy and unconditional warmth proved statistically significant using both an analysis of variance test ($p \leq .01$) and t-tests ($p \leq .05$). Also, the patient's level of process or depth of intrapersonal exploration returned to its previous higher level when the lowered conditions levels were removed. (The earlier higher levels of therapist conditions were reinstated.)

Research Discussion

In interpreting these findings, it must be noted that gross manipulation of therapist variables leaves uncontrolled any other variables which might be correlated with the experimental variables in the present study and there is also the possibility that the patient's level of self-exploration might have some effect upon the therapist's level of conditions. However, previous research, employing an incomplete Latin square design in which a number of patients saw a number of different therapists (Truax and Carkhuff, 1964), established that the level of conditions offered by the therapist is determined by the therapist and not by the patient.

Nevertheless, present findings do not preclude the possibility that the patient's level of self-exploration might also have some effect upon the therapist's level of conditions; this has yet to be experimentally confirmed or denied. What is confirmed is the therapist's direct effect upon the patient's level of therapeutic process or depth of intrapersonal exploration: when the therapist offers lowered conditions of empathy and unconditional positive regard, there is a consequent drop in the patient's depth of intrapersonal exploration, and when the therapist's level of conditions rises, there is a consequent rise in the patient's level of self-exploration or process.

A methodological difficulty concerns the rating of patient statements with full knowledge of the therapist statements and vice versa. In attempting to measure the levels of therapist conditions and the levels of patient self-exploration there is, of course, the possibility of contaminating the measurement of one with the measurement of the other. The raters who judged levels of patient depth of self-exploration also *heard* the responses of the therapist. Might they have been substantially influenced in their rating of level of patient activity by knowledge of what the therapist was doing? Several lines of thought and evidence argue against this latter possibility. First, the ratings were done by raters who were not sophisticated in psychotherapy theory, research, or practice. They were naive college students *not* studying psychology (mostly English majors) who had little if any prior knowledge of psychotherapy. Just as importantly, they were trained on only *one* scale. Thus the raters trained to rate patient self-exploration did *not* even see the scale designed to measure level of therapist accurate empathy. A successful attempt was made to keep the four groups of raters (for the three measures of therapist offered conditions and the one measure of patient activity) completely apart so that they didn't discuss any aspect of their ratings. Thus there was no likely contamination due to the theoretical expectations of the raters, because the raters were naive both with respect to theory and with respect to the measurement of the other variables involved in the study. Further, an immediate question which arises is, "Is it meaningful to separate patient and therapist responses in the rating?" For example, can it be determined whether a patient's response involves depth of self-exploration or is simply an evasion or defensive maneuver in response to the therapist's previous response? Or can, for example, a therapist's response indicating a certain feeling tone and content be separated from the patient's previous response? Here we must add that research is currently under way to determine whether or not separation of therapist and patient responses is meaningful for rating purposes.

There was no evidence from the patients' reactions during the middle portion of the interview to suggest that they ever discerned any quality of "upset" in the therapist or were ever even consciously aware of any change in the levels of conditions. The only possible reaction to the lowered conditions might be found in some of the patients' self-references during the experimental period. For example, one patient said: "I guess I don't make much sense." Such a statement might tend to reflect the therapist's lowered level of accurate empathy.

In general, the findings are clearly suggestive of a causal relationship between the level of some therapist-offered conditions and some of the patient's therapy behavior.

It is significant that the drop in DX occurred concomitantly with the experimental lowering of levels of accurate empathy and unconditional positive regard, *in spite of a rise in therapist genuineness or self-congruence*. This clearly suggests that therapist genuineness, at least within the ranges of the present study, is not crucial of patient self-exploration. The earlier finding with group therapy (Truax,

1961) showing that only a gross absence of therapist self-congruence or genuineness was related to self-exploration, is perhaps confirmed by the present findings: variations in therapist self-congruence within relatively high levels is not related to patient self-exploration.

To be sure, the experimental manipulation of therapeutic conditions raises some critical questions. However, perhaps the most significant methodological finding of the present research is that therapist-offered conditions can be varied experimentally in the natural setting of therapy, with predictable ensuing consequences.

References

Ebel, R. L. "Estimation of the Reliability of Ratings," *Psychometrika,* 1951, *16,* 407–24.

Truax, C. B. "The Process of Group Psychotherapy." *Psychological Monographs,* 1961, *75* (14, Whole No. 511).

Truax, C. B. "Effective Ingredients in Psychotherapy: An Approach to Unraveling the Patient-Therapist Interaction." *Journal of Counseling Psychology,* 1963, *10,* 256–63.

Truax, C. B., & Carkhuff, R. R. "For Better or for Worse: The Process of Psychotherapeutic Personality Change." In *Recent Advances in the Study of Behavior Change.* Montreal, Canada: McGill University Press, 1964. Pp. 118–63.

*

DIFFERENTIAL EFFECTS OF THE MANIPULATION OF THERAPEUTIC CONDITIONS UPON HIGH- AND LOW-FUNCTIONING CLIENTS

TODD HOLDER
ROBERT R. CARKHUFF
BERNARD G. BERENSON

There is extensive evidence to indicate that the levels of empathy, respect, genuineness, concreteness, or specificity of expression and self-disclosure offered by the counselor are related to the depth of self-exploration and constructive personality change of the client (Truax and Carkhuff, 1964). Concerning the question of causation, in general, the evidence suggests (a) that it is the counselor who determines the level of conditions which he offers and (b) that both counselor and client contribute to the client's engagement in self-exploration (Truax and Carkhuff, 1964). In an experimental approach to the question, Truax and Carkhuff (1965) successfully manipulated the level of conditions offered by the counselor and found the intrapersonal exploration of three female inpatient psychotics to be a function of the level of conditions offered by the counselor. However, there is reason to believe that the communication process has broken down for inpatient psychotics, and they may be characterized as functioning at the very lowest levels of facilitative interpersonal dimensions (Carkhuff, 1966a). Thus, it must be anticipated that they would be dependent upon the counselor in the

*This article is reprinted from *Journal of Counseling Psychology,* 1967, *14,* 63–66, by permission of the publisher, the American Psychological Association, and the authors.

communication process of counseling and, therefore, will explore themselves only when the counselor is functioning at high levels of conditions. The purpose of the present study was to determine the effects of the manipulation of therapeutic conditions upon the depth of self-exploration of persons functioning at high levels and persons functioning at low levels of empathy, respect, genuineness, and concreteness.

METHOD

Eleven female college students were cast in the helping role of the counselor, that is, given a mental set to be as helpful as they could in helping a standard interviewee work through some of his problems. The three highest functioning students and the three lowest functioning students were selected to participate as clients in the counseling project. Unknown to each client, an experienced counselor, functioning at high levels of facilitative conditions based upon previous research, offered high levels of conditions during the first third of a clinical interview, low levels during the middle 20 minutes, and reinstituted high levels of conditions again during the last third of the interview in the manner of the earlier research (Truax and Carkruff, 1965) The counselor presented himself as a counselor who was trying to offer "as much help as possible in the time we have together." The counselor did not lower conditions precipitously by being phony, negative in his regard, or destructive. During the experimental period, the counselor attempted simply to withhold the best possible therapeutic responses which he might otherwise make, and his responses appeared instead to be rather innocuous. He attempted to standardize the introduction to the initial and third periods and attempted to continue to make as many responses during the middle period as he did during the other periods.

During the selection phase, random excerpts were taken from the tape-recorded sessions and rated by experienced raters on six 5-point scales (Carkhuff, 1966b) assessing the following dimensions of interpersonal functioning which have been related to constructive change in counseling and psychotherapy: counselor empathy (*E*), respect (*R*), genuineness (*G*), concreteness (*C*), self-disclosure (*SD*), and the degree to which the client explores himself (*Ex*). *E* ranges from Level 1 where the counselor is unaware or ignorant of even the most conspicuous surface feelings of the counselee to Level 5 where the counselor communicates an accurate empathic understanding of the client's deepest feelings. *R* ranges from the counselor's clear communication of negative regard to his communication of a deep caring for the client. *G* varies from the communication of a wide discrepancy between the counselor's experiencing and his verbalizations to his being freely and deeply himself in a nonexploitative relationship. *C* ranges from vague and abstract discussions to the direct discussion of specific feelings and experiences. *SD* moves from Level 1 where the counselor actively attempts to remain detached from the client and discloses nothing about himself to Level 5 where the counselor freely volunteers with appropriate discriminations, information about his personal ideas, attitudes, and experiences. *Ex* ranges from the lowest level where the client does not explore himself at all to the highest level where the client is searching to discover new feelings concerning himself and his world. Pearson *r* rate-rerate reliabilities for the two raters involved were as follows: *E*, .95, .92; *R*, .93, .90; *G*, .92, .89; *C*, .89, .87; *SD*, .91, .93; *Ex*, .90, .95. The intercorrelations between the raters were as follows: *E*, .98; *R*, .99; *G*, .83; *C*, .91; *SD*, .91; *Ex*, .78.

The three high-functioning subjects had been rated to be functioning at the following levels of facilitative conditions when they were cast in the helping role:

Client A, *E*, 2.50; *R*, 3.00; *G*, 3.38; *C*, 3.13.
Client B, *E*, 2.25; *R*, 2.75; *G*, 2.87; *C*, 2.87.
Client C, *E*, 2.13; *R*, 2.13; *G*, 3.00; *C*, 2.13.

Overall, the mean levels of the high subjects were as follows: *E*, 2.29; *R*, 2.63; *G*, 3.08; *C*, 2.71.

The three low-functioning subjects were rated to be functioning at the following levels of conditions:

Client X, *E*, 1.50; *R*, 1.50; *G*, 1.75; *C*, 1.75.
Client Y, *E*, 1.50; *R*, 1.50; *G*, 1.75; *C*, 1.75.
Client Z, *E*, 1.50; *R*, 1.13; *G*, 1.38; *C*, 1.63.

Overall, the mean levels of functioning of the low students were as follows: *E*, 1.50; *R*, 1.38; *G*, 1.54; *C*, 1.67. Thus, all high-rated subjects were functioning above Level 2 on all of the individual dimensions and all of the low-rated subjects were functioning below Level 2 on all of the individual dimensions when cast in the helping role. Even though both groups worked with standard interviewees who readily shared personal problems and experiences, the high group elicited an average *Ex* level of 2.62 while the low group elicited an *Ex* of 2.38.

In previous research the counselor involved had been found to be functioning at the following average levels of facilitative conditions: *E*, 3.75; *R*, 3.50; *G*, 3.33; *C*, 3.08; *Ex*, 3.50.

The "clients" were given a set to discuss any personal problems or experiences which they might have had, "either now or over the past year," which they felt they could share with the counselor. The clients were seen in a random order which was not known to the counselor. It was anticipated (a) that the depth of self-exploration of the low-functioning clients would be a significant function of the level of conditions offered by the counselor, that is, client *Ex* would be lowered when the counselor-offered conditions were lowered, while (b) the intrapersonal exploration of the high-functioning clients would not be affected. That is, the high-functioning clients, having experienced a high level of therapeutic conditions, would continue to function independently in the communication process during the experimental period.

Results

The counselor was able to manipulate successfully the level of therapeutic conditions which he offered to each client. With each client, the counselor offered significantly higher (.01) levels by *t* of the conditions, treated individually, during Periods 1 and 3 than during Period 2, the experimental period. For all clients the counselor-offered conditions were on an average above Level 3 during Period 1, below Level 2 during Period 2, and approximately Level 4 during Period 3.

Figures 1 and 2 demonstrate the depth of self-exploration engaged in by the high- and low-functioning clients during Periods 1, 2, and 3. The high-functioning clients, A, B and C, functioned individually and as a group at significantly higher (.01) levels of conditions than the low-functioning clients, individually and as a group during Periods 1, 2, and 3. Overall, the high-functioning group functioned on an average between levels 3.0 and 4.5 while the low-functioning group functioned between Levels 1.0 and 2.5.

Overall, the high-functioning group tended to function at approximately Level 3 during Periods 1 and 2 with a slight upward trend to Level 4 during Period 3. There were no significant differences between the levels of functioning of Periods 1 and 3 versus 2, although the high clients were exploring themselves at significantly deeper (.01) levels during Period 3 than Period 1.

The low-functioning group tended to function on an average at Level 2 during the initial period, dropped to less than 1.5 during the experimental period, and raised to approximately Level 2.5 during the final period, The low clients explored themselves at sig-

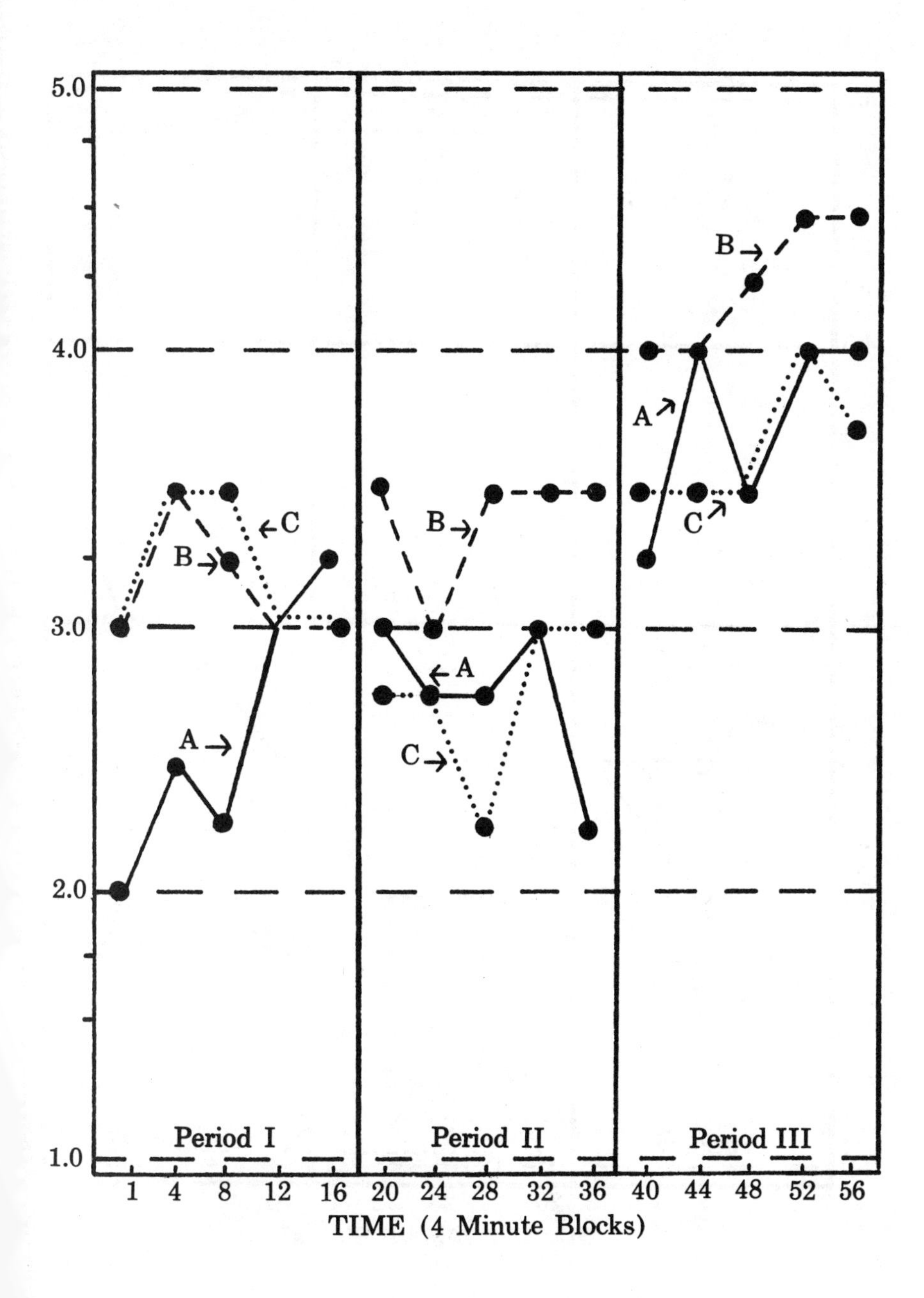

FIG. 1. Levels of depth of self-exploration engaged in by the high-functioning clients, A, B, and C, during Periods 1, 2 and 3.

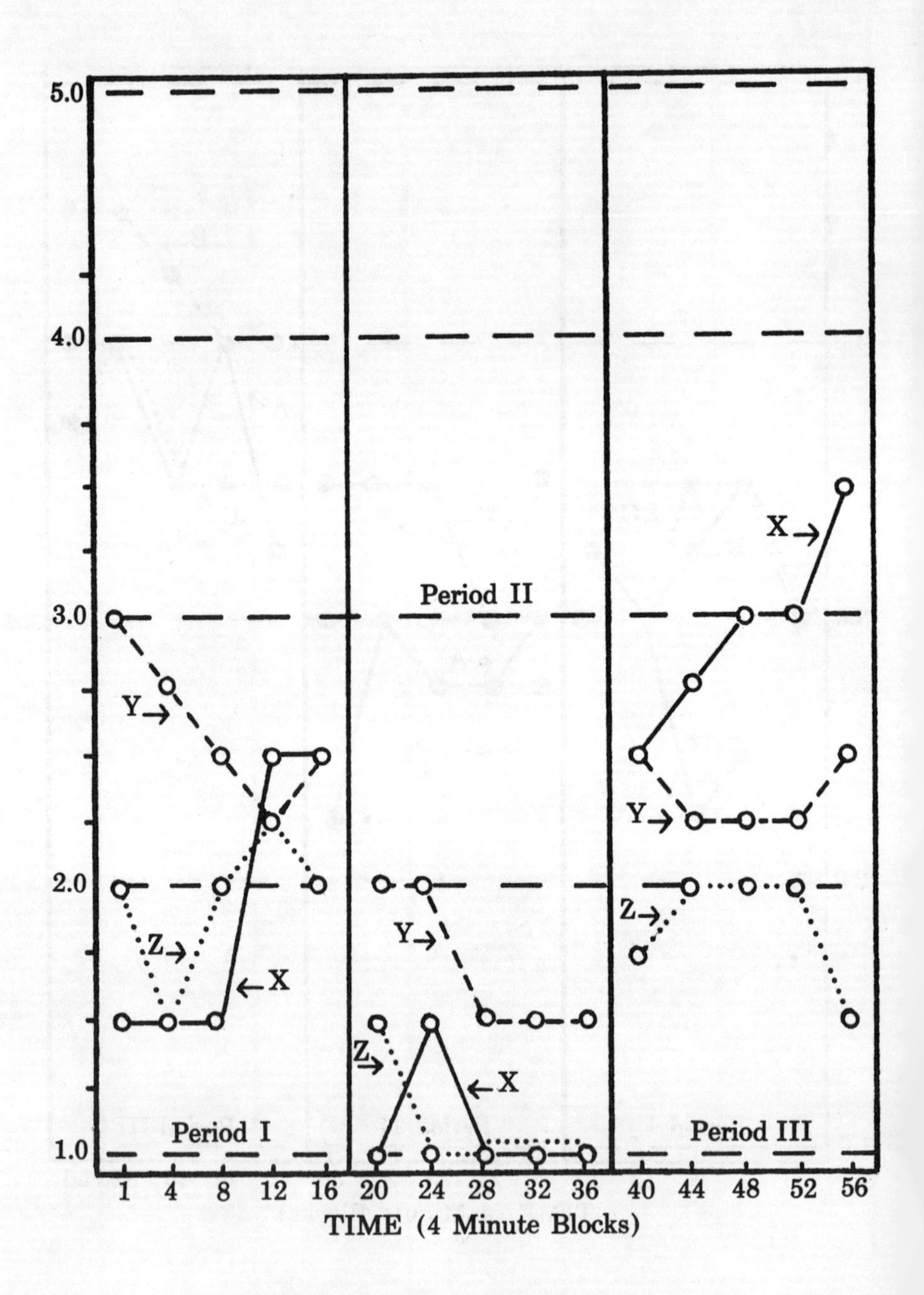

FIG. 2. Levels of depth of self-exploration engaged in by the low-functioning clients, X, Y, and Z, during Periods 1, 2, and 3.

nificantly lower (.01) levels during Period 2 than during Periods 1 and 3. The differences between the levels of self-exploration of Periods 1 and 3 were not significant.

Discussion

Perhaps most significant is the finding that clients who are functioning at higher levels of facilitative conditions explore themselves at higher levels and, thus, in general would appear to make better use of the counseling process than do those who are functioning at lower levels of conditions. The implications for the effective use of counseling and friendship (Martin, Carkhuff and Berenson, 1966) are important.

The finding that higher functioning clients, having established that the counselor is communicating at highly therapeutic levels, go on to function independently during periods when the therapist is functioning at low levels has important implications for counseling and therapy. It supports the proposition that following the establishment of a relatively high level of communication, much of the communication process with high-level functioning, or Level 3 clients, may remain implicit (Carkhuff, 1966a). An initially high level of communication might provide, perhaps, a base for more cognitive pursuits involving the situational stress or choice problems which the Level 3 person most often brings to clinics or counseling centers. It is noteworthy that of the three highest functioning clients two were functioning near Level 3 overall and one was functioning closer to Level 2. Only the one functioning near Level 2, Client C, demonstrated slightly lower self-exploration during the experimental period. Future research might include intermediate levels of client functioning.

The lack of demonstration of significant differences during the experimental period with high-level functioning clients places a very important qualification upon the earlier findings of Truax and Carkhuff (1965). While it would appear that low-level, or Level 1, clients are dependent upon the level of conditions offered by the counselor, it is apparent that high-functioning clients with a high-level counselor are not. The project remains to be replicated with a low-level counselor, although the difficulties in differentiating his level of functioning during an experimental period from all other periods will be great. Nevertheless, differential effects of a low-functioning counselor upon the client's involvement in the counseling process are to be anticipated.

REFERENCES

Carkhuff, R. R. *The Counselor's Contribution to Facilitative Processes.* Urbana, Ill.: Parkinson, 1967. (a)

Carkhuff, R. R. "Toward a Comprehensive Model of Facilitative Interpersonal Processes." *Journal of Counseling Psychology,* 1967, *14,* 67–72. (b)

Martin, J. C., Carkhuff, R. R., & Berenson, B. G. "Process Variables in Counseling and Psychotherapy: A Study of Counseling and Friendship." *Journal of Counseling Psychology,* 1966, *13,* 356–59.

Truax, C. B., & Carkhuff, R. R. "Significant Developments in Psychotherapy Research." In L. E. Abt & B. F. Reiss (eds.), *Progress in Clinical Psychology.* New York: Grune & Stratton, 1964. Pp. 124–55.

Truax, C. B. & Carkhuff, R. R. "The Experimental Manipulation of Therapeutic Conditions." *Journal of Consulting Psychology,* 1965, *29,* 119-24.

EFFECT OF CLIENT DEPTH OF SELF-EXPLORATION UPON HIGH- AND LOW-FUNCTIONING COUNSELORS

ROBERT R. CARKHUFF
MAE ALEXIK[1]

Research of the question, "Who is it who determines therapeutic processes leading to constructive client change or gain?" indicates that (a) it is the therapist who determines the level of facilitative conditions of empathy, respect, and genuineness which he offers and (b) both client and therapist contribute to the client's involvement and self-exploration in the therapeutic process (Truax and Carkhuff, 1964). Evidence involving the effect of the experimental manipula-

*This article is reprinted from *Journal of Counseling Psychology,* 1967, *14,* 350–55, by permission of the publisher, the American Psychological Association, and the authors.

[1]The authors wish to acknowledge the assistance of Winni Barefoot and of David Aspy, Bernard G. Berenson, and John Douds in completing this study and of Daniel Kratochvil for his assistance in statistical analyses.

tion by both high- and low-level functioning counselors upon both high- and low-level clients (Holder, Carkhuff, and Berenson, 1967; Piaget, Berenson, and Carkhuff, 1967; Truax and Carkhuff, 1965) has been presented: In general, the depth to which low-level functioning patients explore themselves is a function of the level of facilitative conditions offered by high-level counselors, while high-level functioning clients continue to explore themselves independently of the experimental lowering of conditions by a high-level counselor; on the other hand, both high- and low-level functioning clients deteriorate in the degree to which they explore themselves over therapy with a low-level functioning counselor.

The influence of client variables upon therapeutic process movement has received sparse attention in the research literature, revolving primarily around the client's expectancies in therapy (Goldstein, 1962) and the client's experience of the level of conditions offered by the counselor (van der Veen, 1965). Thus, while it is reasonable to assume that the degree to which the client explores himself will have an effect upon the level of conditions offered by the counselor, there is no research to indicate such.

In a pilot study, Alexik and Carkhuff (1967) experimentally manipulated client depth of self-exploration by lowering self-exploration during the middle third of a session and studied the effect upon one high- and one low-functioning counselor with differential effects: The low-level functioning counselor was manipulated by the client's self-exploration while the high-level counselor was not manipulated, but instead exhibited a positive increment throughout the session. In the present study, then, it was anticipated (a) that high-level functioning counselors would not be adversely affected by the lowering of client conditions, but would instead continue to function at high levels of facilitative conditions independently of client behavior, while (b) the low-level functioning counselors would be manipulated.

Method

A client saw each of eight experienced counselors for a one-hour interview at the University of Massachusetts Counseling Center. The client was a forty-five-year-old female graduate student in counselor education who, in reality, sought counseling from the senior author concerning the difficulty which she had in implementing the role of the counselor. She was requested to participate, with the full implications considered beforehand, in the study as a real client with a real problem. The client was trained on the research scale involving client self-exploration (Ex) so that she could explore herself at very deep levels and at very superficial levels, or not at all. The counselors, six males and two females, were not aware of the experimental nature of the project, but were each under the impression that he or she was seeing a regular client for a first interview. The counselors were simply asked to record their very next session in order to obtain a representative sample of their work. None of the counselors knew the client at the time of the study. The counselors were seen in the following order: A, E, C, H, F, B, D, and I.

In the initial and last thirds of the interview the client explored at deep levels problems which were very real to her, trying to be as open as she could to the counselor's efforts. During the middle 20 minutes, the client deliberately lowered her depth of self-exploration by introducing material irrelevant to herself and her problem and/or by reverting to a mechanical, unfeeling discussion of any personally relevant material introduced by the counselor.

The counseling hour was divided into 4-minute blocks for rating purposes, so that 5 4-minute blocks were rated by two trained raters in each third of the interview, for a total of 15 4-minute excerpts. Client depth of self-exploration was rated first and the various facilitative dimensions, second. Thus, each 4-minute segment of the taped sessions was rated with the following 5-point scales (Carkhuff, in press):

The scale, "Self-exploration in interpersonal processes" (Ex) ranges from the lowest level, Level 1, in which the interviewee does not explore himself at all, to the highest level, Level 5, in which he is searching to discover new feelings concerning himself and his world. "Empathic understanding in interpersonal processes" (E) ranges from the lowest level, in which the interviewer gives the appearance of being completely unaware or ignorant of even the most conspicuous surface feelings of the other person, to the highest level, in which the interviewer accurately perceives and communicates his understanding of the other person's deepest feelings. "Respect or positive regard in interpersonal processes" (R) varies from Level 1, in which clear negative regard is communicated by the interviewer, to Level 5, in which the interviewer communicates a deep caring for the second person. "Genuineness in interpersonal processes" (G) ranges from Level 1, in which there is a wide discrepancy between the interviewer's experiencing and his verbalizations, to Level 5, in which he is freely and deeply himself in a non-exploitative relationship. "Concreteness or specificity of expression in interpersonal processes" (C) extends from the lowest level, in which the interviewer allows discussion to center around vague and abstract concepts, to the highest level, in which the interviewer is always helpful in guiding the discussion so that the client discusses directly and completely his specific feelings and experiences.

Pearson product-moment rate-rerate reliabilities for a one-week interval were as follows: Ex, .90, .99; E, .95, .96; R, .93, .99; G, .92, .93; and Ex, .92; E, .88; R, .88; G, .80; and C, .90.

Results

The client was able to successfully manipulate her depth of self-exploration. In all cases, the *t*-tests between Periods I and II and between Periods II and III were significant far beyond the .01 level of significance. In general, the client explored herself between Levels 3 and 4 during the first and third periods and between Levels 1 and 2 during the intervening experimental period with all counselors.

When counselors were divided into two groups, (a) those functioning at high levels of facilitative conditions (above Level 3 overall on the scales) and (b) those functioning at lower levels of facilitative conditions, the following results were obtained (see Figure 1 for the average ratings within each period of counselor-offered conditions): (a) counselors originally functioning at high levels of facilitative conditions did not, when the client lowered her self-exploration, lower the level of conditions which they offered; (b) counselors originally functioning at low levels of facilitative conditions were not only manipulated by the client's lowering of conditions, but also failed to reestablish the level of conditions which they offered in the initial period.

In general, the three high-level functioning counselors (A, B, and C) functioned between Levels 3 and 4.5 throughout the three periods of the session. A Friedman two-way analysis of variance by ranks (Siegel, 1956) indicated that the periods had no effect on the levels of functioning of the high counselors ($X_r^2 = .67$). However, the differing process patterns of each of these counselors warrant further consideration. Counselor A, the highest level functioning counselor, steadily increased his level of functioning throughout the interview, offering even higher levels of conditions at the point where the client lowered her self-exploration. Counselor A was functioning at significantly higher levels of conditions, both individually and overall, in Period III than he was in Period I and overall in Period II than Period I, with trends toward significance with overall conditions between Periods II and III (*see* Table 1). Counselor B exhibited a process pattern which is the inverse of that of the client—when the client lowered her level of self-exploration, he increased his level of conditions, and when the client reestablished a high level

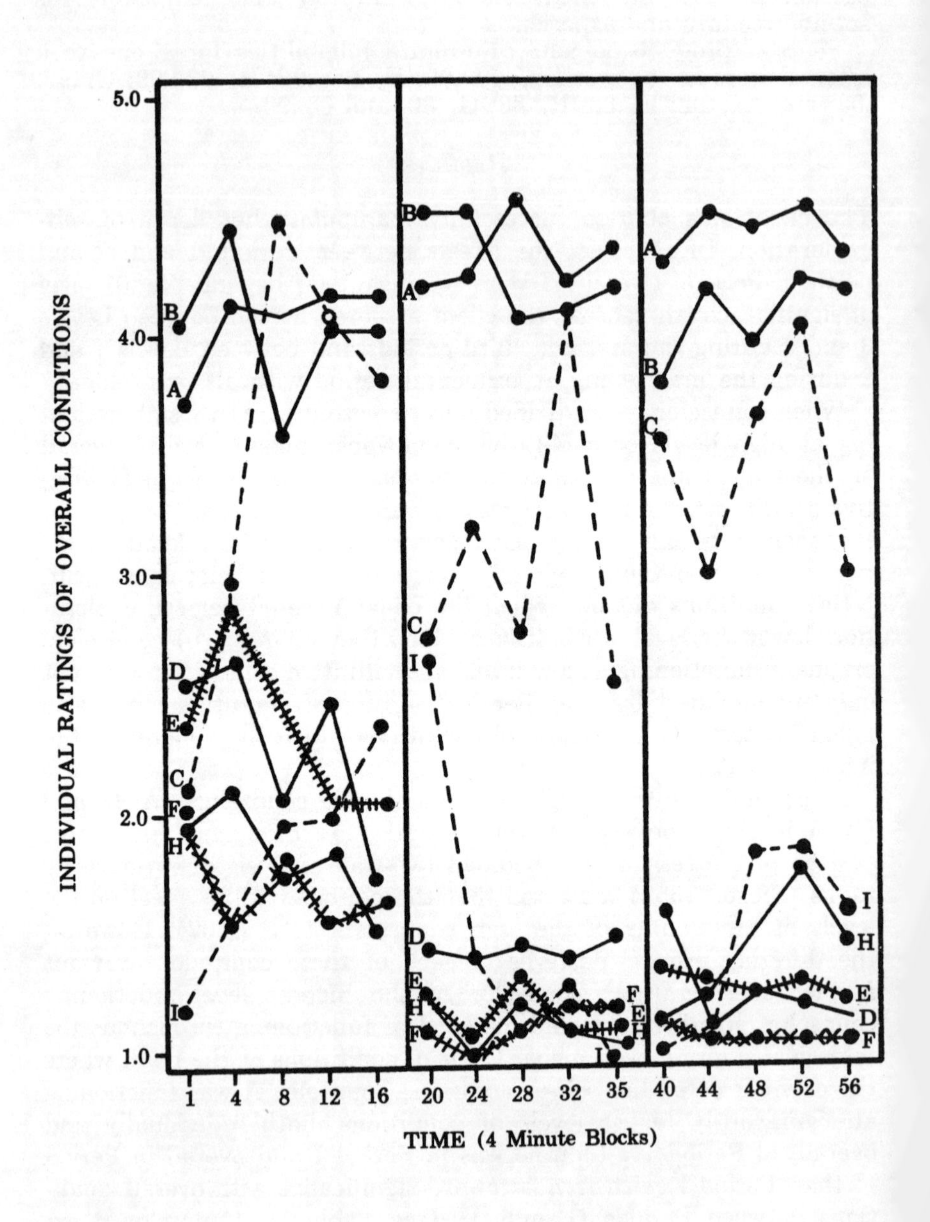

FIG. 1. Overall level of facilitative conditions offered by the eight therapists.

TABLE 1

RESULTS OF *t* TESTS FOR THE DIFFERENCES IN THE LEVELS OF OVERALL AND INDIVIDUAL THERAPEUTIC CONDITIONS OFFERED BY COUNSELORS IN PERIODS I, II, AND III

DIMENSION	*COUNSELOR*							
	A	*B*	*C*	*D*	*E*	*F*	*H*	*I*
	Period I Versus II							
Conditions overall	2.73*	1.82	.92	4.72†	7.26†	5.50†	5.95†	.87
Individual condition:								
Empathy	2.79*	9.00†	.77	3.47†	7.22†	7.48†	2.06	1.98
Respect	1.34	.39	.97	3.15†	9.39†	6.50†	4.91†	.57
Genuineness	1.64	1.26	.21	2.72*	3.71*	2.85*	5.72†	.26
Concreteness	1.00	1.79	1.69	5.74†	5.30†	3.09*	4.40†	2.32*
	Period II Versus III							
Conditions overall	1.49	1.72	1.16	1.38	1.68	1.62	2.71*	.04
Individual condition:								
Empathy	1.23	3.13†	1.06	1.00	3.50†	.00	2.34*	.26
Respect	.89	1.00	1.18	1.46	1.26	1.63	1.37	.16
Genuineness	1.18	1.13	.28	1.37	1.37	1.63	1.06	.29
Concreteness	.58	.73	1.97	.46	1.47	1.37	2.09	.00
	Period I Versus III							
Conditions overall	4.62†	.48	.11	4.82†	6.03†	7.95†	2.14*	1.10
Individual condition:								
Empathy	4.99†	1.00	.00	4.12†	4.71†	7.48†	.32	1.08
Respect	2.89*	.18	.19	4.66†	8.10†	9.48†	2.45*	.51
Genuineness	3.13†	.57	.00	3.14†	6.32†	3.77†	2.10	.00
Concreteness	.67	.94	.24	4.49†	4.02†	9.19†	2.19	2.80*

$^*p < .05$, two-tailed.
$^\dagger p < .01$, two tailed.

of self-exploration, he lowered his conditions to a level which was not dissimilar from that with which he began. Counselor C exhibited a process pattern similar to that of the client; however, because his levels of conditions within each period exhibited such wide variability, the tests of significance did not yield significant results for either the individual or the overall dimensions.

In general, the five low-level functioning counselors averaged between Levels 1.7 and 2.3 during Period I and 1.5 or lower during Periods II and III. The Friedman analysis of variance indicated that the periods had a significant effect on the level of functioning of the low counselors ($X_r^2 = 7.60$, $p < .05$). When we look at the figure we see that among the lower functioning counselors, some functioned higher in the second period than the third and vice versa. Beginning with the client's drop in self-exploration, Counselors D and F consistently lowered the level of conditions which they offered, both failing not only to recover and reestablish higher conditions following the drop in client self-exploration, but actually offering still lower conditions when the client again explored herself in Period III. Counselors E and H demonstrated similar process patterns in that they dropped significantly during the experimental period and rose slightly in their level of conditions during Period III. In general, Counselor I's great variability within each period precluded significant differences between any of the periods, in spite of the apparent drop in conditions from Period I to Period II and the apparent continuation of this level of functioning during Period III in the graphical representation.

Discussion

Again, of greatest importance methodologically was the ability of the client to successfully demonstrate the systematic manipulation of her depth of self-exploration without an awareness on the part of any of the eight counselors. It should be pointed out, however, that the client was not the sole contributor to the level of self-exploration in which she engaged. A rank ordering of the level of client depth of self-exploration during Period III is fairly congruent with a rank ordering of the level of conditions offered by the counselors throughout their sessions. The responsiveness of the client to therapist characteristics evidenced in Period III testified to her genuineness as a *real* client, and this is consistent with the research suggesting that both counselor and client contribute to client-process involvement and exploration.

Although past research has indicated that the level of counselor conditions is characteristic of the counselor and not the client, the present research offers evidence for the differential effect of the client's self-exploration upon the level of conditions offered by the counselor. Apparently, the manipulation of client self-exploration operates to spread out the patterns of the highest and lowest functioning counselors: The pattern of the highest counselor demonstrates continuing positive movement or acceleration; the pattern of the lowest counselor demonstrates continuing negative movement or deceleration. When the levels of the highest and lowest functioning counselors are averaged, there will be no differences between the mean level of functioning during Periods I, II, and III and no apparent effect of the client-process variables upon therapist variables.

Thus, client-process variables, such as the sudden decline in depth of self-exploration studied here, might serve to increase the variability in the counselor-process variables, with some counselors improving and others deteriorating, while not affecting the mean levels of functioning of all counselors combined.

Clinically speaking, it was apparent that during the experimental period, the high-level functioning counselors attempted to relate the client's impersonal expressions to deep and personal experiences of the client. Thus, for a brief example, Counselor A and the client had the following exchange:

Client: Amherst is so very different from Washington . . . geographically. . . .
Counselor: And the people are different—for you.
Client: Well, I have a nice house here. . . .
Counselor: But, it's lonely and no one seems to care.

Indeed, the client acknowledged the great difficulty which she had with high-level functioning counselors during the experimental period in keeping herself from becoming deeply involved in the exploration of her problem areas. In general, when the client lowered her self-exploration, the high-level functioning counselors tended to respond to the client as if this were a "crisis" for the client, and both Counselors A and B increased their levels of functioning during this crisis. On the other hand, the low-level functioning counselors did not acknowledge the client's crisis even to the point of continuing to offer a consistent level of conditions. We can only conjecture concerning the low-level counselor's inability to deal with client crisis: While they do not acknowledge them, they are, to be sure, severely affected by them.

It should also be noted that a rank ordering by the client of her experience with counselors previously unknown to her was quite congruent with the tape ratings. Selections from her immediately recorded impressions characterize the high-level functioning counselors as follows: "stimulating, intelligent, creative, exploring. . . . He offers life. It's like the air he breathes. . . . He is with you and will fight for your life with you. [He] left me feeling more hopeful and more courageous." A composite selection of the client's impressions of the low-level functioning counselor is as follows: "unimaginative, uncreative, boring and pedestrian . . . mechanical, perfunctory . . . never expressing any emotion . . . didn't respond to the feelings I expressed . . . didn't know and couldn't ever know me . . . I invariably left depressed from sessions with these people." The client appeared most impressed with the safe, neutral range of these latter counselors: "The tenacity of these therapists *not* to get involved with anything human was frightening."

REFERENCES

Alexik, M. & Carkhuff, R. R. "The Effects of the Manipulation of Client Depth of Self-Exploration upon High and One Low Functioning Counselor." *Journal of Clinical Psychology,* 1967, *23,* 210–12.

Carkhuff, R. R. (ed.). *The Counselor's Contribution to Facilitative Processes.* Urbana, Ill.: Parkinson (Follett), in press.

Goldstein, A. P. *Therapist-Patient Expectancies in Psychotherapy.* New York: Macmillan, 1962.

Holder, T., Carkhuff, R. R., & Berenson, B. G. "The Differential Effects of the Manipulation of Therapist-Offered Conditions upon High- and Low-Functioning Clients." *Journal of Counseling Psychology,* 1967, *14,* 63–66.

Piaget, G., Berenson, B. G., & Carkhuff, R. R. "The Differential Effects of the Manipulation of Therapeutic Clients." Unpublished manuscript, University of Massachusetts, 1967.

Siegel, S. *Nonparametric Statistics.* New York: McGraw-Hill, 1956.

Truax, C. B., & Carkhuff, R. R. "Significant Developments in Psychotherapy Research." In L. E. Abt & B. F. Reiss (eds.), *Progress in Clinical Psychology.* New York: Grune & Stratton, 1964. Pp. 124–55.

Truax, C. B., & Carkhuff, R. R. "The Experimental Manipulation of Therapeutic Conditions." *Journal of Consulting Psychology,* 1965, *29,* 119–24.

Van der Veen, F. "The Effects of the Therapist and the Patient on Each Other's Therapeutic Behavior." *Journal of Consulting Psychology,* 1965, *29,* 19–26.

*

THE EFFECT OF CLIENT DEMEANOR UPON THE VERBAL RESPONSES OF SCHOOL COUNSELORS

NEAL RICHARD GAMSKY
GAIL F. FARWELL

In recent years, numerous studies have been devoted to various characteristics of the counselor and his behavior in the interview situation. Investigators have studied the influence of experience, age, theoretical orientation (Strupp, 1960), sex (Hiler, 1958), and personality conflicts (Cutler, 1958) on counselor behavior. More recently, there has been an increasing awareness of the need to study how the behavior of the counselor is influenced by certain stimulus characteristics of the counselee.

One aspect which has received limited attention by counselors is the influence of friendly or hostile client demeanor upon the behavior of the counselor. Although there has been widespread recognition that aggression and hostility are fundamental human reactions to frustration (Miller and Dollard, 1939), and counselors have been urged to become more cognizant of these concepts in their work with students (Faries, 1958), this aspect of counselee demeanor and its influence on counselor behavior has been largely neglected. Two studies investigating the effect of client demeanor on counselor behavior, however, are pertinent to the present investigation. Russell and Snyder (1963), using two client-actors and 20 therapists, examined the effect of friendly and hostile client affect on counselor

*This article is reprinted from *Personnel and Guidance Journal, 45,* 477–81, by permission of the publisher, the American Personnel and Guidance Association, and the authors.

anxiety. It was revealed that hostile client behavior led to greater therapist anxiety than friendly client behavior. Heller, Myers, and Kline (1963), in a subsequent study, concluded that hostile client behavior evoked hostile interviewer behavior and friendly client behavior evoked friendly interviewer behavior, but questioned whether more experienced therapists would respond similarly. To this could be added the question as to whether the sex of the counselee and the counselor is an important consideration.

The purpose of the present study was to explore the effect of hostile and friendly client demeanor upon the verbal behavior of school counselors in the initial interview situation from the standpoint of various levels of counselor experience and the counselor-client sex factor. Several questions were developed for investigation. Are there significant differences in the verbal responses of counselors attributable to: (a) professional preparation and experience? (b) sex of the counselor? (c) client demeanor? (d) sex of the client? Also of concern were significant interaction effects relative to the above variables.

The investigators believe that these questions have practical significance for counselors and for graduate programs concerned with counseling techniques and methods.

Method

Four client roles of the "friendly male," "friendly female," "hostile male," and "hostile female" were developed and four student actors obtained from an undergraduate course in theater arts were trained to play these roles. They underwent ten hours of initial training with the principal investigator. One male and one female were trained as "friendly clients." That is, they responded in a pleasant, positive, cooperative manner to the counselor. The other male and female actors were trained as "hostile clients." They responded in a manner generally described as assertive, aggressive, sarcastic, demanding, complaining, and negative. Special effort was made to standardize the clients' intensity of affect and mode of expression.

The roles selected for the client-actors (hereafter referred to simply as clients) were designed to represent typical problems handled by school counselors. In general, the actors portrayed the role of students who had just graduated from high school and who planned to enroll in the University shortly. Their immediate "concern" focused on doubt regarding their educational-vocational plans. After the interview had proceeded for five minutes, however, the clients were instructed to interject their "real problem" which represented parental pressure of various kinds. For example, the "hostile male" client was being pressured by his father to enroll in commerce and eventually to enter the family business, against his will, whereas the "hostile female" client wanted to major in science but her parents were insisting on a more "feminine" program, such as teaching.

Each client was seen by 30 counselors for half-hour interviews. The counselors were led to believe they were seeing real clients. Instruction given to the counselors prior to the interviews gave a fictitious purpose for the study, dealing with the appropriateness of various time limits for initial interviews. The counselors were instructed to use their own preferred techniques in helping the clients with their problems during the half hour and to make recommendations for referral of the client for subsequent disposition of the case. Thus, the counselors not only were made to think that the clients were real, but believed that they were being of help to them. The true purpose of the study was revealed to the counselors following their last interview. There were many indications that all the counselors sincerely believed they were seeing real clients. The design of the study randomized the order in which the counselors participated in the study and the order in which individual counselors saw the various types of clients.

Five male and five female counselors were selected for each of the three counselor groups, viz., inexperienced, moderately experienced, and experienced. The inexperienced group was composed of students who had a maximum of three courses in guidance and counseling and who had not had any supervised field work for other formal counseling experience. They were randomly selected from a total eligible population of 16 students enrolled in an introductory guidance course.

The moderately experienced group represented counselors who had completed all the required courses for a master's degree in counseling and had at least one semester of supervised field experience. They were randomly drawn from a total of 45 student counselors currently on campus.

The experienced group was composed of counselors who had a master's degree in counseling, at least one semester of supervised field experience, and a minimum of one year of counseling experience in a school setting. (The average was four years of counseling experience.) These counselors were randomly chosen from a group of 35 counselors within commuting distance of the University.

The ages of the counselors ranged from twenty-two to fifty-seven, but the mean ages of the three groups were roughly equivalent. All counselors were products of the University of Wisconsin counselor preparation program.

Each interview was recorded by a microphone in the interviewing room which was connected to a tape recorder in an adjoining room. Quantification of the counselor's responses from the tape recordings was accomplished by means of a revision of Bales (1950) System of Interaction Process Analysis, a well-known general purpose framework for describing social interactions. This system commended itself because of: (a) the care that went into its development, (b) its theoretical neutrality with respect to various schools of counseling, (c) the extensive use of it in other studies with satisfactory results.

After several pilot ratings, the category definitions were revised and the scale was extended by subdividing three of the original 12 categories and omitting one that seemed inappropriate. However, the general format of the original Bales categories was retained. The final revision contained the following 14 categories: (1) Gives Reassurance; (2) Shows Approval; (3) Shows Tension Release; (4) Shows Agreement; (5) Gives Suggestion; (6) Gives Interpretation; (7) Reflects; (8) Gives Information; (9) Asks for Information; (10) Asks for Elaboration; (11) Disagrees; (12) Avoids; (13) Shows Disapproval; (14) Shows Antagonism.

The tapes were rated by three female graduate students in counseling. They were not aware of the research questions being investigated, but did know that the clients were actually accomplices. The raters underwent 13 hours of group and individual training in categorizing verbal responses on the Bales scale. Training was stopped when an interjudge mean correlation of .87 was obtained on four pilot interviews.

Prior to the actual rating of the tapes used in the study, the investigators recorded the exact footage on the tape to be rated, beginning with the first moment the client introduced his "problem" and the counselor responded to it, to the last response made at the end of 60 feet of tape, or approximately a 6-minute time interval. It was a relatively easy task to pinpoint the appropriate starting point since the clients were remarkably consistent in introducing their "problems." This "critical incident" technique of selecting tape segments for rating was considered superior to random selection since all the counselors were exposed to the same "problems" presented in the same manner in spite of any previous interaction.

Each tape to be rated consisted of four 30-minute interviews, representing one counselor's interviews with each of the clients. In total there were 30 tapes, with the segments to be rated designated on each. These tape segments were then randomly distributed among three raters. A 10 per cent sample from each counselor group was randomly selected to determine reliability. Rank difference correlation coefficients were computed to determine the degree of interjudge agreement. The mean correlation for all judges was .82.

Although there were many subjective indications that the clients had performed consistently in their designated roles in training and during the study itself, questions could still be raised as to their success in maintaining their specified roles consistently when exposed to a variety of counselors. Thus, the 6-minute tape segments previously selected for rating were presented in randomized order to two judges who were not connected with the study in any other way. They were asked to indicate whether the client appeared "hostile" or "friendly" according to definitions provided for these terms. The two judges independently performed this task without error.

Results

An analysis of variance was employed in examining the main and interaction effects of the four variables under investigation in the study. These variables, viz., counselor experience, counselor sex, client demeanor and client sex, were placed in a four-factor, fully replicated, balanced block design and were analyzed in terms of the scores assigned by the judges for each of the 14 verbal response categories. The 5 per cent level of confidence was selected as determining statistical significance.

With respect to the first research question, it was found that counselor experience was statistically significant in only one verbal response category, i.e., tension release. Lindquist's (1953, p. 93) "critical difference" technique was applied to test the significance of the difference in the observed means for each pair of counselor groups, using the 5 per cent level of confidence. It was determined that the inexperienced counselors used tension release significantly more than either of the other two groups.

In answer to the second research question, it was found that counselor sex has a statistically significant association with the counselor's verbal response, but only for one category, i.e., reassurance. Examination of the mean scores revealed that female counselors used reassurance significantly more often than did the male counselors. However, by inspection of the data for the significant interaction of counselor experience X counselor sex, it was determined that although reassurance was used more often by female than male counselors in all counselor groups, these differences declined rapidly as level of experience increased.

Client demeanor was found to have a significant effect on the counselor's use of approval, reflection, information-giving, requests for information, disagreement and avoidance responses. Inspection of the data revealed that counselors used significantly more reflection, information-giving, disagreement, and avoidance responses, and significantly fewer approval responses and requests for information with hostile as compared to friendly clients.

Finally, the sex of the client was found to have a significant effect upon seven of the 14 verbal response categories. Counselors used significantly more reassurance and fewer agreement, reflection, information-giving, requests for information, elaboration and disagreement responses with male clients than with female clients.

Although several interaction effects were significant, inspection of the data did not reveal any meaningful patterns other than those noted above (Gamsky, 1965).

Discussion and Conclusions

With respect to the major focus of this investigation concerning the effects of client demeanor upon counselors' verbal responses, it was found that the counselors used approval less and disagreement and avoidance more with hostile actor-clients than with friendly actor-clients. If one can assume, as Bales (1950) suggests, that response categories 1 through 4 (i.e., reassurance, approval, tension release, and agreement) generally indicate a positive reaction and categories 11 through 14 (i.e., disagreement, avoidance, disapproval, and antagonism) probably reflect negative reactions while the middle six categories are relatively neutral, then the results indicate that the counselors in this study reacted in a positive manner to friendly clients and in a negative manner with hostile clients. As indicated earlier, Heller, Myers, and Kline (1963) reported similar results. This conclusion is also supported by the counselors' use of antagonism, which was defined in terms of counselor's extreme use of counter-aggression or blatant rejection of the client. Although the F ratio of 3.243 did not reach the 5 per cent level of confidence needed for acceptance, it was sufficiently high (7 per cent level of confidence) to indicate that the counselors tended to be much more antagonistic with hostile actor-clients. Further evidence of this conclusion was obtained from scrutiny of the counselors' evaluations and recommendations forms that were completed following each interview. Many counselors referred to the hostile clients as "sick" or "disturbed" and recommended "psychiatric help," whereas the friendly actor-clients were more often seen as "concerned" or "upset" about their problems, and the counselors recommended "further counseling." These findings are especially significant in view of Bandura's (1960) study which indicated that clients are more likely to drop the hostility topic following a counselor's avoidance reaction. It can be assumed that stronger negative reactions such as disapproval or antagonism would create an even greater deterrent to the clients' expression of hostility.

It was also noted that counselors used more reflection responses and gave information more often to hostile clients than friendly clients, but asked for information less often. At the present time, one may only speculate regarding these findings. It is possible that there is a tendency to reflect negative feelings expressed by a client more than positive feelings. It is also possible that "information giving" may be a form of placating an angry client, whereas with friendly clients, the tendency is to ask more questions in an effort to continue the friendly interaction. Further, some aspects of the experimental situation may have induced certain counselor responses. For example, if the hostile actor-clients were perceived as more demanding for information, the counselors may have felt compelled to supply them with it. Without further definitive research, however, these are only conjectures.

Counselor sex and counselor experience, in this investigation, had little significant effect on the counselors' verbal responses. The latter finding is surprising in view of the obvious attempt to distinguish levels of experience between groups. However, it must be pointed out that the findings are limited to the initial interview situation and to a relatively small sample of school counselors that may not be representative of counselors in general. It is quite possible that different results would have been obtained if the interviews had extended over a longer period of time, if clinically oriented counselors had been used as subjects, or if a larger sample was obtained. Furthermore, counselor remarks were assigned only to verbal response categories in this study. No effort was made to determine the quality or appropriateness of a particular response.

Although client sex was found to have a significant influence on the counselor's verbal responses in several categories, it is difficult to formulate firm conclusions relative to these findings. In fact, they must be regarded with caution since the difference noted could have been the result of extraneous client variations rather than due to the sex factor. However, in view of the findings of this study and others (Fuller, 1963), the influence of client sex and its interaction with counselor sex warrants further investigation.

References

Bales, R. F. *Interaction Process Analysis.* Reading, Mass.: Addison-Wesley Press, 1950.

Bandura, A., Lipsher, D., & Miller, P. "Psychotherapists' Approach-Avoidance Reactions to Patients' Expressions of Hostility." *Journal of Consulting Psychology,* 1960, *24,* 1–8.

Cutler, R. "Countertransference Effects in Psychotherapy." *Journal of Consulting Psychology,* 1958, *22,* 349–56.

Faries, Miriam. "Hostility in Short-Term Counseling." *Personnel and Guidance Journal,* 1958, *36,* 627–28.

Fuller, F. F. "Influence of Sex of Counselor and of Client on Client Expressions of Feelings." *Journal of Counseling Psychology,* 1963, *10,* 34.

Gamsky, N. "Effect of Client Demeanor and Focus of Hostility Upon the Verbal Responses of School Counselors." Unpublished doctoral dissertation, University of Wisconsin, 1965.

Heller, K., Myers, R. A., & Kline, L. V. "Interviewer Behavior as a Function of Standardized Client Roles." *Journal of Consulting Psychology,* 1963, *27,* 117–22.

Hiler, E. W. "An Analysis of Patient-Therapist Compatibility." *Journal of Consulting Psychology,* 1958, *22,* 341–47.

Lindquist, E. F. *Design and Analysis of Experiments in Psychology and Education.* Boston: Houghton Mifflin, 1953.

Miller, N., & Dollard, J. *Frustration and Aggression.* New Haven, Conn.: Yale University Press, 1939.

Russell, P., & Snyder, W. "Counselor Anxiety in Relation to Amount of Clinical Experience and Quality of Affect Demonstrated by Clients." *Journal of Consulting Psychology,* 1963, *22,* 358–63.

Strupp, H. H. *Psychotherapists in Action.* New York: Grune & Stratton, 1960.

*

THE PRESENTATION OF TEST INFORMATION TO COLLEGE FRESHMEN[1]

JUNE E. HOLMES

The presentation of test results by a counselor should benefit the client. Wood (1953) notes that too frequently tests are administered and the results are left in files rather than being presented to students. Wiley and Andrew (1953) state that understanding of test results is essential in helping students to understand themselves. Rogers (1954), Lane (1952), Dressel and Matteson (1950) have investigated the effects of different means of presenting test results to clients.

In general, the few available research studies on method of presenting test results in counseling do not permit definite conclusions about the more desirable methods. This study was therefore undertaken to explore further the matter of method in test presentation. Specifically, the purposes of this study are: (1) to determine the relative effectiveness of four methods used in interpreting test results to college freshmen; (2) to compare the recall of test information with actual scores after a period of one week had elapsed; and (3) to analyze student attitudes toward the test interpretation method used in presenting the scores.

Design and Procedure of the Study

METHOD

Four methods were designed for the study; each followed the theo-

*This article is reprinted from *Journal of Counseling Psychology,* 1964, *11,* 54–58, by permission of the publisher, the American Psychological Association, and the author.

[1]Abstracted from the author's doctoral dissertation, 1959, which was completed under the supervision of Dugald S. Arbuckle.

retical characteristics of the interview: rapport, structuring, discussion, and synthesis. The degree of counselor and student interaction and participation varied in Methods A, B, C, and D.

Method A.—The counselor presented the meaning of each test and referred to the student's standing on his test profile. The counselor answered questions, made suggestions and referrals, and gave his reactions to the student's performance.

Method B.—The counselor encouraged student participation by having the student rate himself on a test profile form prior to receiving the actual scores, and by allowing the student to select the order of tests to be interpreted. The counselor expressed no reactions or opinions to the student's performance but concentrated on eliciting student feelings and attitudes toward the actual test scores and the self-rating.

Method C.—The counselor selected the order of tests to be interpreted and indicated the student's results. He encouraged participation by exploring, clarifying, and reflecting the student's attitudes and feelings about his scores. The counselor made no evaluations or judgments concerning the scores or toward the student's feelings about his standing.

Method D.—There was no discussion of test scores by a counselor since students were mailed a brief summary of the meaning of each test and a test profile on which the scores were plotted.

In general then, all methods were primarily explanatory. One (D) offered only written explanation without exchange of view. All other methods involved conversation between counselor and client and thereby permitted some exchange of views. Method A required that the *counselor* be *dominative* and *evaluative*. Method C also required that the *counselor* be *dominative* at least with regard to the test order, but it also considered the *reflection* of attitude in the course of the interview. Method B required that the student be dominative and involved attitude, but from a *set* arranged by prior student consideration and estimate of his test results. Throughout this paper we shall adopt the following denotation of method:

Method	Denotations of test interpretations in the counseling setting
D	Written
A	Counselor dominative and evaluative
C	Counselor dominative but reflective
B	Student dominative out of learning set

In order to be certain that the four counselors were adhering to the structure of each method they were supposed to employ, they recorded at random three interviews for each method. The taped sessions were later reviewed and the performance of each counselor rated on the Counselor Evaluation Check List. The results of these ratings indicated that the counselors presented test results within the framework of the designated method.

SUBJECTS AND TESTS

One hundred and fifty-four college freshmen at the Boston University School of Education participated in this study. A total of 38 students were assigned to each of Methods A, B, C, and 40 students to Method D.

All tests were administered during the first month of the academic year, with the exception of the College Board Examinations which had been taken prior to admission to the school. The battery of tests included: Otis Quick-Scoring Test of Mental Ability (Gamma), Kuder Preference Record (Form BM), Cooperative English Reading Comprehension (C_2T Form Y), Minnesota Teacher Attitude Inventory, and the Heston Personal Adjustment Inventory. The scores of each test were corrected to stanine scores which were then categorized as follows: 9 and 8 represented High; 7 and 6 Above Average; 5 Average; 4 and 3 Below Average; and 2 and 1 Low. The stanine scores of each student were represented in profile form. The test profile helped to standardize terminology, gave uniformity to all methods, and enabled students to see their performance compared to that of their classmates.

ASSIGNMENT OF SUBJECTS TO METHODS AND COUNSELORS

Age, sex, residence (commuting or dormitory status) and the raw score on the Otis Quick-Scoring Test of Mental Ability were the variables considered in assigning students to one of the four methods. Later statistical tests of method differences for each of these variables indicated that the desired randomization did, in fact, occur.

These same variables were used in assigning students in Methods A, B, and C to one of the four counselors presenting test information. Later tests showed that the counselor's groups were homogeneous in these regards also.

INSTRUMENTS

Two new instruments were designed to carry out this study.

Counselor-Interview Rating Scale.—This scale consisted of 35 statements; 19 measured attitudes toward the counselor, and 16 measured attitudes toward the value of receiving the information. The student indicated the extent of his agreement or disagreement with each statement on a 4-point scale. Those students assigned to Method D responded only to those statements pertaining to the *value* of receiving test information. Students in the other groups completed the scale immediately following the presentation of the test results and one week later as well.

Attitudes toward the counselor were inferred from items like these: "I think the counselor was helpful in assisting me to understand my test results." "I felt free to say anything I wanted during the interview." "I felt that the counselor solved my problems." Attitudes toward the value of receiving the test information were inferred from items like these: "I feel that the test information will help me to understand myself better." "I felt that learning about my traits was a complete waste of time." "I feel that it was of value to learn how my traits compared with other students."

Interpretation Form of the School of Education Test Battery.—One week following the time that a student was given his test results by mail or by personal interview the Counselor-Interview Rating Scale and the Interpretation Form were mailed to each student for completion.

The latter form presented a brief summary of the meaning of each test and a test profile which the student was asked to recall and indicate where he had scored.

Statistical Analysis and Results

STUDENT OPINIONS ABOUT COUNSELORS AND TESTS

The data for analysis were the early and later ratings of the Counselor-Interview Rating Scale. Numerical values were assigned to the four-point rating scale and separate scores obtained for each student on the two parts of the scale, Attitudes Toward Counselor and Attitudes Toward the Value of Information. The correlations .76 based on the scores of the 114 students who met with a counselor, and .75 based on the scores of the total group of 154 students who received their test results show a rather high degree of consistency in rating over a one-week interval.

Analysis of variance was the statistical procedure used to determine if there were significant differences between the four methods. Since the null hypothesis was rejected, t-tests were employed to determine which methods were significantly different from the others.

The students assigned to Methods A, B, and C showed no significant differences in their attitudes toward counselors either immediately after the conference or the week following the interpretation of their results (Table 1). Nor did these students under Methods A, B, and C show any significant difference in attitude toward the value of the tests at either testing time. On the other hand, Method D (tests received by mail) was, in some instances, significantly less effective, and this difference became greater after one week. The mean difference between the initial mean values for Methods B and D was significant at the .01 level; and between Methods A and D, and between B and D at the same level for the later mean differences. From these findings it is concluded (1) that the methods used here by the counselors had little differing effect on student attitudes toward the counselor and toward the considered value of the tests and (2) that students who did not meet with a counselor found the test information to be of least value.

TABLE 1

IMMEDIATE AND DELAYED SCORES ON THE COUNSELOR-INTERVIEW RATING SCALE FOR THE FOUR METHODS

	Attitudes Toward Counselor				*Attitudes Toward Value of Information*			
Method	*Immediate Reaction*		*Delayed Reaction*		*Immediate Reaction*		*Delayed Reaction*	
	Mean	*S.D*	*Mean*	*S.D*	*Mean*	*S.D*	*Mean*	*S.D*
A	17.50	5.49	17.00	6.38	24.32	7.98	25.00	6.90
B	18.18	5.38	17.66	5.62	26.47	6.24	25.89	7.35
C	18.16	5.15	17.87	5.58	23.53	7.30	23.92	7.93
D					22.20*	7.20	20.55†	6.45
Total	17.95	5.34	17.51	5.86	24.10	7.18	23.80	7.16

*Significant .01 level with Method B

†Significant .01 level with Method A and Method B

Further investigations of the data were made to determine if the difference in responses might have been influenced by such factors as the counselor himself, and sex and/or residence status of the student. Of the three variables only one was significant, the counselor. Expressed attitudes during the one-week interval were positive for two counselors and negative toward the other two. Since method of presentation was discounted it was concluded that the counselor himself was a major influence in the formulation of attitudes toward the counselor.

RECALL OF TEST PROFILE

One week after initially seeing their test scores, students, in most instances, did quite well in recalling their test scores.

While test interpretations via mail resulted in the best recall, mailed profiles could have been easily copied, so in the following analysis the mail method (D) is excluded. If the assumption is made that the higher the correlation between actual tests and recalled test scores the better, then Method B was associated with 9½ first places, A with 4 and C with only 1½. Counseling effect seems to last longer if it is student dominative after a learning set for test interpretation has been created.

Conclusions

The purpose of this study was to compare four methods used in presenting test results to freshman students. In addition to the method of presentation the investigation was concerned with the value of the entire experience, especially from the student's point of view. The evidence showed that:

1. Any of the four methods may be used effectively but that students who received their test results through the mail rather than from a counselor considered the results to be less valuable to them.
2. The extent to which student participation was encouraged or minimized by the counselors employing Method A, B, or C did not make a significant difference in their attitudes toward the counselor either immediately or one week later.

The results of this study have brought out the need for evaluating some of the practices that are considered part of the college experience. A review of many college orientation programs shows that testing is a major activity but whether students should be given their results is less clearly known.

The fact that no clear differences were found among counselor methods of presentation gives support to the idea that no one counseling technique lends itself to all counseling situations and it is not what a counselor does as much as what he stimulates his counselee to feel, to do, and to say that is important in the relationship.

References

Dressel, P. L., & Matteson, Rose W. "The Effect of Client Participation in Test Interpretation." *Educational and Psychological Measurement*, 1950, *10*, 728–37.

Lane, D. "A Comparison of Two Techniques of Interpreting Test Results to Clients in Vocational Counseling." Unpublished doctoral dissertation, Teachers College, Columbia University, 1952.

Rogers, Lyle B. "A Comparison of Two Kinds of Test Interpretation Interview." *Journal of Counseling Psychology,* 1954, *1,* 224–31.

Wiley, Roy & Andrew, D. *Modern Methods and Techniques in Guidance.* New York: Harper, 1953.

Wood, H. B. "Testing Used as Part of the Learning Process." *The Clearing House,* 1953. *27,* 454–56.

5

Counselor Role and Function

In recent years there have been a great many role and function studies. Usually, the counselor's role is expressed in terms of his goals and objectives for counseling, while his function is described in terms of the techniques employed to accomplish these goals. In most investigations of role and function, the investigation focuses on function, with the role being inferred from the activities which the counselor prefers or reports to be most appropriate.

There are inherent dangers in this approach to determining role. First, and most obvious, is the danger that the expression of role through inference is not justified. The same activity may be used to accomplish a wide variety of goals. The context of an activity is extremely important in defining its goal or objective, and surveys rarely provide enough information to determine the context in which activities are defined as appropriate by the respondent.

Second, there is danger that counseling practitioners may justify their role and function based upon what is being done rather than what goals ought to be and how they may be most effectively and efficiently achieved. Role and function studies provide a positive beginning point for program development and further research. When they are used as criteria for program evaluation, they serve a negative function.

Role and function studies provide some information about the status of a profession. They point out differences and common elements among perceptions of counseling, and raise questions about these differences. For example, teachers, counselors, counselor educators, and administrators see the counselor's role and function differently. What is the source of these different perceptions? How do these differences affect counseling? Who needs to change, and what change is needed? How may needed change be accomplished —i.e., who are the change-agents in a profession? Role and function studies can serve as the fountainhead for further investigations. It is believed that the studies reported in this chapter present data that raise further questions and should serve as a stimulus to further study.

The Knowles and Shertzer study presents a comprehensive picture of the counselor's role and function as perceived by members of the Association for Counselor Education and Supervision (ACES), the American School Counselor Association (ASCA), and the members of the American Association of School Administrators (AASA) using a Likert-type attitude scale. This study was done on a national scale to determine whether the counselor was viewed as a specialist or a generalist by the members of the three groups surveyed. As the authors point out "the counselor himself takes a middle-of-the-road position, although his attitudes toward his role more closely resemble the individual who trains him than the person who hires him."

The Foster study is similar to the previous one in that it investigated the role and function of the counselor as perceived by others. These others included teachers, administrators, counselors, and counselor educators. The new dimensions added were the perception of the teachers and the limitation to the perceived role and function of the elementary school counselor. The surveyed groups tended to agree on the major importance of the counseling role, but disagreed on the extent to which consultant- and social-worker-type activities were perceived as part of the counselor's role and function.

The Sweeney study narrowed the area of concern to the counselors' role and functions as self-perceived and as perceived by their principals. The major area of disagreement presented revolves around the desire of the administrator for the counselor to operate more as a leader and quasi-administrator than he does, and more than is perceived as appropriate by the counselor.

The study by Perrone, *et al.* used a modification of an instrument designed originally by Francis P. Robinson. The instrument requests the respondent to indicate the amount and kind of counseling appropriate for 14 stereotypes of students. The study reported here is an investigation of perceptions of the counseling function, and includes teachers, students, and parents. This is the only study that investigates parents' perceptions of the role and function of the counselor. It is interesting to note that parents tended to favor more intensive counseling than did either the students or the teachers. This expresses interesting differences in perception between those who work with and observe counselors, and those whose observations are less direct. Does this perhaps mean that teachers and students have become disillusioned with the value of counseling? It may also suggest that parents have unrealistic expectations related to the effectiveness of outside resources in solving the problems of their children.

The Heilfron study utilized the same instrument as was used in the study by Perrone. Heilfron used the Robinson instrument responses as indications of students' perceptions of the counselor's role. Experimental and control groups were selected, and Heilfron attempted to influence the perceptions of the counselor by the experimental group to bring them into agreement with her perceptions of the counselor's role. This was accomplished by utilizing individual interviews with the members of the experimental group. The author found that the counselor role perceived by the experimental group differed in the desired direction from the control group. As a further result of her work, the experimental group indicated that more counseling should be available and was appropriate for more kinds of students than the control group.

Of particular research interest in the present chapter is the instrument developed and used by Knowles and Shertzer. Factor analysis of responses provides a basis for some confidence that expressions of counselor attitude will be analyzed in ways that indicate the context in which the attitudes are held. Therefore, when the counselor's role is inferred, it can be expressed as a pattern of attitudes rather than isolated expressions with little consideration given to the relationship of individual expressions.

Foster developed an instrument that approached the same problem from a somewhat different tack. He developed paired expressions of counselor function that, when analyzed, would provide quantitative expressions of preferred activities. These in turn could be used to infer the role of a person who might provide the function emphasis indicated by the questionnaire. In this instance, the respondent was required to relate functions as he chose between paired choices designed to express context as well as activities.

The analysis of data ranged from graphic presentations (Foster) to *t*-tests and chi-squares. The importance of inference is clear in the studies of these chapters. It was far more difficult to develop findings. Instead, the data "suggest" or "seem to indicate." The authors have used caution in the expression of their findings. In no instance is it believed that the authors go beyond their data. It is hoped that the tentative nature of the findings of these studies will serve as the stimulus necessary to further investigation of the effect of varying perceptions of role and function.

*

ATTITUDES TOWARD THE SCHOOL COUNSELOR'S ROLE[1]

RICHARD T. KNOWLES
BRUCE SHERTZER

Background of Study

Definition of the secondary school counselor's role has been the subject of much controversy, and attempts to isolate issues involved in a systematic way have been lacking. Groups most involved in defining this role have been counselor educators, guidance supervisors, secondary school counselors and secondary school administrators. Attitudes of these groups toward the counselor's role were thought to be very significant in terms of the actual performance of a school counselor's job. Sargent's [*3*] definition of role would seem to support this belief: "A person's role is a pattern or type of social behavior which seems situationally appropriate to him in terms of the demands and expectations of those in his group."

Attitudes toward the counselor's role may be thought of as belonging to a generalist position or a specialist position. Individuals who define the counselor's role from a generalist position perceive the counselor as performing many diverse activities, while those who view the counselor as a specialist would markedly restrict the range of his activities. Dugan [*1*] defines the generalist as the counselor who gives priority to such functions as orientation, group guidance,

*This article is reprinted from *Counselor Education and Supervision,* 1965, *5,* 9–20, by permission of the publisher and authors.

[1]Based on the senior author's Ph. D. dissertation.

registration, class scheduling, course changes, cumulative record development, testing and other appraisal, special class placement, scholarship and college application information and procedures, etc., in addition to some counseling. He defines the specialist as the counselor who gives the counseling service priority over all other activities and, ideally, as one who performs the counseling service exclusively. Although the terms "generalist" and "specialist" are not often used explicitly, the two viewpoints and the attitudes connected with them can be detected in much of the literature dealing with counselor role.

Procedures

An attitude scale was constructed to differentiate between the generalist and specialist viewpoints. The items were Likert-type in that the subjects were requested to respond to statements in the following manner: Strongly Agree, Agree, Neutral, Disagree, Strongly Disagree. They were also written in such a manner that each item had a generalist direction and a specialist direction. Thus, if a person responded to the generalist direction, he was, in effect, denying the specialist direction for that particular item.

In order to insure that the items reflected generalist and specialist viewpoints and that they could be scored in terms of these viewpoints, ten members of the guidance and counseling staff at Purdue University were requested to classify 137 items as "generalist," "specialist" or "?". Items on which at least seven out of ten judges agreed were accepted for use in the final attitude scale providing the other judges had answered with a "?" response. Items about which there was any disagreement (such as one judge labeling an item as "specialist" and the other nine labeling it as "generalist") were rejected. This resulted in an 80-item attitude scale.

Items on the final form were presented in a random order. In addition, pages on which items were presented were randomized. In order to make some allowance for social desirability and acquiescence, each item was designed in such a way as to appear socially desirable and to elicit an "agree" response. This was accomplished by avoiding very extreme statements concerning counselor role.

A pilot study was conducted in which the 80 items were administered to 9 members of the Purdue University counselor education staff and 28 Advanced NDEA Counseling Institute participants. Institute students scored in the generalist direction significantly more so (.001 level) than did the staff. Using Hoyt's analysis of variance method [2], the estimate of reliability for the pilot study was found to be .90.

The attitude scale was then submitted to a random sample of 500 members of the Association for Counselor Education and Supervision, 500 members of the American School Counselor Association, and 500 members of the American Association of School Administrators. Usable returns were received from 291 (58 per cent) ACES members, 289 (58 per cent) ASCA members, and 287 (57 per cent) AASA members. Chi-square comparisons demonstrated that the respondents from each group were representative of the total membership of their respective organizations in regard to age and sex.

The 80 items were each given a score of 0 to 4, depending upon the direction of the response as previously determined by the judges. The specialist direction was represented by the lower scores (a perfect specialist score would be 0, and a perfect generalist score would be 320). Factor analysis was used to arrive at an empirical grouping of the items which provided a further basis of comparison among the different professional groups. This analysis resulted in five factors, and a score for each factor was obtained by adding the scores for all items comprising that factor. Thus the groups were compared on the basis of total score and on each of the five factor scores. Hoyt's analysis of variance method [2], based upon a random sample of 50 respondents, resulted in the following reliability coefficients: Generalist-specialist total score .92; Factor I (administrative responsibilities) .82; Factor II (philosophical orientation) .72; Factor III (discipline commitment) .83; Factor IV (clinical emphasis) .84; and Factor V (type of student contact) .47. Because negative factor loadings appeared on Factor V, the reliability coefficient may be an underestimate. For comparative purposes, the groups (counselor-educators, school counselors and school administrators) were subdivided on the basis of training and experience in respect to the total score and each of the factor scores.

Results

Table 1 represents results obtained for each of the groups on total attitude scale score.

In respect to the data presented in Table 1, one-tailed *t*-tests were used to determine differences between the means. Significant differences in the predicted direction were found between ACES members and ASCA members (.05), between ASCA members and AASA members (.001), and between ACES members and AASA members (.001). Within ACES and ASCA significant differences (at least at the .05 level) were found between members on the basis of training (course work) and secondary school experience. Among

TABLE 1
A COMPARISON OF THE DISTRIBUTIONS OF VARIOUS GROUPS ON TOTAL TEST SCORE (SPECIALIST-GENERALIST) *

			Mean	*Standard Deviation*
Members of the Association for Counselor Education and Supervision N-291	Counselor Educators with little secondary school experience	N-44	139.2	30.6
	Counselor Educators	N-220	149.0	31.6
	Counselor Educators and Guidance Supervisors	N-291	152.8	30.7
	Guidance Supervisors	N-71	164.3	24.4
	Guidance Supervisors with more secondary school experience	N-48	168.4	24.0
Members of the American School Counselor Association N-289	Counselors with little secondary school experience and more course work	N-33	148.7	32.7
	Counselors with little secondary school experience	N-118	153.5	27.3
	Counselors	N-289	158.8	26.6
	Counselors with more secondary school experience	N-171	162.4	25.6
	Counselors with more secondary school experience and less course work	N-33	165.6	21.3
Members of the American Association of School Administrators N-287	Administrators from large schools and with more course work	N-28	177.4	17.0
	Administrators from large schools	N-149	183.9	16.8
	Administrators	N-287	183.9	24.4
	Administrators from small schools	N-111	185.4	17.2
	Administrators from small schools and with less course work	N-36	184.1	15.7

*Low score tends to specialist position; high score to generalist position

AASA members, no difference was found on the basis of school size. The overall pattern showed that those with greater professional training tended to the specialist position more than those with more secondary school experience.

Table 2 presents results obtained from Factor I (administrative responsibilities) scores. High scores indicated a broad general definition of a school counselor's responsibilities.

Results of *t*-tests indicate a significant difference between ACES members and ASCA members (.001), between ASCA members and AASA members (.001), and between ACES members and AASA members (.001). All were in the predicted direction, that is, those

TABLE 2

A Comparison of the Distributions of Various Groups on Factor I Score (Administrative Responsibilities) *

			Mean	Standard Deviation
Members of the Association for Counselor Education and Supervision N-291	Counselor Educators with little secondary school experience	N-44	44.4	11.7
	Counselor Educators	N-220	45.8	12.1
	Counselor Educators and Guidance Supervisors	N-291	47.0	12.2
	Guidance Supervisors	N-71	50.9	11.5
	Guidance Supervisors with more secondary school experience	N-48	53.1	11.1
Members of the American School Counselor Association N-289	Counselors with little secondary school experience and more course work	N-33	51.9	11.2
	Counselors with little secondary school experience	N-118	52.7	9.6
	Counselors	N-289	53.6	10.1
	Counselors with more secondary school experience	N-171	54.3	10.4
	Counselors with more secondary school experience and less course work	N-33	54.3	9.2
Members of the American Association of School Administrators N-287	Administrators from large schools and with more course work	N-28	58.3	8.1
	Administrators from large schools	N-149	59.4	8.1
	Administrators	N-287	59.5	8.5
	Administrators from small schools	N-111	59.9	8.4
	Administrators from small schools and with less course work	N-36	58.9	6.7

*Low score tends to narrow role definition; high score to broad role definition.

with the most training and least secondary school experience tended toward a narrow role definition for school counselors. Within ACES, significant differences (at least at .01 level) were found in the predicted direction among those grouped by training and experience. No significant differences were found within ASCA or AASA members grouped similarly.

On Factor II, philosophical orientation (*see* Table 3), results indicate the following differences among the three main groups. ACES members were not significantly different from ASCA members on Factor II. However, there were significant differences between ASCA members and AASA members (.001 level) and between ACES

TABLE 3

A Comparison of the Distribution of Various Groups on Factor II Score (Philosophical Orientation) *

			Mean	*Standard Deviation*
Members of the Association for Counselor Education and Supervision N-291	Counselor Educators with little secondary school experience	N-44	15.2	6.1
	Counselor Educators	N-220	15.6	5.9
	Counselor Educators and Guidance Supervisors	N-291	15.7	5.8
	Guidance Supervisors	N-71	15.9	5.5
	Guidance Supervisors with more secondary school experience	N-48	16.0	5.7
Members of the American School Counselor Association N-289	Counselors with little secondary school experience and more course work	N-33	13.8	6.0
	Counselors with little secondary school experience	N-118	13.7	5.1
	Counselors	N-289	14.1	5.2
	Counselors with more secondary school experience	N-171	14.3	5.3
	Counselors with more secondary school experience and less course work	N-33	16.4	4.5
Members of the American Association of School Administrators N-287	Administrators from large schools and with more course work	N-28	17.5	5.5
	Administrators from large schools	N-149	19.4	5.3
	Administrators	N-287	20.1	5.7
	Administrators from small schools	N-111	21.2	5.9
	Administrators from small schools and with less course work	N-36	22.3	5.2

*Low score tends to nonauthoritarian, student-centered, full-time counselor; high score to somewhat authoritarian, institution-centered, part-time counselor.

members and AASA members (.001 level). Those with greater training and less secondary school experience favored a nonauthoritarian, student-centered, full-time counselor more than the other groups. No significant difference was found within the ACES group or within the ASCA group on the basis of training and experience although school size did make a difference within the AASA group (.001 level) with those from larger schools favoring a nonauthoritarian, student-centered, full-time counselor more than those from smaller schools.

On Factor III, discipline commitment (*see* Table 4), the results

TABLE 4

A COMPARISON OF THE DISTRIBUTIONS OF VARIOUS GROUPS ON FACTOR III SCORE (DISCIPLINE COMMITMENT) *

			Mean	*Standard Deviation*
Members of the Association for Counselor Education and Supervision N-291	Counselor Educators with little secondary school experience	N-44	20.2	8.0
	Counselor Educators	N-220	24.7	8.8
	Counselor Educators and Guidance Supervisors	N-291	25.8	8.6
	Guidance Supervisors	N-71	29.0	6.7
	Guidance Supervisors with more secondary school experience	N-48	29.6	6.4
Members of the American School Counselor Association N-289	Counselors with little secondary school experience and more course work	N-33	23.3	8.3
	Counselors with little secondary school experience	N-118	24.8	7.5
	Counselors	N-289	26.7	7.4
	Counselors with more secondary school experience	N-171	28.0	7.0
	Counselors with more secondary school experience and less course work	N-33	28.0	6.1
Members of the American Association of School Administrators N-287	Administrators from large schools and with more course work	N-28	31.8	4.6
	Administrators from large schools	N-149	33.1	4.8
	Administrators	N-287	32.7	4.7
	Administrators from small schools	N-111	32.7	3.9
	Administrators from small schools and with less course work	N-36	32.1	3.7

*Low score tends to psychological viewpoint; high score to educational viewpoint.

indicate the following differences among the three main groups. Again, no significant difference was found between ACES members and ASCA members on Factor III. However, there were significant differences between ASCA members and AASA members (.001 level) and between ACES members and AASA members (.001 level); those with more course work and less secondary school experience favored a psychological viewpoint more than the other groups. Within the ACES group and within the ASCA group the expected significant differences were found on the basis of training and experience (.001 level). No difference was found on the basis of school size.

TABLE 5
A COMPARISON OF THE DISTRIBUTIONS OF VARIOUS GROUPS ON FACTOR IV SCORE (CLINICAL EMPHASIS) *

			Mean	*Standard Deviation*
Members of the Association for Counselor Education and Supervision N-291	Counselor Educators with little secondary school experience	N-44	17.4	4.7
	Counselor Educators	N-220	17.1	4.8
	Counselor Educators and Guidance Supervisors	N-291	17.3	4.7
	Guidance Supervisors	N-71	17.9	4.1
	Guidance Supervisors with more secondary school experience	N-48	17.6	4.4
Members of the American School Counselor Association N-289	Counselors with little secondary school experience and more course work	N-33	13.7	4.8
	Counselors with little secondary school experience	N-118	14.5	4.6
	Counselors	N-289	15.2	4.5
	Counselors with more secondary school experience	N-171	15.6	4.3
	Counselors with more secondary school experience and less course work	N-33	15.2	4.1
Members of the American Association of School Administrators N-287	Administrators from large schools and with more course work	N-28	15.0	4.4
	Administrators from large schools	N-149	14.1	4.4
	Administrators	N-287	14.0	4.3
	Administrators from small schools	N-111	13.7	3.9
	Administrators from small schools and with less course work	N-36	13.9	3.4

*Low score tends to clinical approach; high score to nonclinical approach.

On Factor IV, clinical emphasis (*see* Table 5), no significant differences were found among the three major groups. The clinical approach emphasizes clinical psychology courses and working with emotionally disturbed students. Thus, emphasis on a clinical approach is not found in the ACES group more than in the other groups, as was the trend for total score and the other factor scores. In fact, the opposite trend is suggested; that is, those with more training and less experience may favor a clinical emphasis for the counselor less than other groups. Within the groups, only one difference was found to be significant: Within the ASCA groups, counselors with less secondary school experience were found to emphasize a

TABLE 6

A Comparison of the Distribution of Various Groups on Factor V Score (Student Contact) *

			Mean	*Standard Deviation*
Members of the Association for Counselor Education and Supervision N-291	Counselor Educators with little secondary school experience	N-44	4.7	2.1
	Counselor Educators	N-220	4.9	2.6
	Counselor Educators and Guidance Supervisors	N-291	5.1	2.7
	Guidance Supervisors	N-71	5.7	3.0
	Guidance Supervisors with more secondary school experience	N-48	5.7	3.0
Members of the American School Counselor Association N-289	Counselors with little secondary school experience and more course work	N-33	6.1	2.6
	Counselors with little secondary school experience	N-118	6.5	2.4
	Counselors	N-289	6.8	2.6
	Counselors with more secondary school experience	N-171	7.0	2.6
	Counselors with more secondary school experience and less course work	N-33	7.8	2.1
Members of the American Association of School Administrators N-287	Administrators from large schools and with more course work	N-28	6.4	2.2
	Administrators from large schools	N-149	7.2	2.2
	Administrators	N-287	7.2	2.3
	Administrators from small schools	N-111	7.5	2.3
	Administrators from small schools and with less course work	N-36	7.7	2.7

*Low score tends to personal and educational counseling; high score to information-giving.

clinical approach more (.05 level) than those with more experience, but the combination of training and experience did not result in significant differences within the group.

On Factor V, type of student contact (*see* Table 6), the following differences were noted among the three groups. A significant difference (.001 level) was found between ACES and ASCA members, between ASCA and AASA members (.05 level), and between ACES and AASA members (.001 level) in the predicted direction. Groups with the most training and least secondary school experience emphasized personal and educational counseling more than the other groups. Within ACES and within ASCA the expected significant differences occurred among members grouped by training and experience. Within the AASA group a significant difference (.05 level) was found among members on the basis of school size coupled with training but not on school size alone.

Discussion

The total score (generalist-specialist dimension) results indicated that while scores of ACES, ASCA, and AASA members clustered around the middle of the scale, significant differences were found among the groups in their attitudes toward the secondary school counselor's role. The findings also support the idea that these differences in attitude may be explained in terms of experience and training; that is, those who have had many courses in guidance, counseling, and psychology and little secondary school experience tend to the specialist position, whereas those with more secondary school experience and less course work tend toward the generalist position.

These results indicate that a counselor is probably trained to be a specialist in a counseling setting and hired to be a generalist in the total school setting. The counselor himself takes a middle-of-the-road position, although his attitudes toward his role more closely resemble the individual who trains him than the person who hires him. It would seem imperative that these three groups discuss their differences and come to a closer agreement concerning the role of the secondary school counselor. This agreement might lead to less tension because each group, including counselors, would have more similar expectations concerning counselor role. But, more importantly, it would lead to more effective service to students.

When groups were compared on Factor I (administrative reponsibilities), significant differences were found which may well lead to problems and misunderstandings. For example, based on counselor educator's responses on this factor, a counselor is trained to believe that many of the duties (administrative in nature) included in Factor I are not part of his job. However, an administrator who hires him expects him to perform these duties. Discussion among these groups could result in closer agreement as to the specific administrative duties, if any, that a counselor should perform.

When groups were compared on Factor II (philosophical orientation), both counselors and counselor educators more so than school administrators emphasized that a counselor should be a nonauthoritarian, student-centered, full-time counselor. Because counselors do hold this perception of a counselor, it may alienate them somewhat from administrators. Counselors may be trying to widen the gap between their previous role as teachers and their present role as counselors. Whatever the reason, it seems that counselors will experience difficulty in obtaining full administrative approval of this viewpoint, especially among those administrators associated with smaller schools. In effect, counselors are asking administrators to appreciate how counselors differ from other educators, especially in terms of placing loyalty to students above loyalty to a school.

Factor III was labeled discipline commitment (education versus psychology). Secondary school administrators tended toward an educational point of view more than other groups; that is, they emphasized the importance of teaching experience, education courses, and the educational function of a counselor. These results seem consistent with results of Factor II, on which administrators emphasized a somewhat authoritarian, institution-centered, part-time counselor. Size of a school did not make a difference among administrators on this factor. Significant differences among counselor educators, guidance supervisors, and counselors were found in relation to training and experience; that is, the formula for producing a psychological viewpoint is to increase training and decrease secondary school experience. This viewpoint emphasizes nonteaching experience, psychology courses, and the mental health function of a counselor.

When groups were compared on Factor IV (clinical emphasis), those with the most training and least experience did not favor a clinical emphasis for a school counselor more than those with less training and more experience. In fact, an opposite trend was noted. However, results related to clinical emphasis indicated that counselors with little secondary school experience emphasized a clinical approach to a greater degree than those with more experience. Less experienced counselors may be overimpressed by the status attached to clinical psychology courses to which they were exposed.

Despite a somewhat lower reliability estimate, comparisons between and among groups in Factor V (type of student contact) followed a fairly consistent pattern, a pattern similar to the total score comparisons and to the first three factor comparisons. The four groups emphasized personal and educational counseling in the following order: counselor educators, guidance supervisors, counselors, secondary school administrators. Each group showed significant differences, one from the other. Experience and training produced hypothesized differences, except that experienced and inexperienced counselors did not differ significantly. The size of student population did not make a difference in the attitudes of secondary school administrators on this factor. It should also be noted that out of a possible range of factor scores from 0 to 24, the highest mean was 7.72. Thus, although administrators may have emphasized more the information-giving aspects of a counselor's role, they did not exclude personal and educational counseling.

Conclusions

1. Many attitudes concerning the counselor's role are related to the generalist-specialist frame of reference.
2. Within this frame of reference, there are significant differences among counselor educators, guidance supervisors, counselors and administrators in their attitudes toward the role of the secondary school counselor.
3. Differences are generally consistent with explanations of training and experience; that is, those with more training in guidance and counseling tend to the specialist position, whereas those with more secondary school experience tend to the generalist position.
4. Counselor educators are identified, more than any other group, with the specialist position. The specialist position is one which favors a narrower definition of the counselor's role, emphasizes a nonauthoritarian student-centered, full-time counselor, favors a psychological viewpoint, and stresses personal and educational counseling.
5. Secondary school administrators, more than any other group, are identified with the generalist position. The generalist position is one which favors a broader definition of the counselor's role, emphasizes a somewhat authoritarian, somewhat institution-centered, part-time counselor, favors an educational viewpoint, and stresses the information-giving functions of the counselor.
6. Secondary school counselors hold a position which is located between administrators and counselor educators, and significantly different from both on most dimensions with the following exceptions. Counselors are similar to counselor educators in favoring a nonauthoritarian, student-centered, full-time counselor, and in emphasizing a psychological viewpoint.
7. The specialist position does not emphasize clinical aspects of the counselor's role; that is, those with more training in guidance and counseling do not see the counselor as a clinical psychologist.
8. Secondary school administrators associated with small schools are generally not significantly different from those associated with large schools on all comparisons, with one exception. Those associated with small schools and with little training in guidance and coun-

seling tend to emphasize a somewhat authoritarian, somewhat institution-centered, part-time counselor more than do those associated with large schools who have had greater training in guidance and counseling.

A Note of Caution

In order to isolate areas of disagreement, it became necessary to use education and psychology as reference points. It might be concluded on the basis of this study that counseling is somewhere between these two points of a continuum. Such a conclusion is however not justified since school counseling cannot be defined merely in terms of its differences from other areas. Counseling has its roots in many disciplines but also has features that are unique to it.

References

1. Dugan, Willis E. "Guidance in the 1970's." *School Counselor,* 1963, *10,* 96–100.

2. Hoyt, Cyril. "Test Reliability Estimated by Analysis of Variance." *Psychometrika,* 1941, *6,* 153–60.

3. Sargent, S. S. "Conceptions of Role and Ego in Contemporary Psychology." In J. H. Rohrer and M. Sherif (eds.), *Social Psychology at the Crossroads.* New York: Harper, 1951.

*

THE ELEMENTARY SCHOOL COUNSELOR—HOW PERCEIVED

CAR M. FOSTER

Educators have long contended that guidance services should be available for pupils from grade one to completion of school. Despite this contention, provisions for integrated elementary school guidance programs, staffed by well-prepared counselors, have lagged considerably. However, progress is being made because of several forces: federal financial support to local elementary schools, local educators, counselor educators, and parents who believe that professional assistance must be given the teacher in helping the child at an early age to prevent developing serious problems later.

There is a current and urgent need for a fairly comprehensive elementary counselor education program including preparing elementary counselors and analyzing local school needs so that the elementary counselor will know how best to use his professional knowledge and skills in the schools to which he may be assigned.

Sullivan [*8*] emphasized the importance of the early school years. He considered this period of particular importance in the social development of the individual and believed that anything which interfered with peer relationships would be doubly handicapping. Handicaps would occur, first, in terms of the original faulty learning resulting from social inadequacy and, second, through the lack of opportunity for corrective or new learning. The child who fears error and/or ridicule may fail to expose himself to corrective or new learning with unfortunate results, thus creating a vicious circle. Authors have recently advocated the elementary school guidance program as an essential part of the school but more importantly for its beneficial outcomes for individual pupils. As part of his report on American

*This article is reprinted from *Counselor Education and Supervision,* 1967, *6,* 102–7, by permission of the publisher and author.

secondary schools, Conant [2] recommended that counseling be started in the elementary school and that it be closely articulated with the secondary school program. The White House Conference on Children and Youth [*1*] had this to report: "In the good elementary school the teacher has, and indeed cannot avoid, the primary role for the guidance of children at the school, and specialized services are to be provided to support the teacher in performing this function."

In describing the duties of an elementary school guidance worker, Martinson and Smallenburg [*7*] viewed him primarily as a resource for teachers. Eckerson and Smith [*3*] refer to him as a "guidance specialist." Hill [*6*] maintains that if the elementary school counselor works mainly with problem children, he will not differ much from the usual pattern of the school psychologist.

Authors in the field have concerned themselves with describing the secondary school counselor's role and function, but little effort has been given to defining role and function of the elementary school counselor. If the confusion that presently exists in the field is to be partially eliminated and the counselor is to function to a maximum extent in the educational setting, it seems axiomatic that all perceptions of his functions are important to an understanding of what he is expected to do and can do.

The primary purpose of this study [*4*] was to identify factors associated with the role and function of the elementary school counselor as perceived by elementary school teachers and administrators, elementary and secondary school counselors, and counselor educators. By determining the similarities and differences among the five groups of educators, it was believed that one issue might be partially resolved, i.e., the kind of program needed to prepare elementary school counselors.

Method

Instruments.—Three instruments were developed for this study. The first instrument, consisting of 143 items denoting counselor functions, sought to classify possible roles performed by elementary school counselors. Ten advanced graduate students enrolled in guidance and counseling at Purdue University were asked to classify each of the 143 items within one of seven role-types, each describing a particular activity. The second instrument consisted of 120 acceptable items retained from the administration of the first instrument. A second set of judges, consisting of 50 subjects randomly selected from the total sample, were asked to rate the degree of importance they would accord the items as legitimate responsibilities of the elementary school counselor. They were asked to score the items on a 9-point Thurstone-type scale, ranging from "very important activity" to "not an important activity." The final instrument, the Elementary School Counselor Questionnaire, was used to determine the opinions of the participating groups concerning the elementary school counselor's functions in grades one through six. Paired comparisons were made of all "type activities" according to the rating given each activity, resulting in 84 paired comparisons, each pair of equal importance to the functions of the elementary school counselor. This questionnaire was then administered to five groups of educators, asking them to select from each pair of statements the one statement they believed to be the most legitimate responsibility of the elementary school counselor.

Subjects and Procedure.—The population sample included five groups of educators believed to be interested in helping to define the role and function of the elementary school counselor: 100 elementary school teachers, 90 elementary school administrators, 100 secondary school counselors, 80 elementary school counselors, and 88 counselor educators. Data were analyzed by two-factor analysis of variance with the appropriate analysis of simple effects, and the Newman-Keuls A Posteriori technique was used to test for individual differences. The .05 level of significance was used for all tests.

Results and Findings

Figure 1 is a geometric representation of the activities for each group of educators. The height of the counseling activity in contrast to the height of the administrative type activity indicates the significance of the activity. The crossing of lines indicates the possibility of significant interaction in the remaining activity profile lines.

1. All five groups of educators perceived counseling-type activities as the most important function that the elementary school counselor performs. Administrative-type activities were considered to be the least important function to be performed by elementary school counselors.

2. Elementary school teachers and counselors perceived social-worker-type activities as being second in importance. Counselor educators, secondary school counselors, and elementary school administrators viewed consultant-type activities as second in importance for elementary school counselors.

3. All groups except teachers viewed guidance-type activities as third in importance of the functions to be performed by elementary

school counselors. Teachers viewed psychologist-psychometrist-type activities third most important.

4. Counselor educators and elementary school counselors placed

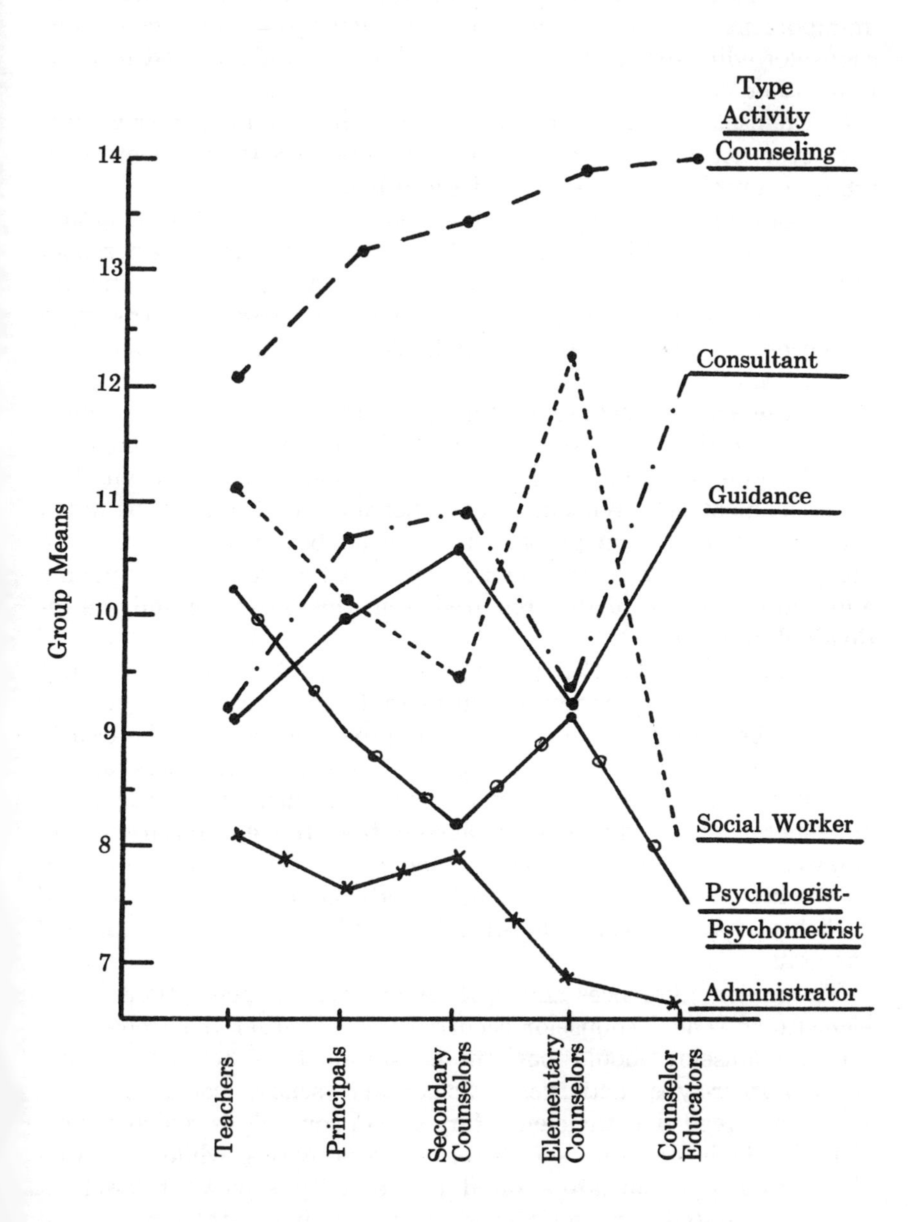

FIG. I. Profiles for groups at levels of activities.

more importance on the elementary school counselor conducting counseling-type activities than did elementary school teachers and principals or secondary school counselors.

5. Although all groups rated administrative-type activities as an unimportant type of function for the elementary school counselor, counselor educators and elementary school counselors rated it lower than other groups of educators.

6. Counselor educators and secondary school counselors saw guidance-type activities as more important functions for an elementary school counselor than did any of the other educators.

7. Total group comparisons indicated that counseling-type activities were of utmost importance as functions of the elementary school counselor. Consultant-, social-worker-, and guidance-type activities were rated next in importance. Psychologist-psychometrist-type activities were rated a weak fourth. Administrative-type activities were rejected by all groups.

8. Teachers and counselor educators displayed the largest difference in how they perceived the role and function of the elementary school counselor, while principals and secondary school counselors were the most homogeneous in their perceptions. It should be noted that this difference in perception occurred between those who are presently employed in the elementary school working with students and those who are further removed from the classroom and the individual student.

Perceptions of the elementary school counselor held by the five groups of educators reflected considerable communality as well as some differences. Communality among groups usually can be clearly stated and is more easily accepted. However, differences among groups raise additional questions that require further investigations. In general, these groups were agreed that the elementary school counselor as a school staff member should be professionally prepared to conduct a counseling relationship with children directed toward such broad areas as personal-social and educational and vocational concerns.

The major differences among these five groups' perceptions of the elementary school counselor occurred over whether the elementary school counselor should perform consultant-type activities versus social-worker-type activities. Elementary school counselors and teachers agreed that the elementary school counselor's role and function should incorporate social-work-type activities, while the other three groups of educators rated this activity somewhat lower. It should be noted that social-worker-type activity statements dealt primarily in the area of out-of-school contacts, whereas consultant-type activities dealt primarily with services offered within the school proper.

Summary and Conclusions

The elementary school counselor, whatever his job is perceived to be, is not looked upon as a "cure-all" for problems existing in the elementary school. He is a staff team member and offers only one of many needed services at the elementary school level. Consensus as to the specific role and function of the elementary school counselor has not been and may never be achieved. It may be inferred from the study that preparation programs for elementary school counselors cannot be specifically prescribed at the present time. The lack of actual practitioners in the field impairs any definite notions as to direction for preparation programs. Individual schools require counselors to adapt their role and function to their specific needs. Elementary school counselors who work in schools that employ social workers would most certainly perform functions that are different from elementary school counselors who work in schools that employed no other special school personnel. Differences in school policies, areas of the country, personnel employed, and the needs of various individuals will necessitate some modification of any idealistic model proposed. The direction for functioning elementary school counselor practitioners will come into existence by trying out a variety of models and selecting the best or choosing from among the best of many.

References

1. *Children in a Changing World! Golden Anniversary White House Conference on Children and Youth.* Washington: U. S. Government Printing Office, 1960.

2. Conant, J. B. *The American High School Today.* New York: McGraw-Hill, 1959.

3. Eckerson, L. & Smith, H. M. "Guidance in the Elementary School." *School Life.* U. S. Department of Health, Education, and Welfare Bulletin, 1962, No. OE–25033.

4. Foster, C. M. "Perceptions of the Role and Function of the Elementary School Counselor." Unpublished doctoral dissertation, Purdue University, 1965.

5. Garry, R. *Guidance Techniques for Elementary Teachers.* Columbus, Ohio: Charles E. Merrill, 1963.

6. Hill, G. E. "Guidance Needs of the Elementary School: Their Relationship to the Preparation, Role and Function of a Full-Time Guidance Specialist." Speech given at the American Personnel and Guidance Association Convention, San Francisco, March, 1964.

7. Martinson, R. & Smallenburg, H. W. *Guidance in Elementary Schools.* New York: Prentice-Hall, 1958.

8. Sullivan, H. S. *The Interpersonal Theory of Psychiatry.* New York: Norton, 1953.

THE SCHOOL COUNSELOR AS PERCEIVED BY SCHOOL COUNSELORS AND THEIR PRINCIPALS

THOMAS J. SWEENEY

It has been with increasing interest that counselors, counselor educators, and state supervisors of guidance have sought to define and delimit the role of the secondary school counselor. Studies conducted in the fifties found counselors to be performing many and varied duties. Studies by Hitchcock (1953), Martyn (1957), Tennyson (1958), and Vassello and Kindred (1957) seemed to suggest that when school counselors did not have a clear concept of their role, they tended to perform more clerical and administrative tasks than they did guidance or counseling functions. Knapp and Denny (1961), after reviewing studies of what counselors were doing, concluded that one inherent difficulty for a new counselor arises from the fact that, unlike the new teacher who can receive direction and support from other teachers on the staff, the school counselor is more often alone in his position. Since the establishment of funds for school guidance and the training of school counselors under the National Defense Education Act of 1958, the number of counselors has grown rapidly. In an effort to assist counselors in their proper role-identification, the staff and members of the Ohio School Counselors Association have sponsored five cooperative studies designed to investigate the role of the school counselor. This paper is a report on one of the five studies completed to date.

*This article is reprinted from *Personnel and Guidance Journal,* 1966, *44,* 844–49, by permission of the publisher, the American Personnel and Guidance Association, and the author.

Problem

The school administrators' assistance and support of the guidance services long have been recognized as a central factor in the establishment of an effective program. From their position as leaders of the educational program in the school, principals play a major part in defining the role of their school counselor. Studies by Kemp (1962), and Chenault and Seegars (1962), led them to believe that counselors and principals may vary in their expectations of the counselor as a person. With the preceding factors in mind, this study was designed to answer the following questions:

1. Do counselors and administrators assign similar priorities to various areas of counselor activity?
2. Do counselors and administrators identify similar types of attributes as necessary for the counselor to be effective in his role?
3. Do certain personal, educational, or experiential factors in the background of the counselors or administrators appear to be related to their perception of the counselor's role or his personal attributes?

Population and Procedure

The populations of counselors and administrators for the study were obtained by sending questionnaires to all certified counselors or pupil personnel workers reported in the 1962–63 Ohio School Principals' Report to the State Department of Education. From a total population of 886 full-time, certified counselors, a random, stratified sample of 220 counselors and their administrators was selected (N = 210, five administrators had two counselors). Chi-square analysis for differences between the original total population of counselors and each population of counselors returning usable instruments showed no significant differences in their educational, experiential, personal, or situational background. Similar tests were made for the administrators and no significant differences were found to exist.

Two instruments in addition to informational questionnaires were utilized. The first instrument was constructed and used by Stevic (1963) as a means of determining the performance of Ohio school counselors in six areas of activity. Sixty forced-choice triads containing statements representative of counselor activities permitted a hierarchial listing of areas when numerical values were assigned to the responses. The items were grouped into six sub-areas of counselor activities. These areas were: (1) providing service to individual students; (2) providing services to groups of students; (3) establishing and maintaining staff relationships; (4) promoting the general school program; (5) establishing and maintaining community relationships; and (6) accepting professional responsibilities.

The personality measuring instrument, the Interpersonal Check List (ICL), (1955), contains 16 variables arranged in a circular continuum. The most recent form contains 128 items, 8 items for each of the 16 variables. Intensity levels were built into the instrument to distinguish between adaptive and maladaptive amounts of the behavior. The octant categories were: managerial-autocratic, competitive-exploitive, critical-aggressive, skeptical-distrustful, modest-self-effacing, docile-dependent, cooperative-overconventional and responsible-overgenerous.

In order to test for differences in the perceptions of the counselors and administrators it was necessary to determine group scores in each of the sub-areas and categories of the two instruments. It then was possible to calculate *t*-tests to rank sub-areas as well as to determine significant differences between the counselors' and administrators' scores. From the information gathered by questionnaires, sub-groups of counselors and administrators were established based upon their personal, educational, or experiential background.

Findings

One of the preliminary questions answered was whether or not counselors had a clear concept of the priorities that they should place upon their activities. The findings reported in Table 1 show that the counselors distinguished priorities among the first four sub-areas of activity but not among the last three. "Promoting the general school program," "providing services to groups of students," and "accepting professional responsibilities" appear to denote areas of activity in which counselors have not established definite priorities. The counselors did rank "providing services to individual students," "establishing and maintaining staff relationships," and "establishing and maintaining community relationships," in that order, as their preference of activity.

Being aware of the administrators' position as leader of the school program, their perceptions of the priorities for counselor activity become even more important in view of the counselors' difficulty in establishing a ranking of all their activities. In Table 2 it is interesting to note that the school administrators ranked the sub-areas of counselor activity with statistically very significant differences between the mean scores. Evidently the administrators have some fairly definite priorities for the counselor's activities.

Table 3 shows that the counselors and administrators rank the

TABLE 1

RANK AND SIGNIFICANCE OF DIFFERENCES IN MEANS FOR SUB-AREAS OF THE ACTIVITIES INSTRUMENT BY THE SCHOOL COUNSELORS
(N = 179)

Sub-Area	*Rank*	*Mean**	*Level of Signifi-cance†*
Providing services to individual students	1	49.46	
			0.01
Establishing and maintaining staff relationships	2	34.46	
			0.01
Establishing and maintaining community relationships	3	26.35	
			0.01
Promoting the general school program	4	24.09	
			No
Providing services to groups of students	5	23.10	
			No‡
Accepting professional responsibilities	6	23.09	

*Highest possible score in each sub-area is sixty.

†Significance figure indicates difference level between the higher area and the area immediately below in the table.

‡An additional *t*-test determined no significant difference between sub-areas 4 and 6.

counselor activities similarly in four of the six sub-areas. However, they placed significantly different emphasis upon four of the sub-areas in which counselors function. Counselor scores in the areas relating to working with individual students and accepting professional responsibilities were significantly higher than the administrators'. The administrators' scores in the areas relating to counselor function in working with staff members and promoting the general school program were significantly higher than the counselors'.

In answer to the first question, then, it was found that counselors and administrators assigned similar priorities to four of six sub-areas of counselor activity. However, they showed significantly different emphasis in four of the six sub-areas. Equally important, only the administrators ranked all six sub-areas with significant differences between the mean scores. The counselors could rank only the first four sub-areas of counselor activity with significant differences between means.

In an effort to answer the second question regarding counselor attributes, the mean scores of each sixteenth of the ICL were tested

TABLE 2
RANK AND SIGNIFICANCE OF DIFFERENCES IN MEANS FOR SUB-AREAS OF THE ACTIVITIES INSTRUMENT BY THE SCHOOL ADMINISTRATORS
(N = 86)

Sub-Area	*Rank*	*Mean**	*Level of Significance†*
Providing services to individual students	1	47.28	
			0.01
Establishing and maintaining staff relationships	2	38.67	
			0.01
Promoting the general school program	3	27.77	
			0.01
Establishing and maintaining community relationships	4	25.12	
			0.01
Providing services to groups of students	5	22.45	
			0.01
Accepting professional responsibilities	6	18.81	

*Highest possible score in each sub-area is sixty.
†Significance figure denotes difference level between the higher area and the area immediately below in the table.

TABLE 3
DIFFERENCES BETWEEN MEAN SCORES OF SUB-AREAS ON THE ACTIVITIES INSTRUMENT FOR SCHOOL COUNSELORS AND SCHOOL ADMINISTRATORS

Sub-Area	*Counselors N = 179*		*Administrators N = 86*		*Level of Significance*
	Mean	*Rank*	*Mean*	*Rank*	
Providing services to individual students	49.46	1	47.28	1	.05
Establishing and maintaining staff relationships	34.46	2	38.67	2	.01
Establishing and maintaining community relationships	26.35	3	25.12	4	No
Promoting the general school program	24.09	4	27.77	3	.01
Providing services to groups of students	23.10	5	22.45	5	No
Accepting professional responsibilities	23.09	6	18.81	6	.01

for significant differences between counselors' and administrators' scores. Very significant differences were found to exist between scores in three of the sixteenths (Table 4). In each case the administrators scored the counselor higher for possessing attributes under the headings of responsible, competitive, and autocratic. In general, the item

TABLE 4

DIFFERENCES BETWEEN MEAN SCORES OF SIXTEENTHS ON THE INTERPERSONAL CHECKLIST FOR SCHOOL COUNSELORS AND SCHOOL ADMINISTRATORS

	Counselors $N = 183$		*Administrators* $N = 105$	
Sixteenth	*Mean*	*Rank*	*Mean*	*Rank*
Cooperative	25.19	1	26.59	1
Over-Conventional	34.28	2	33.20	4
Over-Generous	34.28	3	32.99	3
Responsible*	34.54	4	32.67	2
Managerial	38.90	5	39.03	5
Dependent	40.55	6	39.84	7
Autocratic*	41.01	7	39.24	6
Docile	42.23	8	42.15	9
Self-Effacing	43.49	9	42.75	10
Competitive*	43.62	10	41.88	8
Exploitive	45.90	11	45.60	11
Modest	47.78	12	47.95	13
Aggressive	48.57	13	47.66	12
Distrustful	50.14	14	49.10	14
Skeptical	54.67	15	54.73	15
Blunt	55.06	16	55.13	16

*Difference significant at one per cent level (Lower scores show greater acceptance of the category item).

content of these sixteenths could be interpreted as leadership attributes, e.g., encourages others, self-respecting, forceful. The tendency for the administrators to prefer the counselor as possessing these characteristics to a greater extent than the counselors believed necessary, though not always statistically significant, was in evidence in the ranking of octants, sixteenths, and individual attributes.

The second question can be answered by stating that although counselors and administrators tend to identify similar attributes as necessary for the counselor to be effective in his role, the administrators showed a desire for the counselors to demonstrate a greater degree of leadership characteristics.

Efforts to identify personal, experiential, and educational factors that might be related to counselor and administrator preferences for certain counselor activities or attributes necessary for the counselor were generally unsuccessful. Teaching experience, time assigned to guidance activities, the number of students for whom the counselor was responsible, and membership in a local counselors' organization variously affected responses to some sub-areas of the activities instrument. Willingness to participate in the study, membership in the American Personnel and Guidance Association, number of years in a guidance position, and similar criteria for grouping uncovered no factors relating to any significantly different perception of the counselor's activities. In general, it must be said that regardless of the criteria for grouping the counselors, only scattered relationships were found between the counselors' experiential and educational background and the various criteria.

One notable exception to these findings was the greater agreement which counselors who aspire to school administration positions had with the administrators' responses to the counselor activities. In only one sub-area, "establishing and maintaining staff relationships," did the counselors disagree significantly (.05) with the administrators. In this case the administrators considered this to be more important than the counselors. In effect, then, it suggests that counselors aspiring to administrative positions tend to agree more with the administrators upon the activities that they prefer for the counselor to perform.

Similar efforts to identify background information about the school administrators that might relate to differing perceptions of the activities of the counselors were inconclusive. Factors such as possession of junior or senior high school counseling certificates, number of years as an administrator, and experience in counseling practicum were among the criteria for grouping.

Discussion

In response to the first question, it was found that, in general, the counselors and administrators ranked the counselor activity subareas similarly. However, significant differences existed in the degree to which each group believed that certain activities in four areas were important for the counselor to perform. This seems to support Schmidt's suggestion that it may be the lesser matters upon which the counselor and administrator lack agreement (1962).

An example of how disagreement might exist can be constructed hypothetically from an analysis of the counselors' and administrators' scores on items in some of the triads. Mean scores of both groups place "accepting professional responsibilities" as last of the six counselor-activity areas. Counselors' scores in the last three areas could not be ranked, as with the administrators', by statistically significant differences. For some counselors this could mean that their administrators may expect them to score standardized tests, make suggestions to teachers on teaching methods, or do clerical work on pupil personnel records as compared to directing some of their energy toward attending classes to improve their counseling skills or participating in a professional organization. Assuming that the counselor is among those who find it difficult to define his role in these areas, it would seem likely that their administrators' wishes would prevail.

The principals' expectations for clerical and administrative help is especially understandable if counselors show no cause for thinking otherwise. For many principals, the counselor is likely to be seen chiefly as the quasi-administrator of guidance services. This also can explain their preference for slightly more from the counselor in qualities of administrator-type leadership.

Among the major findings of the study was the indication that while counselors and administrators ranked attributes for the counselor similarly, administrators tended to emphasize leadership attributes more strongly than counselors. This tends to corroborate findings of Kemp (1962) and Chenault and Seegars (1962). If administrators interpret the counselor's role from their perceptual frame of references as a quasi-administrator of guidance services, it is understandable that they also would tend to see him in terms of attributes that they consider necessary for an administrator. It is not so much a matter of possessing given attributes as it is the manner in which they are demonstrated. A counselor who is cognizant of the importance of establishing an effective working relationship with the students is likely to hesitate being a leader in supervising discipline in the halls. However, leadership in proposing, coordinating, maintaining, and evaluating the school's guidance program demands every attribute of an effective leader that the counselor possesses. It appears that counselors can do themselves a favor, one which their administrators would seem to welcome, by assuming appropriate leadership for the guidance services, especially as they relate to the general school program. Professional affiliation, in-service training, and constant contact with other counselors should assist all counselors to better establish their professional identity in a manner that permits projection to their various publics. In addition, it is recommended that counselors initiate a statement of objectives of the guidance program. This would provide a meaningful vehicle by which to discuss counselor responsibilities with the school principal. In this way, activities that contribute most directly to objectives of the guidance program would be clearly identified.

References

Chenault, J. & Seegars, J., Jr. "The Interpersonal Diagnosis of Principals and Counselors." *Personnel and Guidance Journal,* 1962, *41,* 118–22.

Hitchcock, W. L. "Counselors Feel They Should." *Personnel and Guidance Journal,* 1953, *32,* 72–74.

Kemp, C. "Counseling and Need Structure of High School Principals and of Counselors." *Journal of Counseling Psychology,* 1962, *9,* 326–28.

Knapp, D. L., & Denny, E. W. "The Counselor's Responsibility in Role Definition." *Personnel and Guidance Journal,* 1961, *40,* 48–50.

La Forge, R., & Suczek, R. F. "The Interpersonal Dimension of Personality, III, An Interpersonal Checklist." *Journal of Personality,* 1955, *24,* 94–112.

Martyn, K. "We Are Wasting the Counselor's Time." *California Journal of Secondary Education,* 1957, *32,* 439–41.

Schmidt, L. D. "Concepts of the Role of Secondary School Counselors." *Personnel and Guidance Journal,* 1962, *40,* 600–605.

Stevic, R. R. "The School Counselor's Role: Commitment and Marginality." Unpublished doctoral dissertation, Ohio State University, 1963.

Tennyson, W. W. "Time: The Counselor's Dilemma." *Personnel and Guidance Journal,* 1958, *37,* 129–35.

Vassello, T., & Kindred, L. "How Counseling Can Be Improved." *Nation's Schools,* 1957, *59,* 58–60.

*

THE COUNSELING FUNCTION AS SEEN BY STUDENTS, PARENTS AND TEACHERS

PHILIP A. PERRONE
MARY L. WEIKING
ELWYN H. NAGEL

Four areas receiving attention when the counseling function in the school is discussed are: the importance of student and teacher perception and its effect on the implementation of the counselor's role (Braden, 1953; Durnall, 1952; Grant, 1954); the failure of students to make the transition from the historical view of the counselor as one who assists them with only vocational decisions to one where he is concerned with the whole person (Heilfron, 1960; Robinson, 1953; Rogers, 1942); the lack of effective communication of the counselor's role (Gibson, 1962; Grant, 1954; Jensen, 1955; Kerr,

*This article is reprinted from *Journal of Counseling Psychology,* 1965, *12,* 148–52, by permission of the publisher, the American Psychological Association, and the authors.

1962; Perrone and Evans, 1964; Swann, 1963; Tyler, 1961); and students evidencing awareness of certain needs and problems and lacking awareness of others (Grant, 1954; Hartley and Hedlund, 1952; Warman, 1960). This study was undertaken with these four areas in mind.

The investigators chose to ask junior high school students, their parents and teachers to express their views of the counseling function. This information was to be used in planning instructional programs for students and parents and in conducting in-service meetings for teachers in communicating the counselor's role, with emphasis upon the counseling function, prior to and during the initiation of a guidance program. In this study answers were sought to the following questions:

1. What student types do junior high school students, their parents and teachers see as requiring counseling and to what degree?
2. Do these three groups differ in the degree of counseling they recommend for the 14 student types?
3. Do students who indicate many problems and those who indicate few problems differ in the degree of counseling they recommend for the 14 student types?
4. Do the parents of students who indicate many problems and the parents of students who indicate few problems differ in the degree of counseling they recommend for the 14 student types?

Method

It was decided to use an instrument which would set forth problems which could be dealt with in varying degrees by a counselor. Such an instrument was developed by Robinson (1953) to study teacher and counselor perceptions of the counseling function and modified by Heilfron (1960) in surveying high school students' perception of the counseling function. Further adaptations were necessary in order to use the instrument with junior high school students and to deal with the criticism of Tyler (1961) that the degree of counseling should also designate the kind of counseling relationship. A preliminary study with another group of junior high school students indicated that the basic image of the student types used by Robinson and Heilfron had been maintained. In addition, the Mooney Problem Checklist was administered to all the students to provide information necessary in answering three of the above research questions.

When analysis of student responses produced no significant intergroup differences among the seventh- and eighth-grade boys and girls, the investigators decided to treat the students as one group.

Similarly, the responses of the parents of girls and the parents of boys were undifferentiated so both sets of parents' responses were combined into one. The revised instrument is presented below with labels added to facilitate discussion.

Counseling Need

Following is a set of descriptions of the counseling that could be offered to junior high school students. Each description has a number so that the least amount of counseling is No. 1 and the greatest amount of counseling is No. 4. Then brief descriptions of different types of students in junior high school are given. Please indicate by number the degree of counseling you feel each student needs.

1. Routine programming conference once each year which could include making up the class schedule, reporting of test scores, information about educational and occupational opportunities.
2. Sitting down with the counselor three or four times a year in addition to a programming conference to discuss school progress or future plans a student might have.
3. Talking with the counselor each month or more frequently in addition to a programming conference so special plans concerning the student's needs or personal problems can be discussed.
4. Referral of student to an agency outside the school or to an individual in private practice for regular counseling.

Student Types

Athlete.—A natural athlete. Even at this grade level is the star in all athletic events held by the school. Studies about the same as other students and gets "C" grades. Is friendly and popular because he isn't conceited.

Bright.—Very bright student who has found school work easy. Particularly likes mathematics and gets "A's" in all his courses with little or no effort. (His success in spite of his poor study habits makes it difficult to convince other students that they might benefit from learning better study methods.) The other kids like him. Often a leader.

Cqueer.—Everyone is aware of his behavior because it is so different. He is nervous, gets upset over little things, and keeps to himself. You never know what he'll do next. Doing very poor school work. The other kids tease and make fun of him.

Dumb.—He has always done poor school work, and in eighth grade he only does fifth grade work in reading and arithmetic. He is older and bigger than other students and is well liked by students.

Engineer.—Has his heart set on becoming an engineer. Has gotten high grades all through grade school and junior high school also. Has many mechanical and electrical hobbies. Not very sociable but is well liked by students.

Failing.—Student studies about the same as others and is getting a "C" in everything but math which he is failing. He is upset by the failing grade. Has always had trouble with math, just as his mother did. Liked by his fellow-students.

Gauche.—Not very popular with the other kids. The way he dresses you can spot him a mile away. Not always clean, has poor manners, seems awkward. Does good work in school, however.

Homely.—She just isn't good looking at all. She has a pleasant personality, gets along well with other people, and other students in class choose her to work on class projects. Outside of school she doesn't get invited to parties and other girls tend to leave her out of social activities. Does good work in school.

Ill.—Constantly has colds. Lately has had a bad cough and has lost weight. Says she doesn't feel good. When she does attend school she does good work and is liked by students.

Jerk.—Does well in school. Always looking for ways to please his teachers. Mama's-boy type, immature and childish in his actions. Disliked by other students.

Kiddish.—Girl shows many forms of immature behavior, baby-talk, depends upon her mother to make all her decisions. However, she behaves in such a "cute" manner that she is popular with many of the boys. Does average work in school because her parents force her to study and they help her with her work.

Lazy.—Never does any school work but gets high test scores. Liked by students, takes part in many school activities. Thinks "C" grades are good enough in junior high, even though he got "A's" and "B's" in elementary school. Plans to go to an expensive private college.

Medicine.—Wants to become a doctor but has gotten many failing grades in the past and in junior high even though he tries hard. Will probably have difficulty even in being admitted to college or, if admitted, will have difficulty staying there.

Not known.—Never chosen by students to work on committees. Does average work in school but doesn't contribute to class discussion. Teachers say nothing about her stands out. Prefers to be alone. Not rejected by students—just considered sort of shy and retiring.

POPULATION

The population studied included 371 seventh and eighth grade students with an approximately even number of boys and girls, 250 pairs of parents and nine classroom teachers in a suburban village of 8200 people in Wisconsin. The mean Henmon-Nelson IQ for eighth graders and the mean Otis IQ for seventh graders were both approximately one standard deviation above the national mean. On the Mooney Problem Checklist the mean number of indicated problems for students in the upper quartile was 53.1 and the mean for students in the lower quartile was 6.5.

The occupations of the fathers of the 371 students using the occupational categories devised by Roe were: Service—9 per cent, Business Contact—10 per cent, Organization—19 per cent, Technology—39 per cent, Outdoor—7 per cent, Science—4 per cent, General Cultural—6 per cent, Arts and Entertainment—1 per cent, not available—5 per cent. In terms of occupational level, 1 per cent were in level 1, 16 per cent in level 2, 34 per cent in level 3, 27 per cent in level 4, 17 per cent in levels 5 and 6, 5 per cent not available. There were 15 per cent of the mothers employed outside the home, 3 per cent of the homes with no mothers, and the remaining 82 per cent of the mothers were identified as full time housewives.

RESULTS

The percentage of students, parents and teachers who specified each degree of counseling for each student type is presented in Table 1. Weights of 1 through 4 were assigned to the four descriptions of counseling and a mean degree of counseling and a measure of variability (S^2) were computed for the responses of the three groups (*see* Table 2). There were almost no statistically significant differences in variability (S^2) of perception of the counseling function for each group on each student type.

The similarity of the rankings of counseling need for the 14 student types by the three groups is seen in the Rho coefficients. These coefficients ranged from .95 between teachers and parents, through .86 between parents and students, to .82 between teachers and students.

A comparison between the three groups for recommended degree of counseling for the 14 student types as a whole using χ^2 produced a significant difference between parents and students and parents and teachers. The χ^2 between parents and students was 96.41 which is significant at the .001 level. The χ^2 between parents and teachers

TABLE 1

DEGREE OF COUNSELING RECOMMENDED FOR CERTAIN STUDENT TYPES BY JUNIOR HIGH SCHOOL STUDENTS, THEIR PARENTS, AND TEACHERS

	Students (N = 371)					*Parents*				*Teachers (N = 9)*			
	Degree of Counseling					*Degree of Counseling*				*Degree of Counseling*			
Student Type	*1* %	*2* %	*3* %	*4* %	*N**	*1* %	*2* %	*3* %	*4* %	*1* %	*2* %	*3* %	*4* %
Athlete	39	51	8	2	248	28	57	14	1	33	55	11	0
Bright	61	31	6	2	249	37	35	23	5	11	88	0	0
Cqueer	2	7	43	48	250	1	1	31	67	0	0	33	66
Dumb	2	11	54	33	249	5	10	49	36	11	0	66	22
Engineer	60	34	4	2	250	43	39	14	4	55	44	0	0
Failing	7	57	32	4	249	4	36	56	4	0	66	33	0
Gauche	5	22	55	18	249	5	15	68	12	0	33	66	0
Homely	19	47	27	7	247	17	37	42	4	44	33	22	0
Ill	19	39	20	22	243	7	11	28	54	11	22	11	55
Jerk	5	22	57	16	248	5	15	50	30	0	22	77	0
Kiddish	5	24	44	27	247	5	19	54	22	0	11	77	11
Loafer	10	51	34	5	249	8	47	39	6	0	99	0	0
Medicine	3	28	50	19	249	5	20	60	15	0	66	33	0
Not Known	6	32	45	17	248	6	31	54	9	0	22	66	11

*All parents did not respond to each student type.

TABLE 2

TEACHERS', STUDENTS', AND PARENTS' RECOMMENDED DEGREE OF COUNSELING FOR DIFFERENT STUDENT TYPES

	Teachers (N = 9)		*Students (N = 371)*		*Parents (N = 243-250)*		*Student-Parent*
Student Type	*X*	*S²*	*X*	*S²*	*X*	*S²*	*t*
Athlete	1.778	.394	1.722	.460	1.867	.421	.837
Bright	1.889	.103	1.485	.482	1.944	.775	6.920*
Cqueer	3.667	.219	3.367	.499	3.636	.328	5.380*
Dumb	3.000	.555	3.181	.501	3.177	.610	.200
Engineer	1.444	.248	1.496	.472	1.788	.687	4.616*
Failing	2.333	.223	2.332	.446	2.598	.403	4.939*
Gauche	2.667	.220	2.854	.574	2.855	.471	.020
Homely	1.778	.172	2.210	.695	2.328	.649	1.743
Ill	3.111	1.211	2.466	1.070	3.292	.834	3.202†
Jerk	2.778	.172	2.844	.540	3.056	.629	3.403†
Kiddish	3.000	.667	2.922	.707	2.939	.585	.255
Loafer	2.000	.000	2.348	.522	2.446	.527	1.650
Medicine	2.333	.224	2.854	.580	2.859	.525	.080
Not Known	2.889	.321	2.733	.654	2.661	.532	1.125

**p* .001; using a two-tailed test.
†*p* .01; using a two-tailed test.

was 13.37 which is significant at the .01 level. The χ^2 between students and teachers was 6.16 which is not statistically significant. This analysis suggests that parents are more in favor of intensive counseling by either school counselors or outside experts than either teachers or students. Students also tend to favor more intensive counseling than teachers.

The significance of the differences between student, parent, and teacher mean degree of counseling recommended for *each* student type was determined by *t* tests. Although χ^2 showed teachers valuing counseling least, when a comparison is made between the three groups, there are no differences between teachers and the parents or students in the recommended degree of counseling for any one of the 14 student types. This lack of significance for individual *t*-tests is probably due to the small *N* for the teachers ($N = 9$). Comparing parents and students, however, parents recommended more counseling for the Bright, Cqueer, Engineer, Failing, Ill and Jerk student types. The values of the *t* ratios and the significance levels for these comparisons are shown in Table 2.

A comparison of students who indicated many problems (X = 53.1 on the Mooney) with students who indicated few problems (X = 6.5 on the Mooney) showed statistically significant differences in the amount of counseling recommended for two student types. Those with fewer indicated problems recommended more counseling for the Cqueer student type and students who indicated more problems recommended greater counseling for the Homely student type. The parents of students who indicated many problems when compared with parents of students who indicated few problems, showed no statistically significant differences in the amount of counseling recommended for any of the student types.

Conclusions

1. The students, parents, and teachers in this study appear in general to agree on the rank order in which they see different pupils needing intensity of counseling service (Rho's = .95, .86 and .82).

2. The parents and students were in close agreement concerning the degree of counseling required by any one student type. Where differences existed, parents indicated a need for more counseling than did the students. These differences were found for student types rated as requiring a low degree of counseling as well as a high degree of counseling. The parent-student differences may be a result of more parent awareness of the probability of a junior high school student's behavior continuing into adult life or the parents and students may focus on different phrases used in describing a student type. Parents can be seen as more in favor of intensive counseling by either school counselors or outside experts than teachers or stu-

dents. This would suggest that parents are ready for more extensive counseling programs (more than even the teachers) and gives some support to the development of such programs in the schools.

3. The students who indicated many problems and those who indicated few problems, in general, do not differ in the degree of counseling they see as necessary for the different student types. Likewise, the parents of these two student groups do not differ in the degree of counseling they recommend for the 14 student types. This suggests that student's and parent's perception of counseling need is not related to the number of problems indicated by the student.

References

Braden, M. M. "Former Students Evaluate Guidance." *Journal of Educational Research,* 1953, *47,* 127–33.

Durnall, E. J. "Students Scrutinize a Guidance Program." *Personnel and Guidance Journal,* 1952, *31,* 187–88.

Gibson, R. "Pupil Opinion of High School Guidance Programs." *Personnel and Guidance Journal,* 1962, *40,* 453–57.

Grant, C. W. "How Do Students Perceive the Counselor's Role?" *Personnel and Guidance Journal,* 1954, *32,* 386–88.

Grant, C. W. "The Counselor's Role." *Personnel and Guidance Journal,* 1954, *33,* 74–77.

Hartley, D., & Hedlund, P. A. *Reactions of High School Seniors to Their Guidance Programs.* New York: University of New York Press, University of the State of New York Bulletin 1411, 1952.

Heilfron, M. "The Function of Counseling as Perceived by High School Students." *Personnel and Guidance Journal,* 1960, *39,* 133–36.

Jensen, R. "Student Feeling About Counseling Help." *Personnel and Guidance Journal,* 1955, *33,* 498–504.

Kerr, W. D. "Students' Perceptions of Counselor Role in the College Decision." *Personnel and Guidance Journal,* 1962, *41,* 337–42.

Perrone, P. A., & Evans, D. L. "The Elementary School Counselor? Coordinator? Or What?" *Counselor Education and Supervision,* 1964, *4,* 28–31.

Robinson, F. P. "Guidance for All: In Principle and in Practice." *Personnel and Guidance Journal,* 1953, *31,* 500–504.

Roe, A. *Psychology of Occupations.* New York: Wiley, 1956.

Rogers, C. R. *Counseling and Psychotherapy.* Boston: Houghton Mifflin, 1942.

Swann, M. H. "The Changing Role of the School Counselor." *School Counselor,* 1963, *11,* 94–101.

Tyler, L. *The Work of the Counselor.* New York: Appleton-Century-Crofts, 1961.

Warman, R. E. "Differential Perception of Counseling Function." *Journal of Counseling Psychology,* 1960, *7,* 269–74.

*

CHANGING STUDENTS' PERCEPTIONS OF THE COUNSELOR'S ROLE

MARILYN HEILFRON

Crisis counseling for the few or developmental counseling for the many is an issue recurring in guidance literature.

Ten years ago Robinson said that in principle counseling and guidance were for all students, but in practice counselors devoted most of their time to those with intellectual and social handicaps [*2*]. Studies by Stewart [*4*] and Heilfron [*1*] have suggested that the *attitudes* of counselors, teachers and students play a role in determining the *kinds of problems* brought to the counselor and the *types of students* who avail themselves of counseling services.

These studies indicate that counseling is commonly considered to be for students with intellectual, social and emotional deficiencies. Neither those students performing well academically and socially who might need help in deciding where best to apply their talents, nor those whose relatively good defenses against certain emotional problems limited their growth in other areas were expected to receive help.

From these considerations the question grew: Assuming that counselors wanted to help students with all types of problems, what could a counseling department do to change the prevailing attitude among students that only those with certain types of problems should seek counseling? One approach that suggested itself was that students be "educated" to change their perception.

---

*This article is reprinted from *The School Counselor,* 1964, *11,* 221–25, by permission of the publisher, the American School Counselor Association, and the author.

METHOD

One hundred thirty-two high school students assigned to the author as counselees for an academic year were selected as the experimental group. The control group consisted of 107 students from another high school who had participated in the earlier study [*1*]. The two student groups had similar socio-economic backgrounds and aspirations. The two schools sent the same proportion of students to college, and their distributions of scores on national tests were approximately the same.

Data from both the control group and the experimental group were responses to a modified version of Robinson's questionnaire [*2*]. The respondent was asked to indicate the amount of counseling needed by each of 14 types of students. Five degrees of counseling, ranging from *minimum* (routine programming conferences only) to *maximum* (extra-school referral for regular and frequent counseling) were defined. A brief description was given of each of the 14 student types.

Both groups were given the questionnaire at the end of the school year. At the beginning of the school year, however, the control and experimental groups were treated differently. With the control group no educative attempts were made to define the role of the counselor. In the experimental group, on the other hand, the function and methods of the counselor were described to each student.

This particular method of "education" and the content of the message given the student regarding the role of the counselors evolved from Rogers' descriptions of the second and third steps in the therapeutic process, defining the helping situation and encouraging free expression of feelings [*3*].

Such perception of the counseling situation by the client usually develops gradually, frequently without awareness or an explicit statement from the counselor. But a high school setting rarely provides an opportunity for the student to have relatively frequent regular meetings with the counselor in order to arrive at any such feeling about the counselor's role.

Therefore the author met in individual half-hour conferences with each of the 132 students during the first two months of the year and in a quiet, slow and friendly manner explained her function as follows:

"I am here to help you find out what you want in terms of school —or a career—or socially—and the ways you might get what you want. I am not here to discipline you or to make you get better grades. Whatever you tell me in a conference is confidential. I will not contact your parents unless we talk about it first, and if your parents contact me I will encourage them to tell you about it or tell you myself.

"*I* asked *you* to come to me this time. From now on you can come to me whenever you want to. You can use the time any way you want—to talk about anything or not talk at all. Sometimes I may ask to see you. You do not have to come if you do not want to, unless I put 'please come' which means we have to get some of the details of your program straightened out. Even then, come only as soon as it is convenient for you.

"There is nothing you can tell me that will shock me. You will never find me prying. If I were in your position, I wouldn't trust me right away; I would test me gradually."

TABLE 1

RELATIVE DEGREES OF COUNSELING BELIEVED NECESSARY FOR SELECTED TYPES OF STUDENTS

Rank Position	*Type of Student*	*Column 1 Degree of Counseling (No. Respondents = 132)* 1	2	3	4	5	*Column 2 Rank Scores*
1.	Athlete	45	53	31	3	0	256
2.	Bright	48	53	18	12	1	261
3.	Engineer	33	57	39	2	1	277
4.	Failing	1	32	66	30	3	398
5.	Ill	11	32	46	24	19	404
6.	Homely	5	34	49	33	11	407
7.	Not Known	2	15	56	44	14	446
8.	Kiddish	4	13	50	45	20	460
9.	Gauche	2	18	27	65	20	479
10.	Loafer	2	6	39	73	12	483
11.	Medicine	3	7	38	62	22	489
12.	Jerk	5	10	27	49	41	507
13.	Dumb	0	4	26	61	41	535
14	Cqueer	1	1	3	42	85	605

RESULTS

The *number* of respondents (132) who specified each degree of counseling for each type of student is presented in column 1 of Table 1. Therefore the first row is read: 45 respondents designated 1 for the degree of counseling; 53 indicated 2; 31 specified 3 for degree of counseling; etc.

In column 2 appears the rank score for each type of student which was derived from the formula:

RS = N(x).

where:

RS = rank score
N = number of respondents selecting a specific degree
x = degree of counseling.

Thus one arrives at the rank score for "athlete" by: 45(1) + 53(2) + 31(3) + 3(4) + 0(5) = 256. Since there were 132 respondents, all of whom for any one type of student could have specified 1 or 5 degrees of counseling, the rank scores, possible range is from 132 (132 x 1) to 660 (132 x 5).

After all the rank scores had been computed, the 14 types of students were arranged in Table 1 according to rank position, *i.e.*, from low to high rank scores, to permit quick inspection of the relative positions of each type. The lower the rank position or rank score for an individual the more frequently respondents indicated a lesser degree of counseling, while the higher the rank position or rank score the greater the percentage of respondents who specified a greater degree of counseling. Thus students believe that "Athlete" requires the least amount of counseling while "Cqueer" requires the greatest amount.

The major question in this study was: How did the experimental group differ in its performance from the control group? To answer this question it was necessary to compare the rank scores of the two groups. However, the rank scores for the control group, taken from an earlier study, first had to be "corrected" in order to account for the difference in the total population of the two groups. This difference equaled 25 students.

It was assumed that an additional 25 students in the control group would have distributed themselves along the "degree of counseling" continuum in proportionately the same way as did the total 107. Therefore the corrected rank scores for the control group were derived by multiplying each rank score by .234 (25 is 23.4 per cent of 107) and adding the amount to the original rank score. The percentage differences between the rank scores of the control and experimental groups were computed with the corrected rank score for the control group as a base. The results appear in Table 2.

Discussion

Several changes between the control and experimental groups might have occurred. The percentage differences in the amount of counseling considered desirable might have: (1) consistently increased, (2) consistently decreased or (3) shown an inconsistent pattern in which an increase was considered necessary for some students and a decrease for others.

TABLE 2
COMPARISON OF RANK SCORES
BETWEEN CONTROL AND EXPERIMENTAL GROUPS

Type of Student	*Control Group Original*	*Control Group Corrected*	*Experimental Group*	*Percentage Difference*	
Athlete	194	239	256	7.1%	increase
Bright	207	255	261	2.4	"
Engineer	214	264	277	4.9	"
Failing	274	338	398	17.7	"
Ill	285	352	404	14.8	"
Homely	299	369	407	10.3	"
Not Known	344	425	446	4.9	"
Gauche	363	448	479	6.9	"
Kiddish	363	448	460	2.7	"
Loafer	364	449	483	7.6	"
Medicine	376	464	489	5.4	"
Dumb	422	521	535	2.7	"
Jerk	436	538	507	5.8	decrease
Cqueer	483	596	605	1.5	increase

With one exception the experimental group felt that an increased amount of counseling was appropriate for all types of students.

This finding lends support to the suggestion that a counseling department may play an active role in creating its image in the eyes of the student body.

Although the conclusion must be tentative until other research is undertaken with more rigorous control of variables to allow the significance of the results to be tested, the finding indicates that it would be worthwhile for counseling departments to participate in educative programs.

If a high school counseling department wishes to reach the needs of all students, even though only for brief support, it is highly possible that it is not necessary to proceed gradually by helping students and hoping the student "grapevine" will carry the word.

The particular educative program may vary. In this study *each student* was approached because this was the only means available to the investigator. It is possible that students may be approached in small groups either through classrooms or in special meetings. It is possible that contact with parents would advance the desire of the department to reach more students.

Naturally, the first question a counseling department must ask itself is, "What do we want to do?" If the answer is, "Make out programs, provide test scores, check on the academic failures and the emotionally disturbed who have become discipline problems," then our studies suggest that there is no need to educate students about these functions. They already expect counselors to do these things.

But if a department wishes to define its functions differently and feels qualified to perform other functions, then it seems possible to accomplish some change in student perceptions through a direct educational program.

Summary

The question investigated in this study was: Can the perceptions high school students have of the counselor be changed by defining his role explicitly? That is, can students be encouraged to view the counselor as a person who is available to help *all* students with *all types* of problems

Two groups of students were studied: the control group consisted of 107 students; the experimental group, 132 students.

At the beginning of the school year the counselor's role was defined verbally in individual conferences with each student in the experimental group. The control group was given no definition. At the end of the school year each group was given a questionnaire asking for the degree of counseling 14 different types of students should receive.

In every case except one, the experimental group indicated that more counseling should be given the different types of students than the control group indicated. The finding suggests that if a counseling department wishes to reach students who present a variety of problems, an educational program involving a simple and direct statement of the counselor's role may be successful in encouraging more students to avail themselves of counseling services.

References

1. Heilfron, Marilyn. "The Function of Counseling." *Personnel and Guidance Journal,* 1960, *39,* 133-36.
2. Robinson, Francis P. "Guidance for All: In Principle and Practice." *Personnel and Guidance Journal,* 1953, *31,* 500–504.
3. Rogers, Carl. *Counseling and Psychotherapy.* Boston: Houghton Mifflin, 1942.
4. Stewart, Lawrence H. "Teachers and Counselors Look at Students." *Personnel and Guidance Journal,* 1957, *35,* 565–68.

6

Counselor Education and Supervision

As the reader might gather by the time he reaches this point, there is a great deal that remains unknown about counseling theory and practice. Despite this handicap, the need for counselors continues to grow, and pressure continues on counselor education institutions to expand their programs to increase the number of counselors being prepared. As a result, counselor educators find themselves caught in the middle of the proverbial Gordian knot. They are asked to prepare more counselors to meet existing needs. This includes investigating the possibility of preparing counselors on the undergraduate level. They are also asked to increase the minimum length of training to two years to produce more highly trained counselors. To complicate further their situation, they must also be continuously involved in the development and testing of more adequate theory and practice.

Placed in this demanding predicament, counselor educators find themselves in the position of planning and implementing training programs with little time or evidence to support what they do. For example, there are certain questions which must be answered if we, as counselor educators, hope more effectively to fulfill our function. Several of the questions that need to be researched include the following:

1) What background should the individual have who wishes to enter the counseling profession? For example, should school counselors have training and experience in teaching?

2) When we engage in counselor education, are we primarily concerned with selecting and educating persons who have the personal qualities required of a counselor, or are we concerned with both modification of personality and education for the profession of counseling?

3) Should student counselors in practicum settings work primarily with the age and problem group typical of their future work setting, or is counseling a process in which practice is relatively unrelated to types of clients or the setting?

4) What should be the content and experiences that will best prepare a person for work as a counselor? Is there a particular sequence of content and experience that is more effective than others?

5) What criteria of adequacy of preparation should be applied in counselor education? Who should determine the criteria and evaluate the extent to which they are satisfied?

These questions are but a few of those that bedevil the counselor educator. Most have been the subject of statements by leaders in the field. However, we need more than opinion to substantiate current practice and to point the way to new and better ways of educating the counselor of tomorrow.

In selecting the articles for this chapter, the editors found a number of reports of current theories and practices in counselor education. However, studies built on research were few. There were no studies reporting the success or failure of the para-professional, supporting a recommended structure of counselor education programs, or providing evidence to assist in the evaluation of counselor education and supervision.

The study by Gazda, *et al.* investigates the controversial question of the relative importance of teaching experience as a prerequisite for admittance to and/or success in school counseling. The results seem to corroborate the findings of others by indicating that teaching experience is of no help, and may even be a hindrance to students attempting to meet the demands of the counselor education program in which they are enrolled. The question remains as to whether or not teaching experience is necessary for the role of the counselor as defined by administrators and other school personnel.

O'Hern describes an instrument that may have applicability for measuring sensitivity of counselor trainees. The instrument apparently is not yet ready for such application, yet the findings suggest such use may be feasible for this or similar instruments. Further development by such methods as factor analysis may lead to the refinement of her instrument for effective use. In its present form, the investigator did find a relationship between performance on the sensitivity instrument and supervisor's evaluation of counselor effectiveness.

Carkhuff and Truax describe an approach to counselor training that may result in more rapid and adequate preparation of counselors. The approach seems to be primarily experiential with little attention to the theoretical basis for counseling. The findings in this study have major implications for the preparation of counselors in considerably less than the minimum recommended two years. Further study is certainly warranted based upon the outcomes of this initial experience.

The study by Johnston and Gysbers surveys the response of counselor supervisors to various strategies of supervision, and classifies these strategies according to implied general types. The study is useful for several reasons. First, it helps to point up differences among techniques of supervision. Second, it raises an interesting question about the justification of the supervisory approaches that seem to receive extensive support by counselor educators. A substantial majority of the supervisors believe in a democratic relationship with direct personal involvement between the supervisor and student in an unstructured situation. How then does the supervisor satisfy his evaluative and certification responsibility?

The articles that follow utilize a number of instruments that may have value in further studies. The design of the investigations provide information related primarily to a single set of conditions and approach to counselor education rather than evaluation of different conditions and approaches. The O'Hern study design may have provided comparative data related to differences among trainees had the instrument been further refined. But at present, there is little information upon which practice may be based.

The research in this chapter suggests that there is a need for studies that will test the effectiveness of alternative approaches to the selection of counselor trainees and their preparation. It further suggests that there may be need for creative effort directed toward finding new approaches to the task. Only one of the studies described an approach that differed from a primarily didactic instructional program. None of the studies investigated different methods of selection of students who were to become counselors. The investigations reported provide a basis for some comparative work that may serve to advance counselor education beyond what seems to be didactic course work—practicum dichotomy of instruction and experience. This is clearly an area in great need of future effort.

*

RESPONSE SETS OF NEOPHYTE COUNSELORS

GEORGE M. GAZDA
HUBERT M. CLEMENTS
JACK A. DUNCAN
CAROL L. MARTIN

During the height of the controversy regarding the advisability of requiring teaching experience as a prerequisite for counselor certification, both camps cited the need for research to assist in resolving the controversy. At the risk of resurrecting the controversy, certain individuals have, in fact, attempted to research the issue. In 1962, Campbell [*1*] found that counselors with a background of teaching or administrative experience used significantly more advising, tutoring, and information-giving in their counseling than did counselors without teacher/administrative backgrounds. In a recent study by Mazer, Severson, Axman, and Ludington [*6*], former teachers who were enrolled in a counselor education program used evaluative responses three times more than similar enrollees who had *no* previous teaching experiences. Furthermore, Mazer, *et al.* found that there was little difference in the number of evaluative responses between those counselors who had two years teaching experience when compared with those having at least seven. In other words, two years of teaching experience appeared sufficient to instill an evaluative attitude in enrollees in the counseling curriculum which was not significantly changed by the accumulation of at least five more years of teaching experience. This finding is all the more ironic since most states requiring teaching experience for counselor certificates require *at least two years.* [*7*]

*This article is reprinted from *Counselor Education and Supervision,* 1967, *6,* 151–56, by permission of the publisher and authors.

Hopke [5] reported a study of enrollees in an Advanced Guidance Institute in which he found that experienced counselors devoted one-half of their responses to probing or questioning; the next most numerous response employed was interpretation. The study reported herein is similar to Hopke's in design and outcome; however, this study concerned itself with beginning counselors; employed a larger sample; used four judges instead of one, determined inter-judge reliability; and utilized role-playing rather than actual counselee interviews.

In addition to resurrecting the controversial teaching-experience-versus-no-teaching-experience requirement for counselor certification, the results of this study also resurrect the old teacher-counselor issue because the subjects of this study are all former teachers just removed from the classroom and embarking on the study of counseling. The way this group of former teachers reacted to a standard role-playing session is very likely the manner they, and possibly the majority of teachers, routinely "counsel" their students.

With the increasing demands upon counselor educators to prepare counselors for vocational rehabilitation, the Employment Service, the Office of Economic Opportunity, and still other organizations on the horizon, the time may be at hand when counselor educators must look beyond the teaching field for other sources of potential counselor candidates. The findings of this study and the research of others cited above *suggest* that previous teaching experiences *may*, in fact, prove to be a liability rather than an asset for prospective *counselors*.

Procedures

The senior author typically has all his new students respond, as they perceive a counselor would respond, to a structured client role in order that he as practicum supervisor and they as potential counselors have some understanding of their present concept of counseling. The subjects of the present study were prospective counselors enrolled in the University of Georgia's Counseling and Guidance Institutes of 1963-64 and 1964-65. The first assignment of the senior author's pre-practicum groups was to have each student play the counselor's role in a structured ten-minute role-playing session. A member of the pre-practicum group was arbitrarily selected to play the structured role for the nine members of the group, and then one of the other members played the student's role to enable the original student role-player to play the role of the counselor. (In all instances the role-player-counselee was a female.) The role-playing was observed by all members of the group and by the supervisor; however, no discussion or evaluation of the role-playing was done until *after* all students had assumed the role of counselor.

The role-played problem concerned a teacher-student confrontation in which a senior high school girl and a male teacher had a brief, but heated, exchange of words during an extra-curricular school activity. This confrontation led to the girl's being referred to the counselor by her homeroom teacher the following day.

Subjects

Subjects were N.D.E.A. Guidance and Counseling Institute enrollees who had been teaching the year prior to their admission to the Institute. More precisely, all enrollees were simply ex-teachers.

There were nine females in the group—three were married. Their ages ranged from 23 to 40 with an average of 27.5. Of the 16 males, only one was single; their age range was 21-42, the average 32. The average age for the combined group was 30.6 years.

No enrollee was eligible for the Institute if he had earned more than 20 or less than 5 quarter hours of work in counseling and guidance; the average quarter hours earned was 10. Since the core of the counseling and guidance courses was taught in the Institute, the 10 hours earned prior to the enrollee's beginning the Institute were earned in areas such as psychology, sociology, and educational psychology, and would not likely greatly influence the neophyte's counseling techniques in the role-playing session.

All enrollees held at least the B.S. or B.A. degree. Two held the master's degree—one in theology and one in education. Six enrollees were English majors, and seven were social studies or history majors. Business and science each contributed three majors; two were sociology majors; and there was one major in each of the following areas: French, industrial arts, mathematics, and Bible.

The majority (21) of the enrollees was previously teaching in the South; four had been teaching in the North.

All enrollees had to be eligible for admission to the Graduate School of the University of Georgia, and thus all had earned at least B averages as undergraduates. Scores made by the subjects on a number of different standardized tests for graduate students ranged from the lowest quintile to the highest quintile.

Years of teaching experience ranged from 1 to 15 with a mean of 5.75.

Instrument

The instrument employed for evaluating the role-playing sessions was the instrument devised by Porter [*10*] with minor revisions made by the authors—including the addition of a category for "unclassifiable" responses. The remaining response categories were Evaluative, Interpretive, Supportive, Probing, and Understanding.

Inter-judge reliability was established for the instrument by first having several training sessions during which the judges practiced on role-played tapes similar to those they were to judge as part of the research reported in this study. After approximately eight hours of practice with the Porter instrument, the judges rated independently each counselor response for all 25 trainees, approximately four hours and ten minutes of structured role-played sessions. Inter-judge reliability is therefore based on the same 25 tapes used for obtaining the counselor-response categorizations. Three of the four judges hold the Ed.D. with majors in counseling and guidance, and the fourth was a candidate for same.

In order to give the judges as much help as possible in judging the meaning of the counselor response, the tape recorder operator would play a segment of tape including client response/counselor response/client response or vice versa and then wait until all four judges independently rated the response before proceeding with the next series. Segments were replayed as often as a judge desired before his judgment was made. Since all judges rated exactly the same segments or counselor responses, the inter-judge reliability could be obtained by per cent of agreement among judges. Overall or perfect agreement among all four judges for all response categories was 71.31 per cent. However, for purposes of this study, a response was considered correctly classified when three of four judges were in agreement. This was true for 91.07 per cent of judgments; or, three out of four judges agreed on the classification of 765 of 840 counselor responses.

Results

Table 1 indicates the per cent and number of counselor responses given by neophyte counselors to a structured ten-minute role-playing session.

Without regard to variables of age, sex, or amount of previous teaching experience, the findings of this study are very similar to those of Hopke. [*5*] Hopke found the majority of responses of counselors with previous counseling preparation were probing (50 per cent) compared with approximately 60 per cent of the responses in the present study; 75 per cent of the responses in Hopke's study consisted of Probing, Interpretation, and Evaluation, and 73 per cent in the present study were so classified. Twenty-four per cent of experienced counselors' responses in Hopke's study were Supportive or Understanding compared with approximately 15 per cent for the neophyte counselors described in this study.

TABLE 1

RESPONSE CATEGORIES OF TWENTY-FIVE NEOPHYTE COUNSELORS

Response Category	*Number of Responses**	*Per Cent of Total Responses**
Probing	462	60.4
Unclassifiable	94	12.3
Evaluative	75	9.8
Understanding	73	9.5
Supportive	37	4.8
Interpretive	24	3.2
Total	765	100.0

*Based on responses with perfect agreement in classification by three of the four judges.

DISCUSSION

The results of this study appear to be in essential agreement with studies of a similar nature by Campbell [*1*], Hopke [*5*], and Mazer, *et al.* [*6*] To present more conclusive results, of course, further studies should be done in which neophyte counselors or prospective counselors of varied preparation would be compared with prospective counselors from backgrounds in teaching. Nevertheless, there is beginning to build up a body of research which tends to support suggestions made by Cohen [*2*], Hobbs [*4*], Dugan [*3*], Wrenn [*11*], and McCully [*8*], among others, regarding the need for counselor educators to carefully re-appraise the requirement of previous teaching experience as a prerequisite for counselor preparation and/or certification.

The research studies cited above suggest that counselor educators who question the validity of teaching experience as a prerequisite for admission to counseling programs and/or certification have at least as much evidence to support their hypotheses as do those who cite surveys of school administrators' preferences for hiring counselors with previous teaching experience or similar allegations that counselors with previous teaching experience "get along better" with school personnel.

The writers believe it is quite possible, though far from conclusive, that we are paying too high a price in the time spent by counselor education in helping prospective counselors *unlearn* attitudes and practices developed as teachers which may be antithetical to counseling. Proposals such as Noble's [*9*] for beginning counselor education in the third year of undergraduate school, and the suggestions by Hobbs [*4*] that our poorest candidates might be those who ". . . plodded through undergraduate majors in psychology and education," must now be given serious attention.

References

1. Campbell, R. E. "Counselor Personality and Background and His Interview Subrole Behavior." *Journal of Counseling Psychology,* 1962, *9,* 329–34.

2. Cohen, Nancy K. "Must Teaching Be a Prerequisite for Guidance?" *Counselor Education and Supervision,* 1961, *1,* 69–71.

3. Dugan, W. E. "An Inward Look: Assumptions and Aspirations." *Counselor Education and Supervision,* 1962, *1,* 174–80.

4. Hobbs, N. "The Compleat Counselor." *Personnel and Guidance Journal,* 1958, *36,* 594–602.

5. Hopke, W. E. "How Are School Counselors Counseling?" *Counselor Education and Supervision,* 1964, *3,* 162–65.

6. Mazer, G. E., Severson, J. L., Axman, A. L., & Ludington, Karan A. "The Effects of Teaching Background on School Counselor Practices." *SPATE Journal,* 1965, *4,* 81–84.

7. McCully, C. H. "A Rationale for Counselor Certification." *Counselor Education and Supervision,* 1961, *1,* 3–9.

8. McCully, C. H. "The School Counselor: Strategy for Professionalization." *Personnel and Guidance Journal,* 1962, *40,* 681–89.

9. Noble, F. C. "The Two-year Graduate Program in Counselor Education: A Re-examination." *Counselor Education and Supervision,* 1965, *4,* 160–62.

10. Porter, E. H., Jr. *An Introduction to Therapeutic Counseling.* Boston: Houghton Mifflin, 1950.

11. Wrenn, C. G. *The Counselor in a Changing World.* Washington, D. C.: American Personnel and Guidance Association, 1962.

*

SENSITIVITY: A MEASURABLE CONCEPT?

JANE S. O'HERN
DUGALD S. ARBUCKLE

Research on the selection of school counselors has been limited in both scope and specificity. Hill and Green [*1*] state that "perhaps the most severe handicaps of such research have been: (a) lack of certainty as to ends sought, (b) lack of basic studies evaluating guidance practices, and (c) failure to communicate research findings through professional publication." It seems safe to assume that the complexity of the problem requires better research and a wider distribution of this research in order to improve the profession of counseling.

Since the goal of counselor education is to produce effective counselors, it would appear necessary to define the nature of effectiveness. There seems to be general agreement in the field that personality factors in general and interpersonal attitudes in particular are primary contributory factors in counseling effectiveness. While the importance of attitudes has been stressed in recent writings, there is a need for research designed to find a set of variables predictive of success in the field of counseling. Hill and Green [*1*] state that "basic longitudinal research on the selection, education and subsequent effectiveness of guidance and personnel workers was not found." Santavicca [*4*] found that the predominant emphasis in the selection of students in counselor education was upon academic competence. Personal qualifications, as judged by interviews, letters of recommendation, rating scales, and staff judgments, were also considered. An instrument for the measurement of student-counselor

---

*This article is reprinted from *Personnel and Guidance Journal,* 1964, *42,* 572–76, by permission of the publisher, the American Personnel and Guidance Association, and the authors.

attitudes is necessary if counselor educators are to measure objectively the amount of change during the education of the student-counselor. In the present study only one of these traits, that of expressed sensitivity, was investigated.

The Problem

The primary problem of this study was the development of an instrument measuring the degree of sensitivity possessed by potential counselors. In addition, the study was concerned with the effect of the following variables on one's measured degree of sensitivity: (1) age, (2) education, (3) intelligence, (4) personal security, (5) occupation, (6) religion, (7) sex, (8) undergraduate grade-point average, and (9) years in occupation.

Design of the instrument

The instrument prepared for this study was a tape consisting of 30 different client problems, each followed by counselor responses.

1. *Selection of Client Problems.*—Professional counselors were requested to role-play, on tape, some typical client problems that met the following criteria:

a. Client problems that contained enough information so that they could be used out of context.

b. Problems that *could* be of a threatening nature to the counselor, such as areas concerning death, interpersonal relationships, religion, and sex.

c. Problems that represented those of both male and female clients.

2. *Acquisition of Responses.*—In order to obtain a range of responses, 13 individuals with varied backgrounds were requested to respond to the stimulus tape. This group included full-time counselors, graduate students in counseling, and advanced undergraduates.

Each of the 13 individuals listened to the client problems that had been prerecorded on tape. During a 30-second time interval between each client problem, each of the individuals was requested to record his response on a second recorder. If more than 30 seconds was desired, the individual was instructed to stop the recorder playing the client problems.

The 30 taped responses of each of the 13 individuals in this study were spliced and placed on one tape preceded by the client problem.

3. *Selection of Judges.*—A professional jury of seven counselors participated in this study. Each counselor had completed his doc-

toral work in the field of counseling, had counseling experience, and was directly or indirectly involved in counselor education. An effort was made to include counselors who adhered to various counseling philosophies, in order to prevent the influence of any one philosophical bias.

Each member of the professional jury was sent a tape and typescript of the client problems and responses. Each was requested to listen to each response and then rate its degree of sensitivity on a four-point scale. The definition and the four categories of sensitivity were defined as follows:

Sensitivity: The capacity to perceive or the awareness of what is happening in the treatment process from the verbal statements and the verbal behavior of the client. The counselor understands quickly and accurately the emotional basis, the moods, and the conflicts that underlie the client problem.

Categories:

3. The person's initial response was extremely perceptive. He responded accurately to the emotional meaning or underlying feelings of the client's problem.

2. The person's response was relatively perceptive. He responded to part of the client's affect, but failed to perceive the main trend of communication.

1. The person responded to the verbal content of the client's problem, but failed to understand the emotional meaning or underlying feelings of the problem.

0. The person failed to respond to either the affect of the verbal content; or the response showed evidence of bias, marked defensiveness and/or emotional distance by the counselor.

4. Coding of the Responses.—For an item to be included in the refined instrument it was required that (1) at least four of the seven judges agree on a response category, and the ratings of the minority be distributed no more distant than one category position to either or both sides of the modal selections, or (2) five of the seven agree, and the distribution of the minority responses be disregarded. For the purpose of assigning scores to each response, the categories were dichotomized. The acceptable division included responses that were extremely or relatively perceptive, while the unacceptable division was composed of responses that were marginal or showed evidence of a lack of sensitivity.

A code was designed so that the degree of change of one's sensitivity could be measured by means of pre- and post-testing. Each of the four possible answers for each response was assigned an ordinal value as follows:

3. Agreed with judges as to both division and category.
2. Agreed with judges as to division only.
1. Answer was in alternate division, but the selected alternative within the division was closer to the favored division.
0. Answer was in alternative division, but the selected alternative was furthest from the favored division.

5. *Selection of Responses for the Final Instrument.*—The group used for the item analysis was randomly selected from the total sample, and their sensitivity scales were scored according to the previously discussed scoring code. Since the investigator was seeking to identify those items or responses that significantly differentiated between the top and bottom groups, the top and bottom 33 per cent of the sample were isolated. Analysis was determined by a two-by-two chi-square test [*3*]. Due to small cell entries, probabilities of those responses which were significant at the 5 per cent level of confidence or higher were computed by Fisher's Exact Method [*2*].

Results indicated that 94 of the original 294 responses included in the refined instrument were significantly differentiating. The inclusion of a preponderance of significant items which the jury rated as demonstrating a lack of sensitivity was partially offset by incorporating 20 nonsignificant items in the final sensitivity scale.

Method

A total of 212 students enrolled in seven Summer Guidance and Counseling Institutes sponsored by the National Defense Education Act participated in this study. The group was homogeneous in that all enrollees met the criteria established by the U.S. Office of Education.

During the first week of each Institute a battery of tests including the Sensitivity Scale, Concept Mastery Test, and the Security-Insecurity Inventory were administered to each participant. At the conclusion of the Institute, staff and self-ratings based on the definition of sensitivity, practicum grades, and other pertinent data were obtained. Analysis of variance, chi-square, and correlations were the statistical procedures used to determine the effect and relationship of specific variables on the degree of sensitivity possessed by potential counselors.

Results

Scores on the final Sensitivity Scale have a possible range from 0 to 342. The mean score obtained on the Scale for 86 Institute participants was 195.81 with a standard deviation of 30.54. This group had a mean age of 36.47 years and a standard deviation of 8.75 years. They had been employed in their present occupation for 4.92 years and the standard deviation was 5.80 years.[1]

Students who identified themselves as Jewish or Undeclared (N = 5) as to religious preference scored significantly higher on the final Sensitivity Scale than those students identifyng themselves as Catholic (N = 17) or Protestant (N = 64), but caution is suggested due to the limited number in each of the religious categories. The variables age, sex, education, occupation, years in occupation, personal security, intelligence, and undergraduate grade-point average had no significant relationship to scores received on the final Sensitivity Scale. There also was no significant relationship between counseling practicum grades, staff sensitivity ratings, and self-sensitivity ratings with respect to scores received on the final Sensitivity Scale. There was no significant relationship between one's undergraduate grade-point average and effectiveness in a counseling practicum course.

At the conclusion of each Institute, staff members listed those students whom they selected as the five most sensitive and the five least sensitive in counseling practice according to the definition of sensitivity. Twenty-nine students were included in each group.[2] Students judged most sensitive were significantly younger, had attained a lower educational degree, had been employed in their present position fewer years and received practicum grades that were significantly higher than those received by the least sensitive. The following variables did not significantly differentiate between those students judged most sensitive and least sensitive: sex; religion; occupation; personal security; intelligence; score on the Sensitivity Scale; undergraduate grade-point average and self-sensitivity ratings.

A similar study was made with two groups judged most effective and least effective in counseling practice with respect to specific variables. Students judged most effective in counseling practice were significantly younger, scored significantly higher on the final Sensitivity Scale, and received significantly higher practicum grades than those students judged least effective. The variables sex, religion, education, occupation, years in occupation, personal security, in-

---

[1]The marked skewness of this distribution (which ranges from 6 months to 32 years) is attributable to the relatively few subjects with extensive years of professional activity in their present occupation. Their contribution to the arithmetic mean score and variance necessarily results in a description of a truncated distribution.

[2]The other six students were eliminated due to incomplete data and lack of enrollment in a counseling practicum.

telligence, undergraduate grade-point average, and self-sensitivity ratings failed to differentiate significantly between students judged most effective and least effective.

Discussion

Many of the results obtained in this study are far from conclusive in themselves but they suggest further consideration of certain aspects of counselor education. At the present time, teaching experience is a necessary prerequisite for the potential counselor as it has been assumed that experience will provide a more realistic and greater depth of understanding on the part of the counselor. In light of this assumption it is interesting to note that those students who were judged by staff members as being the most sensitive in counseling practice were significantly younger, had attained a lower educational degree, and had been employed in their present position fewer years than those judged to be least sensitive in counseling practice. While the reasons for the above are not known, it might be hypothesized that conformity resulting in rigidity or a high degree of dogmatism might be caused by the pattern of education in various educational settings. It is thus conceivable that the education of the counselor might be more beneficial without prior teaching experience.

A philosophical issue is raised concerning the meaning of grades. It is noteworthy that, of the 24 Institute enrollees judged as being least effective in counseling practice, three received a grade in counseling practice of B+, eleven received a grade of B, three received a grade of B−, one received a grade of C+, and six received a grade of C. Those enrollees judged as being the most effective in counseling practice received grades that were significantly higher, but it appears that either the present selection techniques are excellent, and we assume they are not, or that it is difficult for counselor educators to assign unsatisfactory grades to their students. The validity or meaningfulness of grades when examined in this light seems to be highly questionable.

While some educators have thought that self-evaluation might be a beneficial tool in the development of insight, it appears from this study that the better students seem to be more critical, hence rating themselves lower. The poorer students tend to rate themselves higher. On the other hand, of course, it may be that the staff ratings are invalid.

In contrast to the staff ratings of sensitivity, for which criteria for rating had been specified, the judgments on the dimensions of effectiveness were elicited with the absence of any specified or structured instructions. Insofar as a pronounced agreement exists between these two sets of ratings despite the operational differences, there appears some basis to assert that the concepts of effectiveness and sensitivity overlap. The results of the analysis indicating the instrument's ability to differentiate high and low counseling effectiveness but not sensitivity may be due in large measure to seven students not judged equally effective and sensitive, and who appear in the analysis of the effective group. The difference, if it is meaningful, would lead one to believe that the final Sensitivity Scale is a better measure of effectiveness than of sensitivity, but a replication of the study is necessary before this can be affirmed.

Conclusions

The results of this study, while limited in scope, seem to imply that success on qualifying exams and an acceptable grade-point average are not directly related to effectiveness in counseling practice. The final Sensitivity Scale may have some predictive value in that potential counselors who were judged most effective in counseling practice scored significantly higher on the Scale than those judged least effective.

The potential usefulness of the Scale is at present unknown, but it is our hope that the results of a replication of this study in addition to an analysis of the Scale by means of the factor analytical approach (now under investigation) may be of help to individuals concerned with research in the area of counselor education. The Scale has many limitations, but the authors hope that they may be moving in a new and challenging direction. The fact that accurate attitude evaluation in an area is difficult to obtain is an argument for more, not less, effort.

References

1. Hill, George E., & Green, Donald A. "The Selection, Preparation and Professionalization of Guidance and Personnel Workers." *Review of Educational Research,* 1960, *30,* 115–30.

2. Maxwell, A. E. *Analyzing Qualitative Data.* New York: Wiley, 1961. 23.

3. McNemar, Quinn. *Psychological Statistics.* New York: Wiley, 1955, 224.

4. Santavicca, G. Gene. "A Summary of a Study Concerning Supervised Experience and Selection of Counselor Trainees." Oxford, Ohio: Miami University, 1958. (Mimeographed.)

*

TRAINING IN COUNSELING AND PSYCHOTHERAPY: AN EVALUATION OF AN INTEGRATED DIDACTIC AND EXPERIENTIAL APPROACH[1]

ROBERT R. CARKHUFF[2]
CHARLES B. TRUAX[3]

A recent attempt (Truax, Carkhuff, and Douds, 1964) was made to implement a view of training in counseling and psychotherapy that would integrate the didactic-intellectual approach which emphasizes the shaping of therapist behavior with the experiential approach which focuses upon therapist development and growth. Briefly, the approach set forth involves the supervisor's didactically teaching the trainee the former's accumulated research and clinical learnings concerning effective therapeutic dimensions in the context of a relationship which provides the trainee with experiences which the research and clinical learnings suggest are essential for constructive change or positive therapeutic outcome. For example, the teacher-supervisor might teach about high levels of empathic understanding while himself attempting to provide high levels of this dimension in his relationships to the trainees. Supervision is itself viewed as a therapeutic process: a learning or relearning process which takes place in

*This article is reprinted from *Journal of Consulting Psychology,* 1965, *29,* 333–36, by permission of the publisher, the American Psychological Association, and the authors.

[1]The authors wish to acknowledge the critical technical contributions of Edward P. William to the training program and data analyses and the cooperative efforts of John Corcella, Robert DeBurger, and Logan Gragg.

[2]Robert Carkhuff's work was supported by Public Health post-doctoral research fellowship number 7 F2 MH-19, 912-02, and the program was supported by Research and Development Grant No. 906-PM to the authors from the Vocational Rehabilitation Administration.

[3]Psychotherapy Research Group.

the context of a particular kind of interpersonal relationship which is free of threat and facilitative of trainee self-exploration.

This integrated approach has grown out of programs of research into the processes of individual and group counseling and psychotherapy which appear to have identified at least four critical process variables in effective therapeutic processes. The dimensions include: (a) therapist accurate empathic understanding; (b) therapist warmth or positive regard; (c) therapist genuineness or self-congruence; and (d) patient depth of self-exploration. There is extensive evidence to indicate that the three therapist-offered conditions predictably relate to the patient process variable of intrapersonal exploration, and all four dimensions have been shown to relate significantly to a variety of positive patient personality and behavioral change indexes (Barrett-Lennard, 1962; Bergin and Solomon, 1963; Braaten, 1961; Halkides, 1958; Rogers, 1962; Tomlinson and Hart, 1962; Truax, 1961; Truax and Carkhuff, 1964a, 1964b; Wagstaff, Rice, and Butler, 1960).

A central part of the training program involves the application of research scales which have been predictive of positive patient outcome in researching these dimensions. With the help of the scales which had successfully measured or estimated the levels of the therapeutic conditions in previous research, the trainees are didactically taught the therapeutic conditions involved. The beginning counselors are then exposed to tape-recorded samples of counseling or psychotherapy rated at various levels of therapist-offered conditions and client-process involvement. The trainees get practice at discriminating levels of therapist and client conditions. Further, the trainees receive empathy training in which the trainee listens to patient statements and then is asked to formulate his response in terms of the feeling and content of the communication. The trainees then role-play, and finally their initial clinical interviews with hospitalized patients are recorded and then rated so as to give them immediate and concrete informational feedback on how well they are learning to put into operation the concepts involved.

Two separate, but essentially identical, training programs have been successfully implemented. The first program involved 12 advanced graduate students, ranging in age from the twenties to the thirties, in a regular university graduate course in "Individual Psychotherapy." The second and simultaneously run program involved five volunteer but otherwise unselected lay hospital personnel, ranging in age from the thirties to the fifties. These five volunteers consisted of three aides, a volunteer worker, and an industrial therapist. Only the industrial therapist had a college education. The programs lasted one semester of 16 weeks. The classes met twice a week for 2 hours on each occasion. In addition, the trainees spent approximately two additional hours per week listening on their own to recorded therapy.

METHODOLOGY

During the last week of the semester of training, each trainee had a single clinical interview with each of three hospitalized patients. From the three tapes of each trainee, six 4-minute excerpts were randomly selected, two excerpts from each tape. For purposes of comparison, excerpts of therapy interviews were similarly selected from the recordings of sessions in which 11 patients from a similar patient population were seen by experienced therapists in the Schizophrenic Project of the Wisconsin Psychiatric Institute. In addition, random excerpts were obtained from the publicly dispersed tapes of therapy interviews of four prominent therapists. The combined experienced therapists included the following: Albert Ellis, William Fey, Eugene T. Gendlen, Rollo May, Allyn Roberts, Carl R. Rogers, Jack Teplinsky, Charles B. Truax, Julius Seeman, Al Wellner, and Carl Whitaker. The experienced therapists ranged in age from the thirties to the sixties.

Following the pattern of rating upon which much of the extensive body of research in support of the four dimensions has been built, undergraduate students who were not psychology majors and who were naive concerning therapeutic practices were trained on the particular individual scales involved to a degree of intrarater reliability of not less than .50 in order to insure that the ratings were not random. While .50 was the cut-off level, in most cases the rate-rerate reliabilities hovered in the seventies and eighties. In the rater training, the prospective raters were exposed to therapy excerpts selected because of a high degree of rating agreement by a variety of raters, including experienced therapists, at the various levels of the scales involved in order to insure a spread in the therapy process levels which the prospective raters were to rate. In the Wisconsin Schizophrenic Project and the Kentucky Group Therapy Project and in the analyses of data from other resources such as Chicago and Stanford, the therapy process ratings of undergraduate students trained on these particular individual scales successfully predicted therapeutic outcome (Rogers, 1962; Truax and Carkhuff, 1964a, 1964b). Four raters were trained to rate the therapist accurate empathy scale; four different raters rated patient depth of self-exploration; two other raters rated therapist positive regard; and two still different raters rated therapist congruence.

The therapist accurate empathy (AE) scale is a 9-point scale attempting to specify stages along a continuum. At the lowest stage, for example, ". . . the therapist seems completely unaware of even the most conspicuous of the client's feelings. . . ." At the highest stage, Stage 9, the therapist ". . . unerringly responds to the client's full range of feelings in their exact intensity. . . ." The product-moment correlations between the four raters employed on the AE training data ranged in the .40's and .50's with one correlation falling to .24.[4]

The scale measuring therapist unconditional positive regard (UPR) is a 5-point scale running from the lowest point where ". . . the therapist is actively offering advice or giving clear negative regard. . . ." to the highest point where ". . . the therapist communicates unconditional positive regard without restriction. . . ." The product-moment correlation between the two raters employed was .48.[5]

Therapist self-congruence (TSC) is estimated by a 7-point scale where Stage 1 is indicated by a ". . . striking evidence of contradiction between the therapist's experiencing and his current verbalization. . . ." and Stage 7 is noted when ". . . the therapist is freely and deeply himself in the relationship. . . ." The correlation between the two raters employed was .62.[6]

Client depth of self-exploration (DX) is measured by a 9-point scale running from the lowest stages where ". . . the patient actively evades personally relevant material. . . ." to the highest stages where ". . . the patient is deeply exploring and being himself. . . ." The product-moment correlations between the four raters employed on the DX training data ranged in the .50s and .60s with only one correlation falling below .47.[7]

Results

The results appear in Tables 1 and 2. It can be readily seen that, with the notable exception of the critical DX variable, where the lay therapists' mean scores were approximately equal to those of the students and the experienced therapists, the groups consistently performed in the following rank order: (a) the experienced therapists; (b) the graduate students; and (c) the lay personnel. While a hierarchy of performance was established, the experienced therapists did not effect significantly better process levels than the graduate stu-

[4]All intercorrelations for the ratings on all scales were significant beyond the .01 level.

[5]See footnote 4.

[6]See footnote 4.

[7]See footnote 4.

dents on any dimensions, and the latter were not significantly higher than the lay group on any indexes. The only significant difference was found in the comparison of the experienced and the lay groups on the therapist self-congruence dimension.

TABLE 1
MEAN SCALE OF THERAPY PROCESS VARIABLES FOR GROUPS OF TRAINEES AND EXPERIENCED THERAPISTS

Scale	Number of Points	Lay* (n = 5)	SD	Students* (n = 12)	SD	Experienced (n = 15)	SD
AE	(9)	4.58	.30	5.14	.69	5.22	.84
UPR	(5)	2.82	.62	3.05	.32	3.16	.40
TSC	(7)	4.86	.35	5.23	.48	5.51	.45
DX	(9)	4.66	.30	4.56	.60	4.86	.56

*Personnel involved in training program.

TABLE 2
t-TESTS FOR SIGNIFICANT DIFFERENCES OF THERAPY PROCESS VARIABLES FOR GROUPS OF TRAINEES AND EXPERIENCED THERAPISTS

Scale	Students Versus Lay	Students Versus Experienced	Lay Versus Experienced
AE	1.750	.267	1.641
UPR	1.045	.786	1.417
TSC	.487	1.556	2.955*
DX	.357	1.304	.741

*Significant at the .01 level.

DISCUSSION

The results suggest that in a relatively short training period, i.e., approximately 100 hours, both graduate students and lay hospital personnel can be brought to function at levels of therapy nearly commensurate with those of experienced therapists.

It is notable that on the empathy dimension all of the groups functioned near Stage 5, which is characterized by the ". . . therapist accurately respond[ing] to all of the client's more readily discernible feelings. . . ." All groups hovered around Stage 3 of the unconditional positive regard scale where ". . . the therapist indicates a positive caring for the patient or client but it is a semipossessive caring. . . ." On the therapist self-congruence scale all groups functioned near Level 5 where ". . . there are no negative cues suggesting any discrepancy between what he says and what he feels, and there are some positive cues indicating genuine response to the patient. . . ."

The patients of all the groups of therapists are engaged in the therapeutic process of self-exploration at Levels 4 and 5 where ". . . personally relevant material is discussed . . ." and frequently, ". . . either with feeling indicating emotional proximity, or with spontaneity. . . ." To sum: It may be said that the trainees, both students and lay personnel, engaged almost as well as the more experienced therapists in what would commonly be characterized as *effective psychotherapy.*

For purposes of comparison, there is Bergin and Solomon's (1963) analysis of six different supervisory groups of post-internship fourth-year graduate students from a more didactically and psychoanalytically oriented clinical training program of a school of some repute in the field on an expanded version of the empathy scale. By inserting a stage between Levels 2 and 3 of the present scale, the authors obtained the following average ratings, with many of the ratings between Levels 2 and 3 and all of those above Stage 3 tending to be inflated if compared to assessments employing the 9-point empathy scale: Group A, 2.14; Group B, 3.84; Group C, 3.20; Group D, 2.02; Group E, 1.91; Group F, 2.08. It should be noted here that Bergin and Solomon also found empathy to be positively related to outcome. While we have only empathy ratings for comparison, it can easily be seen that the highest of these levels of functioning on empathic understanding is nowhere near those produced by the integrated program described here.

That the experienced therapists are significantly higher than the lay personnel, as well as relatively higher than the graduate students, on the self-congruence dimension, suggests that with experience the therapists come to be more freely, easily, and deeply themselves in the therapeutic encounter. In this regard, one handicap with which the lay personnel may have been operating is the lack of any real theoretical orientation to indicate to them where they were going in their encounters. The very notion that counseling and therapy may take place devoid of any theoretical knowledge is currently being assessed in a lay group counseling treatment study. While the present program did not emphasize outside readings, the graduate students tended to glean from other sources some direction for themselves and their activities.

It is perhaps noteworthy that the lay personnel, consistently the lowest on all scales assessing the level of therapist-offered conditions, engage their patients in a depth of intrapersonal exploration commensurate with that of the experienced therapists and the students. The suggestion is that other dimensions come into play in effecting patient self-exploration which, in turn, is so highly correlated with patient outcome criteria. Perhaps the oft-noted social class variables are relevant here in the sense that lower socio-educational class therapists are in some way more facilitative in engaging their patient counterparts in the therapeutic process.

References

Barrett-Lennard, G. T. "Dimensions of Therapist Response as Causal Factors in Therapeutic Change." *Psychological Monographs,* 1962, *76* (43, Whole No. 562).

Bergin, A. E., & Solomon, Sandra. "Personality and Performance Correlates of Empathic Understanding in Psychotherapy." *American Psychologist,* 1963, *18,* 393.

Braaten, L. J. "The Movement of Non-Self to Self in Client-Centered Psychotherapy." *Journal of Counseling Psychology,* 1961, *8,* 20–24.

Halkides, Galatia. "An Investigation of Therapeutic Success as a Function of Four Variables." Unpublished doctoral dissertation. University of Chicago, 1958.

Rogers, C. R. "The Interpersonal Relationship: The Core of Guidance." *Harvard Educational Review,* 1962, *32,* 416–29.

Tomlinson, T. M., & Hart, J. T., Jr. "A Validation Study of the Process Scale." *Journal of Consulting Psychology,* 1962, *26,* 74–78.

Truax, C. B. "The Process of Group Psychotherapy." *Psychological Monographs,* 1961, *75* (14, Whole No. 511).

Truax, C. B., & Carkhuff, R. R. "For Better or for Worse: The Process of Psychotherapeutic Personality Change." Chapter in Blossom T. Wigdor (ed.), *Recent Advances in Behavior Change.* Montreal, Canada: McGill University Press, 1964. (a).

Truax, C. B., & Carkhuff, R. R. "Significant Developments in Psychotherapy Research." Chapter in L. Abt and B. F. Riess (eds.), *Progress in Clinical Psychology,* Vol. VI. New York: Grune & Stratton, 1964. (b).

Truax, C. B., Carkhuff, R. R., & Douds, J. "Toward an Integration of the Didactic and Experiential Approaches to Training in Counseling and Psychotherapy." *Journal of Counseling Psychology,* 1964, *11,* 240–47.

Wagstaff, A. K., Rice, L. N., & Butter, J. M. "Factors in Client Verbal Participation in Therapy." *Counseling Center Discussion Papers,* University of Chicago, 1960, *6* (9), 1–14.

*

PRACTICUM SUPERVISORY RELATIONSHIPS: A MAJORITY REPORT

JOSEPH A. JOHNSTON
NORMAN C. GYSBERS

A number of recent articles have focused on supervisory relationships in counseling practicums [*1*, *2*, *3*]. While they add to our knowledge and understanding of supervision, they also illustrate that divergent views exist. This study examines normative data on practicum supervisors' reactions to selected alternatives for handling typical supervisory situations in an effort to report on current practices.

Backgrounds and Methods

Nine situations were devised illustrative of typical supervisory contacts with counselor candidates in practicum, and numerous alternatives for handling them were provided. Practicum supervisors were asked to indicate the nature of their agreement or disagreement with each alternative (strongly agree, agree, undecided, disagree, or strongly disagree).

In February, 1965, the situations were sent to most colleges and universities in the North Central Region of ACES where a counselor education program was known to exist. A selected number of schools from other regions was also included.

The individual contacted at each school was asked to give copies of the situations to three supervisors currently concerned with prac-

---

*This article is reprinted from *Counselor Education and Supervision,* 1966, *6,* 3–10, by permission of the publisher and authors. It was adapted from a presentation made at the 1965 APGA Convention at Minneapolis, Minnesota.

ticum supervision. A respondent could choose to remain anonymous, supplying only the name of the institution represented and his total years of experience as a supervisor. Of 51 institutions contacted, 41 were represented in the final data analysis.[1] One hundred supervisors comprised the final sample.

Results

Each situation was generally followed by 15 alternatives to which the respondent indicated the nature of his agreement or disagreement. If a majority (two-thirds or more) indicated "strongly agree" or "agree," the alternative was taken as representative of accepted practice. If a similar number indicated "strongly disagree" or "disagree," the alternative was classified as involving some practice supervisors did not see as acceptable. The situations and the alternatives that fit these categories follow. After each alternative is the actual tally of responses to the item.[2]

SITUATION 1

A counselor candidate, enrolled in practicum for the first time, realized early in the semester that he will soon see his first client. He becomes quite concerned about what he feels is a lack of adequate preparation for the experience and goes to his supervisor for some direction in preparing for it. In dealing with this situation a supervisor should . . .

Accepted practice (strongly agree and agree responses combined):

a) Explore in a sympathetic, understanding way, the counselor candidate's concern about his initial performance. (97%)

b) Suggest the counselor candidate role-play an initial interview with another candidate. (72%)

c) Attempt to see this situation as a counseling relationship and deal with it accordingly. (77%)

d) Discuss with the counselor candidate how he feels a supervisor might be of help to him and proceed accordingly. (66%)

Not accepted practice (strongly disagree and disagree combined):

e) Assure the counselor candidate that he will be provided with all the necessary preparation he needs prior to his first interview. (78%)

f) Reassure him that his preparation has been adequate. (71%)

SITUATION 2

You are observing a counselor candidate's first counseling interview.

[1]An institution could return as many as three sets of situations. Some, however, either had fewer than three individuals engaging in supervision or had some supervisor(s) who chose not to respond.

[2]SA = Strongly Agree; A = Agree; U = Undecided; D = Disagree; SD = Strongly Disagree.

The counselee is a high school senior who stated as his reason for wanting to talk to a counselor, "I would like to discuss my plans about going to medical school." From the available high school records you note that he is considerably above average scholastically and is highly recommended by his teachers.

As you watch the interview from behind the one-way mirror, you notice the counselor candidate is having a difficult time. He is completely dominating the interview, cutting the client off repeatedly. There is apparently little attempt to listen to the client. For the most part the interview has turned into a quasi-lecture by the counselor candidate about the merits of various medical schools. In dealing with this situation a supervisor should . . .

Accepted practice (strongly agree and agree responses combined):

a) Let the interview continue as it is since it is important for the counselor candidate to learn from his mistakes and develop his own style of counseling. (77%)
b) After the interview, suggest to the counselor candidate that he should prepare an analysis of his behavior during the interview. (68%)
c) Suggest that the counselor candidate go over the tape in a supervisory session as soon as possible after the interview, hoping that an immediate review of his performance would help him discover the nature of counseling. (87%)
d) After the interview, explore with him his ideas regarding his performance during the interview. (97%)

Not accepted practice (strongly disagree and disagree combined):

e) Directly intervene in the interview by sitting in on the rest of the session and participating as needed. (94%)
f) Knock on the door and ask the counselor candidate to step out of the room for a moment and discuss the situation with him. (77%)
g) Enter the counseling situation and demonstrate on the spot what might be a more acceptable way of handling the situation. (97%)
h) Ignore his performance unless he expresses concern about the interview and then work with his expressed needs. (90%)
i) Don't make an issue of his performance unless there has been a consistent pattern of this type—in the latter case suggest he seek psychotherapy or else he cannot expect to receive any endorsement for a counseling position. (81%)
j) Assume that his behavior is only a manifestation of a "larger" problem and wait until he is ready to discuss it. (75%)

SITUATION 3

A beginning counselor has an initial interview that lasts about one-half hour. Parts of it were especially good and then parts were quite bad. What the counselor would do well one time, he would do poorly the next time. After the interview the counselor makes an appointment with his supervisor to go over the tape of the interview. In dealing with this situation a supervisor should . . .

Accepted practice:

a) Explore thoroughly the counselor candidate's feelings regarding the interview and deal primarily with his personal evaluations. (74%)

b) Invite the counselor candidate to use the supervisory interview for a discussion of how he sees his interview performance relating to his personal and professional development as a counselor. (77%)

Not accepted practice:

c) Discuss only the positive parts of the interview performance hoping that reinforcement of his behavior will carry over to subsequent interviews. (80%)

d) In playing the tape, stop only where the counselor candidate makes a serious error, i.e., misses completely what the client is saying or experiencing. (80%)

e) Politely and tactfully avoid listening to the tape since that is not usually the most productive use of supervisory time. (95%)

SITUATION 4

A counselor candidate in a one-semester practicum is doing a rather poor job of working with clients. His commitment to counseling is definite but he sees his role with clients much like a teacher with a student. He asks his supervisor about the middle of the semester for an appointment to discuss his progress. The supervisor has observed a number of his interviews. In dealing with this situation the supervisor should . . .

Accepted practice:

a) Explore with the counselor candidate his feelings regarding his work. (97%)

b) Invite him to discuss the criteria a supervisor and counselor might use in checking progress and then apply these criteria to his performance over the semester. (68%)

c) Use the counselor candidate's concern about progress as a means of exploring his expectations from the practicum and a supervisor. (82%)

d) Give the counselor candidate a rather honest expression of your feelings about his performance and work with his reactions to these feelings. (74%)

e) Explore with the counselor candidate his perceptions of a counselor's role and how these perceptions may be related to his personal needs. (93%)

f) Give the counselor candidate some frank feedback regarding his performance and invite him to discuss his feelings about the feedback. (78%)

Not accepted practice:

g) Avoid a discussion of the counselor candidate's personal feelings about his overall performance and instead take his immediate concerns as the basis of discussion. (79%)

SITUATION 5

Mr. Jim, a beginning counselor candidate, is rather cool and aloof in his contacts with clients in practicum. As the result of his dissatisfaction with his performance, Mr. Jim asks his supervisor for an appointment. During their discussion, he revealed that his home had always been Spartan-like and any show of affection was a sign of weakness. His experiences as a teacher had reinforced his idea that a certain aloofness was necessary in the classroom or students would take advantage of you. In dealing with this situation a supervisor should . . .

Accepted practice:

a) Explore with him whether he would like to do something about his relationships and how he thinks it might be accomplished. (95%)

b) Discuss with him whether he feels he might profit from further explorations into the antecedents of his aloofness. (84%)

c) Invite him to discuss ways in which he might accommodate some change in his approach to clients. (78%)

Not accepted practice:

d) Suggest he drop the course and forget about counseling as a career. (86%)

e) Give the counselor candidate an incomplete until he can develop warmer relationships with people. (68%)

f) Omit references to his aloofness and concentrate upon his techniques. (94%)

g) Give him some personality tests (or review the results of any already given) to discover his problem. (84%)

h) Give him a coached client who also tends to be aloof in hopes that his inadequacies in dealing with the client will motivate him to seek changes in his behavior. (73%)

i) Subtly suggest the counselor candidate read portions of some standard textbooks which stress the importance of relationships to counseling effectiveness. (67%)

SITUATION 6

Mr. Blue is a "loner" in practicum. In a sense, he was an independently functioning counselor candidate, wanting neither to participate in any small group discussions nor to discuss his counseling experiences with his supervisor. Again and again he makes excuses why a tape recorder did not record or why a particular client was unhappy whenever recordings were made of interviews. On one occasion, he lost a tape, on another he (or someone else) disconnected the microphone from the recorder. In dealing with this situation a supervisor should . . .

Accepted practice:

a) Confront him with his feelings about the counselor's possible discomfort with his supervision. (68%)

b) Discuss with him his expectations from the practicum. (93%)

c) Invite him to use the supervisory session as a means of exploring his relationship with clients and others in the practicum. (87%)

Not accepted practice:

d) Assign him a coached client so as to have some evaluation of his performance. (67%)
e) Pay very little attention to his evasive behavior until he indicates a desire for assistance. (82%)
f) Ignore his behavior and spend time with counselor candidates who seek assistance. (97%)

SITUATION 7

A counselor candidate completes an interview involving a test interpretation of an interest inventory and an aptitude test battery. It is observed that while he established a particularly good relationship with the client, he made a number of mistakes in interpreting the tests. (These mistakes were corrected before the client left the premises so there was no harm done to the client.) The counselor candidate feels pretty good about the interview and wants a supervisory session. In dealing with this situation a supervisor should . . .

Accepted practice:

a) Suggest the counselor candidate first go over the tape by himself paying particular attention to his interpretation of the tests. (67%)
b) Take the opportunity during the supervisory session with the counselor candidate to review some points concerning test interpretations. (71%)
c) In a supervisory session clarify any test misinterpretation made and reinforce the positive aspects of the relationship he developed. (87%)
d) Begin by giving the counselor candidate an opportunity to express fully his feelings about his performance. (97%)
e) Invite the counselor candidate to explore ways in which he feels he may improve as the result of his experience. (92%)

Not accepted practice:

f) Deal with the counselor candidate relationship with the client and leave the test interpretation for later clarification. (71%)
g) Tell the counselor candidate to check the manuals, tests, etc., where he might obtain the necessary clarification for proper test interpretation, but try not to have this discussion become a part of the supervisory interview. (69%)
h) Reinforce the positive aspects of the interview and attempt to cover the negative in more general ways at other times, i.e., in small group meetings, lectures, through assigned readings, etc. (66%)

SITUATION 8

In an interview a counselor candidate does an excellent job of relating occupations to test scores for a client, but it is at the expense of the relationship. The client becomes disinterested in the interview, but the counselor fails to see this. The counselor, in fact, feels he had done a good job and wants to go over the tape with his supervisor. In dealing with this situation a supervisor should . . .

Accepted practice:

a) Suggest the counselor candidate first go over the tape by himself paying particular attention to the nature of the relationship he established. (75%)

b) Provide the counselor candidate with some observations about the counselor-client relationship he established and work with his reactions. (75%)

Not accepted practice:

c) Reinforce the positive aspects of the interview and attempt to cover the negative at other times, i.e., in more general ways during small group meetings, lectures, readings, etc. (77%)

d) Establish at any cost the "reality" of the interview since this is a unique part of the supervisory role. (66%)

e) Assume the counselor candidate is not going to be very open to criticism and attempt to create a felt need for some assistance. (72%)

f) Avoid any direct confrontation with the counselor about his performance with this client and spend the time discussing how the counselor candidate perceives the client. (73%)

g) Ignore this particular situation and wait to provide feedback until the counselor candidate senses his relationships are not as good as they might be. (84%)

h) Suggest that the counselor candidate consider psychotherapy as a means of relating more easily to other people. (75%)

SITUATION 9

A counselor candidate who is enrolled in a one-semester practicum in counseling and who seems to be quite well adjusted and doing an excellent job working with clients, comes to his supervisor and asks for some concrete evaluation of his performance to date. This is the middle of the semester. The supervisor has watched a number of his interviews through the one-way mirror. The counselor starts by stating he feels he hasn't received sufficient evaluation to date. In dealing with this situation a supervisor should . . .

Accepted practice:

a) Try to get the reason for the counselor candidate feeling the need for such concrete evaluation at this point. (80%)

b) Discuss with the counselor candidate his expectations from a supervisory session. (85%)

c) Show your acceptance and understanding of how frustrated he must feel in such a situation and invite further discussions. (78%)

Not accepted practice:

d) Assure him of later evaluation but tactfully help the counselor candidate to see the incongruity of such a role for a supervisor at this time. (69%)

e) Accept his need for evaluation and help him attain this in other ways, such as from other supervisors, some other objective measures like interview rating forms, or other counselors in the practicum but avoid, if possible, making it a part of the supervisory relationship with him. (69%)

Discussion and Implications

Eliciting responses to alternatives for handling given situations avoids some shortcomings of the questionnaire-type instrument. Caution must be exercised in the analysis of the results, however, since this approach leaves considerable latitude for inference concerning actual practice. In this article, for example, it is inferred that agreement with an alternative for handling a given situation would be indicative of agreement with approaches for handling other situations. It is also inferred that the stimuli presented in a situation or an alternative to a situation are perceived in like manner by all respondents. There was evidence, however, in individuals' written comments concerning some of the alternatives that such was not always the case. Further, some alternatives involved multiple stimuli that respondents found difficult to reconcile in a forced response.

Despite limitations in the instrument, several observations seem warranted.

1. Relationship.—Alternatives listed for the nine situations can be classified in terms of the relationship with counselor candidates being advocated or rejected by supervisors. An examination of alternatives chosen by a majority of supervisors in this study suggests that, at least initially, they would involve themselves in one of three types of relationships with counselor candidates.

One type seems paternalistic in nature. In a paternalistic relationship, supervisors would not encourage counselor candidates to participate in planning supervisory activities. In fact, supervisors, in traditional teacher-pupil fashion, would assume major responsibility for deciding on learning activities for counselor candidates.

Another type seems democratic. In this relationship, supervisors would encourage counselor candidates to participate in planning supervisory activities. Candidates would share responsibility for planning practicum learning experiences.

Still another type seems laissez-faire in nature. In a laissez-faire relationship, supervisors would either avoid involvement or provide assistance only on request.

Of the three types of relationships identified, practicum supervisors expressed preference for situational alternatives that placed them in democratic relationships with counselor candidates (examples: 1a, 2d, 3a, 4a, 5a, 6b, 7d, 8b, 9a). Alternatives that suggested paternalistic (examples: 1e, 2g, 3c, 4g, 5f, 6d, 7f, 8e, 9d) or laissez-faire (examples: 2j, 6f, 8g) relationships were generally deemed inappropriate.

2. Strategy.—The alternatives also suggested numerous strategies supervisors would use in handling the situations. A dimension of strategy was supervisor involvement. Alternatives would either demand supervisors remain personally involved, such as in a demonstration, intervention, evaluation or discussion, or they would suggest a referred activity in which the supervisor was not involved, e.g., a role-playing exercise with another counselor, suggestion of a tape analysis of an interview by the counselor himself, referral for diagnostic testing, conference with someone else, or perhaps avoidance of any specific help at this time.

Supervisors repeatedly chose alternatives in which they remained personally involved. About the only "referred" learning activities that received support were role playing (1b) and activities termed "behavioral analysis" (2b, 7a, 8a). (Examples of other alternatives in which supervisors were not personally involved included 2h, i, j, 3e, 5g, h, i, 6f, 7g, 8g, h, 9e.)

3. Structure.—The initial relationship most frequently chosen by supervisors working with counselor candidates can best be described as democratic. In the democratic relationship, supervisors generally elected discussion as the most appropriate supervisory strategy. An examination of this strategy reveals a pattern concerning the amount of structure supervisors would give to these discussions. Using a threefold classification of structure (minimal, some, or much) supervisors almost invariably expressed preference for alternatives classified as minimal.

Conclusions

Practicum supervisors seem to see their initial approach in supervisory relationships with counselor candidates as involving the strategy of "minimally structured" discussion in a democratic atmosphere. They generally do not approve of initial strategies involving intervention, demonstration, or referral in either paternalistic or laissez-faire relationships. This seems to be in contradiction of the data gathered by Walz and Roeber [5] which suggested that "the relationship between supervisor and counselor (is) more like that of the subject matter teacher and pupil" than like counselor and client. Perhaps reaction to specific responses on an interview typescript evokes a different response set than a situation in which alternate practices are stated as broad, general strategies for candidate-supervisor relationships.

On the other hand, the relationship seems to be a learner-centered type similar to the supervisor relationship which Patterson [*4*] feels "should be more like (that) of counseling and psychotherapy than didactic teaching."

Left unanswered is the question of how practicum supervisors can be self-congruent in a democratic, minimally structured relationship and still manage to handle common supervisory roles, such as instruction and evaluation, or administrative roles, such as endorsement for certification.

References

1. Arbuckle, D. S. "Supervision: Learning, Not Counseling." *Journal of Counseling Psychology,* 1965, *12,* 90–94.

2. Clark, C. M. "On the Process of Counseling Supervision." *Counselor Education and Supervision,* 1965, *4,* 64–67.

3. Gysbers, N. C. & Johnston, J. A. "Expectations of a Practicum Supervisor's Role." *Counselor Education and Supervision,* 1965, *4,* 68–74.

4. Patterson, C. H. "Supervising Students in the Counseling Practicum." *Journal of Counseling Psychology,* 1964, *11,* 47–53.

5. Walz, G. R. & Roeber, E. C. "Supervisors' Reactions to a Counseling Interview." *Counselor Education and Supervision,* 1962, *2,* 2–7.

7

Evaluation of Counseling Effectiveness

A major reason for the difficulty in conducting research on counseling lies in the inability to arrive at satisfactory criteria of success. Most research into counseling falls short of being definitive because the criteria usually amount to little more than a value judgment implicit in an instrument or on what happens to the counselee after counseling which is assumed to be desirable.

The reasons underlying whatever decision or adjustment the counselee makes, what self-understanding he achieves, or his ability to accept his life as it is, too often remain unknown. Those involved in counseling usually have no way of knowing whether their efforts result in "success" because of counseling, in spite of counseling, or because whatever environmental stresses produced the initial problem were removed.

The research reported in this chapter represents attempts by the authors to investigate the important area of counseling effectiveness. The articles presented fall logically into two groups. The first three articles are attempts to evaluate counseling either by the use of counselee ratings, or by judgments of the counseling process by external evaluators. The last three articles are based on designs that apply criteria external to the counselee that express changes that may have occurred as a consequence of counseling.

The first study by Linden, Stone, and Shertzer presents the data underlying the development of the Counseling Evaluation Inventory (CEI). This instrument is a refinement of the Anderson and Anderson Interview Rating Scale (IRS) and the Correll modification discussed in Chapter 1 and included in Appendix A. The study involves a factor analysis of the IRS producing a short form with three final factors: counseling climate, counselor comfort, and client satisfaction. The findings indicate that the instrument has acceptable reliability and some discriminative validity when related to practicum grades. It is recommended as having usefulness for further research into the meaning of client ratings of counselors for both supervisory evaluations and counseling effectiveness judgments. The basis of information rests in the perceptions of the counselee.

The Minge article investigates counselee readiness for change and its relationship to the counseling readiness of clients. The investigator used the Edwards Personal Preference Schedule (EPPS) to provide an opportunity for self-study which, it was hypothesized, would result in greater change in self-rating among both clients and non-clients than would occur among clients and non-clients who did not complete the EPPS. The changes in rating scores were significantly greater with those who had completed the EPPS. It was also found that clients with personal-social concerns made greater changes in self-ratings than did clients with educational-vocational concerns. Minge suggests that changes in self-rating of clients and counseling readiness are related, and, further, that activities such as the administration of the EPPS can enhance counseling readiness. As in the previous study, the base of evaluation was within the client. Minge suggests that other research indicates a client will change because he is ready to do so. This implies that the nature of a specific counseling experience will have less significance than the desire to change. Evaluation of counseling should thus take into account counseling readiness of clients as well as evidences of change associated with counseling.

The Rice study investigates the relationship between therapist experience, style, and case outcome. Her study identified three types of therapist style through factor analysis of three aspects of therapist behavior expressed qualitatively and evaluated through tape recordings of counseling interviews. The investigator found that only one of the three types of therapist style related significantly to the success of counseling on three of the five criteria of success used. These three criteria were a therapist questionnaire filled out at termination of counseling, a pre- and post-*Q*-sort score differential, and the change score on the Taylor Manifest Anxiety (MA) scale.

The other two criteria investigated were a client questionnaire following counseling, and the change score on the Barron Ego Strength (ES) scale.

The next group of three articles were efforts to apply more objective criteria than client self-ratings to the effectiveness of counseling. The article by Schmieding reports the results of individual counseling and other guidance activities employing certificated school counselors with failing junior high school students. His findings include the effects of parent and teacher conferences and "other forms of environmental manipulation" in which the counselors were involved. Following treatment, the experimental group rated statistically better than the control group on grade-point average, teacher ratings of student characteristics, and a number of problems identified on the Mooney Problem Check List. The procedures were equally effective with students failing one subject and those failing more than one subject. Despite the limitations in this study associated with the presence of uncontrolled and undefined variables, it holds promise for both practice and further research. The results of the study are supportive evidence of the effectiveness of professionally educated school counselors in improving the functioning of failing students.

Kinnick and Shannon provided an investigation of the effects of both group and individual counseling on a group of students identified as socially rejected. The instrument used to identify the students was the Ohio Social Acceptance Scale (OSAS) administered to a group of high school sophomores. A control group was also provided. The criterion of success was improvement in acceptance by classmates as indicated by pre- and post-administration of the OSAS. The findings showed greater gains by those students who had received counseling although the effects of regression to the mean were also present and apparently were in part responsible for the favorable findings.

The Campbell study represents an extremely rare type of investigation, a longitudinal study of the effect of counseling on counselees. Twenty-five years after counseling, an experimental group that received counseling was compared with a control group which had not sought counseling. Criteria used included academic success, patents, publications, income, and contributions to society. Differences were small but showed a tendency to favor the counseled group. The scale reported by Campbell called "Contribution to Society" may present possibilities for future longitudinal research.

The significance of the Campbell study is more suggestive than definitive. The experimental group had sought counseling, suggesting their feeling of a need for assistance. The control group had indicated no such concern, thus indicating the possibility of other and unspecified differences in the two groups. While the original Borden and Williamson study indicated marked short-term concomitants of counseling, the Campbell study suggests that even after many years, the differences persist. The findings lead to much speculation. Do those who feel the need to seek counsel perform better than those who do not? Would those who sought counseling have been less adequate adults if they had received no assistance than those who did not seek counseling? Campbell's success in being able to compare the lives of this large number of persons illustrates the practicability of designing studies that provide evidence of the long-term effects of counseling.

The studies included in the present chapter are encouraging for those concerned with the development of the practice of counseling, and with investigations that provide evidence of the value of counseling. Two general investigative procedures warrant comment. First, the use of factor analysis in two of the six studies suggests that counseling is still so new a profession that it is necessary to utilize statistical analyses to express both the nature of the process and the reactions of the counselees. The use of such analysis is encouraging in that it suggests that counseling has advanced at least beyond the point where instrumentation is based upon construct validity related to assumptions concerning both the process and its outcomes.

Second, studies are being undertaken that utilize changes in rather objective, broadly expressed areas of counselee behavior. The studies by Schmieding and Campbell are especially significant in that they express in objectively defined terms effects associated with counseling. The examples they provide may serve as guides and inspirations for others in the evaluation of counseling based on criteria uncontaminated by the judgments of those with personal or professional commitments to counseling.

It seems apparent that the profession of counseling is still in its infancy. Much more needs to be done in terms of the evaluation of counseling effects and outcomes. Analysis of the dimensions of life that are expressed both qualitatively and quantitatively and extend longitudinally need to become common. A more precise expression of the nature of various approaches to counseling and their effects on counselees needs to be introduced into research designs. This includes a careful analysis based on the counseled–non-counseled dichotomy.

*

DEVELOPMENT AND EVALUATION OF AN INVENTORY FOR RATING COUNSELING

JAMES D. LINDEN
SHELLEY C. STONE
BRUCE SHERTZER

Counselor educators agree that present counselor selection and retention procedures are inadequate (Santavicca, 1959; Hill and Green, 1950; Hill, 1961; Patterson, 1962; Stripling and Lister, 1963). Although it has been recommended (APGA, 1963) that selection and retention criteria be applied to the personal qualities of counselor candidates as well as to their ability to master academic and professional skills, a review of the literature indicates that little provision has been made for the assessment of nonintellective variables. Wrenn noted some time ago (1952) that it is easier to measure intellectual factors; consequently, as Stoughton indicated, emphasis seems to have been placed here despite the observation that "good scholarship doesn't guarantee counseling ability" (1957).

For at least a decade, limited evidence has suggested that counselors could be differentiated from noncounselors by measured nonintellective variables (Cottle and Lewis, 1954; Cottle, Lewis and Penny, 1954). Using psychological testing procedures, counselors, for example, have been shown to reflect greater needs for intraception, exhibition and affiliation than noncounselors (Kemp, 1962). Several such studies have also suggested that counselors are understanding, sensitive, and friendly, that they value others and tend to exhibit tolerance for ambiguity in given interpersonal relationships (Fiedler, 1950a, 1950b, 1953; Grater, Kell, and Morse, 1961; Coutts, 1962; Rogers, 1962).

*This article is reprinted from *Personnel and Guidance Journal,* 1965, *44,* 267–76, by permission of the publisher, the American Personnel and Guidance Association, and the authors.

However, nonintellective measures seldom have demonstrated efficiency in discriminating between so-called effective and ineffective counselors. Arbuckle (1956), Brown (1960) and Stefflre and his colleagues (Stefflre, King, and Leafgren, 1962) have found that counselors judged effective or ineffective were differentiated to a limited degree by data obtained from a few Strong Vocational Interest Blank (SVIB, Male) scales, namely, the Psychologist Scale and the social service scales of SVIB Group V. It should be noted, however, that the distinctions between the effective and ineffective counselor largely seem due to differences in the intensity of given characteristics rather than to the presence or absence of the given characteristics themselves within the individual counselor (Kazienko and Neidt, 1962; Stefflre, King, and Leafgren, 1962).

The diversity of the methods employed in published studies of counselor effectiveness attests to a lack of satisfaction with the results obtained. In part, the limited success of past research is attributable to the lack of sensitivity of available measures of nonintellective variables. Also intimately related to this dissatisfaction is the problem of the definition and measurement of adequate effectiveness criteria for assessing counseling activity. Despite these crucial factors, some criteria do appear to be regarded as more promising than others. Users of sociometrics and the Q-technique have expressed the belief that these are fruitful methods worthy of continued investigation. Ratings by expert judges, supervisors and/or peers typify other criteria which are considered useful even though possessing limitations. In general, past efforts to establish criteria for evaluating counselor effectiveness have yielded sparse success (Hill and Green, 1960). Despite numerous recommendations to the contrary, client ratings seldom have been investigated as a source of effectiveness criteria (Shoben, 1953; Grigg and Goodstein, 1957; Goodstein and Grigg, 1959; Patterson, 1959; Pohlman and Robinson, 1960; Mueller, Gatsch, and Ralston, 1963). In 1957, Grigg and Goodstein stated:

> Some appraisal of the client's reaction to the counselor and to counseling should be obtained before we can say that we have any comprehensive understanding of who makes a good counselor and what constitutes successful counseling techniques (p. 32).

Specifically, this research was an effort to modify and refine for client use the 50-item Interview Rating Scale (IRS) devised by Anderson and Anderson (1962) and employed as a criterion measure by Correll (1955) and Brams (1961) in studies pertaining to communication in the counseling relationship. It was intended that such an instrument might provide a vehicle for subsequent research by the authors or others in exploring the value of client ratings as a criterion of counselor effectiveness.

The Development of the Counseling Evaluation Inventory

A 68-item Counseling Evaluation Inventory (CEI) which included the Anderson and Anderson IRS items was sent nationwide to 703 randomly selected school counselors and to 386 high school students who had been counseled by practicum students at Purdue University. To control any counselor-student variance associated with the degree of social favorability attributed by these subjects to the items included in the CEI, each counselor and student was asked to rate every item for social favorability on a nine-point Thurstone scale. Returns from 446 counselors and 289 students showed no counselor-student rating difference significant at the .05 level; consequently, all 68 items were retained for further study.

With the CEI response format changed to a five-point Likert scale, additional returns were obtained from 336 secondary students who were asked to evaluate their counseling experience at Purdue University. The responses of these students were scored according to provisional weights arbitrarily determined from the social desirability data noted above.

An intercorrelation matrix for the 68-item responses and a CEI total score were computed and factor-analyzed by the Thurstone Multiple Group Centroid Method (Thurstone, 1947). Communalities for this analysis were estimated by the image covariance procedure developed and reported by Guttman (1953). This method yielded four correlated factors of significance. The factor matrix was rotated, using an IBM 7090 digital computer program, according to the biquartimin criterion described by Carroll (1957).

Table 1 presents an abstract of the rotated factor matrix including only those data relevant to the items retained in the final form of the CEI. To be retained an item had to meet a dual criterion in that the item had to load .40 or greater on one factor but less than .40 on all other factors.

The four correlated factors exhibited item content that led the authors to label them Counseling Climate (X), Counselor Comfort (Y) and Client Satisfaction (Z-1 and Z-2). Nine items were retained in Scale X, five items met criteria for Scale Y and seven items constituted Scale Z (a combination of correlated factors Z-1 and Z-2).

TABLE 1
ABSTRACT OF ROTATED FACTOR MATRIX

Item No.	*Factor 1*	*Factor 2*	*Factor 3*	*Factor 4*
	Cumulative Per Cent of Trace			
	49.72	61.80	67.34	71.21
	Factor Loadings			
1	.44*	.01	.12	.20
2	.16	.24	.16	.48*
3	.45*	.00	.14	.23
4	—.12	.70*	.14	—.12
5	.06	.04	.66*	—.13
6	.53*	.26	—.12	—.21
7	.22	.18	.11	.49*
8	.15	.51*	.09	—.31
9	.42*	—.06	.20	.01
10	.05	.06	.58*	.02
11	.47*	—.03	.15	.23
12	.14	.60*	—.17	—.02
13	.02	.14	.46*	.27
14	.50*	—.03	.11	.08
15	.06	—.08	.52*	—.06
16	.02	.65*	—.19	.28
17	.57*	.14	—.13	—.03
18	.05	.00	.58*	.06
19	.43*	—.07	.15	.07
20	—.14	.70*	.13	.19
21	.40*	.09	.27	—.15

*A factor loading of .40 or greater was defined as exhibiting practical significance.

Table 2 summarizes data relevant to the item content of these factors, scoring weights, factor loadings, test-retest reliability of the final instrument and the social desirability rating of the items. These items were retained among those of the original long-form inventory (CEI-LF) and also set forth in a new short form (CEI-SF) that included only the 21 critical items ordered at random. The empirical scoring weights of all responses to the critical items were determined by item-analysis procedures using a sample of 336 clients. Interim scoring weights based on the rounded square of the factor loading were used to score the scales provisionally for item-analysis purposes. The upper and lower 27 per cent of these scores were identified and final response weights derived for each item using the Flanagan *r* statistic.

THE RELIABILITY OF THE COUNSELING EVALUATION INVENTORY

Two reliability studies were undertaken employing separate client samples. Two weeks following the conclusion of a terminal counseling interview, a copy of the CEI-LF was mailed to each of 132 high school student clients who had completed counseling at Purdue University during April and May, 1963. Each student was asked to complete and return the inventory. Approximately 100 days later, a second CEI and similar instructions were sent to the same counselees. This time, alternately, the CEI-LF and CEI-SF were sent to the 132 students, thus providing one sample of counselees who had completed a CEI LF-LF combination and another sample that had completed a CEI LF-SF combination. Complete data from 103 students were obtained, yielding, with one follow-up, a 78 per cent return for this 100-day reliability study.

In addition, 174 high school students who had been counseled at Purdue University during the summer of 1963 were asked to complete the CEI prior to leaving campus following the termination of their last counseling session. At this time, half of these students were given the CEI-LF to complete and half were asked to use the CEI-SF. Two weeks later, a second CEI was mailed to these students with a request that they complete the inventory and return it to Purdue University. As was the case for the first administration of the CEI, half of the students received the CEI-LF and half were provided the CEI-SF, but on the second administration of the inventory half of the counselees completed the same form of the CEI that they completed earlier and half were given the alternate form of the inventory. This procedure assured that all possible combinations of CEI form completions and order of form presentations were accomplished. Of the 174 student clients included in this latter study, 163 responded, yielding, with one follow-up, a 93.6 per cent return.

Analyzing both CEI-LF and CEI-SF test-retest data obtained from the samples of 103 and 163 secondary students described above, all but 3 of the 21 critical items were shown to be reliable at or beyond the .05 level for both groups, respectively. Of the three items that failed to demonstrate repeated reliability, one was found to be reliable when presented in the CEI-LF format and the other two suggested adequate reliability when included in the CEI-SF.

In the interest of brevity, only the two most critical comparisons have been presented: (1) short-form versus short-form comparisons which provide data on the final form of the CEI; and (2) the final 21 items abstracted from the original long-form instrument which indicates the stability of the retained items over a longer time span. Table 3 presents these reliability data. An inspection of Table 3 reveals that the lowest scale score of CEI total score test-retest coefficient obtained was .62 (Factor X, 100-day sample) and the highest coefficient was .83 (CEI total score, 14-day sample). The

TABLE 2

IDENTIFICATION, CONTENT AND DESCRIPTIVE DATA RELEVANT TO THE ITEMS INCLUDED IN THE FINAL FORM OF THE CEI

Item No.	*Item Content*	*Final Scoring Weights‡*	*Factor Loading*	*Relia-bility†*	*Median Social Desirability Ratings§ Counselors*	*Students*
	Factor X	*Counseling Climate*				
17	I distrusted the counselor.	1 1 1 0 2	.57	.39*	.63	.78
6	The counselor acted cold and distant.	1 1 1 1 2	.53	.44*	.96	1.17
14	The counselor was very patient.	2 0 1 1 1	.50	.39*	7.71	7.56
11	I believe the counselor had a genuine desire to be of service to me.	2 1 0 1 1	.47	.35*	7.66	7.55
3	The counselor acted as though he thought my concerns and problems were important to him.	2 1 0 1 1	.45	.57*	8.01	7.57
1	I felt the counselor accepted me as an individual.	2 0 1 1 1	.44	.33*	8.17	7.54
19	The counselor insisted on being right always.	1 1 1 0 2	.43	.50*	.76	1.44
9	In our talks, the counselor acted as if he were better than I.	1 1 1 0 2	.42	.53*	.87	1.33
21	The counselor acted as if he had a job to do and didn't care how he accomplished it.	1 1 1 0 2	.40	.32*	1.13	1.26
	Factor Y	*Counselor Comfort*				
4	The counselor acted uncertain of himself.	1 1 0 1 2	.70	.55*	2.11	1.90

20	The counselor gave the impression of "feeling at ease."	3	0	0	1	1	.70	.25	7.32	7.35
16	In opening our conversations, the counselor was relaxed and at ease.	3	0	0	1	1	.65	.42*	7.33	7.28
12	The counselor was awkward in starting our interviews.	1	1	0	0	2	.60	.42*	2.59	2.17
8	The counselor seemed restless while talking to me.	1	1	0	1	2	.51	.42*	2.34	2.12
	Factor Z	*Client Satisfaction*								
5	The counselor helped me to see how taking tests would be helpful to me.	2	1	0	1	1	.66	.43*	6.91	6.91
18	The counselor's discussion of test results was helpful to me.	2	1	0	1	1	.58	.38*	7.30	7.22
10	The counselor's comments helped me to see more clearly what I need to do to gain my objectives in life.	2	1	0	0	1	.58	.41*	7.44	6.96
15	Other students could be helped by talking with counselors.	2	1	0	1	1	.52	.67*	7.06	7.76
7	I felt at ease with the counselor.	2	1	0	1	1	.49	.58*	8.09	7.69
2	I felt comfortable in my interviews with the counselor.	2	1	0	1	1	.47	.53*	7.31	7.15
13	I felt satisfied as a result of my talks with the counselor.	2	1	0	0	1	.46	.57*	7.06	7.21

‡In sequence, respectively: Always, Often, Sometimes, Rarely, Never.
†Test-retest estimates, 14-day interval, N = 41.
*Coefficients significant at or beyond .05 level.
§Rated on a 0 through 8 scale from least desirable to most desirable.

TABLE 3

Item No.	*Short Form* *(k = 21)* *14-Day* *Interval* *N = 41*	*Long Form* *(k = 86)* *100-Day* *Interval* *N = 52*
1	.33*	.40*
2	.53*	.48*
3	.57*	.40*
4	.55*	.60*
5	.43*	.45*
6	.44*	.47*
7	.58*	.61*
8	.42*	.46*
9	.53*	.46*
10	.41*	.50*
11	.35*	.37*
12	.42*	.31*
13	.57*	.60*
14	.39*	.12
15	.67*	.67*
16	.42*	.28*
17	.39*	.77*
18	.38*	.42*
19	.50*	.36*
20	.25	.40*
21	.32*	.18
X Score	.78*	.67*
Y Score	.63*	.62*
Z Score	.74*	.71*
Total Score	.83*	.76*

*Significant at or beyond .05 level.

median coefficient computed among all the scale score or total score indices was .72.

The Validity of the Counseling Evaluation Inventory

Utilizing counselor candidates' practicum grades as a provisional criterion, congruent or discriminative validity significant at or beyond the .05 level was demonstrated for the factor scales or CEI total score of the 21-item CEI-SF. Correlational (Table 4) and analysis of variance (ANOV) procedures (Tables 5–8), respectively, were employed to analyze the data for the congruent and discriminative validity studies. Where appropriate, ANOV main or simple effects were tested by Newman-Keuls analyses (Winer, 1962) for ordered data means (Figure 1 and Tables 5–8). The data so analyzed were the practicum grades quantified on a nine-point scale and the median CEI scale score and total score client ratings given to 139 (101 male and 38 female) masters-level school-counselor candidates at Purdue University during the 1962–63 academic year and the 1963 summer session. At least five clients rated each counselor involved in the study. Counselors having fewer ratings were dropped from the sample.

TABLE 4

CORRELATION MATRIX FOR CEI SCORES AND PRACTICUM GRADE

	Mdn X Score	*Mdn Y Score*	*Mdn Z Score*	*Mdn Total Score*	*Practicum Grade*
	Males (N = 101)				
Mdn X		.29*	.48*	.74*	.25*
Mdn Y			.44*	.68*	.21*
Mdn Z				.73*	.17
Mdn Total					.25*
Practicum Grade					
	Females (N = 38)				
Mdn X		.53*	.56*	.53*	.19
Mdn Y			.60*	.70*	.50*
Mdn Z				.66*	.32*
Mdn Total					.42*
Practicum Grade					
	Males and Females Combined (N = 139)				
Mdn X		.36*	.50*	.66*	.22*
Mdn Y			.48*	.67*	.29*
Mdn Z				.70*	.24*
Mdn Total					.32*
Practicum Grade					

*Significant at or beyond .05 level.

As indicated in Table 4, all correlations computed among the CEI scale scores and total score exhibited significant departures from zero-order relationship. In addition, the counselor comfort (Scale Y) and CEI total scores for both male and female counselors demonstrated significant relationships with practicum grades. However, the grade criterion was shown to be associated significantly with only the clients' ratings of counseling climate (Scale X) given to male counselors and the clients' ratings of counseling satisfaction (Scale Z) accorded female counselors.

Tables 5–8 reveal that a significant interaction between practicum grade and sex of counselor was evident for the CEI total score ANOV data. Figure 1 summarizes the exploration of the ANOV simple effects for these latter data which revealed that females graded *B* were rated higher by clients than those graded *A* or *C*.

TABLE 5
COUNSELING CLIMATE
ANALYSIS OF VARIANCE SUMMARY TABLE

Source	*SS*	*df*	*MS*	*F*
Practicum Grade	3169.84	2	1584.92	3.39*
Sex	517.75	1	517.75	1.11
Interaction	1027.88	2	513.94	1.10
Error	62116.56	133	467.04	

NEWMAN-KEULS TESTS FOR ORDERED PRACTICUM GRADE MEANS

Main Effect Level	a_3	a_2	a_1
Practicum Grade	C	B	A
Ordered Means	143.73	151.81	158.01
Difference Between Pairs			
a_3		8.08*	14.28*
a_2			6.20*
a_1			
Truncated Range *r*		2	3
$q_{.95}$ (*r*, 120)		2.80	3.36
$q_{.95}$ (*r*, 120) $\sqrt{MS\ error/n}$		5.12	6.15

*$F_{.95}$ (2,125) = 3.07.

TABLE 6
COUNSELOR COMFORT
ANALYSIS OF VARIANCE SUMMARY TABLE

Source	*SS*	*df*	*MS*	*F*
Practicum Grade	6006.73	2	3003.36	4.84*
Sex	4770.53	1	4770.53	7.69*
Interaction	2173.31	2	1086.65	1.75
Error	82503.44	133	620.33	

NEWMAN-KEULS TESTS FOR ORDERED PRACTICUM GRADE MEANS

Main Effect Level	a_3	a_2	a_1
Practicum Grade	C	B	A
Ordered Means	55.82	71.91	76.12
Difference Between Pairs			
a_3		16.09*	20.30*
a_2			4.21
a_1			
Truncated Range *r*		2	3
$q_{.95}$ (*r*, 120)		2.80	3.36
$q_{.95}$ (*r*, 120) $\sqrt{MS\ error/n}$		5.91	7.09

*$F_{.95}$ (2,125) = 3.07.

TABLE 7

CLIENT SATISFACTION

ANALYSIS OF VARIANCE SUMMARY TABLE

Source	*SS*	*df*	*MS*	*F*
Practicum Grade	2256.33	2	1128.16	3.69*
Sex	228.83	1	228.83	0.75
Interaction	639.16	2	319.58	1.05
Error	40666.55	133	305.76	

NEWMAN-KEULS TESTS FOR ORDERED PRACTICUM GRADE MEANS

Main Effect Level	a_3	a_2	a_1
Practicum Grade	C	B	A
Ordered Means	83.91	94.71	96.14
Difference Between pairs			
a_3		10.80*	12.23*
a_2			1.43
a_1			
Truncated Range r		2	3
$q_{.95}$ $(r, 120)$		2.80	3.36
$q_{.95}$ $(r, 120)$ $\sqrt{MS\ error/n}$		4.14	4.97

$*F_{.95}$ (2,125) = 3.07.

TABLE 8

TOTAL SCORE

ANALYSIS OF VARIANCE SUMMARY TABLE

Source	*SS*	*df*	*MS*	*F*
Practicum Grade	40623.12	2	20311.56	6.45
Sex	7177.75	1	717.75	2.28
Interaction	22653.03	2	11326.52	3.60*
Error	418657.00	133	3147.80	

NEWMAN-KEULS TESTS FOR PRACTICUM GRADE BY SEX CELL MEANS

Practicum Grade by Sex†	ab_{32}	ab_{31}	ab_{21}	ab_{11}	ab_{12}	ab_{22}
Ordered Cell Mean	248.40	282.42	306.62	323.31	327.74	355.78
Difference Between Pairs						
ab_{32}		34.02*	58.22*	74.91*	79.34*	107.38*
ab_{31}			24.20*	40.89*	45.32*	73.36*
ab_{21}				16.69*	21.12*	49.16*
ab_{11}					4.43	32.47*
ab_{12}						28.04
ab_{22}						
Truncated Range r		2	3	4	5	6
$q_{.95}$ $(r, 120)$		2.80	3.36	3.69	3.92	4.10
$q_{.95}$ $(r, 120)$ $\sqrt{MS\ error/n}$		13.33	15.99	17.56	18.66	19.52

$*F_{.95}$ (2,125) = 3.07.

†A: a_1 = Grade A, a_2 = Grade B, a_3 = Grade C.
B: b_1 = Males, b_2 = Females.

Male counselors were rated as was expected (i.e., *A* students were rated higher than *B* students who, in turn, were rated higher than *C* students). The ANOV's further showed that females were rated higher than males on Scale Y (Counselor Comfort). No sex difference was indicated by the ANOV's for Scale X (Counseling Climate) or Scale Z (Client Satisfaction). However, on all three factor scales, counselors graded *A* in practicum were rated significantly higher than those evaluated as *C*-grade practicum students. Moreover, Scale X data indicated that counselors graded *B* were ranked significantly less effective in fostering an adequate counseling climate than counselors graded *A*. At the same time, clients evaluated *B*-grade counselors as significantly more effective in producing an adequate counseling climate than they did counselors graded *C*.

The results of the correlational analyses required that certain of the ANOV findings presented in Tables 5–8 be interpreted with caution. Although no significant sex difference was found for either the counseling climate or the client satisfaction scales, only male counseling climate scores and female client satisfaction scores were shown to be correlated significantly with the practicum grade criterion. Consequently, it is possible that the ANOV finding that the counseling-climate ratings distinguished among *all* practicum grade groups is applied best to the evaluations made for male counselors. Similarly, the suggestion that client-satisfaction ratings may distinguish between *C*-grade counselors and others perhaps is restricted to evaluations of female counselors.

Overall, female counselors were rated by their clients as exhibiting greater comfort within the counseling relationship than did the male counselors. Since this factor scale score was shown to be related significantly to final practicum grades in the case of both male and female counselors, this finding may be generalized with greater confidence and may cast some light upon the sex by practicum grade interaction reported for the ANOV computed to evaluate the CEI total score data.

Other research recently completed at Purdue University (Johnson, 1964) suggested that practicum supervisor evaluations may have been influenced by the observed friendliness of male counselors and by the perceived efficiency of female counselors when determining practicum grades. In Johnson's research, the quality of practicum grade was related to certain objectively measured personality characteristics which supported this conclusion. Consequently, the sex by practicum grade interaction found for the CEI total score data may indicate that a dual supervisor standard operated in assigning practicum grades while clients utilized only a single criterion in

FIGURE 1

SUMMARY OF NEWMAN-KEULS TESTS FOR SIGNIFICANT ANOV MAIN EFFECTS OR SIMPLE EFFECTS*,†

Counseling Climate

(1) Ordered Practicum Grade Means
A_3‡ $\quad A_2 \quad A_1$

Counselor Comfort

(2) Ordered Practicum Grade Means
$A_3 \quad \underline{A_2 \quad A_1}$

Client Satisfaction

(3) Ordered Practicum Grade Means
$A_3 \quad \underline{A_2 \quad A_1}$

Total Score

(4) Ordered Practicum Grade by Sex Cell Means
$AB_{32} \quad AB_{31} \quad AB_{21} \quad \underline{AB_{11} \quad AB_{12} \quad AB_{22}}$

*Cells underlined by a common line do not differ from each other.

†Abstracted from Tables 5 through 8.

‡Code figures and numbers indicate the conditions as follows:

A: Practicum Grade	B: Sex
1—A	1—males
2—B	2—females
3—C	

rating their respective counselors. It is possible that the practicum supervisors gave high grades to the friendly male counselors and to the efficient female counselors, but the clients responded primarily to what warmth and friendliness they experienced in the counseling relationship regardless of the sex of their counselor.

It should be recognized that the final practicum grades represent a relatively gross index of counselor effectiveness in settings such as the one in which this research was conducted. Repeated observation and reviews of taped sessions do not absolutely assure a common base of evaluation. As a global index of counseling effectiveness, practicum grades can, and probably do, rest upon implicit as well as explicit factors deemed important to specific supervisors. The factors contributing to grades may vary somewhat from supervisor to supervisor. Notwithstanding efforts among experienced staff supervisors to arrive at equitable pooled evaluations, it is possible that some supervisors may base grades primarily upon efficient administrative management of a given client's case, others may emphasize comprehensive case presentation in supervisory sessions, while still others may stress observed counselee-counselor interaction. Future efforts at validation of the CEI should include the use of practicum performance criteria which are explicitly defined, subjected to prior test to determine their reliability and relevance and, finally, employed in situations where adequate safeguards can be maintained to minimize factors not directly related to counseling effectiveness as measured by the CEI.

Conclusions

In short, despite their brevity, all CEI factor scales and the CEI total score exhibited adequate reliability and at least limited discriminative validity for practicum grades. Most scales and the total score demonstrated significant congruent validity when related to practicum grade, especially in the case of female counselors. Although each factor scale thus indicated some merit for continued experimental exploration, the significant intercorrelations found among the three factor scales and the relatively greater reliability and discriminative and congruent validity suggested for the CEI total score supported speculation that the latter score may be the most parsimonious measure to employ for any practicable use now made of the CEI.

References

American Personnel and Guidance Association. "A Statement of Policy. The Counselor: Professional Preparation and Role." *Personnel and Guidance Journal,* 1963, *41,* 480–85.

Anderson, R. P., & Anderson, G. V. "Development of an Instrument for Measuring Rapport." *Personnel and Guidance Journal,* 1962, *41,* 18–24.

Arbuckle, D. S. "Client Perception of Counselor Personality." *Journal of Counseling Psychology,* 1956, *3,* 93–96.

Brams, J. M. "Counselor Characteristics and Effective Communication in Counseling." *Journal of Counseling Psychology,* 1961, *8,* 25–30.

Brown, D. J. "An Investigation of the Relationships Between Certain Personal Characteristics of Guidance Counselors and Performance in Supervised Counseling Interviews." Unpublished doctoral dissertation, Ohio State University, 1960.

Carroll, J. B. "The Biquartimin Solution for Oblique Rotation in Factor Analysis." *Science,* 1957, *126,* 1114–15.

Correll, P. T. "Factors Influencing Communication in Counseling." Unpublished doctoral dissertation, University of Missouri, 1955.

Cottle, W. C., & Lewis, W. W., Jr. "Personality Characteristics of Counselors: II Male Counselor Responses to MMPI and GZTS." *Journal of Counseling Psychology,* 1954, *1,* 27–30.

Cottle, W. C., Lewis, W. W., Jr., & Penny, M. M. "Personal Characteristics of Counselors: III An Experimental Scale." *Journal of Counseling Psychology,* 1954, *1,* 74–77.

Coutts, R. L. "Selected Characteristics of Counselor Candidates in Relation to Levels and Types of Competency in the Counseling Practicum." Unpublished doctoral dissertation, Florida State University, 1962.

Fiedler, F. E. "A Comparison of Therapeutic Relationships in Psychoanalytic, Nondirective and Adlerian Therapy." *Journal of Consulting Psychology,* 1950, *14,* 239–45. (a)

Fiedler, F. E. "The Concept of an Ideal Therapeutic Relationship." *Journal of Consulting Psychology,* 1950, *14,* 239–45. (b)

Fiedler, F. E. "Quantitative Studies on the Role of Therapists' Feelings Toward Their Patients." In O. Hobart Mowrer (ed.), *Psychotherapy: Theory and Research.* New York: Ronald Press, 1953, 296–315.

Goodstein, L. D., & Grigg, A. E. "Client Satisfaction, Counselors and the Counseling Process." *Personnel and Guidance Journal,* 1959, *38,* 19–24.

Grater, H. A., Kell, B. L., & Morse, J. "The Social Service Interest: Roadblock and Road to Creativity." *Journal of Counseling Psychology,* 1961, *8,* 9–12.

Grigg, A. E., & Goodstein, L. D. "The Use of Clients as Judges of the Counselor's Performance." *Journal of Counseling Psychology,* 1957, *4,* 31–36.

Guttman, L. "Image Theory for the Structure of Quantitative Variates." *Psychometrika,* 1953, *18,* 277–96.

Hill, G. W. "The Selection of School Counselors." *Personnel and Guidance Journal,* 1961, *39* 355–60.

Hill, G. E., & Green, D. A. "The Selection, Preparation and Professionalization of Guidance and Personnel Workers." *Review of Educational Research,* 1960, *30,* 115–30.

Johnson, Dorothy. "A Study of Interests and Personality Characteristics of Counselor Trainees and Counseling Effectiveness." Unpublished doctoral dissertation, Purdue University, 1964.

Kazienko, L. W., & Neidt, C. O. "Self-Descriptions of Good and Poor Counselor Trainees." *Counselor Education and Supervision,* 1962, *1,* 106–23.

Kemp, C. G. "Counseling Responses and Need Structures of High School Principals and Counselors." *Journal of Counseling Psychology,* 1962, *9,* 326–28.

Mueller, W. J., Gatsch, C. M., & Ralston, J. K. "The Prediction of Counselor Interview Behavior." *Personnel and Guidance Journal,* 1963, *41,* 513–17.

Patterson, C. H. "Client Expectations and Social Conditioning." *Personnel and Guidance Journal,* 1958, *37,* 136–38.

Patterson, C. H. "Selection of Rehabilitation Counseling Students." *Personnel and Guidance Journal,* 1962, *41,* 318–24.

Pohlman, E., & Robinson, F. P. "Client Reaction to Some Aspects of the Counseling Situation." *Personnel and Guidance Journal,* 1960, *38,* 546–51.

Rogers, C. R. "The Interpersonal Relationship: The Core of Guidance." *Harvard Educational Review,* 1962, *32,* 416–29.

Santavicca, G. G. "Supervised Experience and Selection of Counselor Trainees." *Personnel and Guidance Journal,* 1959, *38,* 195–97.

Shoben, E. J. "Some Problems in Establishing Criteria of Effectiveness." *Personnel and Guidance Journal,* 1953, *31,* 287–94.

Stefflre, B., King, P., & Leafgren, F. "Characteristics of Counselors Judged Effective by Their Peers." *Journal of Counseling Psychology,* 1962, *9,* 335–40.

Stoughton, R. W. "The Preparation of Counselors and Personnel Workers." *Review of Educational Research,* 1957, *27,* 174–85.

Stripling, R. O., & Lister, J. L. "Selection, Preparation and Professionalization of Specialists." *Review of Educational Research,* 1963, *33,* 171–78.

Thurstone, L. L. *Multiple-Factor Analysis.* Chicago: University of Chicago Press, 1947.

Winer, B. J. *Statistical Principles in Experimental Design.* New York: McGraw-Hill, 1962.

Wrenn, C. G. "The Selection and Education of Student Personnel Workers." *Personnel and Guidance Journal,* 1952, *31,* 9–14.

*

COUNSELING READINESS AS READINESS FOR CHANGE

M. RONALD MINGE[1]

Counseling readiness (CR) is a vital concept for counselors, for it is an important determinant of what occurs in and results from counseling. Despite the utility of the concept of CR, the term has been used ambiguously, perhaps because it is influenced by a complex composite of many determining factors. A consensus of authors produces a definition on this order: CR involves (a) a transitory state of discomfort generally including anxiety, (b) recognition that a difficulty exists, (c) willingness and ability to change, and (d) belief that another person with greater knowledge can help to resolve the difficulty.

Essentially CR means that persons who seek counseling are likely to change in a counseling relationship because they are ready to do so. There is substantial evidence to support this. The client is by definition in need of change, as most authors have considered CR to be largely a result of temporary discomfort or dissatisfaction (Brammer and Shostrom, 1960; Doleys, 1964; Parker, 1961; Rogers, 1951). Also, counselors have found from experience that persons who actively seek counseling are more likely to benefit from it than are those who do not seek it. Reluctance to force therapy upon

*This article is reprinted from *The Journal of College Student Personnel,* 1966, 7, 197–202, by permission of the publisher and author.

[1]This article is abstracted from the author's doctoral dissertation.

potential clients is exemplified by the statement that " . . . sound counseling practice and ethics demand that counseling be voluntary" (Brammer and Shostrom, 1960, p. 122). Additional evidence is supplied by Rogers and Dymond (1954), who found that clients who did not receive counseling improved their self-ratings. The implication is that they were ready to change and did so. Conversely, counselors are aware that some persons who seek and receive counseling do not appear to benefit from it. Clients' apparent lack of progress sometimes is considered to be a function of inadequate readiness for counseling.

CR as readiness for change also is indicated by the claimed success for a wide variety of therapeutic techniques. Frank (1961) has been outspoken here, contending that methods ranging from voodoo healing to psychoanalysis work because they possess an element in account for claimed universal successes. That is, most persons who common: their practitioners are confident and persuasive. However, readiness for change is another common element which might better seek therapy, regardless of its nature, are ready to modify that behavior which is distressing.

Three other criteria have been used for consideration of CR, but while these are useful, they have severe limitations. These criteria are: whether the client seeks, remains in, and benefits from counseling. The first is limited in that counselors often encounter voluntary clients who are not ready to discuss problem areas. Also, it must be assumed that many persons with difficulties suitable for counseling do not request help because they are unaware of counseling facilities or misperceive their purpose and function. In a recent survey concerning awareness of the existence and functions of a university student counseling center, large differences were found among various segments of the student population (Minge and Cass, 1966).

Duration of counseling as a criterion for CR also has severe limitations, although it is easily quantified. It has been used recently by Heilbrun (1961a, 1961b, 1964) and Heilbrun and Sullivan (1962). This criterion is tautological and virtually precludes the possibility of successful short-term counseling. It is essentially a *post hoc* criterion, for with it CR cannot be determined until counseling has been terminated. Further, its use assumes that counseling-ready clients are those who remain in counseling long enough for some benefits to accrue. The difficulty with this assumption is that it has not been established how long persons must be counseled for important gains to be made.

The third criterion is whether the client benefits from counseling. This is another after-the-fact criterion of little use for predictive purposes. More importantly, a lack of standards by which the outcome of counseling might be evaluated severely handicaps the use of this criterion. A compounding difficulty is the general complexity of changes in human behavior.

CR has been viewed in this study as readiness for change, or more specifically, as readiness to modify self-perception. This approach was suggested by client-centered counselors' emphasis upon the discrepancies between a client's self-perception and what he experiences. Because the client is in need of change and a major purpose of counseling is to facilitate changes in self-perception, treating CR as readiness to modify self-perception appears highly appropriate.

Persons who seek counseling are likely to modify self-perceptions in a counseling relationship because they are ready to do so. This implies that they also might change self-perceptions when confronted with other settings which require self-evaluation. That is, the counselor may be a stimulus for change, but other stimuli also may be appropriate for facilitating change. For example, a book on study skills might help the client with educational difficulties to reappraise his self-expectations. Vocational problems might be alleviated by exposure to vocational information. Similarly, a task which requires consideration of personality dimensions might particularly benefit clients with personal problems. The present study investigated CR by measuring changes in self-perception which occurred when college students were given an experimental task which required self-evaluation on a number of personality dimensions. The hypotheses tested were:

1. Completion of a task requiring self-evaluation facilitates changes in self-perception.
2. College students who seek counseling are more ready to modify self-perceptions than are students who do not seek counseling.
3. Clients with personal problems are more ready to modify self-perceptions concerning personality than are clients with vocational and educational difficulties.

METHOD

SELF-EVALUATION BATTERY

Completing a personality inventory was considered to be a task which would require self-evaluation and therefore might stimulate the modification of self-perception. In this sense it is somewhat analogous to a counseling interview. The Edwards Personal Preference Schedule (EPPS) was chosen because it was designed primarily for counseling and research purposes with college students and was intended to ". . . provide quick and convenient measures of a number of relatively *normal* personality variables" (Edwards, 1959, p. 5). It purports to measure 15 personality variables taken from Murray's need system, but its purpose here was as a structured stimulus situation which required the student to evaluate himself.

A rating scale was developed to measure the changes made in self-description as a result of completing the EPPS. The scale consisted of 15 descriptive statements based upon the 15 needs measured by the EPPS. *S*'s were asked to rate themselves, with respect to each statement, along a seven-point continuum. The scale was not developed to measure personality, nor was it intended as a means by which an accurate profile of *S*'s' self-perceptions might be gained. Rather, it was intended as a task, or as a vehicle for determining the amount of change in self-perceptions made by *S*'s.

The rating scale was administered first, then collected, and *S*'s were given the EPPS. The scale was readministered upon completion of the EPPS. Completion of the scales took from 3 to 5 minutes each, and the EPPS required approximately 40 minutes for most *S*'s. *S*'s were not told in advance that the second scale would be given, so that they would not make a particular effort to remember their ratings on the first scale.

Rating changes were tabulated for each statement by determining how many points the second rating was discrepant from the first. Thus, a change of rating from one on the first scale to a rating of five on the second scale was counted as a change of four points. A change of rating from seven on the first scale to four on the second was counted as a change of three points. The changes of the 15 subscales were then added for a total change score for each *S*.

SUBJECTS AND PROCEDURE

The three hypotheses were tested by administering the battery to several groups of *S*'s and comparing resultant change scores. Hypothesis One was tested by comparing *S*'s' change scores made *with* and *without* the EPPS. Fifteen students who requested counseling (clients) at the Student Counseling Center (SCC), Washington State University, were administered the rating scale as an intake test. Then they were asked to return in 50 minutes for further testing, which was unspecified. When they returned, the scale was administered again. Fifteen non-clients who met as a small discussion group for an introductory psychology course were asked to complete the scale as part of a psychological study. It was given at the beginning of a 50-minute class period and then administered again as a surprise test at the end of the period. Changes made *without* the EPPS were thus attained for clients and non-clients.

To determine whether the EPPS facilitated changes, 72 clients and 54 non-clients were administered the scale *with* the EPPS. Non-clients were undergraduates enrolled in psychology courses who had volunteered for an undefined experiment. None had ever been a client at the SCC. Client and non-client groups were similar with respect to academic class, sex, marital status, and college residence.

Clients were administered the scales and EPPS as an intake battery of tests. They first completed an individual information form routinely required at the SCC and then were asked to complete the battery before being seen by a counselor. Clients either completed the battery immediately or made arrangements to complete it soon thereafter. In no case were the tests administered after the client had seen a counselor. Only four clients refused to take part, explaining that the current press of examinations would cause a hardship. The battery was completed in the testing room at the SCC during regular office hours. Clients worked individually on the battery, but there usually were other students completing tests in the same room.

Most non-clients were given the battery in small groups in the early evening. A small university classroom which was nearly the same size as the SCC testing room was used. A few non-clients completed the task in the SCC during regular office hours because it was more convenient for them.

Hypothesis One was tested by comparing the difference in change scores between (a) clients *without* the EPPS and clients *with* the EPPS, and (b) non-clients *without* the EPPS and non-clients *with* the EPPS.

Hypothesis Two was that clients are more likely to change self-perceptions than are non-clients. It was tested by comparing the change scores of 72 clients and 54 non-clients, both of which groups had completed the EPPS.

The testing of Hypothesis Three involved dividing the client group into two subgroups. Students who seek counseling do so for a variety of reasons. While individual problems vary greatly, it is possible to categorize clients according to their major difficulty. The classification system used at the SCC is a widely used trichotomy. It distinguishes vocational, educational, and personal problems. Although the classifications are not mutually exclusive and it is sometimes difficult to demarcate them, they are useful and fairly stable.

Change scores of 30 clients with personal problems were compared with scores of 41 clients with vocational and educational difficulties.

One client could not be classified in the trichotomy. Hypothesis Three was that personal counseling clients would modify their self-perceptions more than would vocational and educational clients.

Results

RATING CHANGES WITHOUT EPPS

The difference between the mean change scores of the 15 clients and 15 non-clients *without* the EPPS is shown in Table 1. This difference and the three following differences were all evaluated by simple analysis of variance (McNemar, 1962).

TABLE 1
CHANGE SCORES OF CLIENTS AND NON-CLIENTS WITHOUT EPPS

	Range	*Mean*	*Sigma*	*F*	*(df = 1,28)*
Clients	2-10	4.87	2.77	1.45	(P >.05)
Non-Clients	0-10	3.67	2.49		

The mean change scores of the clients were higher than those of the non-clients, but the difference was not significant at the .05 level. The change scores of the two groups were considered sufficiently low to warrant use of the scales with the intervening EPPS.

CHANGES WITH AND WITHOUT EPPS

The change scores of the 72 clients who completed the EPPS were compared with the change scores of the 15 clients who did not take the EPPS. The same comparison was made between change scores of the 54 non-clients who completed the EPPS and the 15 non-clients who did not. The results are shown in Table 2.

TABLE 2
CHANGE SCORES OF SUBJECTS WITH AND WITHOUT EPPS

	Without EPPS		*With EPPS*			
	Mean	*Sigma*	*Mean*	*Sigma*	*df*	*F*
Clients	4.87	2.77	9.13	4.25	1,85	13.44*
Non-Clients	3.67	2.49	8.06	3.53	1,67	19.66*

*P<.001

The mean rating change scores of both clients and non-clients were fairly low when the EPPS was not administered. The increase in change scores with the intervening EPPS can be attributed to the effect of the EPPS. This supported the contention of Hypothesis One that completion of a personality inventory is analogous to a counseling interview, as they both require the client to think about himself.

CLIENTS AND NON-CLIENTS

The difference between the change scores of the 72 clients and 54 non-clients who had completed the EPPS is shown in Table 3. The difference was not significant, although it was in the direction predicted. Therefore, the experimental hypothesis that clients would modify their self-perceptions more than would non-clients was not supported.

TABLE 3
CHANGE SCORES OF CLIENTS AND NON-CLIENTS

	Mean	*Sigma*	*F*	*(df = 1,124)*
Clients	9.13	4.25	2.21	(P>.05)
Non-Clients	8.06	3.53		

PERSONAL AND VOCATIONAL-EDUCATIONAL CLIENTS

The difference between the mean change scores of personal and vocational-educational clients is shown in Table 4. The difference was significant at the .01 level, thus supporting Hypothesis Three.

TABLE 4
CHANGE SCORES OF PERSONAL AND VOCATIONAL-EDUCATIONAL CLIENTS

	Mean	*Sigma*	*F*	*(df = 1,69)*
Personal Clients	10.37	4.86	7.02	(P<.01)
Voc-Ed Clients	7.90	2.82		

DISCUSSION

There are several implications resulting from the present study. First, readiness for change appears to be a most useful criterion of CR. It can be evaluated by a number of methods, including changes on rating scales, personality tests, operant conditioning, educational material to be read, and a variety of other experimental tasks. Further, such changes are capable of objective measurement.

A second implication is that appropriate measures of change should be used to evaluate CR. The difference in change scores between personal and vocational-educational clients indicated that the personality-oriented self-evaluation battery used was most appropriate for the former group. Vocational and educational clients' problems were generally of a fairly specific nature, not necessarily involving concerns about personality. Future research should compare changes made by clients with similar problems, and appropriate tasks and measures should be used. For example, educational clients could be given material to read concerning study techniques or motivation for academic work, and changes following this exposure then could be determined.

Another area which warrants future consideration is the appropriateness of changes made by *S*'s. Difficulty might be encountered in determining the appropriateness of change, however. This study has considered CR as readiness for change, but has not supposed that greater CR would be reflected in more accurate or appropriate changes in self-perception. On the contrary, persons who could make appropriate changes might be less likely to seek help from a counseling facility.

The means and variances of rating changes made by the client and non-client groups were quite similar. This similarity suggests that readiness for change was characteristic of some clients and some non-clients but not characteristic of others. In other words, some *S*'s, both clients and non-clients, were ready to modify their self-perceptions and did so. Perhaps it is not surprising that some clients changed as much as they did, since the college years are generally considered to be a period of extensive modification of self-perceptions. It appears that some students who were ready to change came to the SCC but other students, also ready to change, did *not* request counseling help. The difference between them might best be accounted for in terms of whether the changes in self-perception involved problems which they felt required professional counseling assistance.

Considering CR as readiness for change has much promise for future research. A variety of experimental tasks designed to require the *S* to consider himself and his problem may be used to evaluate subsequent change, but the task should be appropriate to the problems for which the client seeks counseling. Readiness for change may then be evaluated as a criterion of CR by correlating it with subsequent duration of and benefits from counseling.

References

Brammer, L. M., & Shostrom, E. L. *Therapeutic Psychology: Fundamentals of Counseling and Psychotherapy*. Englewood Cliffs, N. J.: Prentice-Hall, 1960.

Doleys, E. J. "Differences Between Clients and Non-Clients on the Mooney Problem Check List." *Journal of College Student Personnel,* 1964, *6,* 21–24.

Edwards, A. L. Manual for the *Edwards Personal Preference Schedule*. New York: The Psychological Corporation, 1959.

Frank, J. D. *Persuasion and Healing*. New York: Schocken, 1961.

Garrett, H. E. *Statistics in Psychology and Education*. New York: Longmans, Green, 1958.

Heilbrun, A. B. "Client Personality Patterns, Counselor Dominance, and Duration of Counseling." *Psychological Reports,* 1961a, *9,* 15–25.

Heilbrun, A. B. "Male and Female Correlates of Early Termination in Counseling." *Journal of Counseling Psychology,* 1961b, *8,* 31–36.

Heilbrun, A. B. "Further Validation of a Counseling Readiness Scale." *Journal of Counseling Psychology,* 1964, *11,* 290–92.

Heilbrun, A. B. "Counseling Readiness: A Treatment-Specific or General Factor?" *Journal of Counseling Psychology,* 1965, *12,* 87–90.

Heilbrun, A. B., & Sullivan, D. J. "The Prediction of Counseling Readiness." *Personnel and Guidance Journal,* 1962, *41,* 112–17.

McNemar, Q. *Psychological Statistics*. New York: Wiley, 1962.

Minge, M. R., & Cass, W. A. "Student Perceptions of a University Counseling Center." *Journal of College Student Personnel,* 1966, *7,* 141–44.

Parker, C. A. "The Predictive Use of the MMPI in a College Counseling Center." *Journal of Counseling Psychology,* 1961, *8,* 154–58.

Rogers, C. R. *Client-Centered Therapy*. Boston: Houghton Mifflin, 1951.

Rogers, C. R., & Dymond, Rosalind F. *Psychotherapy and Personality Change*. Chicago: University of Chicago Press, 1954.

*

THERAPIST STYLE OF PARTICIPATION AND CASE OUTCOME[1]

LAURA NORTH RICE

Until recent years, psychotherapy research has focused largely on the question of the effectiveness of psychotherapy, yet the problem is still far from a satisfactory resolution. The last few years have seen a shift toward examination of the characteristics of the client, the therapist, and the therapy process itself. This shift seems to stem not from the conviction that the effectiveness of psychotherapy has been unequivocally demonstrated but rather from the realization that a part of the problem arises from treating psychotherapy as a homogeneous "treatment" variable in outcome designs, an assumption that ignores the tremendous variation which we know to exist even within a single theoretical orientation. It may be that some psychotherapy situations are no more effective in bringing about personality change than is the mere passage of time, whereas others will prove to be demonstrably more effective. There is some evidence that such differences in effectiveness do not rest on differences of theoretical orientation but rather on more subtle aspects of the structure of the situation, the characteristics each member of the dyad brings to the situation, and the nature of the ensuing interaction. If these aspects can be identified and shown to be meaning-

---

*This article is reprinted from *Journal of Consulting Psychology,* 1965, *29,* 155–60, by permission of the publisher, the American Psychological Association, and the author.

[1]This study was supported in part by Research Grant MH 04609 from the National Institute of Health, United States Public Health Service and in part by a grant from the Ford Foundation (Psychotherapy Research Project).

We wish to express our appreciation to Desmond Cartwright and Donald W. Fiske for making case recordings and test data available to us.

fully related to case outcome, there will be considerably more light on the whole question of the effectiveness of psychotherapy.

Perhaps the most direct attempts to get an understanding of differential outcome are those that scrutinize the nature of the interaction in the therapy hour, making the assumption that characteristics of the therapist, client, and therapeutic setting, if they are in fact relevant, will manifest themselves in the events of the therapy hour. But as the focus of interest shifts increasingly toward the events of psychotherapy, it becomes apparent that we have little language available for describing events in process terms. Much of what is available, for example, "resistance" or "transference," refers more to interpretation or explanation of the phenomena, rather than serving to characterize the phenomena themselves. Furthermore, it is not even very certain what the events of therapy are, that is, what variables should be scrutinized.

The writer has stated elsewhere the conviction that the most fruitful approach to a field in which there is uncertainty even about the variables to be measured or controlled is that of systematic, quantifiable, naturalistic observation (Butler, Rice, and Wagstaff, 1963). The approach outlined in the above volume and used in the present study starts with a classification system into which the observed behaviors are classified. The data thus classified are treated by a method of vector analysis designed to test for structural relations underlying classes of behavioral events. The quantitative relationship between classes, the metric of the system, emerges from the analysis rather than being built into the classification system.

The purpose of the present study was to construct and test a process language for describing the events of the therapy hour. The term "process" here refers to characteristics, both lexical and vocal, of the therapist's style of participation. Although content is involved in the lexical aspects of the therapist's message, the concern here is with the way in which a theme is expressed rather than with specific content.

The classification system was designed to yield a descriptive rather than an explanatory language. That is, the process terms used here refer to subclasses containing behaviors of the therapist that are similar *as* behavior, rather than containing diverse behaviors assumed on the basis of theory to have similar meaning. The "syntax" of the process language is established by the manner in which the classes of behavior relate to each other on an occasion and over a series of occasions. It was further decided that the behaviors to be observed should be those that seemed to be vehicles of therapy rather than concomitants. Some kinds of behavior seem to be carriers of the therapy process in the sense that they could not be changed without markedly changing the character of the process, whereas others are associated with crucial variables but are not themselves influential in the process. Finally, it was decided that the classes should focus on behaviors characterizing the moment-by-moment interaction rather than on behaviors that remain constant for an interview or for a person.

METHOD

THERAPIST CLASSIFICATION SYSTEM

The theoretical position that guided the selection of categories has been discussed elsewhere (Butler and Rice, 1963). Summarized briefly, the position is that one of the primary functions of the client-centered therapist, or indeed of any therapist, is to help the client to generate new inner experience. Even when the content of the therapist's response is within the client's internal frame of reference, as is usual in a client-centered interview, there is a range of possible responses, all equally accurate perhaps, but with different stylistic qualities, having sharply different kinds of stimulus value for the client. The more expressive the verbal and vocal behavior of the therapist, the more the client is stimulated to generate new experience. The more constricted the therapist's behavior, the more the client tends to be confined within the grooves of his own repetitive thinking processes. The term "expressiveness" as used here does not mean simply activity or loudness, but rather the degree to which the therapist's behavioral style functions as a stimulus tending to expand or contract the range of new experience which the client is able to generate.

Brief descriptions of the three aspects and their subclasses are given below. The names assigned are not intended to define the classes, but are simply short terms for designating the behaviors included. The definition of each class lay in the series of taped examples that were used in training the raters. The raters themselves were given only letters and numbers to designate classes.

Aspect A: Freshness of Words and Combinations.—Some kinds of language are clearly far more connotative than others, in the sense of arousing in the listener more trains of association, a greater wealth of inner experience. Two kinds of language use were distinguished.

FRESH, CONNOTATIVE LANGUAGE: The total response may have a metaphorical quality with high imagery, auditory and kinaesthetic as well as visual, or there may be only a few fresh, stimulating words or combinations.

ORDINARY LANGUAGE: Responses are made up of commonplace words and phrases.

Aspect B: Voice Quality.—Investigations of the significance of vocal qualities in different forms of interpersonal communication have usually followed one of two strategies. Studies by Soskin and Kauffman (1961) and Starkweather (1961) have focused on the emotional state expressed in the voice of the speaker and the extent to which this could be identified independently of the content of the message. Other investigators, working within the framework of linguistics, have made "microscopic" analyses, aiming for a fairly complete transcription of the interview into linguistic and paralinguistic terms (McQuown, 1957; Pittinger, Hockett, and Danehy, 1960). The present study followed a third strategy. An attempt was made to locate a limited number of voice patterns that varied among therapists, showed considerable variation over sessions and within sessions, and seemed to differentiate meaningfully among sessions that had previously been characterized clinically as to quality. Once such patterns had been isolated, they were described as closely as possible in terms of pace, hesitations, pitch range, patterns of emphasis, etc. These descriptions, together with taped samples covering the range of each of the three subclasses, were given to the judges.

EXPRESSIVE: The voice is characterized by high energy used in a controlled but not constricted way. Color and range are present in the voice, but not to the extent of emotional overflow. The pitch range is wide, and although there is considerable emphasis, it is irregular and appropriate to the structure.

USUAL: A moderate amount of energy is present, and the pitch range is limited. Inflection is moderate and natural, although not usually conversational.

DISTORTED: Energy may be high or relatively low. Pitch variation is marked. The most distinguished feature is the regular emphasis, seemingly for effect rather than for spontaneous meaning. There is a subtly cadenced or sing-song quality, in which emphasis is shifted from its natural location.

Aspect C: Functional Level.—It seems probable that the stance which the client takes toward his own experience may be much influenced by the expressive stance that the therapist takes in responding to his message. Three such stances or functional levels were defined, with a fourth subclass for responses so far outside the client's frame of reference as to make them unscorable on this aspect.

INNER EXPLORING: Here the focus is on exploration of the client's immediate inner experience. The emphasis is on the idiosyncratic quality of the experience rather than on finding a label for it.

OBSERVING: The therapist joins the client in observing and analyzing the self as an object.

OUTSIDE FOCUS: The therapist's responses are within the client's frame of reference but refer to and focus on something outside the client.

UNSCORABLE.

SUBJECTS

Taped interviews of 20 client-therapist pairs were studied. All were clients seen at the University of Chicago Counseling Center by therapists with a Rogerian orientation, who ranged from highly experienced to relatively inexperienced. The clients were representative of the population seen at the Center at that time, except that there was a somewhat high proportion of males: only 5 were females. Eleven were students while 9 were from the community. The age range was from nineteen to forty-seven with a median of twenty-five. The educational level ranged from high-school graduate to 4 years of graduate work. Almost all were self-referred. The 20 cases were sampled from a larger block of 94 research cases in such a way as to be fairly representative in terms of rated success and case length. The range of case length was 6–68 interviews, with a median of 21 interviews. The proportion of long and short cases was balanced for success and failure cases. Nine of the clients had been rated by their therapists as having had successful therapy (6–9 on a 9-point scale). Four had been rated as having moderate but limited success (5 on the scale). Seven had been rated as having made little or no progress (1–3 on the scale). None had been rated 4. For each client-therapist pair the second and next-to-last interviews were selected for analysis.[2]

RATING METHOD

The unit used for classification was the total response, which was defined for the therapist as everything said between two client reponses. Each interview was divided into thirds on the basis of elapsed time, and from each of these thirds 10 consecutive therapist responses were taken. Thus there were 30 therapist responses from each interview, 10 each from the beginning, middle, and end of each interview. Each response was placed in one and only one subclass of each of the three aspects.

All classifications were based on listening to tapes. No transcripts were used. Interviews were coded so that judges knew nothing about the case. Raters listened to preceding client responses only when necessary to understand antecedents to pronouns, etc. They did not listen to the client's response to the therapist's statement. Response

[2]The matrix that was factor analyzed included 20 additional interviews, 16 middle interviews from clients included in the study, and second interviews from each of four attrition clients. Inspection of the factor plots indicates that the analysis would have yielded approximately the same factorial structure had these additional interviews not been included.

classification was done by five advanced graduate students, all of whom had received training in client-centered therapy and were currently seeing clients. Each tape was independently rated by two judges, with a third judge invoked to break ties.

RELIABILITY

The problem of interjudge agreement in classifying the responses was handled in a manner dictated by the goals and conditions of the study and could be viewed as a system of quality control. It was concluded that an index of judge agreement such as kappa (Cohen, 1960) could exceed chance with a probability of .05 and still be substantially below the agreement obtainable with further training of judges. Therefore, for each of the three main classes a standard was set which was between a lower bound set by significance above chance and an upper bound set by the degree of agreement reached by the constructors of the classification system. A judge was considered trained when he reached this degree of agreement with the standard judges on three successive training tapes. Periodically, judges were asked to classify a taped standard set of responses in order to control the tendency of judges to drift from the original standards over a period of time.

ANALYSIS

The method of analysis used was one analogous to factor analysis and was developed by Butler, Rice, and Wagstaff (1963) for the analysis of sequences of qualitative data.[3] In contrast to the more usual analysis, which starts with a matrix of intercorrelations of scores, the present analysis involved a matrix, the entries of which represented, on a scale between zero and unity, the similarity between interviews. That is, the entries expressed the degree to which different interviews shared the same behaviors, occurring in the same general sequence. After communality estimates had been added, this matrix was factored in the usual way by the principal axis method. The first three factors extracted accounted for 95 per cent of the sum of the latent roots, with successive factors accounting for small and approximately equal proportions. Therefore, only the first three factors were rotated and interpreted. Rotation was carried out by the normal varimax solution.[3] Inspection of the factor plots indicated

[3]A 3-page table, giving the rotated factor matrix for the original sample of 60 interviews, has been deposited with the American Documentation Institute. Order Document No. 8286, from ADI Auxiliary Publications Project, Photo-

that an oblique solution would have closely approximated the structure obtained.

Results

DESCRIPTIONS OF INTERVIEW TYPES

The loadings of each interview on each of the three factors were obtained. The three interview types isolated by the analysis can best be described by examination of the therapist behaviors that are characteristic of interviews that have relatively pure loadings on a given factor. The following descriptions of interview types are based on the most frequently appearing behaviors in interviews with loadings of .50 or above on a given factor and loadings of less than .30 on the other two factors.

Type I interviews are characterized by therapist responses expressed in language that is commonplace rather than fresh and connotative. The voice quality tends to be even and relatively uninflected, seldom expressive and never distorted. The functional level of the responses was primarily that of reflecting client self-observation, with only a few at the level of inner exploration, and none focused outside the client. Inspection of successive thirds of the interviews showed no clear time trends. Clearly then, in interviews with substantial loadings on Factor I, the therapist's style of participation can be characterized as ordinary or "garden variety" on all three aspects.

Type II interviews differ from Type I interviews chiefly with respect to the therapist's voice quality. In more than half of the responses there is a distorted voice quality. Only a few of the responses are expressed in fresh, connotative language. The functional level is primarily that of self-observation with a few responses on the level of exploration. There is some suggestion of a time trend toward less connotative language and less exploration from the first to the last third of the interview.

Type III interviews differ from Type I interviews on all three aspects. The therapist uses somewhat more fresh, connotative language. Over two-thirds of the responses are characterized by an excessive voice quality. More than half of the responses are on the functional level of inner exploration. The only suggestion of a time trend lies in a drop in the expressiveness of the voice quality in the final third of the interview.

---

duplication Service, Library of Congress, Washington, D. C. 20540. Remit in advance $1.25 for microfilm or $1.25 for photocopies. Make checks payable to: Chief, Photoduplication Service, Library of Congress.

RELATIONSHIP TO OTHER VARIABLES

The next step was to test for a relationship between the interview types identified by the analysis and other variables relevant to the process and outcome of therapy. Two kinds of external variables were available, e.g., various outcome measures and the level of experience of the therapist.

Five outcome criteria were used. The first was from the therapist's vantage point and consisted of a composite score derived from a questionnaire filled out by the therapist at the time of termination. Questions asked concerned the degree of satisfaction of the therapist with the outcome and the degree to which the client had changed. The other four measures were from the vantage point of the client. The first was a questionnaire that paralleled the one above and that also yielded a composite score. The second was a change measure derived from the 100-item *Q*-sort developed by Butler and Haigh (1956). Dymond's (1953) *Q*-adjustment score was obtained from each client's self-sort before and after therapy. The measure used was the difference between these two scores. The last two measures, also change scores, were two scales from the MMPI, the Taylor Manifest Anxiety (*MA*) scale and the Barron Ego Strength (*Es*) scale.

The behavior descriptions corresponding to the three interview factors emerging from the analysis suggest the nature of the relationship to be expected between factor loadings and outcome criteria. It seems probable that therapies in which the therapists manifest a high proportion of Type II behaviors would be less likely to be successful than would therapies in which there was little of such behavior. On the other hand one would predict that the presence of Type III therapist behavior would be associated with therapeutic success. The probable effect of Type I behavior is less predictable, perhaps being associated with success, but to a limited extent.

Table 1 shows the rank order correlations (rho) of the factor loadings of the early and next-to-last interviews on each of the three therapist factors with each of the five outcome criteria. Turning first to early interviews, Type II therapist behavior is significantly related in a negative direction to success of therapy as viewed by the therapist and by the client on the post-therapy questionnaire. With the three change measures, the relationship is negative but does not reach significance. The predicted positive relationship between Factor III and success does not appear. The relationships between Factor I behavior and success are positive but reach significance only in the case of change on the Barron *Es* scale.

TABLE 1
RANK-ORDER (RHO) CORRELATIONS OF THREE INTERVIEW TYPES WITH OUTCOME CRITERIA ($N = 20$)

	Second Interviews			*Next-to-Last Interviews*		
Outcome Measures	*I*	*II*	*III*	*I*	*II*	*III*
Therapist questionnaire	.37	—.46*	.21	.14	—.44*	.40*
Client questionnaire	.35	—.49*	—.07	.33	—.50*	.36
Q-adjustment change score	.08	—.30	.31	—.14	—.35	.42*
Taylor *MA* change score (sign reversed)	.21	—.27	.20	.18	—.31	.50*
Barron *Es* change score	.39*	—.27	—.11	.12	—.26	.29

*$p < .05$, one-tailed test.

To sum up, the presence of Type II therapist behavior early in therapy is predictive of an unsuccessful outcome, but the presence of Type I or Type II behavior does not permit a clear prediction, although there is some suggestion that Type I behavior may be followed by successful outcome.

When we turn to the next-to-last interviews, the picture is more clear-cut. There is again a significantly negative relationship between Type II behavior and therapist's and client's judgments, while relationships with the three change scores are negative but do not quite reach significance. The relationship between Type III behavior and therapist's judgment is significantly positive, as are also relationships with positive changes on the *Q*-adjustment score and the Taylor *MA* scale. Relationships with client's judgment and change on the Barron *Es* measures are positive but do not reach significance. Type I behavior no longer shows significant relationship with any of the outcome criteria.

To sum up, the presence of Type II therapist behavior either early or late in therapy is characteristic of therapies that are seen as unsuccessful by both therapist and client. The appearance of Type III behavior earily in therapy seems to be relatively unrelated to outcome, but its appearance late in therapy is clearly related to successful outcome as viewed by both therapist and client. In other words, Type III behavior seems to be a correlate but not a predictor of therapeutic success. There is some suggestion that the appearance of Type I behavior early in therapy may be predictive of successful outcome. If it continues or appears late in therapy, however, there seems to be no relationship with favorableness of outcome.

The second test of the external productivity of the classification system concerns the relationship between style of participation and the therapist's level of experience. The therapists of these 20 clients were divided into two groups on the basis of years of experience. Group 1 consists of 9 therapists with a minimum of 3 years of experience. Group 2 consists of 11 therapists at the internship level with more than 1 but less than 2 years of experience.

In Table 2, comparisons are made by means of the Mann-Whitney *U* test between experienced and inexperienced therapists with respect to the amount of Types I, II, and III behavior appearing in the early and late interviews. Type I behavior does not distinguish between experienced and inexperienced therapists either early or late in therapy. Inexperienced therapists exhibit significantly more Type II behavior than do the experienced ones both in early and in late interviews. On the other hand experienced therapists show significantly more Type III behavior than do the inexperienced ones both early and late in therapy.

TABLE 2

COMPARISON BETWEEN EXPERIENCED (E) AND INEXPERIENCED (I) THERAPISTS WITH RESPECT TO EARLY AND LATE INTERVIEW LOADINGS ON FACTORS I, II, AND III MANN-WHITNEY *U* TESTS

Comparisons Made and Predicted Direction	n_1	n_2	*U*
Early interviews			
E > I on Factor I	9	11	42
I > E on Factor II	9	11	27*
E > I on Factor III	9	11	19†
Late interviews			
E > I on Factor I	9	11	46
I > E on Factor II	9	11	27*
E > I on Factor III	9	11	20†

*$p = .05$.
†$p < .025$.

CONCLUSION

Clearly, then, style of participation is related to the therapist's level of experience as well as to favorableness of case outcome. These two relationships suggest that these stylistic characteristics may be vehicles whereby the more experienced therapists are able to provide a more satisfactory experience for their clients. The data at hand do not permit us to make a third comparison, relating level of experience with favorableness of outcome, since the 20 cases were sampled from the available pool of cases in such a way as to balance the proportion of success and failure cases in relation to experience or inexperience of the therapist. It is necessary also to weigh the contribution of the client's style of participation before attempting to draw substantive conclusions concerning a direct influence of the therapist process on the outcome of therapy.

These findings do indicate, however, that this classification system taps aspects of behavior, both verbal and vocal, that vary widely even among therapists of a single orientation, that vary over the course of a single therapeutic case, and that are clearly related to independently assessed characteristics of therapists and case outcome.

References

Butler, J. M., & Haigh, G. V. "Changes in the Relation Between Self-Concepts and Ideal Concepts Consequent Upon Client-Centered Counseling." In C. R. Rogers & Rosalind F. Dymond (eds.), *Psychotherapy and Personality Change.* Chicago: University of Chicago Press, 1954. Pp. 55–75.

Butler, J. M., & Rice, Laura N. "Audience, Self-Actualization, and Drive Theory." In J. Wepman & R. Heine (eds.), *Concepts of Personality.* Chicago: Aldine Press, 1963. Pp. 79–110.

Butler, J. M., Rice, Laura N., & Wagstaff, Alice K. *Quantitative Naturalistic Research.* Englewood Cliffs, N. J.: Prentice-Hall, 1963.

Cohen, J. "A Coefficient of Agreement for Nominal Scales." *Educational and Psychological Measurement,* 1960, *20,* 37–46.

Dymond, Rosalind F. "An Adjustment Score for Q-sorts." *Journal of Consulting Psychology,* 1953, *17,* 339–42.

McQuown, N. A. "Linguistic Transcription and Specification of Psychiatric Interview Materials." *Psychiatry,* 1957, *20,* 79–86.

Pittinger, R. E., Hockett, C. F., & Danehy, J. J. *The First Five Minutes.* Ithaca, N. Y.: Paul Martineau, 1960.

Soskin, W. F., & Kauffman, P. E. "Judgment of Emotion in Word-Free Voice Samples." *Journal of Communication,* 1961, *11,* 73–80.

Starkweather, J. A. "Vocal Communication of Personality and Human Feelings." *Journal of Communication,* 1961, *11,* 63–72.

*

AN INVESTIGATION OF . . . EFFICACY OF COUNSELING AND GUIDANCE PROCEDURES WITH FAILING JUNIOR HIGH SCHOOL STUDENTS

ORVILLE A. SCHMIEDING

The junior high school occupies a paradoxical position in the structure of American public education. It is comparable to the elementary school in that attendance is compulsory. It is similar also to the senior high school in (1) a formal curricular emphasis, and (2) a traditional marking system that tends to define clearly those who can and those who cannot meet minimum academic standards. The junior high school is different from the elementary school because of its departmentalization and limited course selection. It differs from the senior high school in attendance requirements and limitations and prescription of course choice.

In 1959, 47 states had compulsory attendance laws [*12*]. Unquestionably, many failing junior high school students are trudging to school because of legal requirements; they are not there by choice. It is reasonable to hypothesize that for many students junior high school is a stressful experience and that the threat posed by the compulsory attendance law does not function as an academic motivator.

There is evidence of both success and failure in counseling with failing or underachieving students. Investigations that have shown

*This article is reprinted from *The School Counselor*, 1966, *14*, 74–80, by permission of the publisher, The American School Counselor Association, and the author.

significant or near significant gains in achievement have been conducted by Calhoun [*4*], Turney and Morehead [*11*], Baymur [*3*], and McLaughlin [*6*]. Lund [*5*], Adams [*1*], Newland and Ackley [*7*], Serene [*9*], and Stasek [*10*] report achievement gains but use no statistical tests. Watson and Musselman [*13*] found no evidence that counseling had any significant effect on academic performance. Calhoun [*4*] and Randall [*8*] showed that teachers' perceptions of counseled students changed when measured by a rating scale.

The purposes of this investigation were to assess the effects of counseling and guidance procedures with failing junior high school students and to determine whether or not counseling and guidance procedures were more effective with students failing only one course than with students failing more than one course.

SAMPLE

Subjects for this investigation were chosen from four junior high schools. Selection was limited to those from the seventh and eighth grades who had failed at least one academic course. Depending upon the number of courses failed, these pupils were placed into either a moderate (one-failure) or a severe (two or more failures) group. Experimental and control groups were formed randomly and contained equal numbers of students who had failed one course and students who had failed more than one course. Initially, 94 subjects constituted the sample; 80 remained in the four groups at the conclusion of the investigation. Twenty-four experimental and 24 control students made up the one-failure groups, while 16 experimental and 16 control students were included in the more-than-one-failure groups.

INSTRUMENTS

The following instruments were utilized to gather the data in this investigation. The Iowa Tests of Basic Skills and the semester grade point averages were used to measure academic achievement. The rating scale employed to measure teacher perception was developed by the Arkansas State Department of Education [2]. The number of problems reported by each individual was assessed by a completed Mooney Problem Check List. A *Q*-sort of 50 items, 25 positive statements and 25 negative, was developed by the investigator to measure self-concept.

Method and Procedure

Three counseling sessions of a minimum of 30 minutes each were planned for each experimental student in one semester's time. All of these students were called in for the first counseling session. The decision concerning the continuance of counseling thereafter was agreed upon mutually by the student and the counselor. Many students requested assistance beyond the three sessions planned for the study. The mean number of counseling sessions was 3.7; the median was three. Two students terminated counseling after two sessions, and several had as many as five sessions.

Counseling was provided by eight experienced and professionally educated school counselors in the regular school setting. All the counselors were state certified and each had a master's degree in guidance or its equivalent. All but one had had experience in a supervised practicum, and they had subsequently taped interviews on a regular basis as a means of professional improvement. Four of the counselors were near the doctorate in guidance and counseling. Counseling and guidance procedures undertaken as a part of this investigation had the following objectives: (1) to increase counselee self-understanding; (2) to assist the counselee in making choices and decisions based on increased understandings; (3) to help the counselee accept responsibility for decisions reached; and (4) to aid the counselee in formulating plans of action for implementing decisions. The methodology focused on helping the student to recognize his feelings and to become aware of new information concerning himself and his opportunities. In addition to the specific counseling interviews, counselors engaged in related activities designed to help individuals reach these goals. Wherever it was deemed appropriate, parent conferences, teacher conferences and other forms of environmental manipulation were used to help these junior high school students progress through the above steps. Counseling was adapted to the individual counselor and counselee. The six most popular major topics which these students elected to discuss were peer relationships, study habits, school problems, home problems, educational planning, and vocational planning. A number of interviews were recorded.

Group means were compared at the conclusion of the investigation on semester academic grade-point average, grade-equivalent scores on the Iowa Tests of Basic Skills, teacher-rating of student characteristics, number of problems reported on the Mooney Problem Check List, and z' transformations of Q-sort correlations. To determine whether randomized procedures resulted in nearly equal means on the various criterion measures at the beginning of the investigation, analysis of variance was performed on pre-scores. In all cases the results obtained were nonsignificant.

The rating scale consisted of nine characteristics, each of which contained five response categories. Ratings for the nine characteristics made by a particular teacher for a given individual were summed and the mean was then calculated for use as a single index for that individual. Teachers did not know whether a given pupil was in the experimental or in the control group.

Each individual was instructed to sort the *Q*-sort statements into a forced normal curve distribution of nine piles. First, the individual was instructed to sort the cards to describe "yourself as you see yourself today (self)." Then he was instructed to sort the cards to describe "the person you would most like to be like (ideal self)." A correlation was obtained between the real self and the ideal self, and for purposes of analysis these correlations were transformed into z's. When 14 other individuals sorted these self-statements into the nine piles and repeated the same procedure four weeks later a correlation of .69 was obtained. For the ideal-self statements the correlation was .63.

Results

The basic design used in this investigation was analysis of variance and analysis of covariance in double entry tables. One of the purposes of the study was to determine if counseling and guidance procedures were more effective with students who failed only one course than with students who failed more than one course. In order to analyze the levels effect, it was necessary to pool those students failing one course into one group. The same procedure was necessary for those students failing more than one course. Analysis of variance tests were used for this purpose and in all cases, except grade equivalent on the Iowa Tests of Basic Skills, the results permitted collapsing the data into a two by two table to analyze the levels effect.

Hypothesis H_1.—There are no differences in mean grade-point averages for the experimental and control populations following the treatment period.

Table 1 clearly shows that there is a significant difference in treatment effects with reference to mean grade-point averages. The significant levels effect ($F = 6.3$) is to be expected in this case (GPA = Criterion) because of the way in which the levels groups were established in the first place. Examination of Table 2 shows that the mean grade-point average for the counseled group is 3.20 and for the non-counseled is 2.42. Thus, the hypothesis is rejected and the alternate hypothesis that there is a statistically significant difference between the experimental and control populations following the treatment period is accepted. The difference is in favor of the experimental population.

TABLE 1
ANALYSIS OF VARIANCE OF THE MEAN GRADE-POINT AVERAGES OF EXPERIMENTAL AND CONTROL INDIVIDUALS AT THE CONCLUSION OF THE TREATMENT PERIOD

Source of Variance	*df*	*ss*	*ms*	*F*
Treatment	1	12.20	12.20	6.22*
Levels	1	12.35	12.35	6.30*
T x L	1	.64	.64	.33
Within	76	149.09	1.96	
Total	79	174.28		

*Significant at the .05 level

TABLE 2
TABLE OF MEANS AT CONCLUSION OF TREATMENT PERIOD

	GPA		*Teacher Rating*		*Problems*		*Q-Sort z'*	
	Coun.	*Non-Coun.*	*Coun.*	*Non-Coun.*	*Coun.*	*Non-Coun.*	*Coun.*	*Non-Coun.*
One-Failure Group	3.45	2.81	25.23	23.91	19.42	30.38	.49	.37
Multiple-Failure Group	2.83	1.83	23.86	20.86	23.50	31.31	.41	.25
Combined	3.20	2.42	24.68	22.69	21.05	30.75	.46	.32

Hypothesis H_2.—There are no differences in mean composite grade equivalents on the Iowa Tests of Basic Skills for the experimental and control populations following the treatment period.

There was no significant difference between the groups when grade equivalent scores on the Iowa Tests of Basic Skills were the criterion. Preliminary analysis led to the decision not to pool data. It was necessary to analyze data on this criterion by schools, disregarding the levels effect. The combined school mean of the counseled was .62 grade equivalents higher than that of the controls, but analysis of variance, and analysis of covariance, with initial scores held constant, failed to produce significant statistical results.

Hypothesis H_3.—There are no differences in mean teacher ratings for the experimental and control populations following the treatment period.

It is evident from Table 3 that a statistically significant difference exists between the populations following the treatment period. It can be seen in Table 2 that the mean teacher rating for the counseled is higher than for the non-counseled; therefore, hypothesis H_3 is rejected and the alternate hypothesis accepted. The significant levels effect ($F = 5.18$) in this case (teacher rating = criterion) can be expected if there is a high correlation between level of performance and teacher rating.

TABLE 3

ANALYSIS OF VARIANCE OF MEAN TEACHER RATINGS OF COUNSELED AND NON-COUNSELED STUDENTS AT THE CONCLUSION OF THE TREATMENT PERIOD

Source of Variance	*df*	*ss*	*ms*	*F*
Treatment	1	79.50	79.50	4.40*
Levels	1	93.63	93.63	5.18*
T x L	1	13.50	13.50	.75
Within	76	1373.33	18.07	
Total	79	1559.96		

*Significant at the .05 level

Hypothesis H_4.—There are no differences in mean number of problems reported by the experimental and control populations following the treatment period.

The F ratio (see Table 4) associated with number of problems reported is significant. When reference is made to Table 2, it can be seen that the counseled group reported fewer problems after the treatment period. Hypothesis H_4 is rejected.

TABLE 4

ANALYSIS OF VARIANCE OF MEAN NUMBER OF PROBLEMS REPORTED BY COUNSELED AND NON-COUNSELED STUDENTS AT THE CONCLUSION OF THE TREATMENT PERIOD

Source of Variance	*df*	*ss*	*ms*	*F*
Treatment	1	1,881.80	1,881.80	4.41*
Levels	1	121.00	121.00	.28
T x L	1	47.51	47.51	.11
Within	76	32,426.89	426.67	
Total	79	34,477.20		

*Significant at the .05 level

Hypothesis H_5.—There are no differences in mean transformation of Q-sort correlations for the experimental and control populations following the treatment period.

It is shown in Table 5 that the *F* ratio associated with treatment ($F = 3.01$), although elevated, is not significant. Analysis of covariance was then used with pre-scores held constant. The results, again non-significant, are shown in Table 6.

TABLE 5

Analysis of Variance of z′ Transformation for Q-Sort Correlations of Counseled and Non-Counseled Students at the Conclusion of the Treatment Period

Source of Variance	*df*	*ss*	*ms*	*F*
Treatment	1	.37	.37	3.08
Levels	1	.20	.20	1.67
T x L	1	.01	.01	.01
Within	76	9.35	.12	
Total	79	9.93		

TABLE 6

Analysis of Covariance of z′ Transformations for *Q*-Sort Correlations to Test for Treatment Effect

Source of Variance	I^2	*IF*	F^2	*Adj ss*	*df*	*ms*	*F*
Treatment	.45	.41	.37	.17	1	.17	1.54
Within	13.01	3.69	9.35	8.31	75	.11	
Total	13.46	4.10	9.72	8.48	76		

A separate hypothesis was tested regarding differential treatment effects upon the means of each of the criterion measures. None of the tests resulted in interaction effects large enough for statistical significance.

Summary and Discussion

Depending on the number of academic subjects failed, 94 individuals were placed randomly into one of four groups. Eighty were still included at the conclusion of the investigation. Two of the groups received individual counseling and the use of other guidance procedures as initiated by the counselors in the various school settings. The other two groups formed the controls. After the treatment period, the groups were compared on the following criteria: grade-point average, grade equivalents on the Iowa Tests of Basic Skills, teacher rating of student characteristics, problems reported on the Mooney Problem Check List, and *Q*-sort correlations. Pre-scores indicated no statistically significant differences between groups.

The results showed that groups that were provided with counseling and guidance procedures rated statistically higher on three of the five variables. On the other two variables (grade equivalents and *Q*-sort), no statistically significant differences were noted, although the means of the experimental groups were higher. On none of the variables was there sufficient interaction between treatment and levels to reach statistical significance. Thus, it has not been demonstrated that counseling and guidance procedures help one level of failing student more than the other.

A noteworthy result was obtained when comparing initial and final teacher ratings. The means of the experimental groups remained nearly the same, while the control means dropped decidedly. One could hypothesize that counseling and guidance procedures help to maintain a constant relationship between teachers and failing individuals. Not to have these procedures available apparently leads to a worsening relationship.

Many researchers attempt to explain personality change as a result of some particular counseling theory. This investigation attempted to supplement counseling efforts with systematic guidance activities on the part of parents, teachers, and counselors. The counselors in this investigation were experienced and professionally educated in counseling and guidance procedures.

Conclusions

1. Counseling and guidance procedures applied by experienced and professionally educated school counselors result in:

   a. Higher academic achievement among failing students as determined by semester grade-point average.
   b. Better teacher-pupil relationships between teachers and failing students.

2. Counseling and guidance procedures applied by experienced and professionally educated school counselors are equally effective in improving academic achievement among junior high school students

failing one as contrasted with those failing more than one academic course.

3. When counseling and guidance procedures are withheld from failing junior high school students, teacher-pupil relationships existing between teachers and these students worsen.

4. After counseling and guidance procedures have been applied by experienced and professionally trained school counselors to one group of failing junior high school students and withheld from another, the number of problems reported by the counseled group is less.

References

1. Adams, R. C. "The Personal Interview and Achievement." *Vocational Guidance Magazine,* 1932, *10,* 358–60.

2. Arkansas Department of Education. "The Use of Individual Inventory Forms in the Guidance Program." *Occupational Information,* under the direction of Dolph Camp, State Supervisor of Occupations and Guidance.

3. Baymur, Feriha B., & Patterson, C. H. "A Comparison of Three Methods of Assisting Underachieving High School Students." *Journal of Counseling Psychology,* 1960, *7,* 83–90.

4. Calhoun, Samuel Reed. "The Effect of Counseling on Achievement Motivation." Unpublished doctoral dissertation, University of Indiana. *Dissertation Abstracts,* 1958, *18,* 480.

5. Lund, S. E. Thorsten. "The Personal Interview in High School Guidance." *School Review,* 1931, *39.* 196–207.

6. McLaughlin, Edward. "A Study of the Effectiveness of Personal Counseling with 7th-Grade Pupils." Unpublished doctoral dissertation, University of Houston. *Dissertation Abstracts,* 1956, *16,* 2089.

7. Newland, T. Ernest, & Achley, W. E. "An Experimental Study of the Effect of Educational Guidance on a Selected Group of High School Sophomores." *Journal of Experimental Education,* 1936, *5,* 23–25.

8. Randall, Lon D. "An Investigation of the Influence of Counseling on Certain Pupil Behavior Characteristics as Perceived by Teachers." Unpublished doctoral dissertation, Indiana University. *Dissertation Abstracts,* 1959, *20,* 1272–73.

9. Serene, M. F. "An Experiment in Motivational Counseling." *Personnel and Guidance Journal,* 1953, *31,* 319–24.

10. Stasek, Erwin. "The Effects of Specialized Educational Counseling with Selected Groups of Underachievers at the Secondary Level." Unpublished doctoral dissertation, Northwestern University. *Dissertation Abstracts,* 1955, *15,* 2107.

11. Turney, A. H., & Morehead, Charles G. "An Experimental Evaluation of a Small High School Counseling Program." Lawrence, Kansas: *University of Kansas Bulletin,* 1954, *8,* 74–77.

12. United States Department of Health, Education and Welfare. "State Legislation and School Attendance." Office of Education, O.E. 24000, Circular No. 615, January 1960, 3–16.

13. Watson, William H., & Musselman, D. L. "An Investigation of the Effect of Counseling." *School Counselor,* 1962, *9,* 107–9.

*

THE EFFECT OF COUNSELING ON PEER GROUP ACCEPTANCE OF SOCIALLY REJECTED STUDENTS

BERNARD C. KINNICK
JACK T. SHANNON

Most school counselors would agree that one of their functions is to aid in the social development of the high school youth. Very few research studies, however, have investigated the effects of such counseling efforts.

Cook [3], an educational sociologist, studied the effects of individual guidance upon the social adjustment of a class of tenth-grade high school students. He found improved social adjustment, as measured by a sociogram, for ten of fifteen problem students. He also found an increased volume of social interaction for the group as a whole. No control was used, however, to help determine the effect of extraneous variables upon the results.

Aldrich [1] conducted a controlled study of social guidance among college freshman girls. She found that the experimental group significantly exceeded the control group on three different scales of social adjustment. The experimental group also participated in more group social activities, felt they had more friends, and were less critical of the university social program than the control group. Similar results favoring the experimental group were found in a follow-up study conducted by Aldrich [2] eight years later. At this time the experimental group exceeded the control group both in

*This article is reprinted from *The School Counselor,* 1965, *12,* 162–66, by permission of the publisher, the American School Counselor Association, and the authors. The research was conducted at Central High School in Grand Forks, North Dakota, where the authors were NDEA Counselor trainees at the University of North Dakota.

mean number of college activities, committees, and offices and in percentage of students graduating.

Despite the positive findings of these two studies, little additional research appears to have been done.

Purpose

The purpose of this study was to investigate the effects of individual and group counseling upon the peer group acceptance of socially rejected tenth-grade high school students. The problem of peer group acceptance was selected as one of the most pressing social adjustments which the first year high school student must make.

Method

Measurement.—The Ohio Social Acceptance Scale (OSAS) was used as the selection instrument and the criterion. The OSAS requires that the student rate each of his classmates on the following scale: (1) "My very, very best friends;" (2) "My other friends;" (3) "Not friends, but okay;" (4) "Don't know them;" (5) "Don't care for them;" and (6) "Dislike them." A paragraph describing the activities one is willing to undertake with the student is provided for each of these six steps on the scale.

Additional information describing the OSAS can be found in Rathe [*5*, *6*], Elliot [*4*], Rothney [*7*], and Thorndike and Hagen [*8*].

Subjects.—The subjects were all sophomore high school students in their first year at Grand Forks Central High School in North Dakota. Previous to enrolling at Central High School, the students had attended at least three different junior high schools in the city of Grand Forks.

Students in each of five sophomore English classes were asked to complete the OSAS as part of a University research project. All students receiving an average score of 3.5 or higher on the scale were arbitrarily identified as social rejects. Forty-three subjects out of 142 tested were selected in this manner. By means of random assignment, 18 students were placed in the experimental group and 25 students were placed in the control group.

The experimental group consisted of 9 boys and 9 girls. The control group contained 14 boys and 11 girls.

Information on home environment, parents' occupations, extracurricular activities, and vocational plans was obtained from each student by means of a one-page questionnaire. The experimental group did not significantly differ from the control group on any of these variables. It is noteworthy, however, that the mean number of extra-curricular activities in which both groups participated was considerably less than one. Over half of the students in both groups did not participate in a single extra-curricular school activity at the time of the study.

Treatment.—Six counselors, all second-semester graduate students in the 1962-63 Academic Year NDEA Counseling and Guidance Institute at the University of North Dakota, took part in the study. The purpose of the study was explained to each of the counselors. They were told to employ any techniques which they felt might improve the peer group acceptance of each of their clients.

The counselors had all received similar training in counseling theory and techniques as part of their NDEA graduate study program. This training emphasized a modified client-centered approach to counseling problems as described in Tyler [*9*]. The general approach to the client was based upon the principles of counseling given in Tyler. In addition, the counselors were asked to present complete notes describing what took place in each counseling session.

The subjects were not informed at any time as to the nature of the research project. They were simply asked to see the student counselor as a routine matter. Nearly every student in the school is seen sometime during the year in a similar fashion.

Students in the control group received no counseling. If a student in the control group had requested counseling, he would have been treated as any other self-referred counselee.

Each counselor arranged to see three of the students in the experimental group approximately once a week over an eight-week period. In addition, the counselors worked in pairs conducting group counseling sessions. Each group was composed of six students randomly assigned.

All counseling with the students took place in an eight-week period (excluding vacations) extending from February through April, 1963. Each of the experimental subjects received at least six sessions of individual counseling and a minimum of three group counseling sessions.

Procedures.—The following null hypotheses were tested:

1. There is no significant difference between the mean OSAS scores received by the experimental and control groups after counseling.
2. There is no significant difference between the mean OSAS

scores received by the experimental group before and after counseling.

3. There is no significant difference between the mean OSAS scores received by the control group before and after counseling.

If counseling was effective, hypotheses 1 and 2 should be rejected. Unless other unknown factors are at work, hypothesis 3 should be accepted.

The second and third hypotheses were tested by means of the two-tailed *t*-test whereas the first hypothesis was tested using the one-tailed *t*-test of significance (Walker and Lev [*10*]).

Results and Discussion

The means and standard deviations on the OSAS scale for the experimental and control groups both before and after counseling are shown in Table 1. As would be expected on the basis of random assignment, the mean of the experimental group on the OSAS scale before counseling is not significantly different from the mean of the control group ($t = 1.24$; $p > .05$).

TABLE 1

The Means and Standard Deviation on the OSAS Scale for the Experimental and Control Groups Both Before and After Counseling

Group	*N*	*Mean*	*S.D.*
Experimental Group			
Pre-Counseling	18	3.73	.259
Post-Counseling	18	3.37	.344
Control Group			
Pre-Counseling	25	3.85	.377
Post-Counseling	24*	3.60	.445

*One student in the control group withdrew from school during the course of the study.

The difference between the means of the experimental group and the control group after counseling (Mean diff. = .23) is significant at the .05 level of confidence ($t = 1.87$). The null hypothesis must be rejected. After receiving counseling, the experimental group received significantly lower scores on the OSAS than did the control group.

The difference between the means of the experimental group before and after counseling (Mean diff. = .35) is significant beyond chance at the .01 level of confidence ($t = 3.38$). The second null hypothesis under test must also be rejected. The mean OSAS score of the experimental group is significantly lower after counseling than before. The group apparently gained in peer group acceptance.

Interestingly, the third null hypothesis is also rejected. The mean difference between the control group before and after counseling (Mean diff. = .25) is significant at the .05 level of confidence ($t = 2.06$). The control group showed improvement in peer group acceptance despite the fact that it received no counseling or special treatment.

The results of the study support the use of individual and group counseling as procedures for facilitating the peer group acceptance of sophomore students.

Inspection of the counselor's notes suggests that the majority of the counseling sessions were conducted in a nondirective manner. The students were allowed to choose the topics to be discussed. Nearly all the counselees began by discussing educational and vocational plans. The subject matter of the interviews soon shifted, however, to items of a personal-social nature. Overall, approximately 75 per cent of the counseling time was spent discussing personal and/or social adjustment problems. In nearly all cases, the counselors felt that points relevant to the counselee's lack of acceptance by his peers were eventually considered.

The counselors felt that the students became more acceptable for a variety of reasons including increased insight into the dynamics of their own behavior, improved motivation to get along with others, and better understanding of techniques for gaining social approval.

It is noteworthy that the control group also showed significant improvement in peer group acceptance. This can be explained in part by regression toward the mean. It is a common occurrence in measurement studies that groups with extreme scores upon retesting will regress toward the mean of the population of which they are a member. It is also possible that the mere passage of time together in the classroom may have served to make the students somewhat more acceptable to their classmates. The fact that the control group showed significant improvement *without* counseling points up the absolute necessity for employing a control group in a study such as this. Without the use of a control group, a distorted picture of the change in the experimental group would have been given.

With the present design it is not possible to say what counseling techniques were most effective in bringing about better social adjustment of the students. Additional research is needed to investigate the differential effects of individual versus group counseling in social guidance. Different types of individual and group counseling (e.g., highly structured versus relatively unstructured counseling) should also be compared.

The criteria of social adjustment also need to be more broadly developed. There are many criteria affecting social adjustment which may be studied in future research of this type. The number of school and community activities in which one participates, the number of elective positions held, and the number of social contacts made in a given period of time may be typical of this type of phenomenon.

Summary and Conclusions

1. The peer group acceptance for a sample of socially rejected tenth grade high school students was significantly improved following an eight-week program of individual and group counseling. The improvement in peer group acceptance was significantly greater for the experimental group than for a control group.

2. The control group of students also showed significant improvement in peer group acceptance, although not as great as the experimental group, without the benefit of counseling. The importance of utilizing a control group in evaluating the effects of counseling was stressed.

3. Additional research is needed to determine which *specific* techniques of counseling are most beneficial in improving one's social adjustment. The criteria of social adjustment should be broadened to include aspects other than simply peer group acceptance.

References

1. Aldrich, Margaret G. "An Exploratory Study of Social Guidance at the College Level." *Educational and Psychological Measurement,* 1942, *2,* 209–16.

2. Aldrich, Margaret G. "A Follow-up Study of Social Guidance at the College Level." *Journal of Applied Psychology,* 1949, *33,* 258–64.

3. Cook, L. A. "An Experimental Sociographic Study of a Stratified 10th Grade Class." *American Sociological Review,* 1945, *10,* 250–61.

4. Elliot, M. H. "Ohio Guidance Tests for Elementary Grades." In O.K. Buros (ed.), *The Mental Measurements Yearbook.* Highland Park, N.J.: Gryphon Press, 1949. Pp. 113–14.

5. Rathe, L. "Identifying the Social Acceptance of Children." *Educational Research Bulletin,* 1943, *22,* 72–74.

6. Rathe, L. "Evidence Relating to the Validity of the Social Acceptance Test." *Educational Research Bulletin,* 1947, *26,* 141–46.

7. Rothney, J. W. M. "Ohio Guidance Tests for Elementary Grades." In O.K. Buros (ed.), *The Mental Measurements Yearbook.* Highland Park, N.J.: Gryphon Press, 1949, Pp. 114–15.

8. Thorndike, E. L., & Hagen, Elizabeth. *Measurement and Evaluation in Psychology and Education,* (2nd ed..). New York: Wiley, 1961.
9. Tyler, Leona E. *The Work of the Counselor,* (2nd ed.). New York: Appleton-Century-Crofts, 1961.
10. Walker, Helen M., & Lev, J. *Statistical Inference.* New York: Henry Holt, 1953.

*

ACHIEVEMENTS OF COUNSELED AND NON-COUNSELED STUDENTS TWENTY-FIVE YEARS AFTER COUNSELING[1]

DAVID P. CAMPBELL

This is a report of a 25-year follow-up of students from an earlier study of counseling effectiveness conducted by Williamson and Bordin during the mid-1930's (Williamson and Bordin, 1940). In their research, they selected approximately 400 students who had come to the University of Minnesota Student Counseling Bureau before November of their freshman year—of the years 1933-36—to consult with a counselor about educational, vocational or other personal problems. This group was designated *the experimental group* and selected solely on the basis of having complete counseling folders. One year later, these students were matched individually with other non-counseled students on college entrance test score, English proficiency test score, high school rank, age, sex, size and type of high school, and college class. This second group was *the control group.* All were registered in the College of Science, Literature and the Arts (SLA). There were 384 pairs, 768 students in the final sample. Half were men; half were women.

*This article is reprinted from *Journal of Counseling Psychology,* 1965, *12,* 287–93, by permission of the publisher, the American Psychological Association, and the author.
[1]The research reported herein was supported by the Cooperative Research Program of the Office of Education, U.S. Department of Health, Education, and Welfare.

When they were sophomores, both groups were interviewed and rated on their adjustment to college. Williamson and Bordin reported that the counseled students had made a better adjustment to college, and were making significantly better grades, 2.18 versus 1.97, on a 4.00 scale.

In 1961-62, the data from this earlier study were resurrected, and an attempt was made to locate these individuals to assess the effects of counseling over a 25-year period. Various aspects of this project have been reported earlier (Campbell, 1963, 1964a, 1964b, 1965; Rossmann, 1964).

Surprisingly, virtually all of these former students were located, 761 of the 768. Of these, 731 were still alive and each of them was asked to do four things. Those, and the percentage completing each, were:

Complete a detailed 30 page questionnaire	84%
Have an hour interview	90%
Complete the Strong Vocational Interest Blank	84%
Take the University of Minnesota's current entrance examination	87%
All four of above	80%
At least one of the above	92%

Information Collected

In general the requested information concerned their achievements, and their satisfaction with their job and general station in life. The questionnaire, which was administered by mail, contained mostly multiple-choice or completion questions concerning these topics. The interview, though it contained open-end questions allowing more opportunity for personal expression, was conducted in a highly systematic manner using a specified series of questions in an interview booklet. The interviewer, usually a graduate student in psychology, read the questions in a predetermined order to the subject and made short notes on the booklet, condensing the individual's answer.

Some data were also available on each individual from University records, such as scholastic performance, honors won, high school rank, and score on a college entrance test.

Final Sample Used

The original Williamson-Bordin study used 384 pairs of students. In this follow-up study, several of these pairs were unavailable.

Thirty people had died, seven were unlocated and about 10 per cent would not cooperate. In another 62 cases, the control member of the pair had since come to the Student Counseling Bureau for guidance which meant that these pairs could not be used in the counseled versus non-counseled comparisons.

Because these disruptions occurred in over 100 pairs, the final analyses were done by counseled ($N = 427$) versus non-counseled ($N = 297$) groups rather than by pairs. Although some statistical power was lost by not using the matched pair procedure, it was offset to some degree by the inclusion of some 200 people who would otherwise have been discarded.

There is, of course, a serious problem in the experimental design as the counseled students sought out counseling, the non-counseled ones did not. There may have been differences between the groups other than the counseling they received. In another place (Campbell, 1964a) the author has reported the results of several studies of counseled and non-counseled students, using data collected before the counseling. Only a few mild differences were discovered, and none of them appeared relevant to the variables discussed in this report. But the possibility of some third, confounding factor cannot be dismissed.

Academic Achievement

While the main topic of this report is adult achievement, some mention of the difference in academic achievements between the two groups should be made. The comparability of these two groups on variables related to college achievement is summarized in Table 1.

TABLE 1
Comparison Between Counseled and Non-Counseled Students on Academic Aptitude Measures

	Males				*Females*			
	Counseled		*Non-Counseled*		*Counseled*		*Non-Counseled*	
	Mean	*S.D.*	*Mean*	*S.D.*	*Mean*	*S.D.*	*Mean*	*S.D.*
HSR	67	24	69	24	79	20	79	19
CAT Percentile	64	26	62	25	63	25	61	25
N	238		159		214		155	

The differences between groups were small and none of them were statistically significant. Thus these variables can be ignored in the subsequent discussion. The counseled students clearly achieved more during their academic careers than did the non-counseled ones. They earned significantly better grades (2.20 versus 2.06 on a 4.00 scale); they graduated in roughly one-fourth greater numbers (59 versus 48 per cent); they were more often elected to Phi Beta Kappa (six versus two per cent); they earned more M.A.s (six versus two per cent) and more Ph.D.s (two versus 0.3 per cent); they reported more participation in campus activities and were more often elected to offices in those activities. (For details, see Campbell, 1964a)

Current Achievements

These data were gathered during 1962–63 when these people were roughly 45 years old. The first attempt to measure current achievement asked the individual to list his honors or awards, such as patents, artistic prizes, invited addresses, publications, etc. This was, at best, a crude approach. It used the individual's self-report and people vary in what they consider to be an honor. Also some people, because of their situation, had more opportunities to win awards than the average person. For example, a research engineer, even a mediocre one, is likely to report more patents than the average college graduate. But hopefully these situational restrictions were randomly distributed between the counseled and control groups.

SPECIFIC HONORS AND AWARDS WON

Table 2 lists each question asked and the frequency of each group replying positively. This figure is the percentage of each group saying something other than "none." There was a mild tendency for the counseled individuals to report more intellectual accomplishments while the non-counseled reported more military and business achievements. Perhaps these trends could be explained by the larger number of M.A. and Ph.D. degrees among the counseled group.

Some of the differences were statistically significant, but the establishment of statistical significance when the proportions are low and the magnitudes small is of dubious merit. Perhaps a cautious conclusion that there was a tendency for mild differences in favor of the counseled group is the best summarizing statement.

Several other objective questions, which presumably measured achievement, were included in the questionnaire. These questions were based on the rationale that if a person is successful, he will more often speak publicly and more often be elected to offices of one sort or another. The replies are listed in Table 3. Again there was only the mildest of trends in favor of the counseled group.

TABLE 2

HONORS, AWARDS, AND ACHIEVEMENTS OF COUNSELED AND NON-COUNSELED STUDENTS

	Counseled Per cent	*Non-Counseled Per cent*
Nonfiction articles and books published	8	3
Other publications not indicated elsewhere	9	5
Athletic Awards	8	5
Invitational Address (i.e., Wm. James lecture at Harvard)	4	2
Patents	2	0
Technical articles or books published	15	14
Awards for music	1	0
Fiction articles and books published	2	2
Awards for dramatic productions and performances	1	2
Civic Awards	9	10
Armed Forces decorations awarded on individual basis	8	10
Awards for art	0	2
Professional or Business Awards	8	11
Has your spouse received anything of the above nature?	16	11

TABLE 3

PUBLIC APPEARANCES AND ELECTED OFFICES OF COUNSELED AND NON-COUNSELED STUDENTS

	Percentage Replying "Yes"	
Questions Asked	*Counseled*	*Non-Counseled*
Have you given any speeches in the past 2 years?	47	42
Have you ever been on T.V.?	25	22
Have you been elected to any offices in the past 2 years?	54	54

INCOME AS A MEASURE OF ACHIEVEMENT

The use of the student's income 25 years after counseling as a criterion of counseling effectiveness has many disadvantages, e.g., average salaries differ widely from occupation to occupation; some people inherit money with a subsequent rise in income, etc. But still, in our current society there is a fairly sizeable relationship between income and achievement. The man who is achieving in his occupation is likely to be one of the better paid members of that occupation. And certainly, in an informal way, most people consider a man's income to be very relevant data concerning his achievements. For a woman, the situation is different—she has far less control over the family income. Although data for both sexes are presented here because these figures are intrinsically interesting, more emphasis should be placed on the comparison between the counseled and non-counseled males.

The income reported was total family income, including spouse's income, rental income, investment income and so forth. Usually the husband's salary accounted for the largest portion.

For the counseled males, the annual incomes ranged from $1,600 to $150,000 with a median of $14,670. For the non-counseled males, the range was from $4,000 to $70,000 with a median of $13,500. It is painful to report that this $1,200 difference in median income (certainly a practical difference) was not statistically significant. Though the mild difference was in favor of the counseled group, the distributions were almost identical.

For the counseled females, the family income (mostly the husband's salary) ranged from $1,500 to $200,000 with a median of $13,300. For the non-counseled females, the range was from $4,900 to $100,000 with a median of $13,000. This difference was neither statistically nor practically significant.

An Ultimate Criterion for Counseling Research

In the work reported in this section, an attempt was made to draw together all of the achievement data into one subjective rating of global accomplishment. The scale—called "Contribution to Society" —may represent, more than anything else, the investigator's personal values but it also certainly has much in common with widely accepted criteria of achievement. Perhaps its most controversial aspect is the complete ignoring of any emphasis on the individual's internal satisfaction and happiness, but results in those areas have been reported elsewhere (Campbell, 1964a). This section restricts itself to achievement, with or without satisfaction.

The rating scale had five points. Brief descriptions of each of those points are presented below.

Men's Rating Scale

5—HIGHEST RATING. Very valuable asset to our society. Possible examples are U. S. Congressman, outstanding literary figures, creative research scientists and outstanding business leaders.

4—SUBSTANTIAL CONTRIBUTORS. Individuals who are making less spectacular, but very worthwhile contributions.

3—THE SOLID MIDDLE OF COLLEGE EDUCATED MEN. Men with fairly important jobs, but where there is no evidence of anything outstanding either on or off the job.

2—THE SOLID MIDDLE OF THE AMERICAN CITIZENRY. Those persons whose major contributions are those of the average American citizen.

1—THE BURDENS. Individuals who depend on society or others for their existence.

Women's Rating Scale

5—VERY OUTSTANDING WOMEN. Women making unusual contributions vocationally. Also women with very outstanding records of community service.
4—VALUABLE CONTRIBUTORS. Homemakers involved in more than the average amount of volunteer activities. Includes single women or working married women in occupations which are more than routine.
3—AVERAGE COLLEGE EDUCATED WOMEN. The average homemaker with average children who have average problems.
2—"JUST A HOUSEWIFE." Includes women where there is evidence that she or her family is doing little more than just getting by from day to day.
1—THE BURDENS. Women dependent on others, contributing to no one.

Each subject was rated by three psychologists working independently. Sixteen raters participated, all faculty members of the University of Minnesota. Thirteen of them had Ph.D.'s and the group had a median of ten years of counseling and research experience.[2]

INFORMATION USED IN RATINGS

The raters were given all of the information available on each person with the following exceptions: (1) any material from the earlier Williamson-Bordin study; (2) test scores or grades; (3) job satisfaction information; and (4) whether they were counseled or non-counseled.

Virtually everyone still alive in this sample was rated. For 600 individuals, both the questionnaire and interview notes were available to the raters; for another 16, the questionnaire; and for another 51, the interview notes. For the remaining 49, a credit report from the Retail Credit Association was used. While this may have been a devious procedure, this latter group contained some individuals who were obviously very unsuccessful, and it seemed unwise to eliminate them from the study.

RELIABILITY OF THE RATINGS

Each person was rated three times by raters working independent-

[2]I am indebted to the following for help in making these ratings: Emanuel Berger, Alice Christian, Rene Dawes, Marvin Dunnette, Patricia Faunce, Laurine Fitzgerald, Vivian Hewer, Al Hood, Lloyd Lofquist, Cornelia McCune, Jack Merwin, Gerhard Neubeck, Al Raygor, Ruth Roberts, Don Watley, Lenore White.

ly. Initially, in 3 per cent of the cases, the raters differed by two or more points. In these instances they were asked to review their decision. This re-rating brought all raters within one point of each other. There was perfect agreement in 299 of the 724 cases, about 41 per cent. In the remaining 59 per cent, two raters agreed and the third deviated by one point.

RESULTS OF THE RATINGS

The results are reported in Table 4. While the differences were all in favor of the counseled students, none of them was statistically significant.

TABLE 4
DISTRIBUTION OF "CONTRIBUTION TO SOCIETY" RATING FOR COUNSELED AND NON-COUNSELED GROUPS

	Men		*Women*		*Total*	
	Counseled	*Non-Counseled*	*Counseled*	*Non-Counseled*	*Counseled*	*Non-Counseled*
N	217	148	210	149	427	297
Mean	10.15	9.84	10.30	10.15	10.22	9.99
S.D.	2.48	1.98	2.15	2.10	2.33	2.05
t-test	not significant		not significant		not significant	

Because this comparison was crucial, a further, more powerful statistical test was conducted, using only the pairs of students, one counseled, the other not, matched on ability and background variables in the original Williamson-Bordin group. A matched-pair *t*-test was run for both sexes.

For the 123 pairs of males, the average difference, in favor of the counseled group, was 0.58 and the $SE_{diff} = .27$. Thus the $CR = 2.15$ indicates a difference significant at the 5 per cent level. For the 121 pairs of females, the mean difference was 0.15, the $SE_{diff} = .27$, the $CR = 0.52$; thus there was no significant difference between the counseled and non-counseled women.

The counseled men rated significantly higher on this criterion, but is this an important finding? Is six-tenths of a point on a 13 point scale a practical difference? The answer to that question must be a subjective one; it cannot be answered by empirical statements. Perhaps the main point is that a detectable difference has been found 25 years later between counseled and non-counseled men, one that is large enough so we can be fairly confident that it did not arise by chance. Moreover, this observed difference probably represents a lower limit of the real difference as the gross measures used, the lack of an adequate control group, and the random sources of error introduced by 25 years of living would tend to obscure the true effect of counseling. That even the slightest difference appeared is most surprising.

CORRELATION WITH OTHER MEASURES

The "Contribution to Society" rating was correlated with the other variables and the resulting correlations above .20 are reported in Table 5. Though all the correlations were low, the general thread

TABLE 5
CORRELATIONS BETWEEN "CONTRIBUTION TO SOCIETY" SCALE AND OTHER VARIABLES

MALES		*FEMALES*	
Variables	*Correlations*	*Variables*	*Correlations*
Current Family Income	.49*	Current Family Income	.35*
Total Work Satisfaction Scale	.47	Total Work Satisfaction Scale	.27
Occupational Satisfaction	.45	Occupational Satisfaction	.26
Job Satisfaction	.40	Job Satisfaction	.23
Interviewer Rating of Affluence	.36	Interviewer Rating of Affluence	.26
College Grade Point Average	.29	Minnesota Scholastic Ability Test	.25
High School Rank	.23	High School Rank	.24
Minnesota Scholastic Ability Test	.22	College Grade Point Average	.23
Williamson-Bordin Rating of Adjustment 25 Years Ago	.18	Williamson-Bordin Rating of Adjustment 25 Years Ago	.20
SVIB Scales		SVIB Scales	
Occupational Level	.30	Physician	.22
City School Superintendent	.27	Social Science Teacher	.22
Specialization Level	.26	Psychologist	.21
Lawyer	.26	Librarian	.20
Public Administrator	.22		
Psychologist	.20	Buyer	−.20
		Office Worker	−.21
Accountant	−.20	Steno-Secretary	−.21
Aviator	−.20		
Farmer	−.23		
Industrial Arts Teacher	−.24		
Office Man	−.25		
Policeman	−.25		
Printer	−.27		
Carpenter	−.33		

*Included in materials used by raters.

of achievement ran through them. Prior college achievement, high school achievement, test scores, and the earlier rating of Adjustment from the Williamson-Bordin study all correlated positively with current achievement. This rating was also correlated with both Work Satisfaction and General Satisfaction with Life.

The highest correlation for both sexes was with current income, but this was likely an inflated figure as this information was included in the materials used by the raters.

The correlations with the scales on the Strong Vocational Interest Blank are also reported. For both sexes, social service interests were positively related to this rating, business and skilled trades were negatively related.

Conclusions

What conclusions and implications are suggested by the preceding data? First, these data indicate a very mild difference in achievement between counseled and non-counseled students 25 years later, especially among the men. Although the differences on the specific criteria of achievement were not large and often not statistically significant, they were consistently in favor of the counseled students.

Second, the data support the general conclusion that counseling did indeed exert a beneficial effect on the student's achievement. This effect was most apparent on immediate criteria such as grades and graduation but, though it withered considerably, the impact did not completely disappear over 25 years. This is not surprising. Counselors are more effective in dealing with problems immediately at hand and, for college students, these frequently concern grades and graduation.

Counseling is still best justified as an immediate help to the student bewildered by the increasingly complex maze of educational and occupational opportunities. In this maze, most institutions will recognize their responsibility to help the student explore his potentials and possibilities in an orderly manner. The provision of professional people in counseling services is one way to achieve that. And it is comforting that this method was supported by the analyses in this study, certainly over the short four year academic period and, in a milder way, over the lengthier span of a quarter of a century.

References

Campbell, D. P. "A Counseling Evaluation with a Better Control Group." *Journal of Counseling Psychology,* 1963, *10,* 334–38.

Campbell, D. P. "Twenty-five Year Follow-up of Educational-Vocational Counseling." Cooperative Research Project No. 1346, Office of Education, U. S. Department of Health, Education, and Welfare. 1964a.

Campbell, D. P. "What Students Say About Their Counseling Twenty-five Years Later." Paper presented to the APGA Convention, 1964b.

Campbell, D. P. "A Cross-sectional and Longitudinal Study of Scholastic Abilities Over Twenty-five Years." *Journal of Counseling Psychology,* 1965, *12,* 55–61.

Rossmann, J. "An Investigation of Maternal Employment Among College Women—A 25 Year Follow-up." Unpublished doctoral dissertation, University of Minnesota, 1963.

Williamson, E. G., & Bordin, E. S. "Evaluating Counseling By Means of a Control-Group Experiment." *School and Society,* 1940, *52,* 434–40.

*

APPENDIX A

Interview Rating Scale *Form A*

INSTRUCTIONS

It is essential that all ratings be made by you as *honestly* as possible.

Your task is to rate your counseling experience at the present time. Rate your experience in terms of "what is now," *not* "what ought to be."

Look at the following example which has been filled out to show you how to use the scale.

1. The counselor is a nice person

Always		Occasionally		Never
☐	☐	☒	☐	☐

The person who marked this thinks that his counselor is occasionally a nice person. You are to answer all the questions by placing a check in the box *which best expresses what you feel about your interviews at the present time.* Use *any one of the five boxes* for rating each statement according to the extent it holds true in your own experience.

Here are some hints to help you:

1. Work rapidly. There is no time limit, but do not spend much time on any one item.
2. Mark all items according to your feelings today.

Now proceed to answer the questions on the following pages.

Remember:

1. Try to answer each question as honestly as you can right now.
2. This is *not a test.*

INTERVIEW RATING SCALE

Name ______________________________ *Date* ____________________

Items	*Scale*				
	Always		*Occasionally*		*Never*
1. The counselor gives the impression of being intellectually aloof from the client.	A		O		N
	☐	☐	☐	☐	☐
(1)	1	2	3	4	5
(2)	0	—2	—1	0	+3
2. The counselor creates a feeling of "warmth" in the relationship.	A		O		N
	☐	☐	☐	☐	☐
	5	4	3	2	1
	+3	+3	—3	—3	—2
3. The counselor has a condescending attitude.	A		O		N
	☐	☐	☐	☐	☐
	1	2	3	4	5
	0	—3	—1	0	+3
4. The counselor insists on being always "right."	A		O		N
	☐	☐	☐	☐	☐
	1	2	3	4	5
	—1	0	0	0	+3
5. The client feels secure in his relationship with the counselor.	A		O		N
	☐	☐	☐	☐	☐
	5	4	3	2	1
	0	+3	—3	—3	0
6. The client has confidence in the counselor.	A		O		N
	☐	☐	☐	☐	☐
	5	4	3	2	1
	0	+3	—3	—2	0
7. The counselor is uncertain of himself.	A		O		N
	☐	☐	☐	☐	☐
	1	2	3	4	5
	—2	—3	—1	+2	+3
8. The counselor is artificial in his behavior.	A		O		N
	☐	☐	☐	☐	☐
	1	2	3	4	5
	0	—3	—1	+3	+3
9† The client feels like a misguided delinquent around the counselor.	A		O		N
	☐	☐	☐	☐	☐
	1	2	3	4	5
	0	0	—2	0	+3
10.† The client feels the counselor will jump on him if he says the "wrong" thing.	A		O		N
	☐	☐	☐	☐	☐
	1	2	3	4	5
	0	0	0	0	+3

(1) Weights assigned for scoring by the authors.
(2) Weights determined through Phi coefficient analysis by Correll.
†Items found by Correll not to differentiate between "good" and "poor" interviews.

Item	A		O		N
11. The counselor's tone of voice conveys the ability to share the client's feelings.	□ 5 +3	□ 4 +3	□ 3 —3	□ 2 —3	□ 1 —2
12. The counselor acts as if he had a job to do and didn't care how it was accomplished.	□ 1 0	□ 2 —1	□ 3 0	□ 4 +1	□ 5 +1
13. The counselor "communicates" the attitude that the client's problem is of real importance.	□ 5 +3	□ 4 +1	□ 3 —3	□ 2 —3	□ 1 0
14. The counselor is very patient.	□ 5 +3	□ 4 +3	□ 3 —3	□ 2 —2	□ 1 0
15. The counselor is a warm, sincere individual.	□ 5 +3	□ 4 +3	□ 3 —3	□ 2 —3	□ 1 0
16. The atmosphere of the interview helps the client to see more of himself.	□ 5 +3	□ 4 +3	□ 3 0	□ 2 —3	□ 1 —3
17.† The counselor frightens the client.	□ 1 0	□ 2 0	□ 3 —1	□ 4 0	□ 5 +2
18. The client feels blocked and frustrated in his attempt to relate to counselor.	□ 1 0	□ 2 —3	□ 3 —3	□ 4 +3	□ 5 0
19. The counselor acts cold and distant.	□ 1 0	□ 2 0	□ 3 —3	□ 4 +2	□ 5 +3
20. The client feels the counselor has a genuine desire to be of service.	□ 5 +3	□ 4 +3	□ 3 —3	□ 2 0	□ 1 0
21. The client feels accepted as an individual.	□ 5 +2	□ 4 +3	□ 3 —3	□ 2 —3	□ 1 0
22.† The counselor pushes the client into saying things that aren't really true.	□ 1 0	□ 2 0	□ 3 0	□ 4 0	□ 5 0

†Items found by Correll not to differentiate between "good" and "poor" interviews.

Item	A		O		N
23. The counselor behaves as if the interview(s) is a routine, mechanical process.	□ 1	□ 2	□ 3	□ 4	□ 5
	—1	—3	—3	+3	+3
24. The client feels a sense of satisfaction from the counseling sessions.	□ 5	□ 4	□ 3	□ 2	□ 1
	0	+3	—2	—3	—3
25. The counselor accepts expression of the client's thoughts and desires without condemnation.	□ 5	□ 4	□ 3	□ 2	□ 1
	+3	0	—2	0	0
26. The counselor shows a flagging of interest.	□ 1	□ 2	□ 3	□ 4	□ 5
	0	0	—3	+2	+1
27. The counselor's techniques are obvious and clumsy.	□ 1	□ 2	□ 3	□ 4	□ 5
	—3	—1	0	+3	+3
28. The counselor is restless while talking to the client.	□ 1	□ 2	□ 3	□ 4	□ 5
	—1	0	—3	+3	+3
29. The counselor has a casual relaxed manner of opening the interview.	□ 5	□ 4	□ 3	□ 2	□ 1
	+3	+3	—1	—3	—3
30.† The client is tricked into relating confidences he did not wish to disclose.	□ 1	□ 2	□ 3	□ 4	□ 5
	0	0	0	0	0
31. The counselor communicates little understanding of the client.	□ 1	□ 2	□ 3	□ 4	□ 5
	—3	—3	—2	+3	+3
32. The client can talk freely about his innermost feelings.	□ 5	□ 4	□ 3	□ 2	□ 1
	+3	+3	0	—3	—3
33. The counselor's remarks make things clearer for the client.	□ 5	□ 4	□ 3	□ 2	□ 1
	+3	+3	0	—3	—3
34. The client feels frustrated with the counselor.	□ 1	□ 2	□ 3	□ 4	□ 5
	—2	—2	—3	+2	+2

†Items found by Correll not to differentiate between "good" and "poor" interviews.

Item	A		O		N
35. The client distrusts the counselor.	☐	☐	☐	☐	☐
	1	2	3	4	5
	0	0	−3	0	+3
36. The counselor is awkward in starting the interview.	☐	☐	☐	☐	☐
	1	2	3	4	5
	0	−3	−3	+2	+2
37. The counselor is (to the client) a very "human" person.	☐	☐	☐	☐	☐
	5	4	3	2	1
	+2	+3	−3	−3	0
38.† The counselor makes far-fetched remarks.	☐	☐	☐	☐	☐
	1	2	3	4	5
	0	−1	0	0	0
39.† The counselor has a good sense of humor.	☐	☐	☐	☐	☐
	5	4	3	2	1
	0	+3	−1	0	0
40. The counselor's tone of voice encourages the client.	☐	☐	☐	☐	☐
	5	4	3	2	1
	+2	+3	−3	−3	−1
41. The client feels grateful for the counselor's help	☐	☐	☐	☐	☐
	5	4	3	2	1
	+1	+3	−3	−1	0
42. The counselor understands completely the client's feelings.	☐	☐	☐	☐	☐
	5	4	3	2	1
	0	+3	0	−3	−3
43. The counselor's language is confused.	☐	☐	☐	☐	☐
	1	2	3	4	5
	0	0	−3	+3	0
44. The client is open, honest, and genuine with the counselor.	☐	☐	☐	☐	☐
	5	4	3	2	1
	0	+3	−3	0	0
45.† The counselor is a "clock-watcher."	☐	☐	☐	☐	☐
	1	2	3	4	5
	0	0	0	0	+1
46. The counselor gives the impression of "feeling at ease."	☐	☐	☐	☐	☐
	5	4	3	2	1
	+3	+3	−3	−2	−3

†Items found by Correll not to differentiate between "good" and "poor" interviews.

Statement	A		O		N
47. The client feels more like a "case" than an individual.	☐	☐	☐	☐	☐
	1	2	3	4	5
	—2	—3	0	0	+3
48. The client is comfortable in the counseling situation.	☐	☐	☐	☐	☐
	5	4	3	2	1
	0	+3	—3	—3	0
49. The counselor is a co-worker with the client on a common problem.	☐	☐	☐	☐	☐
	5	4	3	2	1
	+3	+3	—3	—2	—0
50. The client respects the counselor's ability.	☐	☐	☐	☐	☐
	5	4	3	2	1
	+2	+3	—3	—1	0

*

APPENDIX B

Client and Patient Preferences Regarding the Characteristics and Procedures of Counselors and Psychotherapists

ALBERT ROSEN

In the literature on counseling and psychotherapy, considerable attention has been devoted to the expectations of counselors and clients regarding the counseling process and especially to the characteristics of desirable clients from the standpoint of the counselor.[1] Relatively neglected has been consideration of the *preferences of clients* with respect to the characteristics and behavior of counselors. In fact, there appears to be almost a taboo concerning the study of certain kinds of preferences of *both* clients and counselors, such as religion, race, marital status, or physical attractiveness.

A comprehensive overview of the literature revealed only three studies clearly on client preferences in medical settings. The other investigations involved preferences of university and high school students and clients. These studies, as well as clinical impressions, suggest that potential and actual clients have explicit and implicit notions concerning the characteristics they would like manifested in their counselors. Such preferences might determine whether or not they seek counseling, length of counseling, aspects of client-counselor interaction, and effectiveness of counseling.

TABLE 1*

STUDIES OF CLIENT PREFERENCES FOR CHARACTERISTICS AND PROCEDURES OF COUNSELORS AND PSYCHOTHERAPISTS

Category	*Setting*	*Subjects*	*Client Preferences Investigated (or Found)*
COUNSELOR ATTRIBUTES			
Fuller (1963)	Univ. counseling center	Clients	Sex of counselors
Fuller (1964)	Univ. counseling center	Clients	Sex of counselors
Koile & Bird (1956)	University	Freshmen	Sex of counselors
Pohlman & Robinson (1960)	University	Freshmen	Physical handicap, religion, race, age, sex
Rosen (1967)	College for the deaf	Students	Hearing status of counselors
Worby (1955)	High school	Students	Sex and age of counselors
COUNSELOR PERSONALITY			
Arbuckle (1956)	Graduate school	Students	Test scores of preferred counselors
Grater (1964)	Univ. counseling center	Clients	Affective versus cognitive traits
Pohlman (1961)	Univ. counseling center	Clients	Friendliness, confidence, etc.
Stefflre, *et al* (1962)	Graduate school	Students	Test scores of preferred counselors
Stefflre & Leafgren (1964)	Graduate school	Students	Test scores of preferred counselors
COUNSELING PROCEDURES			
Kanfer & Marston (1964)	University laboratory	Students	Interpretation, response frequency
Luchins (1951)	Clinic	Psychotics	Directiveness
Maher (1952)	High school	Students	Directiveness
Mendelsohn (1963)	University laboratory	Students	"Personal" or "objective" interview
Pohlman (1961)	Univ. counseling center	Clients	Advising, evaluating, reflecting
Pohlman (1964)	Univ. counseling center	Clients	Preferred procedures and outcome
M. Rogers (1957)	College	Students	Directiveness
Sonne & Goldman (1957)	High school	Seniors	Directiveness, and client personality

PROBLEMS AND TOPICS			
Grant (1954)	High school	Students	Educational-vocational problems
Holman (1955)	High school	Students	Aversion to selected problems
Jenson (1955)	High school	Students	Educational-vocational problems
King & Matteson (1959)	University	Students	Educational-vocational problems
Parloff, *et al* (1958)	Hospital or clinic	Psychotics	Unspecified
Pohlman (1961)	Univ. counseling center	Clients	Study habits, vocations, religion
Talland & Clark (1954)	Mental hospital	Outpatients	Sex, symptoms, shame, quarrels
Warman (1960)	Univ. counseling center	Clients	Vocational-education problems
COUNSELING RESOURCES			
Grant (1954)	High school	Students	Counselors only for ed.-voc. problems
Jenson (1955)	High school	Students	Counselors only for ed.-voc. problems
Kerr (1962)	High school	Students	Parents, *re* college attendance
Koile & Bird (1956)	University	Freshmen	Psychological counselor
Stotsky (1956)	Mental hospital	Patients	Relative aversion to psychotherapy

*This table is a supplement to Rosen, A. "Client Preferences: An Overview of the Literature," *Personnel and Guidance Journal,* 1967, *45,* 785–89. It lists all the references cited in the above article (plus two located subsequently). The two new references are: Luchins, A. L., "Patients View the Therapist: A Training and Research Device." *Journal of Consulting Psychology,* 1951, *15,* 24–31; Talland, G. A. & Clark, D. H., "Evaluation of Topics in Therapy Group Discussion," *Journal of Clinical Psychology,* 1954, *10,* 131–37.

The following kinds of information are needed with respect to potential and actual clients: (a) Preferences concerning counselors' age, marital status, race, religion, sex, personality characteristics, physical features, professional discipline, therapy procedures; (b) Personality and cultural background as related to these preferences; (c) Effect of preferences on counseling interaction and outcome.

Procedure

In this exploratory stage, a survey design involving "questionnairing" and interviewing of clients in a variety of clinical settings in different regions of the country would be profitable. Since a questionnaire or interview guide must be tailored to fit a given situation, a general form is attached. Although it is designed for college students, it can be easily modified for other subjects. It may be administered with the following variations.

1. Frequency: Before, during, or after counseling, or more than once.
2. Method:
   (a) Questionaire only.
   (b) Interview, using questionnaire as a guide.
   (c) Open-ended questionnaire or interview without suggesting preferred variables (e.g., "If you were interested in seeing a counselor [or if you are now seeing one], what kind of person would you want to see. Describe the person as completely as possible. Indicate which things are most and least important").
   (d) Questionnaire or interview dealing with only one variable for a given subject (e.g., preference regarding sex of counselor).
3. Additional variables: Preferred discipline of counselor (psychologist, social worker, psychiatrist, pastor), physical appearance (physique, attractiveness).
4. Type of setting: College, high school, clinic, hospital, private practice.
5. Type of client: Alcoholic, physically disabled, Negro, neurotic, disadvantaged, homosexual, etc.

As with any survey, interview, or laboratory procedure it is most important to try to understand or control for the biases of the administrator, interviewer, or experimenter, and the beliefs of the subjects as to what responses are expected of them. This information should play a vital part in interpreting the findings.

Analyses

Several interesting analyses should be possible with the above (and some supplementary) data, such as the relationship of client preferences and

---

[1]For convenience, the term "counseling" as used here refers broadly to the interaction of professional helper (psychological counselor, psychologist, psychiatrist, social worker) and client(s) with educational, vocational, social, or emotional problems of whatever degree of severity in an individual or group setting, regardless of frequency, duration, kinds of techniques used, or place (hospital, clinic, or school). Thus, "counseling" will subsume the terms "therapy" and "psychotherapy," and "client" will stand for "patient" and "counselee."

(a) plans for seeking counseling, or satisfaction with counseling in progress or completed, (b) client personality characteristics, (c) preferences of counselors regarding clients, (d) clients' age, sex, religion, race, etc., (e) client expectations. The interrelationships of the various client preferences would also be of interest.

References

Rosen, A. "Client Preferences: An Overview of the Literature." *Personnel and Guidance Journal,* 1967, *45,* 785–89.

Questionnaire

The last section of the questionnaire which follows, dealing with Counselor Behavior, derives from M. Lorr, "Client Perceptions of Therapists: A Study of the Therapeutic Relation," *Journal of Consulting Psychology,* 1965, *29,* 146–49.

PREFERENCES REGARDING COUNSELORS

We would like to know about the preferences of students with respect to characteristics of counselors. We appreciate your cooperation, for this information will be very helpful. It will be kept confidential; only group results will ever be released. So please say what you really mean regardless of whether or not you think it's what anyone else wants or likes to hear. (If you are to see a counselor, there is no guarantee that you will be assigned one according to your preferences.)

First, please fill in the following items carefully (don't write your name unless it is asked for). The questions about race and religion are important in studying group differences.

Birthdate: ______________________
Month Day Year

Class: Fr So Jr Sr Grad Spec Other
(Circle one)

Age (as of last birthday): _____ Sex: M F
(Circle)

Religion: ______________________________
Please be specific; indicate sect or other subgroup

Major (present or planned: ______________________________
(If not decided, write "None")

Race: ______________________________

Are you planning to see a psychological counselor (not a faculty advisor) soon? Yes No
(Circle)

Are you seeing a psychological counselor now? Yes No
(Circle)

Have you seen a psychological counselor either here or elsewhere? Yes No
(Circle)

If your answer was *Yes* to either of the last two questions, please continue.

How many interviews or counseling or therapy sessions did you have?______

For what type of problem, *primarily?*

Personal adjustment Educational Vocational
(Circle *only one*)

How would you rate the results? Good Fair Poor Too early to tell
(Circle one)

We would appreciate your help in learning how students feel about psychological counseling and counselors. The main question is "If you were to see a counselor (*not* a faculty advisor), or if you happen to be seeing one now, regarding a problem of personal adjustment, what kind of person would you want to see with respect to age, sex, etc."

AGE OF COUNSELOR

What are your preferences regarding the counselor's age? Place a number "1" before the most preferred age, a "2" before the next most preferred, and a "3" before the third most preferred. *You don't need to rank the others.* If age is absolutely of no consequence, place a "1" before the last item. State your preferences regardless of the actual ages of counselors who might be available.

_____17-21 years _____37-41 _____52-56 _____67-71

_____22-26 _____42-46 _____57-61 _____Over 71

_____27-31 _____47-51 _____62-66 _____Doesn't Matter

_____32-36

State your reasons for this preference: ____________________

SEX OF COUNSELOR

What is your preference with respect to the counselor's sex? Circle one response and indicate how important it is by also circling one of the three numbers following it. If very important, circle the "1"; if moderately important, circle the "2"; if hardly important, but still a preference, circle the "3".

Female 1 2 3 Male 1 2 3 Doesn't Matter

Your reasons: ____________________

RACE OF COUNSELOR

What is your preference regarding race? Circle one of the four choices, and then indicate importance (as above) by circling one of the three numbers.

Negro 1 2 3 White 1 2 3 Other__________ 1 2 3
(Specify)

Doesn't Matter

Your reasons: ____________________

RELIGION OF COUNSELOR

What is your religious preference with respect to a counselor? Circle one, and then indicate importance, as before.

(Roman) Catholic 1 2 3 Jewish 1 2 3

Protestant 1 2 3 ________________________________
(Specify sect or denomination if you have a preference)

Other ________________________________ 1 2 3 Doesn't Matter
(Specify)

Your reasons: ________________________________

PREFERRED COUNSELOR BEHAVIOR

Here are several ways in which counselors can act. Indicate the order of your preference. Place a "1" on the line *before* the description of the behavior you would most prefer, a "2" before the next most preferred, etc., continuing with "3," "4," and "5."

_____Shows real interest in you; is easy to talk to; is quick to praise you when you are doing well; likes and respects you_____

_____Tells you what to do when you have difficult descisions to make; tries to get you to accept his/her ideas; tells you what to talk about_____

_____Acts impatient, superior, as if he/she doesn't like you; talks down to you_____

_____Encourages you to shoulder your own responsibilities, to help yourself, to work on your problems in your own way, and to make your own decisions_____

_____Knows how you feel and what you mean even if you don't always express it well; understands what your experiences feel like to you_____

Your reasons for this order of preference: ________________________________

"EXPECTED" COUNSELOR BEHAVIOR

Now look at the same five descriptions of counselor behavior once more, but this time you are to indicate how you would *anticipate* the counselor to act (rather than what you would prefer). Place a "1" on the line *after* the described behavior you most expect, a "2" for the behavior next most likely, etc. down to "5."

Your reasons for this order: ________________________________

One last item. How did you feel about answering these questions? Do you think they are important? Was it easy or hard to be frank? Do you believe that you might have answered any differently if your name were requested, or if you had been interviewed?

THANK YOU!

APPENDIX C

Relationship Inventory

G. T. BARRETT-LENNARD

The Relationship Inventory has been revised several times since its original development by Barrett-Lennard (1962) and currently consists of 64 items. Barrett-Lennard used Rogers' conditions of therapy paper (1957) as a starting point for the development of specific items. The preparation of items involved constant interaction between theory and operational expression and resulted in a continuous growth and progressive refinement of meaning relating to each concept. The Relationship Inventory originally measured a person's ability to demonstrate to another person his capacity for (1) level of regard, (2) empathy, (3) congruence, (4) unconditionality of regard, and (5) willingness to be known. The willingness-to-be-known factor was found to correlate highly with the congruence factor and was subsequently eliminated by Barrett-Lennard.

This instrument has demonstrated its usefulness in measuring the defined variables in the context of a significant interpersonal relationship. Barrett-Lennard (1962, pp. 6–7) presented the validation procedures utilized in the development of the original instrument, and many other researchers. Thornton (1960), Berlin (1960), Emmerling (1961), Hollenbeck (1961), Hansen (1963), Clark and Culbert (1965), Van der Veen (1965), Gross and DeRidder (1966) have found this instrument to be of considerable value when attempting to measure particular aspects of an interpersonal relationship.

The technical reliability of earlier versions of the Relationship Inventory has been reported by several researchers: Barrett-Lennard (1962) reported split-half reliability coefficients between .82 (Unconditionality of Regard) and .93 (Level of Regard); Snelbecker (1961) reported split-half reliability coefficients between .75 and .94; Berson (1964) obtained test-retest correlations of .86 for Total Relationship Inventory Scores; Hollenbeck (1965) reported split-half reliabilities between .83 and .95 for the four Relationship Inventory scales, and test-retest correlations (over a six-month interval) of from .61 to .81; and Hough (1965) found split-half reliability coefficients between .82 and .91. On the revised 64-item Relationship Inventory, Barrett-Lennard has obtained reliability coefficients between .86 and .92 on the four scales using a test-retest procedure with two- and six-week intervals.

Presently more than 50 studies are under way using the Relationship Inventory (Barrett-Lennard, 1966), and any researcher wishing to use this instrument would certainly want to become familiar with the references included in this brief introduction.

Relationship Inventory — Form OS–M–64

Below are listed a variety of ways that one person may feel or behave in relation to another person.

Please consider each statement with reference to your present relationship with your counselor.

Mark each statement in the left margin, according to how strongly you feel that it is true, or not true, in this relationship. *Please mark every one.* Write in +3, +2, +1, or —1, —2, —3, to stand for the following answers:

+3: Yes, I strongly feel that it is true.
+2: Yes, I feel it is true.
+1: Yes, I feel that it is probably true, or more true than untrue.
−1: No, I feel that it is probably untrue, or more untrue than true.
−2: No, I feel it is not true.
−3: No, I strongly feel that it is not true.

______ 1. He respects me as a person.
______ 2. He wants to understand how I see things.
______ 3. His interest in me depends on the things I say or do.
______ 4. He is comfortable and at ease in our relationship.
______ 5. He feels a true liking for me.
______ 6. He may understand my words but he does not see the way I feel.
______ 7. Whether I am feeling happy or unhappy with myself makes no real difference to the way he feels about me.
______ 8. I feel that he puts on a role or front with me.
______ 9. He is impatient with me.
______10. He nearly always knows exactly what I mean.
______11. Depending on my behavior, he has a better opinion of me sometimes than he has at other times.
______12. I feel that he is real and genuine with me.
______13. I feel appreciated by him.
______14. He looks at what I do from his own point of view.

_____15. His feeling toward me doesn't depend on how I feel toward him.
_____16. It makes him uneasy when I ask or talk about certain things.
_____17. He is indifferent to me.
_____18. He usually senses or realizes what I am feeling.
_____19. He wants me to be a particular kind of person.
_____20. I nearly always feel that what he says expresses exactly what he is feeling and thinking as he says it.
_____21. He finds me rather dull and uninteresting.
_____22. His own attitudes toward some of the things I do or say prevent him from understanding me.
_____23. I can (or could) be openly critical or appreciative of him without really making him feel any differently about me.
_____24. He wants me to think that he likes me or understands me more than he really does.
_____25. He cares for me.
_____26. Sometimes he thinks that *I* feel a certain way, because that's the way *he* feels.
_____27. He likes certain things about me, and there are other things he does not like.
_____28. He does not avoid anything that is important for our relationship.
_____29. I feel that he disapproves of me.
_____30. He realizes what I mean even when I have difficulty in saying it.
_____31. His attitude toward me stays the same: he is not pleased with me sometimes and critical or disappointed at other times.
_____32. Sometimes he is not at all comfortable but we go on, outwardly ignoring it.
_____33. He just tolerates me.
_____34. He usually understands the whole of what I mean.
_____35. If I show that I am angry with him, he becomes hurt or angry with me too.
_____36. He expresses his true impressions and feelings with me.
_____37. He is friendly and warm with me.
_____38. He just takes no notice of some things that I think or feel.
_____39. How much he likes or dislikes me is not altered by anything that I tell him about myself.
_____40. At times I sense that he is not aware of what he is really feeling with me.
_____41. I feel that he really values me.
_____42. He appreciates exactly how the things I experience feel to me.
_____43. He approves of some things I do, and plainly disapproves of others.
_____44. He is willing to express whatever is actually in his mind with me, including any feelings about himself or about me.
_____45. He doesn't like me for myself.
_____46. At times he thinks that I feel a lot more strongly about a particular thing than I really do.
_____47. Whether I am in good spirits or feeling upset does not make him feel any more or less appreciative of me.
_____48. He is openly himself in our relationship.
_____49. I seem to irritate and bother him.
_____50. He does not realize how sensitive I am about some of the things we discuss.

_____51. Whether the ideas and feelings I express are "good" or "bad" seems to make no difference to his feeling toward me.
_____52. There are times when I feel that his outward response to me is quite different from the way he feels underneath.
_____53. At times he feels contempt for me.
_____54. He understands me.
_____55. Sometimes I am more worthwhile in his eyes than I am at other times.
_____56. I have not felt that he tries to hide anything from himself that he feels with me.
_____57. He is truly interested in *me*.
_____58. His response to me is usually so fixed and automatic that I don't really get through to him.
_____59. I don't think that anything I say or do really changes the way he feels toward me.
_____60. What he says to me often gives a wrong impression of his whole thought or feeling at the time.
_____61. He feels deep affection for me.
_____62. When I am hurt or upset he can recognize my feelings exactly, without becoming upset himself.
_____63. What other people think of me does (or would, if he knew) affect the way he feels toward me.
_____64. I believe that he has feelings he does not tell me about that are causing difficulty in our relationship.

References

Barrett-Lennard, G. T. "Studies in Progress Using the Relationship Inventory." An annotated list for private circulation, University of Waterloo, Ontario, Canada, September, 1966.

——— "Dimensions of Therapist Response as Causal Factors in Therapeutic Change." *Psychological Monographs,* 1962, *76,* (43, whole No. 562).

Berlin, J. I. "Some Autonomic Correlates of Therapeutic Conditions in Interpersonal Relationships." Unpublished doctoral dissertation, University of Chicago, 1960.

Berzon, Betty. "The Self-Directed Therapeutic Group: An Evaluative Study." *Western Behavioral Sciences Institute Reports.* No. 1 of a series on "The Intensive Group Experience," 1964.

Clark, J. V., & Culbert, S. A. "Mutually Therapeutic Perception and Self-Awareness in a T Group." *Journal of Applied Behavioral Science,* 1965, *1*(2), 180–94.

Emmerling, F. C. "A Study of the Relationships Between Personality Characteristics of Classroom Teachers and Pupil Perceptions of these Teachers." Unpublished doctoral dissertation, Auburn University, 1961.

Gross, W. F., & DeRidder, L. M. "Significant Movement in Comparatively Short-Term Counseling." *Journal of Counseling Psychology,* 1966, *13*(1), 98–99.

Hansen, J. C. "Relevance of the Supervisory Relationship to Counselor Trainee's Level of Experiencing and Self-Awareness." Unpublished doctoral dissertation, Ohio State University, 1963.

Hollenbeck, G. P. "The Use of the Relationship Inventory in the Prediction of Adjustment and Achievement." Unpublished doctoral dissertation, University of Wisconsin, 1961.

Hough, J. B. "The Dogmatism Factor in Human Relations Training of Pre-Service Teachers." Paper presented at American Educational Research Association, Chicago, Illinois, February, 1965.

Rogers, Carl R. "The Necessary and Sufficient Conditions of Therapeutic Personality Change." *Journal of Consulting Psychology,* 1957, *21*(2), 95–103.

Snelbecker, G. E. "Factors Influencing College Students' Person-Perceptions of Psychotherapists in a Laboratory Analog." Unpublished doctoral dissertation, Cornell University, 1961.

Thornton, B. M. "Dimensions of Perceived Relationship as Related to Marital Adjustment." Unpublished master's thesis, Auburn University, 1960.

Van der Veen, F. "Dimensions of Client and Therapist Behavior in Relation to Outcome." (American Psychological Association) *Proceedings of the 73rd Annual Convention (1965) of A.P.A.* Pp. 279–80.

*

INDEX

THE BOOK MANUFACTURE

Research in Counseling was composed by Kopecky Typesetting, Inc., Geneva, Illinois. Offset printing and binding was by Kingsport Press, Kingsport, Tennessee. The paper is Perkins & Squire Company's Glatfelter Old Forge. Internal design and case design was by John Goetz. The type in this book is Century Schoolbook with Craw Clarendon Book headings.